(Night of the Full Moon)

(Correction for Volume 6)

Last time, I wrote that *paope* means "middle-aged woman," and I received another letter about it. Actually, it means "fool," not "middle-aged woman."

Consequently, *paope human* means "foolish human," not "middle-aged woman-human."

Ryu Fujisaki

Ryu Fujisaki's *Worlds* came in second place for the prestigious 40th Tezuka Award. His *Psycho +*, *Wāqwāq* and *Hoshin Engi* have all run in *Weekly Shonen Jump* magazine, and *Hoshin Engi* anime is available on DVD in Japan and North America. A lover of science fiction, literature and history, Fujisaki has made *Hoshin Engi* a mix of genres that truly showcases his amazing art and imagination.

HOSHIN ENGI VOL. 7
The SHONEN JUMP Manga Edition

STORY AND ART BY RYU FUJISAKI
Based on the novel *Hoshin Engi*, translated by Tsutomu Ano,
published by Kodansha Bunko

Translation & Adaptation/Tomo Kimura
Touch-up Art & Lettering/Hudson Yards
Design/Matt Hinrichs
Editor/Jonathan Tarbox

Editor in Chief, Books/Alvin Lu
Editor in Chief, Magazines/Marc Weidenbaum
VP of Publishing Licensing/Rika Inouye
VP of Sales/Gonzalo Ferreyra
Sr. VP of Marketing/Liza Coppola
Publisher/Hyoe Narita

Published by VIZ Media, LLC
P.O. Box 77010
San Francisco, CA 94107

SHONEN JUMP Manga Edition
10 9 8 7 6 5 4 3 2 1
First printing, June 2008

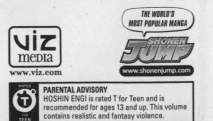

HOSHIN ENGI

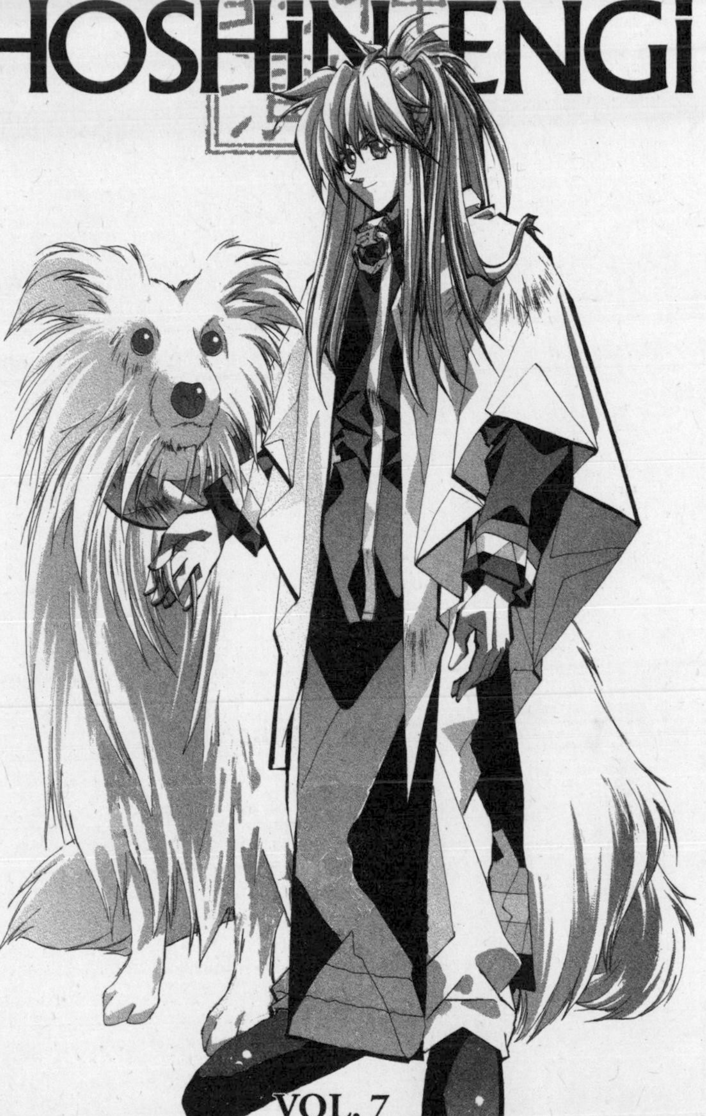

VOL. 7
THE CURTAIN FALLS

STORY AND ART BY RYU FUJISAKI

THE CHARACTERS

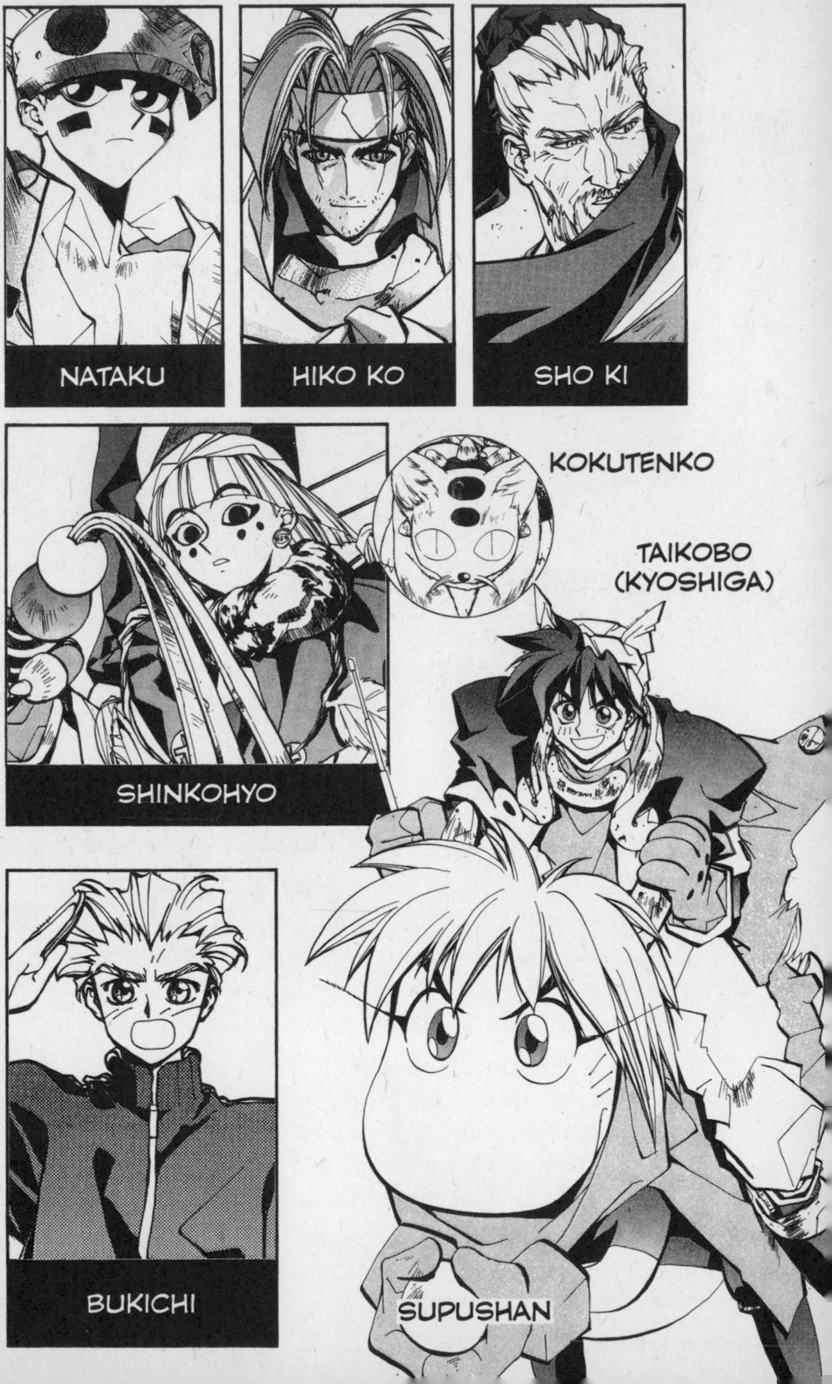
SHO KI
HIKO KO
NATAKU
KOKUTENKO
TAIKOBO (KYOSHIGA)
SHINKOHYO
SUPUSHAN
BUKICHI

KING CHU

BUNCHU

DAKKI

THE MAKA YONSHO

The Story Thus Far

Ancient China, over 3000 years ago. It is the era of the Yin Dynasty.

After King Chu, the emperor, married the beautiful Dakki, the good king was no longer himself, and became an unmanly and foolish ruler. Dakki, a *Sennyo* with a wicked heart, took control of Yin and the country fell into chaos.

To save the human world, the Hoshin Project was put into action. The project will seal evil Sennin and Doshi into the Shinkai, and cause Seihakuko Sho Ki to set up a new dynasty to replace Choka. Taikobo, who was chosen to execute this project, visits Sho Ki in Seiki to encourage him to be the next king.

Seiki finally decides to go to war against Choka, and Taikobo is appointed as the Gunshi of Seiki. However, Sho Ki's health is weakening, and he names his second son Hatsu as his successor.

HOSHiN ENGi

VOL. 7
THE CURTAIN FALLS

CONTENTS

Chapter 52

SUPUSHAN BECOMES BIRD FEED

LISTEN, SHO KI.

I'M GOING TO MAKE A TRIP UP NORTH.

Seiki

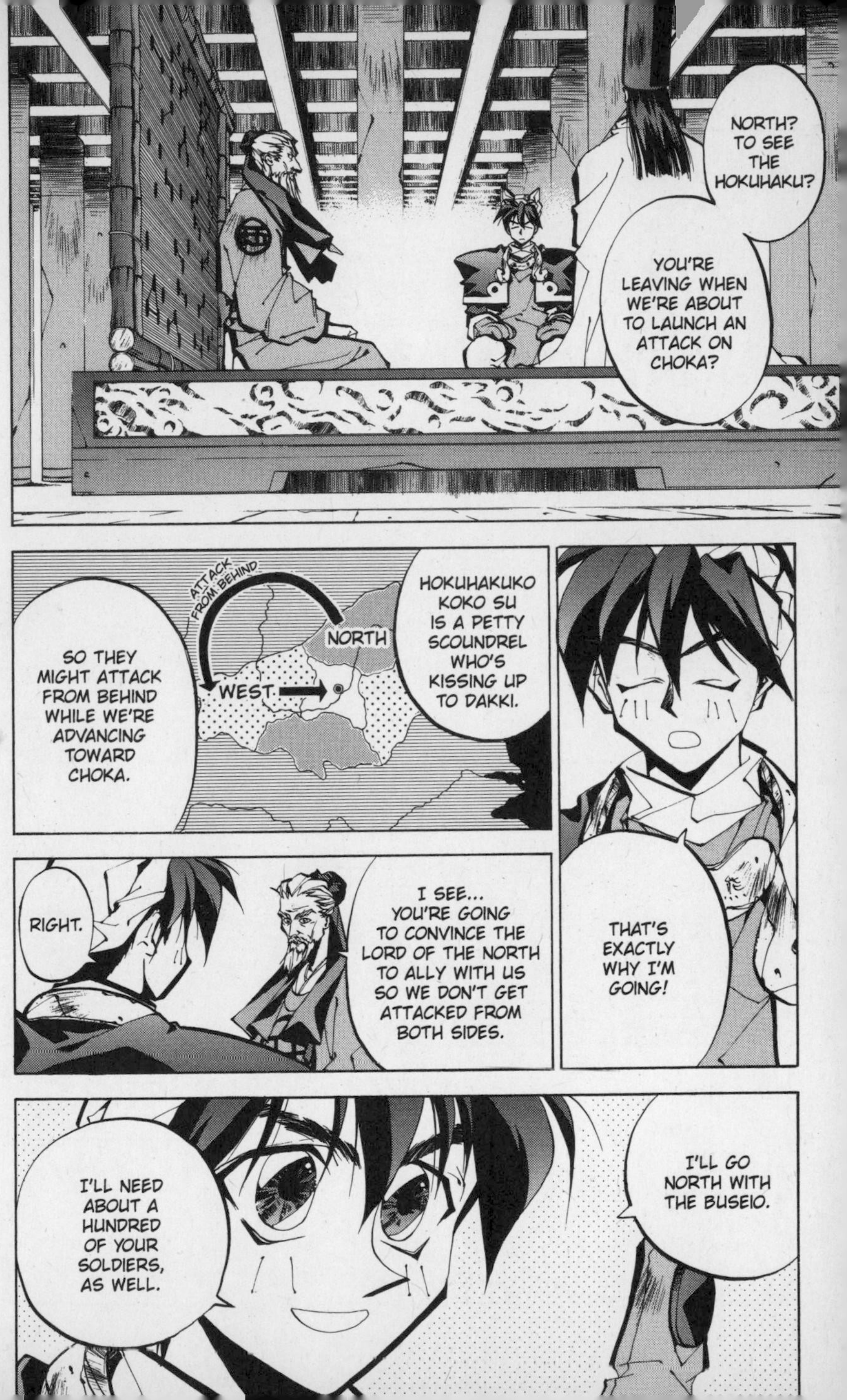
NORTH? TO SEE THE HOKUHAKU?
YOU'RE LEAVING WHEN WE'RE ABOUT TO LAUNCH AN ATTACK ON CHOKA?
THAT'S EXACTLY WHY I'M GOING!
HOKUHAKUKO KOKO SU IS A PETTY SCOUNDREL WHO'S KISSING UP TO DAKKI.
ATTACK FROM BEHIND
NORTH
WEST
SO THEY MIGHT ATTACK FROM BEHIND WHILE WE'RE ADVANCING TOWARD CHOKA.
I SEE... YOU'RE GOING TO CONVINCE THE LORD OF THE NORTH TO ALLY WITH US SO WE DON'T GET ATTACKED FROM BOTH SIDES.
RIGHT.
I'LL GO NORTH WITH THE BUSEIO.
I'LL NEED ABOUT A HUNDRED OF YOUR SOLDIERS, AS WELL.

READ THIS WAY

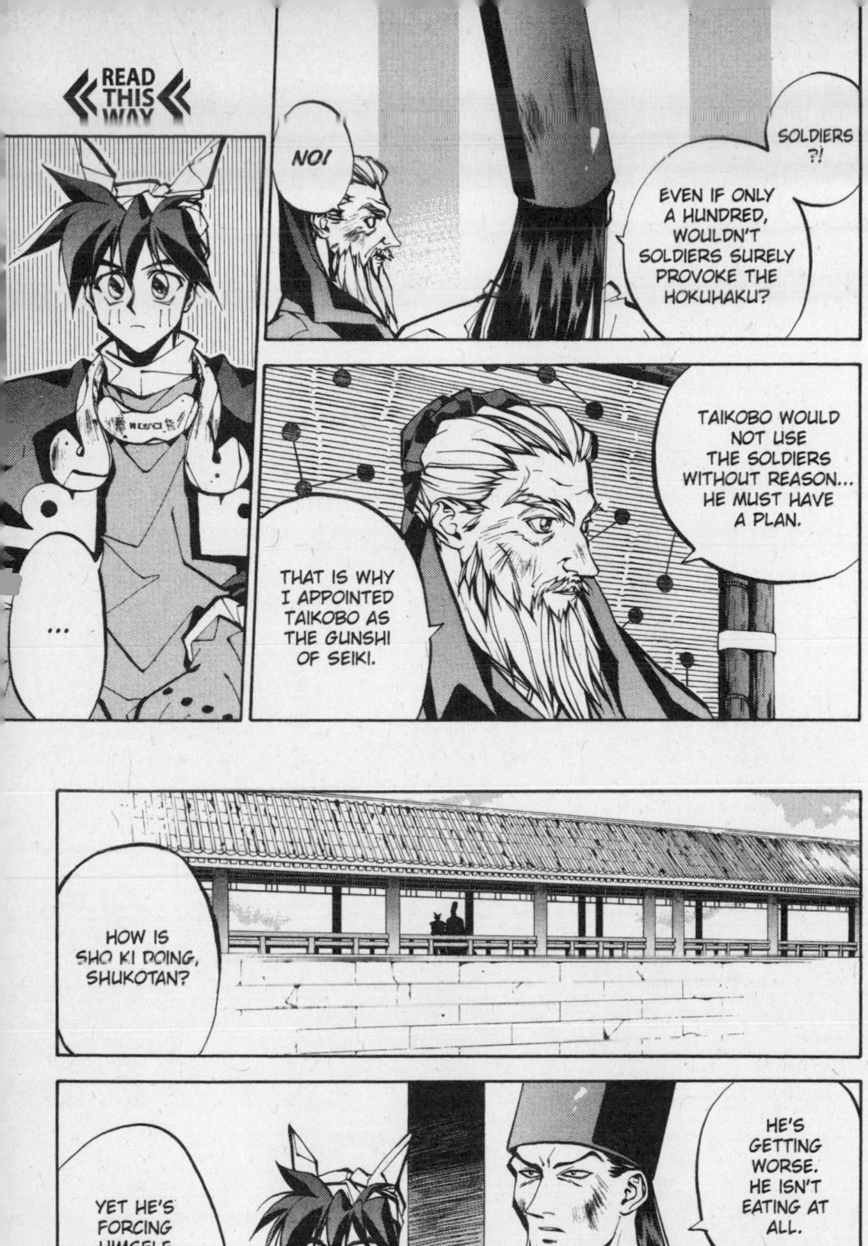
SOLDIERS ?!
EVEN IF ONLY A HUNDRED, WOULDN'T SOLDIERS SURELY PROVOKE THE HOKUHAKU?
NO!
TAIKOBO WOULD NOT USE THE SOLDIERS WITHOUT REASON... HE MUST HAVE A PLAN.
THAT IS WHY I APPOINTED TAIKOBO AS THE GUNSHI OF SEIKI.
...
HOW IS SHO KI DOING, SHUKOTAN?
HE'S GETTING WORSE. HE ISN'T EATING AT ALL.
YET HE'S FORCING HIMSELF TO KEEP WORKING.

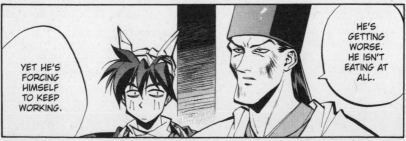

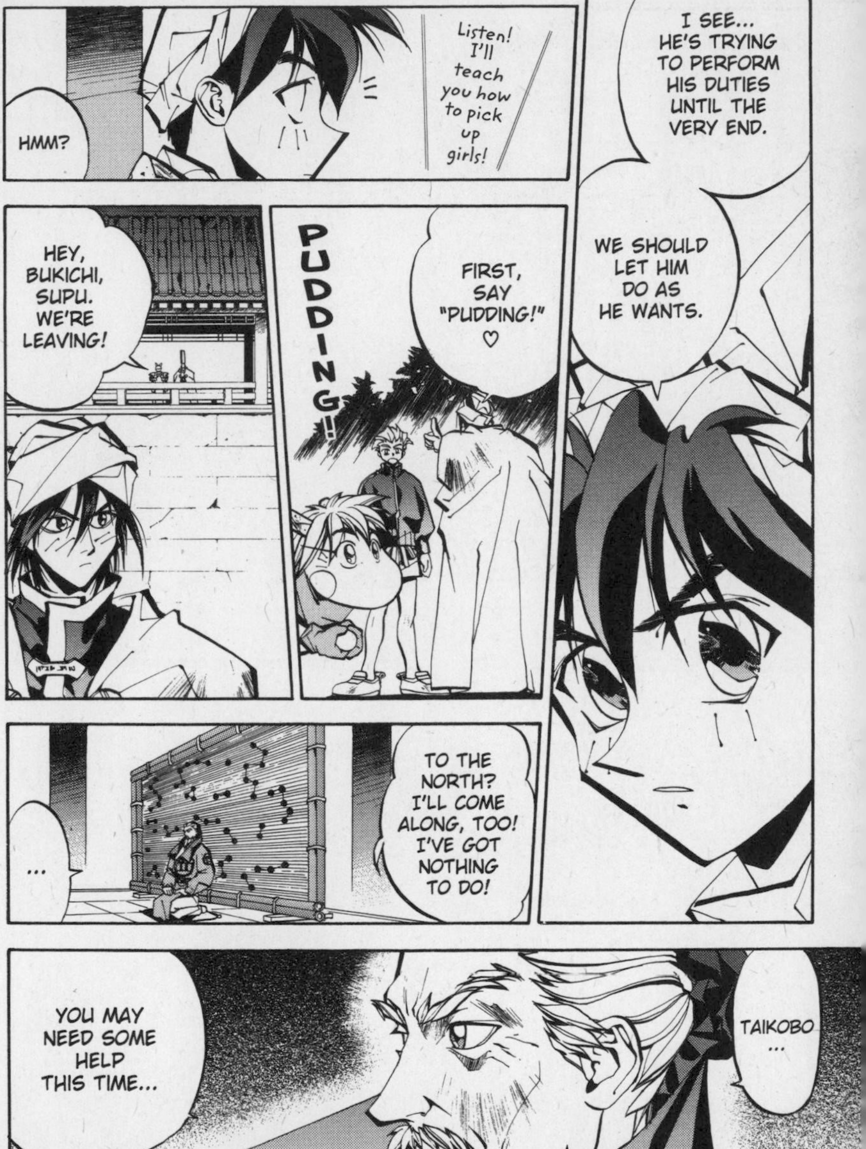
I SEE... HE'S TRYING TO PERFORM HIS DUTIES UNTIL THE VERY END.
WE SHOULD LET HIM DO AS HE WANTS.
Listen! I'll teach you how to pick up girls!
HMM?
FIRST, SAY "PUDDING!" ♡
PUDDING!
HEY, BUKICHI, SUPU. WE'RE LEAVING!
TO THE NORTH? I'LL COME ALONG, TOO! I'VE GOT NOTHING TO DO!
...
TAIKOBO...
YOU MAY NEED SOME HELP THIS TIME...

READ THIS WAY

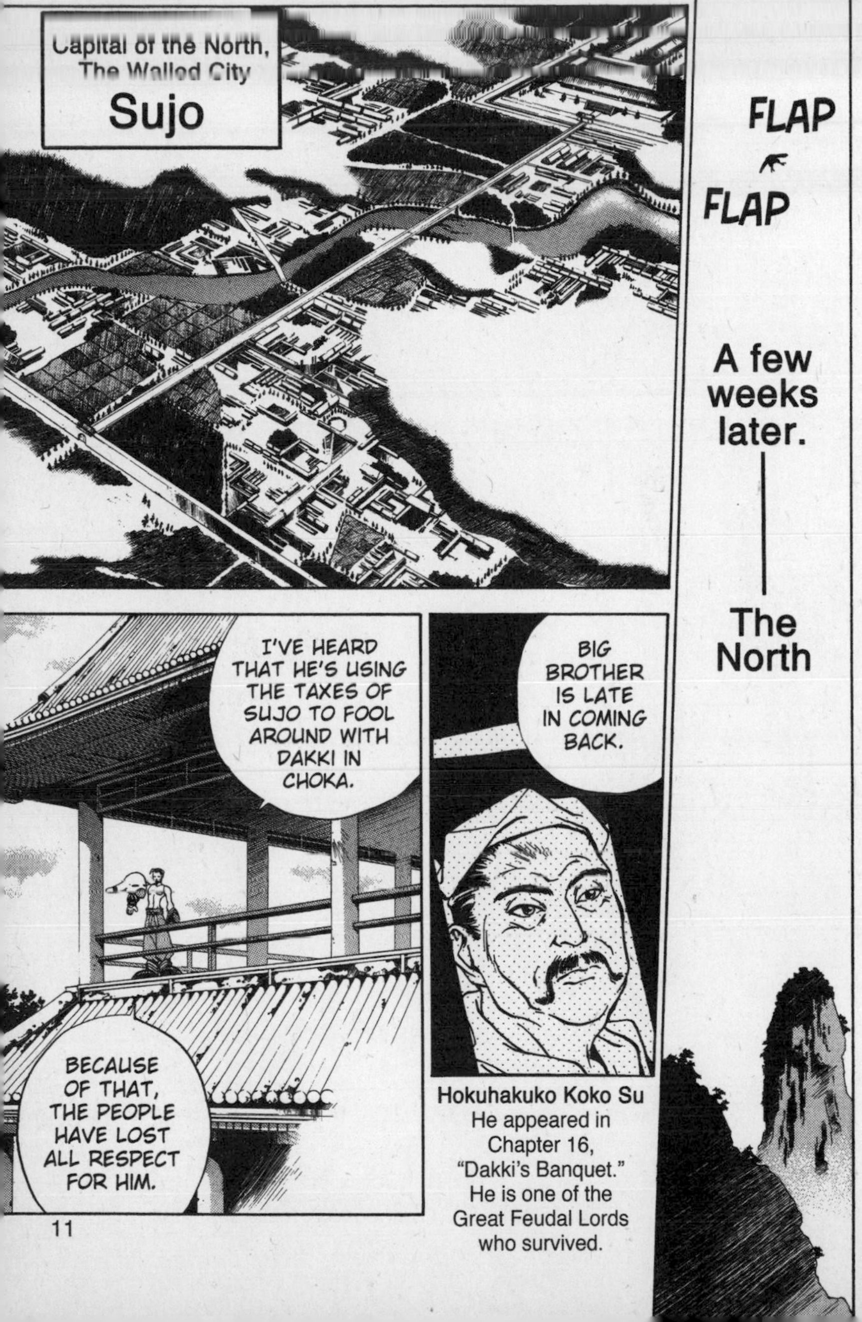
FLAP
FLAP
A few weeks later.
The North
Capital of the North, The Walled City
Sujo
BIG BROTHER IS LATE IN COMING BACK.
Hokuhakuko Koko Su
He appeared in Chapter 16, "Dakki's Banquet." He is one of the Great Feudal Lords who survived.
I'VE HEARD THAT HE'S USING THE TAXES OF SUJO TO FOOL AROUND WITH DAKKI IN CHOKA.
BECAUSE OF THAT, THE PEOPLE HAVE LOST ALL RESPECT FOR HIM.

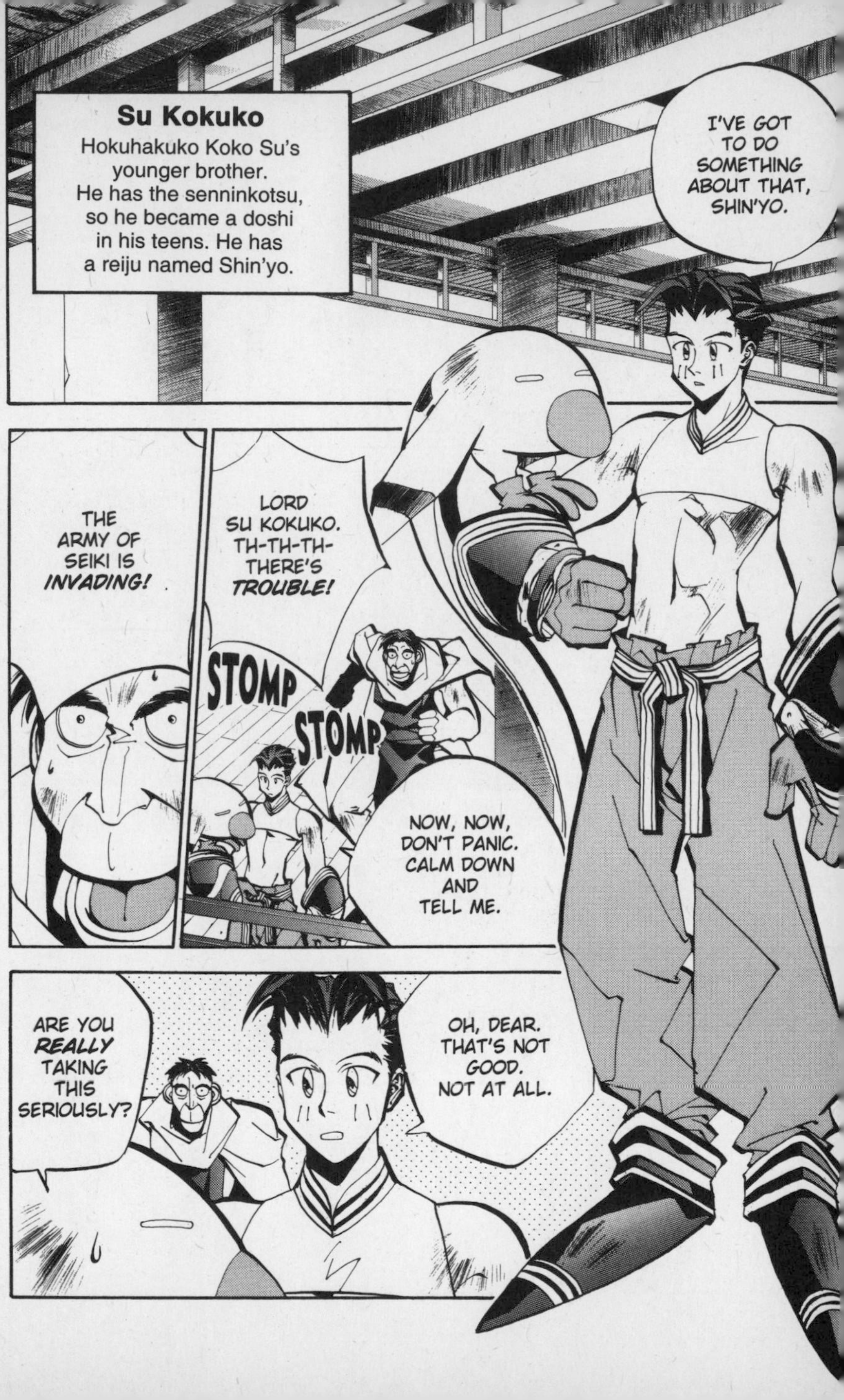

I'VE GOT TO DO SOMETHING ABOUT THAT, SHIN'YO.
Su Kokuko
Hokuhakuko Koko Su's younger brother. He has the senninkotsu, so he became a doshi in his teens. He has a reiju named Shin'yo.
LORD SU KOKUKO. TH-TH-TH-THERE'S TROUBLE!
STOMP
STOMP
NOW, NOW, DON'T PANIC. CALM DOWN AND TELL ME.
THE ARMY OF SEIKI IS INVADING!
OH, DEAR. THAT'S NOT GOOD. NOT AT ALL.
ARE YOU REALLY TAKING THIS SERIOUSLY?

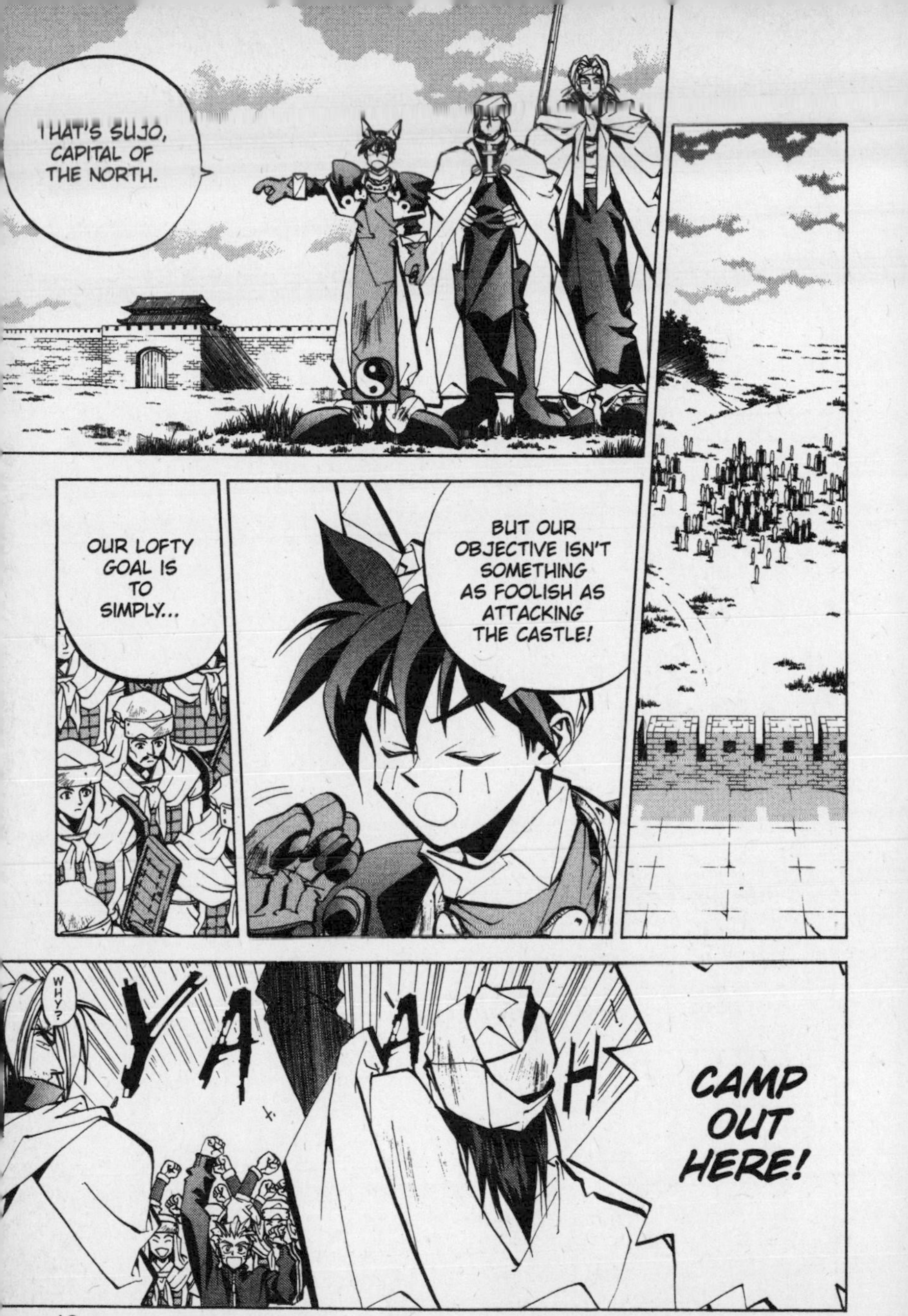
THAT'S SUJO, CAPITAL OF THE NORTH.
BUT OUR OBJECTIVE ISN'T SOMETHING AS FOOLISH AS ATTACKING THE CASTLE!
OUR LOFTY GOAL IS TO SIMPLY...
CAMP OUT HERE!
YAAH
WHY?

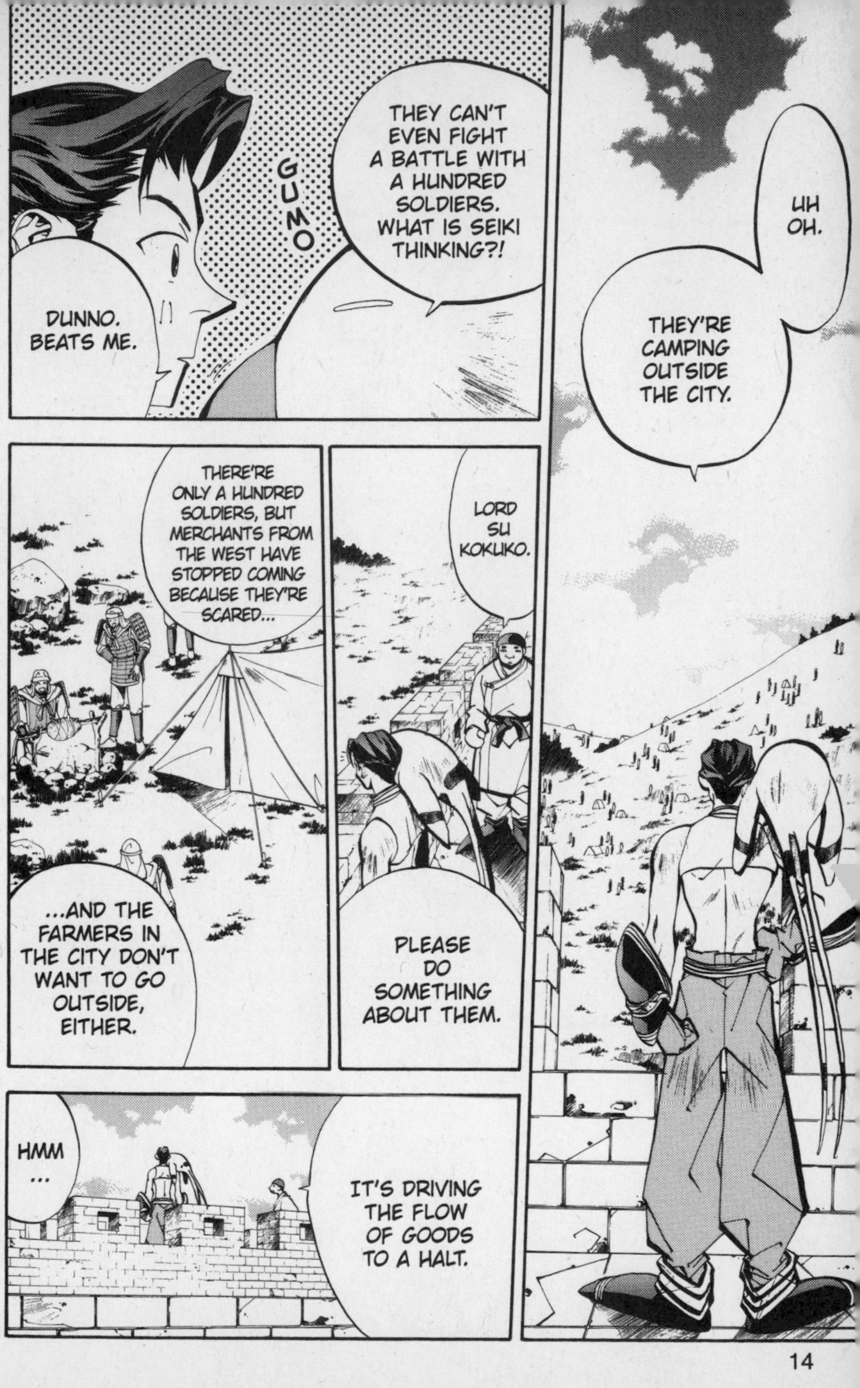
UH OH.
THEY'RE CAMPING OUTSIDE THE CITY.
THEY CAN'T EVEN FIGHT A BATTLE WITH A HUNDRED SOLDIERS. WHAT IS SEIKI THINKING?!
GUMO
DUNNO. BEATS ME.
LORD SU KOKUKO.
PLEASE DO SOMETHING ABOUT THEM.
THERE'RE ONLY A HUNDRED SOLDIERS, BUT MERCHANTS FROM THE WEST HAVE STOPPED COMING BECAUSE THEY'RE SCARED...
...AND THE FARMERS IN THE CITY DON'T WANT TO GO OUTSIDE, EITHER.
IT'S DRIVING THE FLOW OF GOODS TO A HALT.
HMM ...

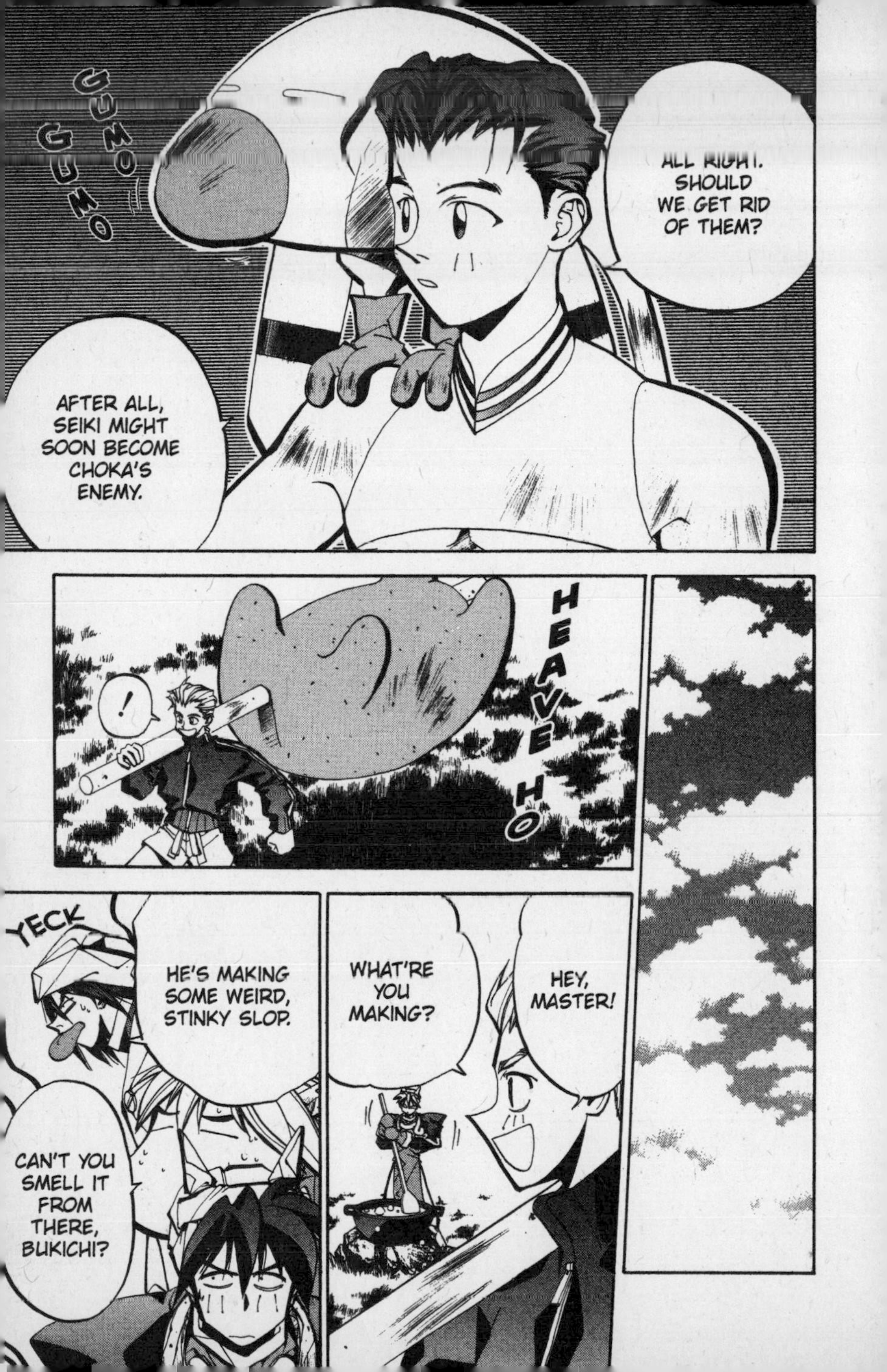
ALL RIGHT. SHOULD WE GET RID OF THEM?
GUMO GUMO
AFTER ALL, SEIKI MIGHT SOON BECOME CHOKA'S ENEMY.
HEAVE HO
!
HEY, MASTER!
WHAT'RE YOU MAKING?
YECK
HE'S MAKING SOME WEIRD, STINKY SLOP.
CAN'T YOU SMELL IT FROM THERE, BUKICHI?

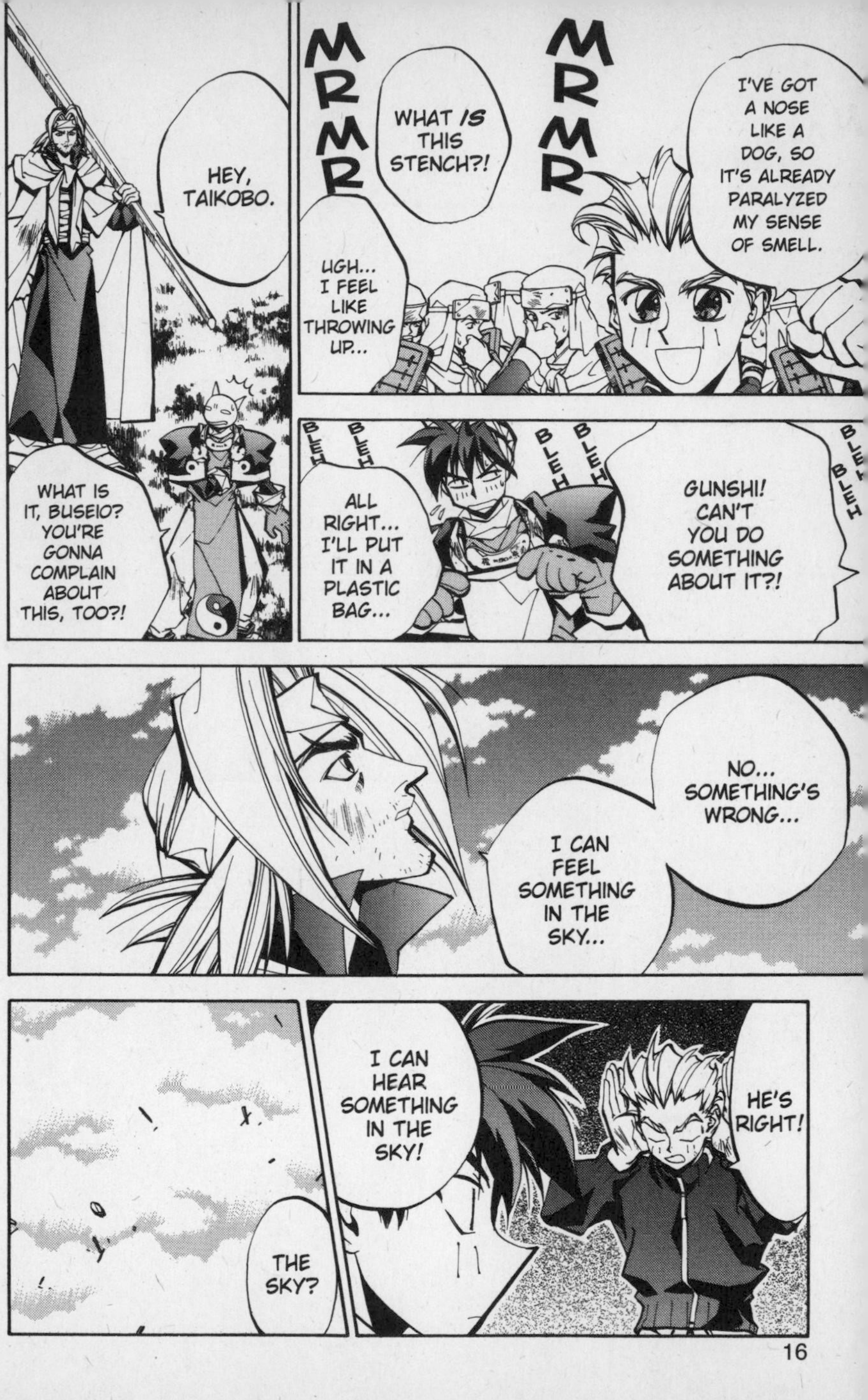
MRMR
I'VE GOT A NOSE LIKE A DOG, SO IT'S ALREADY PARALYZED MY SENSE OF SMELL.
MRMR
WHAT *IS* THIS STENCH?!
UGH... I FEEL LIKE THROWING UP...
BLEH BLEH
GUNSHI! CAN'T YOU DO SOMETHING ABOUT IT?!
BLEH BLEH
ALL RIGHT... I'LL PUT IT IN A PLASTIC BAG...
BLEH BLEH
HEY, TAIKOBO.
WHAT IS IT, BUSEIO? YOU'RE GONNA COMPLAIN ABOUT THIS, TOO?!
NO... SOMETHING'S WRONG...
I CAN FEEL SOMETHING IN THE SKY...
HE'S RIGHT!
I CAN HEAR SOMETHING IN THE SKY!
THE SKY?

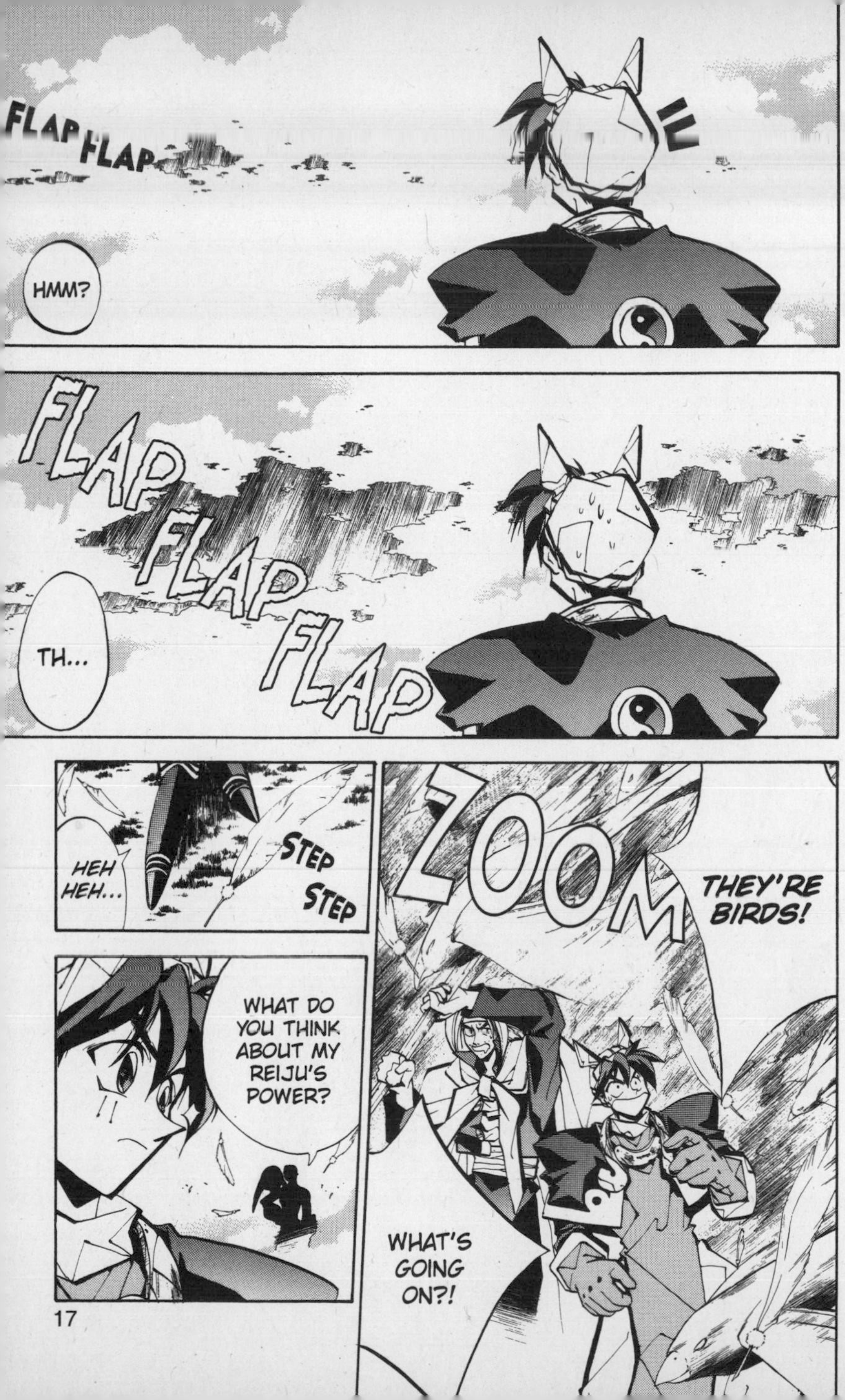
FLAP FLAP
HMM?
FLAP FLAP FLAP FLAP
TH...
ZOOM
THEY'RE BIRDS!
WHAT'S GOING ON?!
HEH HEH...
STEP STEP
WHAT DO YOU THINK ABOUT MY REIJU'S POWER?

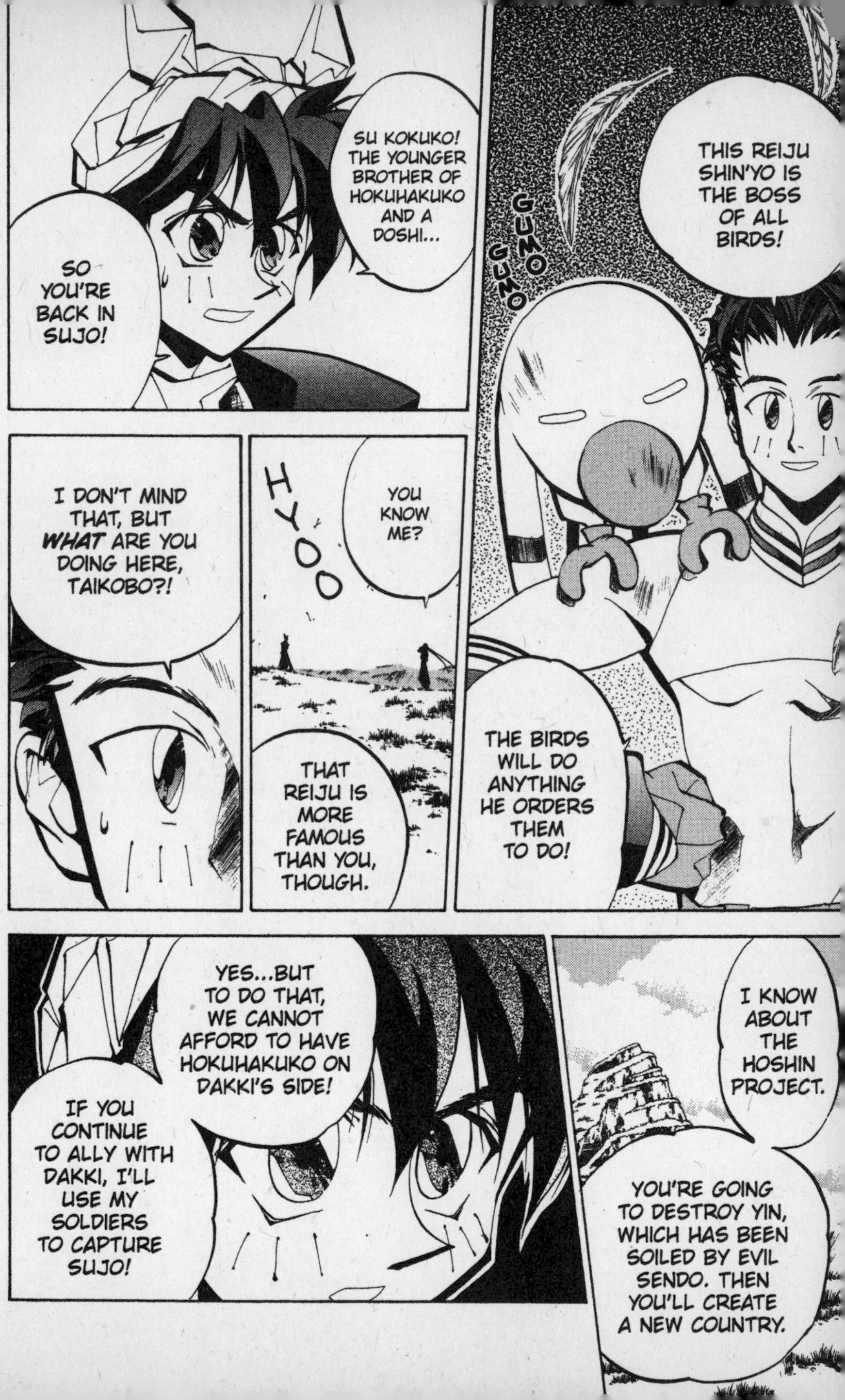
THIS REIJU SHIN'YO IS THE BOSS OF ALL BIRDS!
GUMO GUMO GUMO
THE BIRDS WILL DO ANYTHING HE ORDERS THEM TO DO!
SU KOKUKO! THE YOUNGER BROTHER OF HOKUHAKUKO AND A DOSHI...
SO YOU'RE BACK IN SUJO!
YOU KNOW ME?
HYOO
THAT REIJU IS MORE FAMOUS THAN YOU, THOUGH.
I DON'T MIND THAT, BUT *WHAT* ARE YOU DOING HERE, TAIKOBO?!
I KNOW ABOUT THE HOSHIN PROJECT.
YOU'RE GOING TO DESTROY YIN, WHICH HAS BEEN SOILED BY EVIL SENDO. THEN YOU'LL CREATE A NEW COUNTRY.
YES...BUT TO DO THAT, WE CANNOT AFFORD TO HAVE HOKUHAKUKO ON DAKKI'S SIDE!
IF YOU CONTINUE TO ALLY WITH DAKKI, I'LL USE MY SOLDIERS TO CAPTURE SUJO!

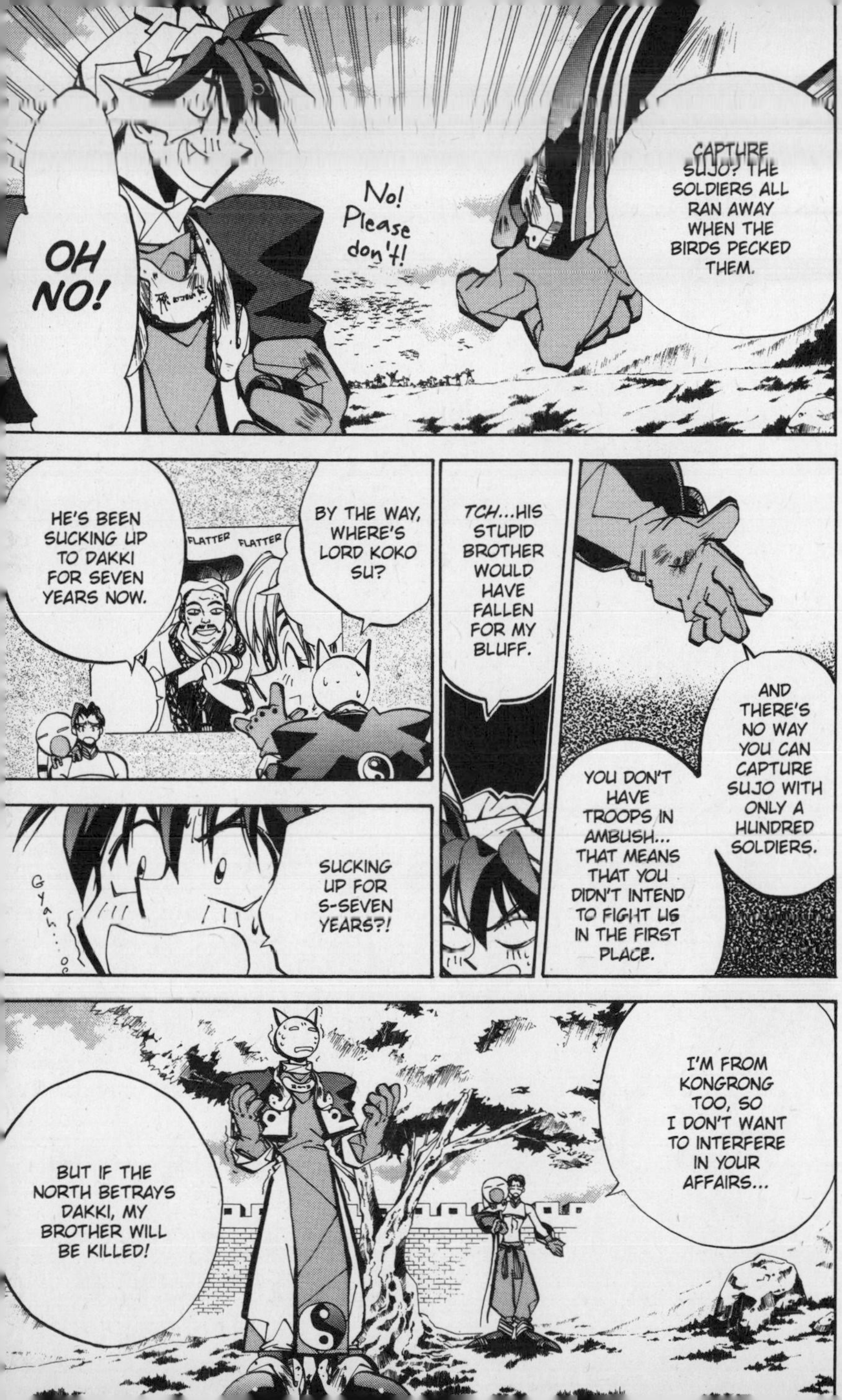
CAPTURE SUJO? THE SOLDIERS ALL RAN AWAY WHEN THE BIRDS PECKED THEM.
No! Please don't!
OH NO!
AND THERE'S NO WAY YOU CAN CAPTURE SUJO WITH ONLY A HUNDRED SOLDIERS.
YOU DON'T HAVE TROOPS IN AMBUSH... THAT MEANS THAT YOU DIDN'T INTEND TO FIGHT US IN THE FIRST PLACE.
TCH...HIS STUPID BROTHER WOULD HAVE FALLEN FOR MY BLUFF.
BY THE WAY, WHERE'S LORD KOKO SU?
FLATTER
FLATTER
HE'S BEEN SUCKING UP TO DAKKI FOR SEVEN YEARS NOW.
SUCKING UP FOR S-SEVEN YEARS?!
Gyah...
I'M FROM KONGRONG TOO, SO I DON'T WANT TO INTERFERE IN YOUR AFFAIRS...
BUT IF THE NORTH BETRAYS DAKKI, MY BROTHER WILL BE KILLED!

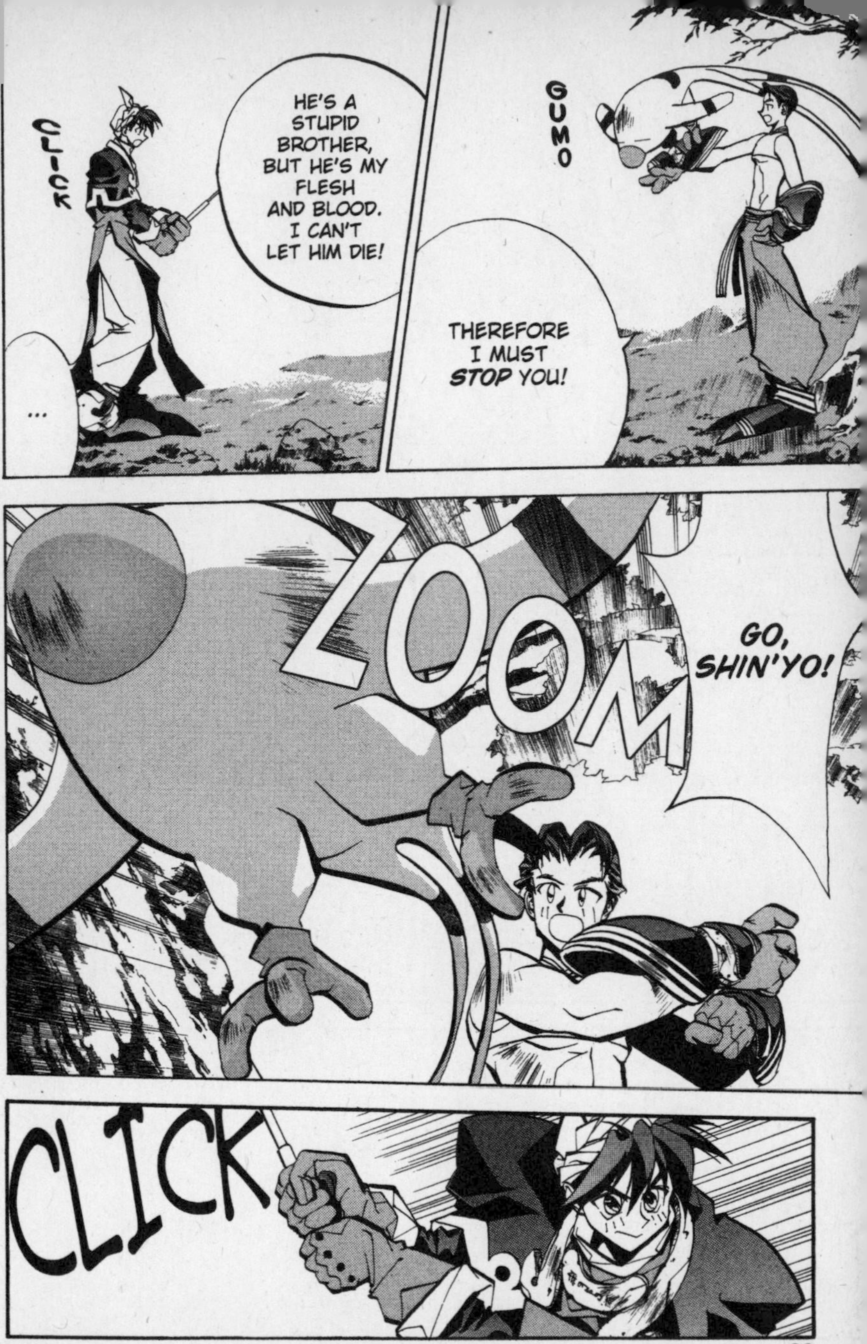
GUMO
THEREFORE I MUST STOP YOU!
CLICK
HE'S A STUPID BROTHER, BUT HE'S MY FLESH AND BLOOD. I CAN'T LET HIM DIE!
...
ZOOM
GO, SHIN'YO!
CLICK

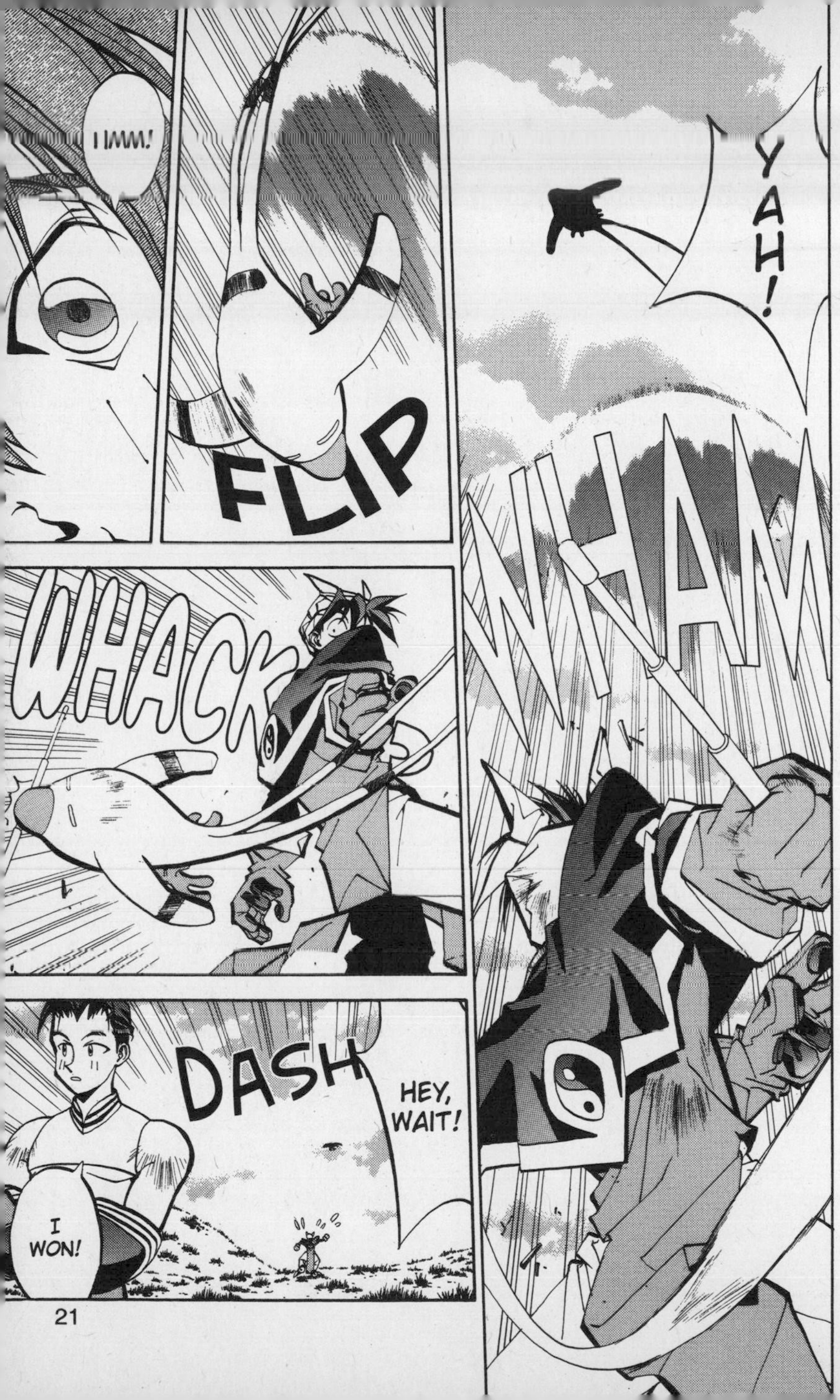
YAH!
WHAM
FLIP
WHACK
HEY, WAIT!
DASH
I WON!

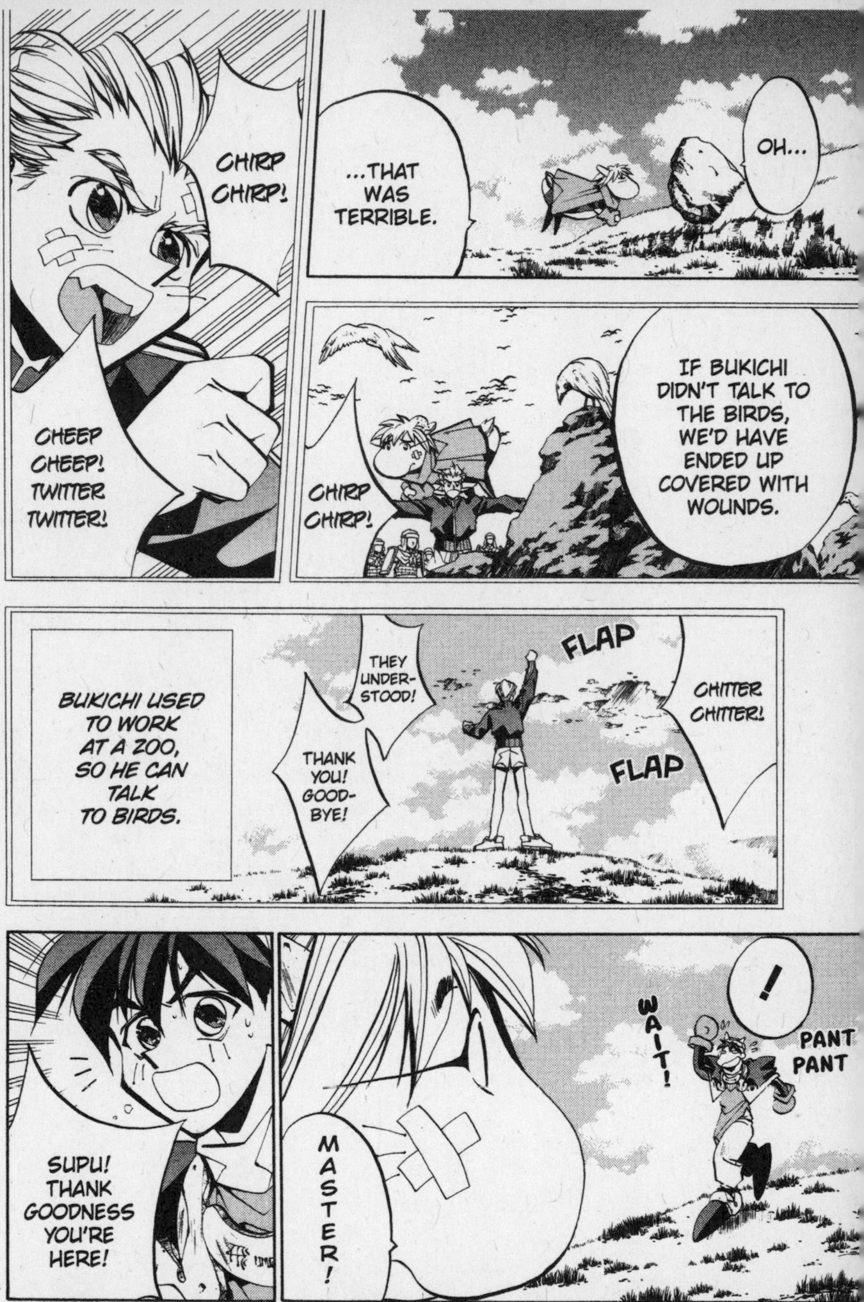
OH...
...THAT WAS TERRIBLE.
IF BUKICHI DIDN'T TALK TO THE BIRDS, WE'D HAVE ENDED UP COVERED WITH WOUNDS.
CHIRP CHIRP!
CHIRP CHIRP!
CHEEP CHEEP! TWITTER TWITTER!
FLAP
CHITTER CHITTER!
FLAP
THEY UNDERSTOOD!
THANK YOU! GOODBYE!
BUKICHI USED TO WORK AT A ZOO, SO HE CAN TALK TO BIRDS.
!
PANT PANT
WAIT!
MASTER!
SUPU! THANK GOODNESS YOU'RE HERE!

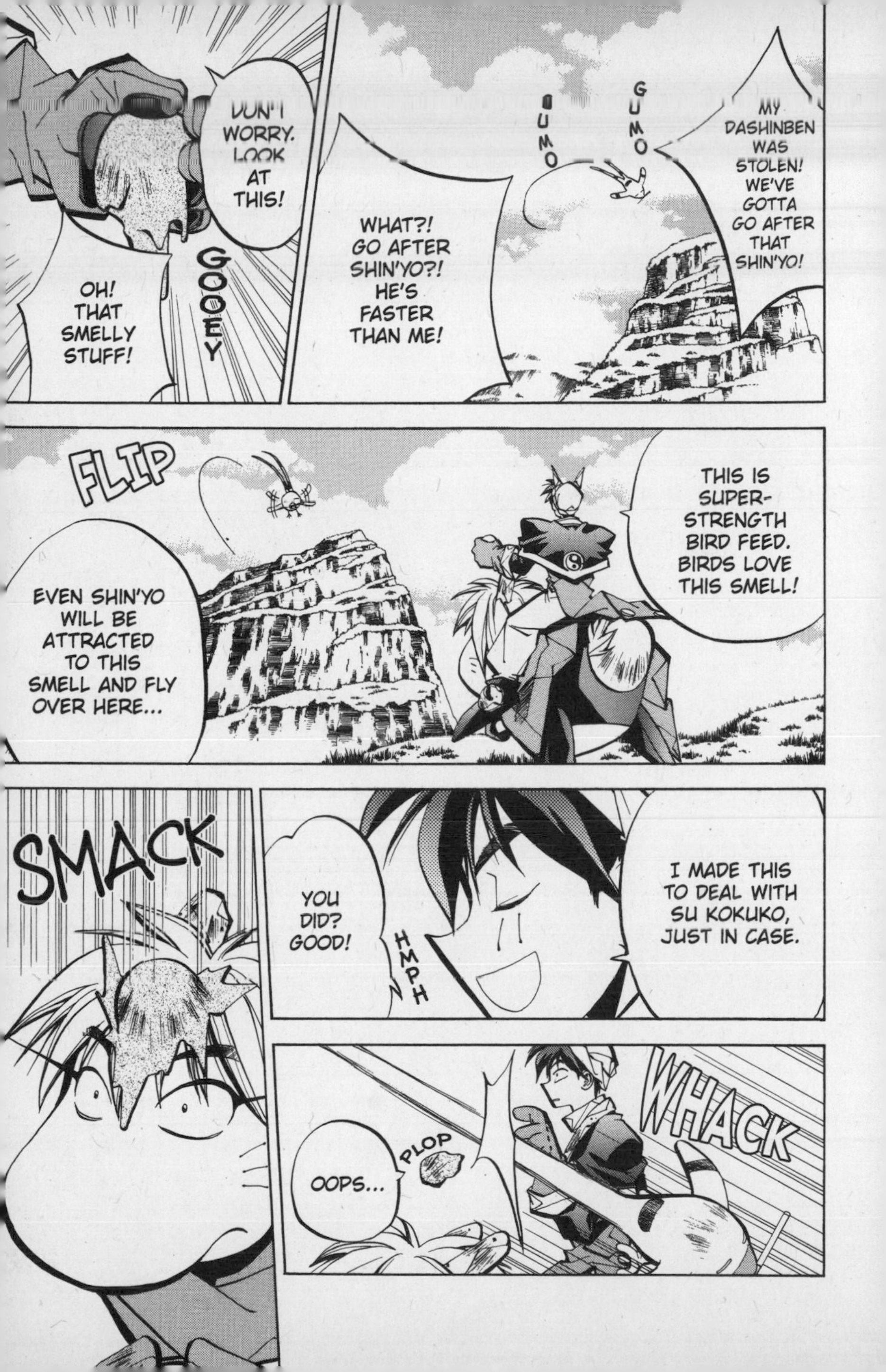
MY DASHINBEN WAS STOLEN! WE'VE GOTTA GO AFTER THAT SHIN'YO!
GUMO
GUMO
WHAT?! GO AFTER SHIN'YO?! HE'S FASTER THAN ME!
DON'T WORRY. LOOK AT THIS!
GOOEY
OH! THAT SMELLY STUFF!
THIS IS SUPER-STRENGTH BIRD FEED. BIRDS LOVE THIS SMELL!
FLIP
EVEN SHIN'YO WILL BE ATTRACTED TO THIS SMELL AND FLY OVER HERE...
I MADE THIS TO DEAL WITH SU KOKUKO, JUST IN CASE.
HMPH
YOU DID? GOOD!
WHACK
PLOP
OOPS...
SMACK

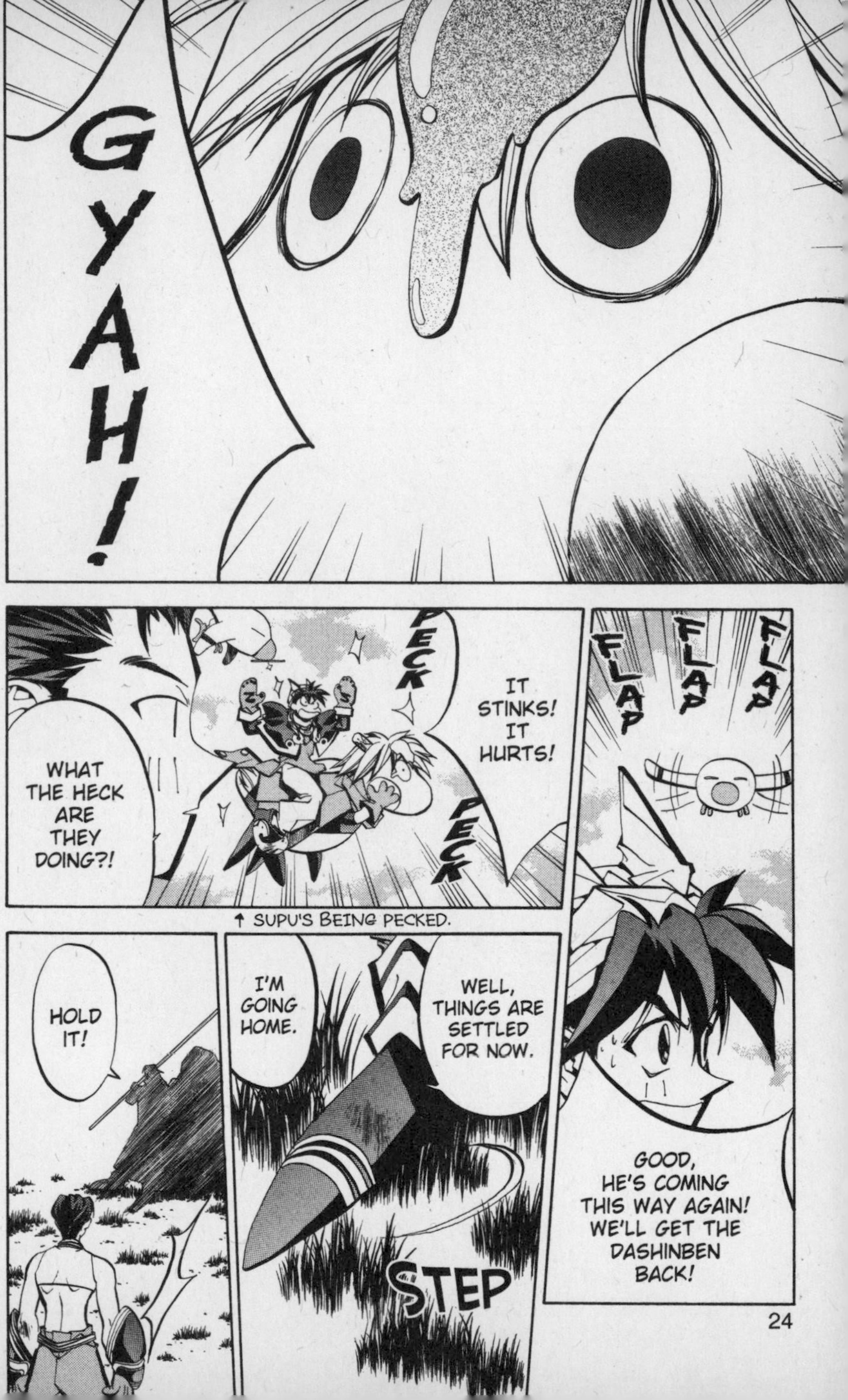
GYAH!
FLAP FLAP FLAP
GOOD, HE'S COMING THIS WAY AGAIN! WE'LL GET THE DASHINBEN BACK!
PECK
IT STINKS! IT HURTS!
PECK
WHAT THE HECK ARE THEY DOING?!
↑ SUPU'S BEING PECKED.
WELL, THINGS ARE SETTLED FOR NOW.
I'M GOING HOME.
STEP
HOLD IT!

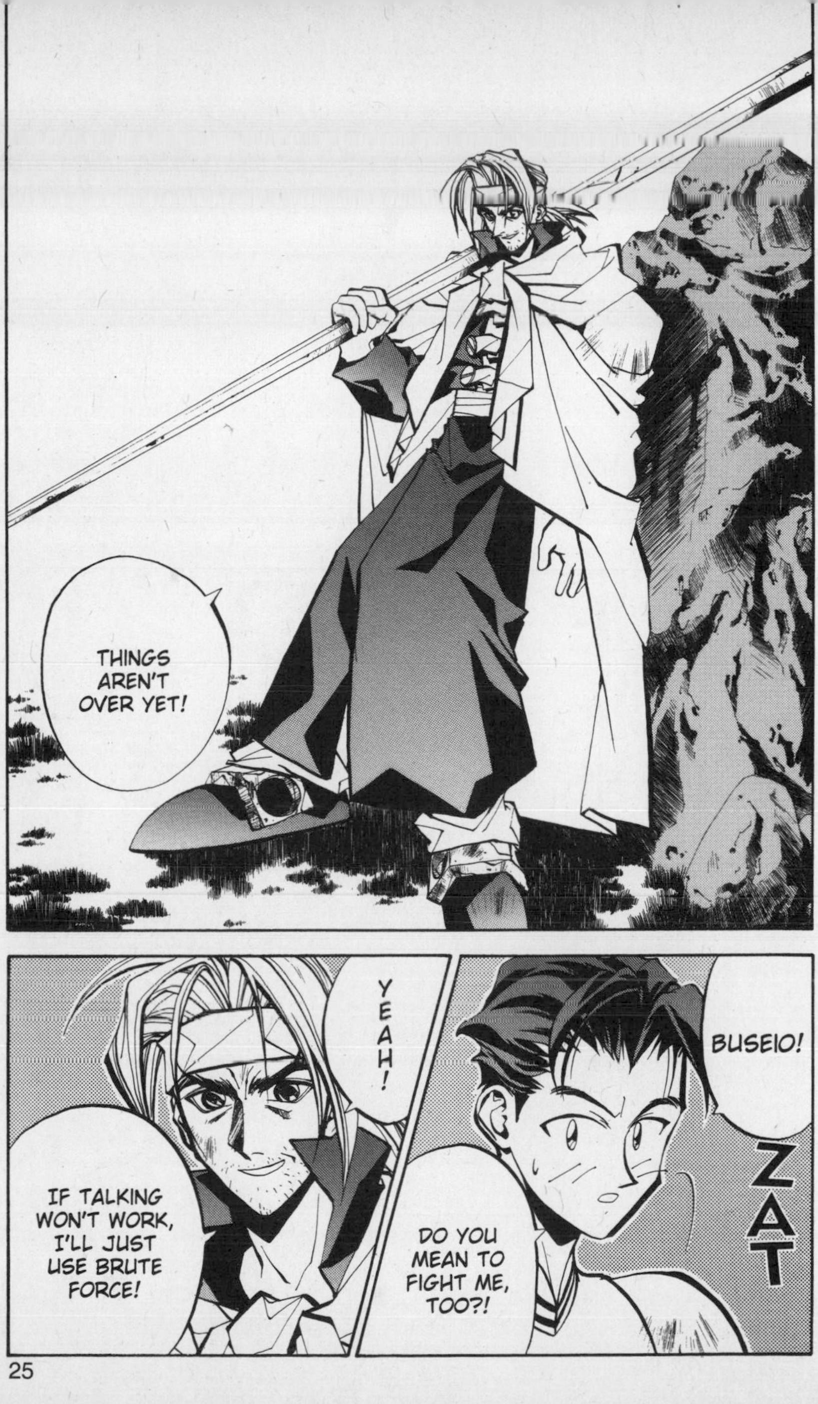
THINGS AREN'T OVER YET!
BUSEIO!
ZAT
DO YOU MEAN TO FIGHT ME, TOO?!
YEAH!
IF TALKING WON'T WORK, I'LL JUST USE BRUTE FORCE!

封神演義

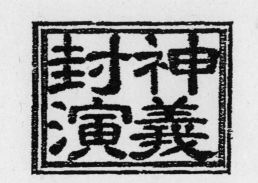

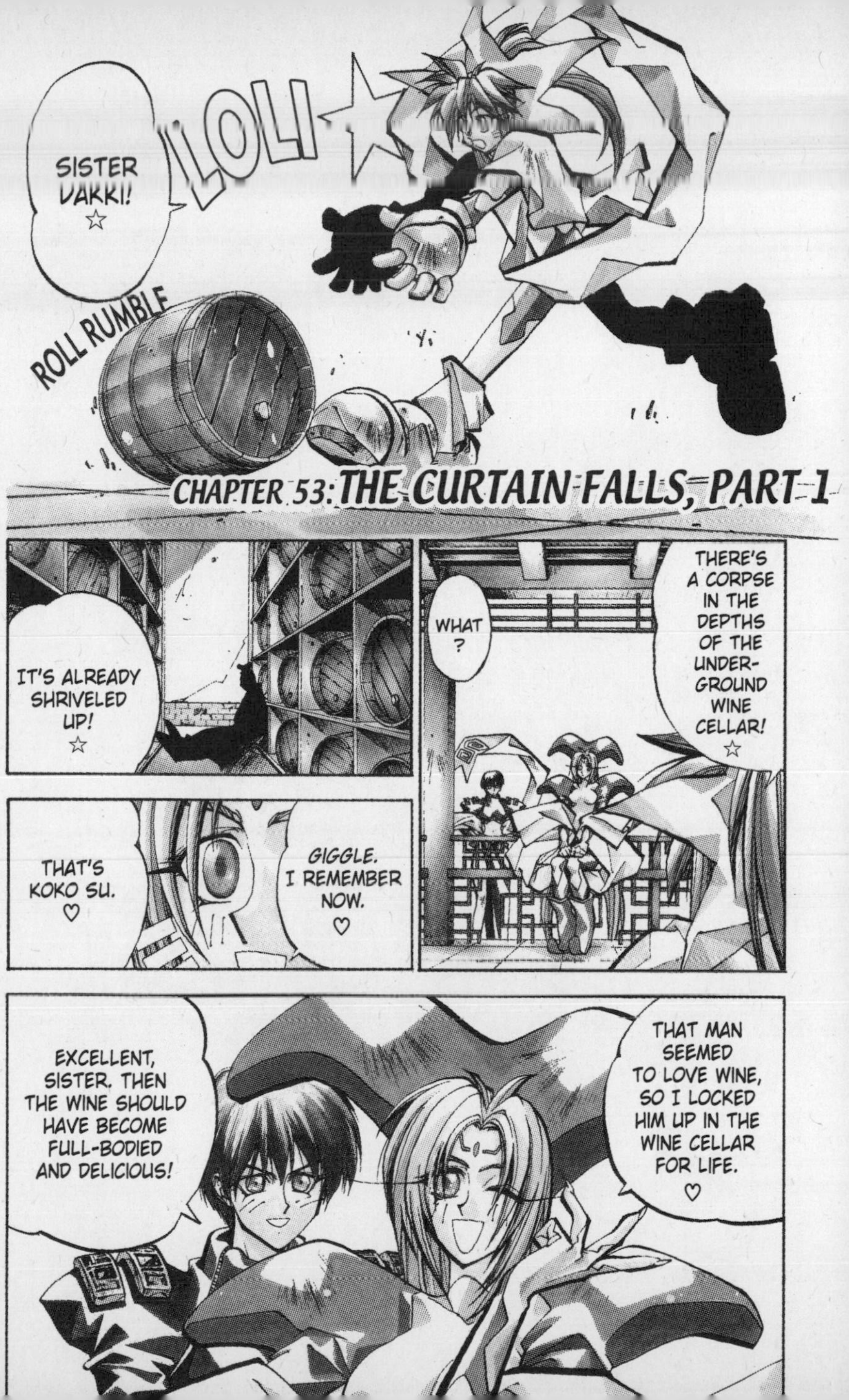
SISTER VAKKI! ☆
LOLI ☆
ROLL RUMBLE
CHAPTER 53: THE CURTAIN FALLS, PART 1
THERE'S A CORPSE IN THE DEPTHS OF THE UNDER-GROUND WINE CELLAR! ☆
WHAT?
IT'S ALREADY SHRIVELED UP! ☆
GIGGLE. I REMEMBER NOW. ♡
THAT'S KOKO SU. ♡
THAT MAN SEEMED TO LOVE WINE, SO I LOCKED HIM UP IN THE WINE CELLAR FOR LIFE. ♡
EXCELLENT, SISTER. THEN THE WINE SHOULD HAVE BECOME FULL-BODIED AND DELICIOUS!

Chapter 53

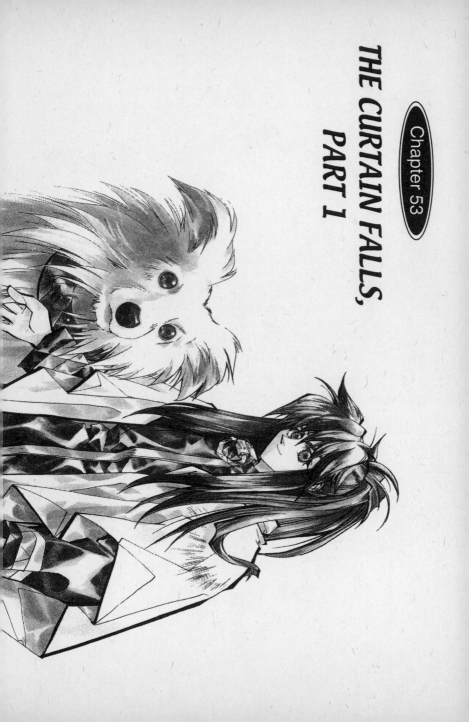

THE CURTAIN FALLS, PART 1

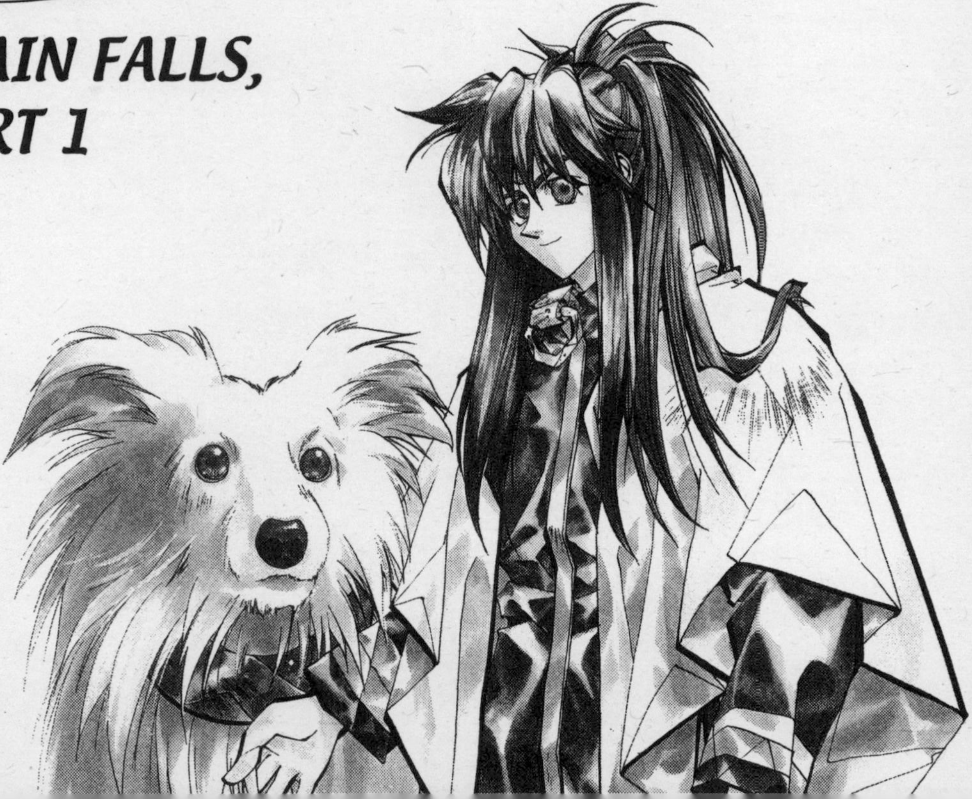

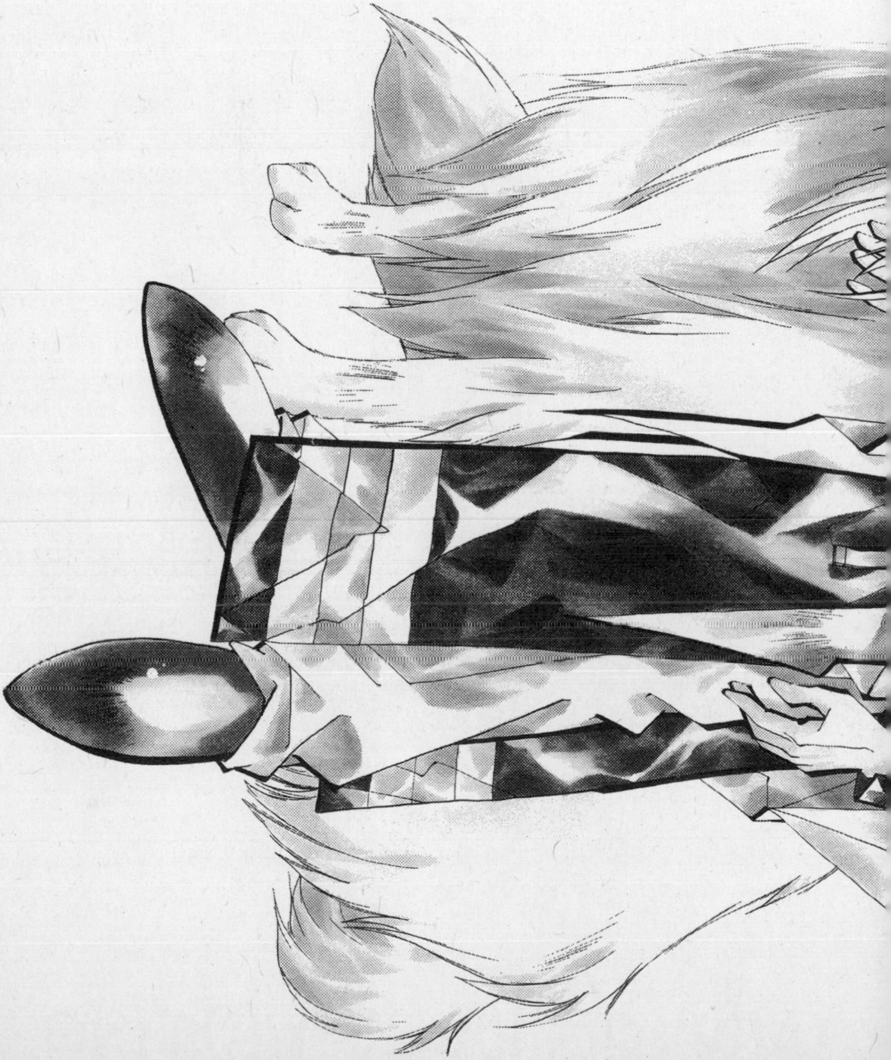

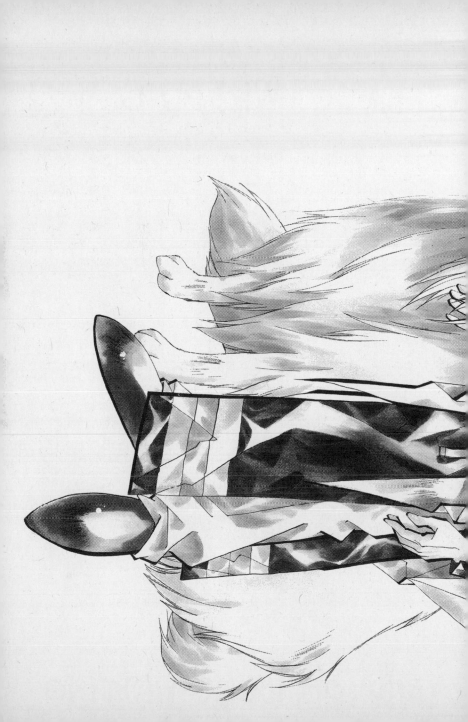

YOU DON'T HAVE TO READ IT, BUT SINCE THERE'S AN EXTRA PAGE:

HACK WRITING V

- △ BECAUSE I CALL THIS SECTION HACK WRITING, I HAVE TO REALLY WRITE VERY TRIVIAL AND BORING STUFF. THAT'S THE FRAMEWORK GIVEN TO ME, AND IS MY MISSION.
- △ I'M BURNING WITH A SENSE OF MISSION TODAY, SO EXCUSE ME FOR WRITING BLUNTLY.
- △ DOES EVERYBODY KNOW ABOUT CHAMBER POTS?
- △ THERE MAY BE SOME PEOPLE WHO DON'T KNOW WHAT THEY ARE. BUT I WON'T EXPLAIN WHAT A CHAMBER POT IS HERE. WELL, I COULD PROUDLY EXPLAIN IN IT DETAIL, BUT IT MIGHT MAKE THE READERS FEEL ILL, SO I WON'T EXPLAIN IT.
- △ WHEN I'M WORKING, I TALK NONSENSE WITH MY ASSISTANTS. ONE DAY, WE HAPPENED TO TALK ABOUT CHAMBER POTS.
- △ I REMEMBER THAT WHAT WE TALKED ABOUT WENT SOMETHING LIKE THIS.
- △ LET'S PRETEND THAT THERE IS AN UNPRECEDENTED CHAMBER POT BOOM AMONG THE PEOPLE WHO CREATE FADS (WE HAD FEMALE SENIOR HIGH SCHOOL STUDENTS BE THESE PEOPLE).
- △ I THINK THERE ARE PEOPLE WHO'LL ALREADY BE SHOUTING "THAT'S IMPOSSIBLE!" BUT THIS IS HACK WRITING, SO IT CAN BE FORGIVEN.
- △ THE CHAMBER POT BOOM TAKES OVER ALL OF JAPAN, AND IT'S CHAMBER POTS RIGHT AND LEFT. IN COMMERCIALS, TOP IDOLS PASSIONATELY SING LOVE SONGS ABOUT CHAMBER POTS. STUDENTS PUT PORTABLE CHAMBER POTS IN THEIR POCKETS AND HAVE THEIR TEACHERS CONFISCATE THEM. IN SHIBUYA AND IKEBUKURO, THERE ARE CHAMBER POT BOXES, AND YOUNG PEOPLE COMPETE TO USE CHAMBER POTS. AND SHAMEFULLY, PEOPLE HUNT FOR CHAMBER POTS BECAUSE THEY WANT THEM SO MUCH. CHAMBER POTS WITH FACES OF BASEBALL PLAYERS PRINTED ON THEM ARE POPULAR AND COMMAND A PREMIUM, SO THEY ARE EASY TARGETS.
- △ AND THEN CHAMBER POTS, THE BIG CRAZE IN JAPAN, START TO GET EXPORTED. THEY ARE APPARENTLY POPULAR IN THAILAND.
- △ BUT FADS DON'T LAST LONG. THE NEXT FAD, CHECKED GINGHAM GIFT ENVELOPES, MADE CHAMBER POTS HISTORY...
- △ SO I OFTEN TALK ABOUT THINGS LIKE THIS WITH MY ASSISTANTS.
- △ THERE ARE OTHER TOPICS SUCH AS COW BURP RESEARCHERS. I'LL WRITE ABOUT IT LATER IF I HAVE THE CHANCE.

END OF HACK WRITING

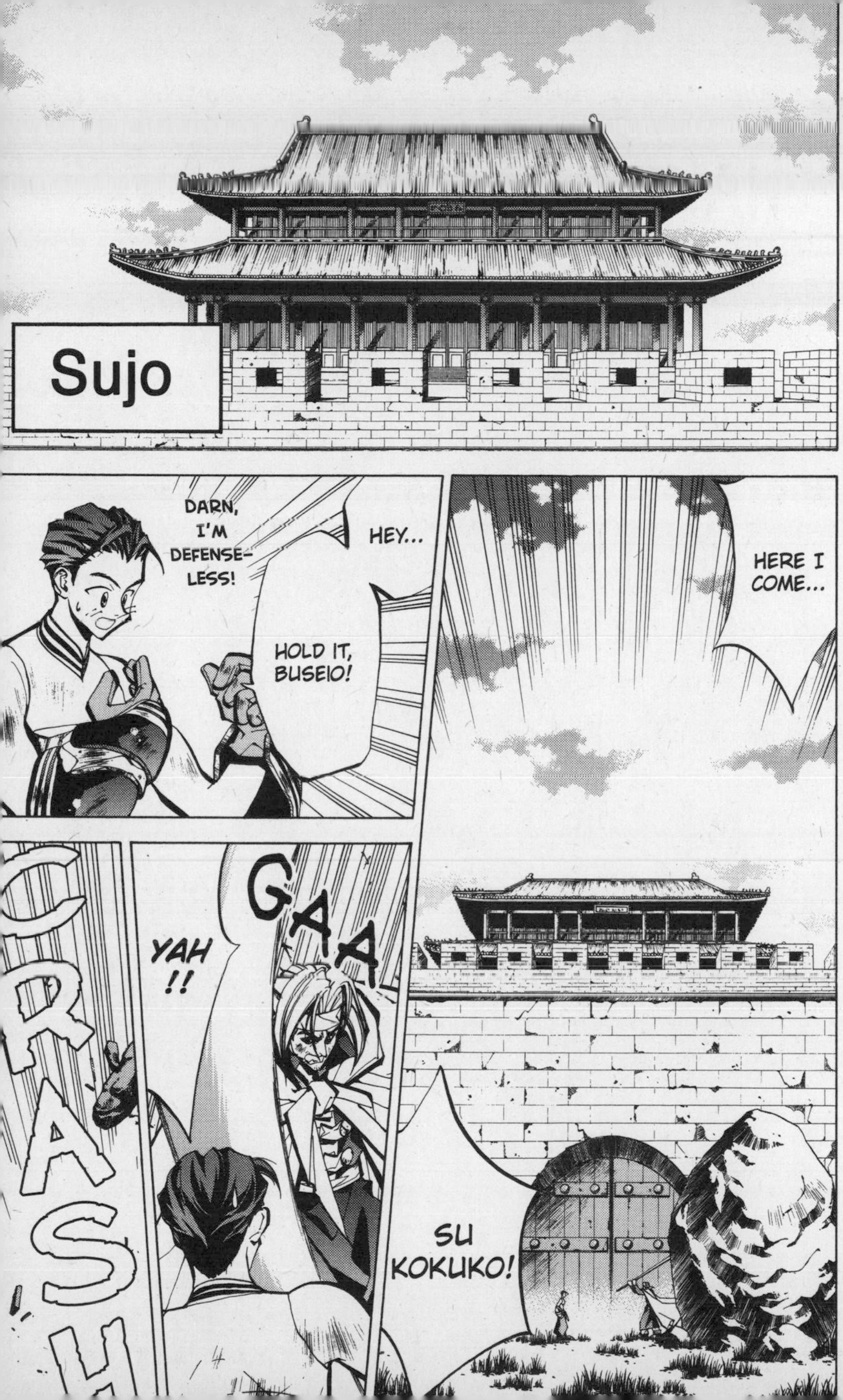
Sujo
HERE I COME...
SU KOKUKO!
HEY...
HOLD IT, BUSEIO!
DARN, I'M DEFENSE-LESS!
GAA
YAH !!
CRASH

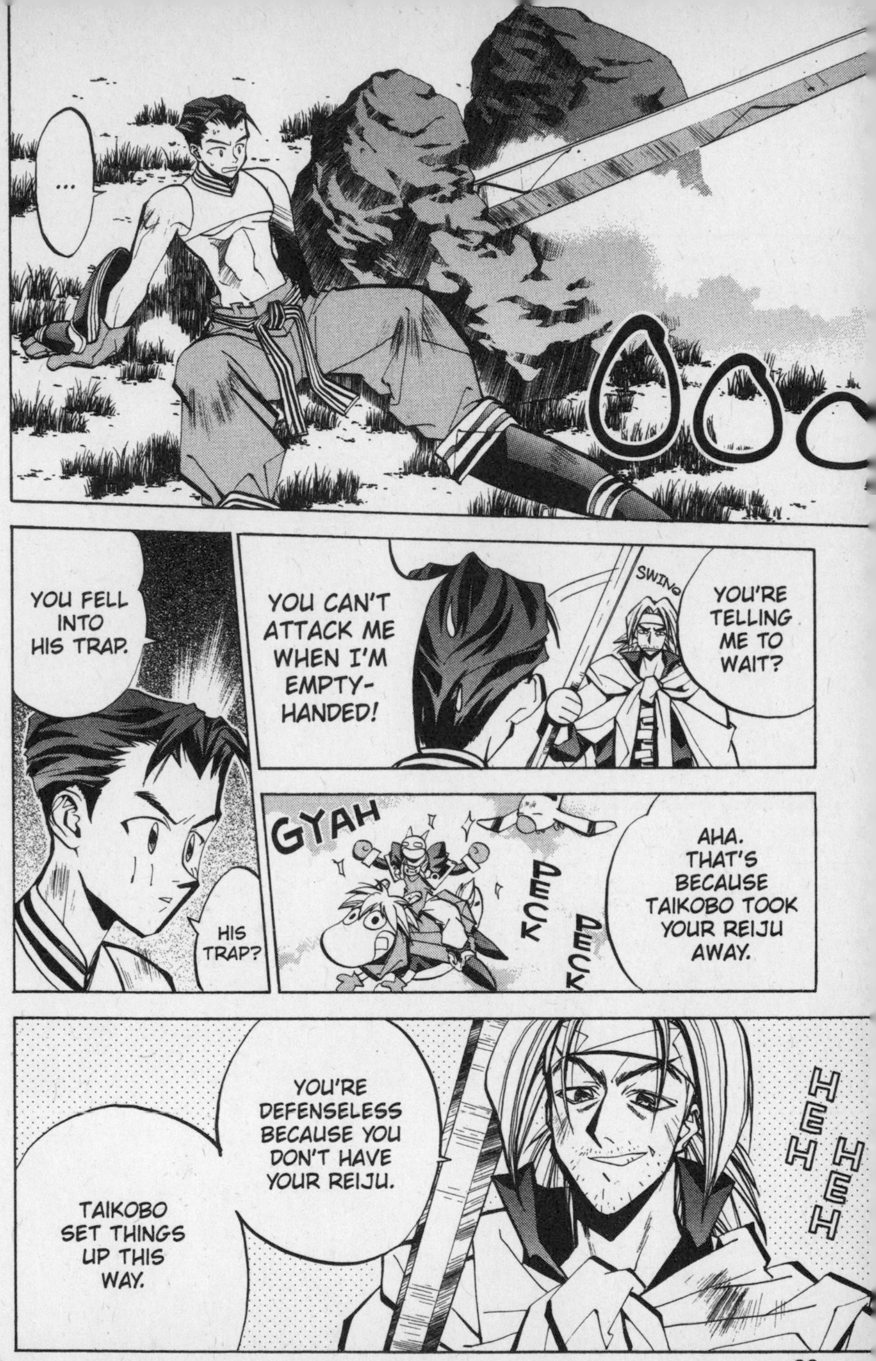
...
YOU'RE TELLING ME TO WAIT?
SWING
YOU CAN'T ATTACK ME WHEN I'M EMPTY-HANDED!
AHA. THAT'S BECAUSE TAIKOBO TOOK YOUR REIJU AWAY.
PECK
PECK
GYAH
YOU FELL INTO HIS TRAP.
HIS TRAP?
HEH HEH
HEH
YOU'RE DEFENSELESS BECAUSE YOU DON'T HAVE YOUR REIJU.
TAIKOBO SET THINGS UP THIS WAY.

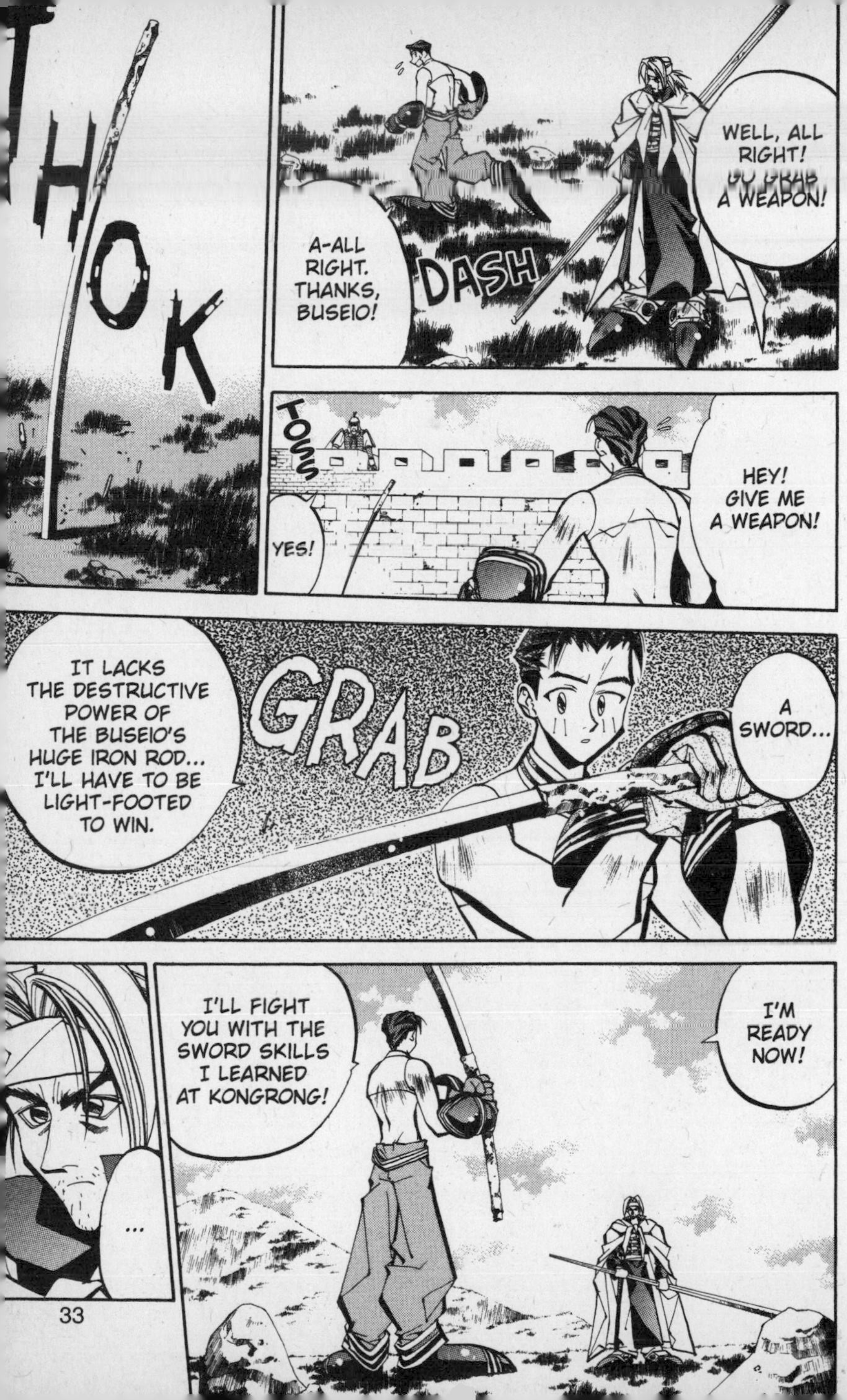
WELL, ALL RIGHT! GO GRAB A WEAPON!
A-ALL RIGHT. THANKS, BUSEIO!
DASH
HEY! GIVE ME A WEAPON!
TOSS
YES!
THOK
A SWORD...
GRAB
IT LACKS THE DESTRUCTIVE POWER OF THE BUSEIO'S HUGE IRON ROD... I'LL HAVE TO BE LIGHT-FOOTED TO WIN.
I'M READY NOW!
I'LL FIGHT YOU WITH THE SWORD SKILLS I LEARNED AT KONGRONG!
...

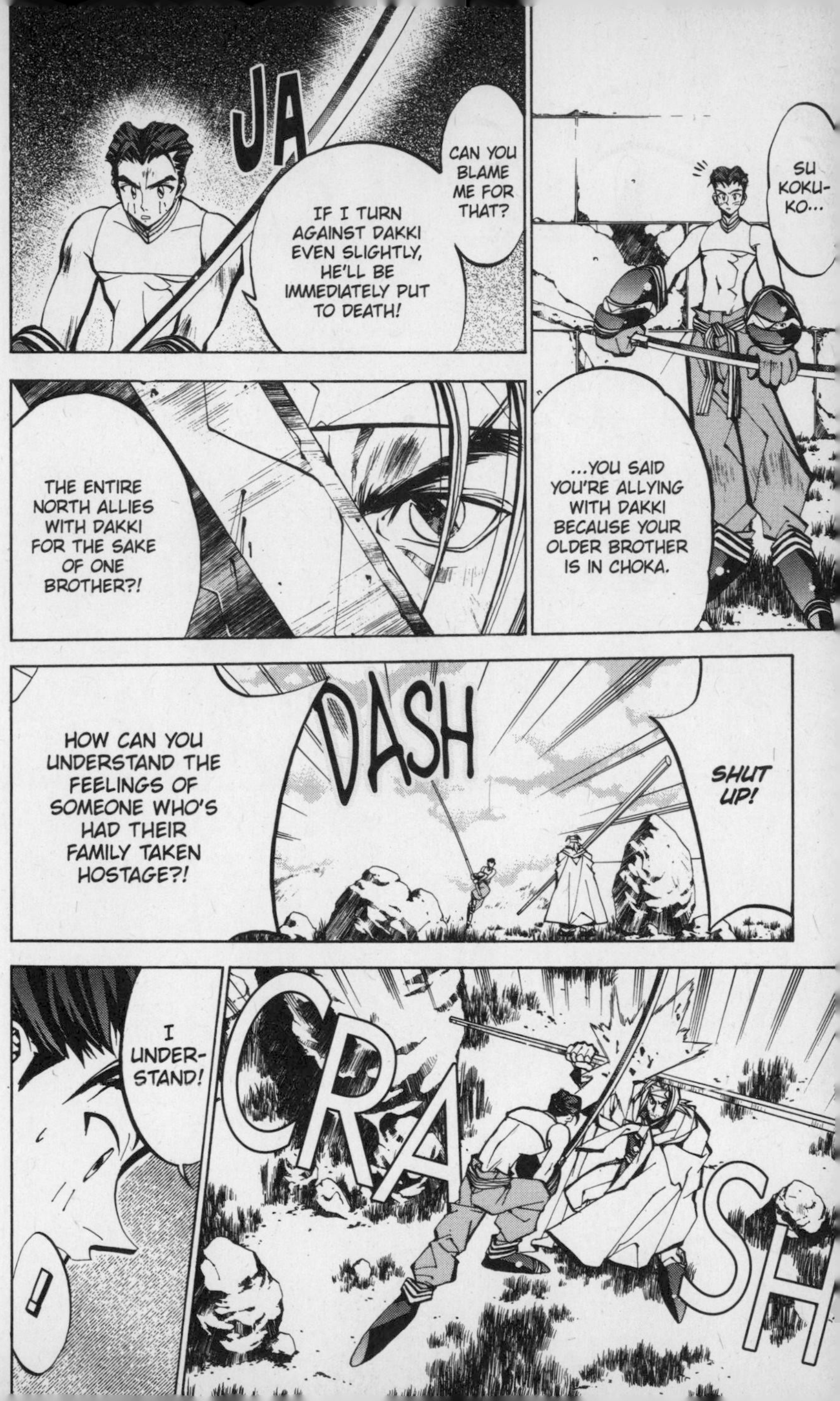
SU KOKU-KO...
...YOU SAID YOU'RE ALLYING WITH DAKKI BECAUSE YOUR OLDER BROTHER IS IN CHOKA.
JA
IF I TURN AGAINST DAKKI EVEN SLIGHTLY, HE'LL BE IMMEDIATELY PUT TO DEATH!
CAN YOU BLAME ME FOR THAT?
THE ENTIRE NORTH ALLIES WITH DAKKI FOR THE SAKE OF ONE BROTHER?!
SHUT UP!
DASH
HOW CAN YOU UNDERSTAND THE FEELINGS OF SOMEONE WHO'S HAD THEIR FAMILY TAKEN HOSTAGE?!
CRASH
I UNDER-STAND!
!

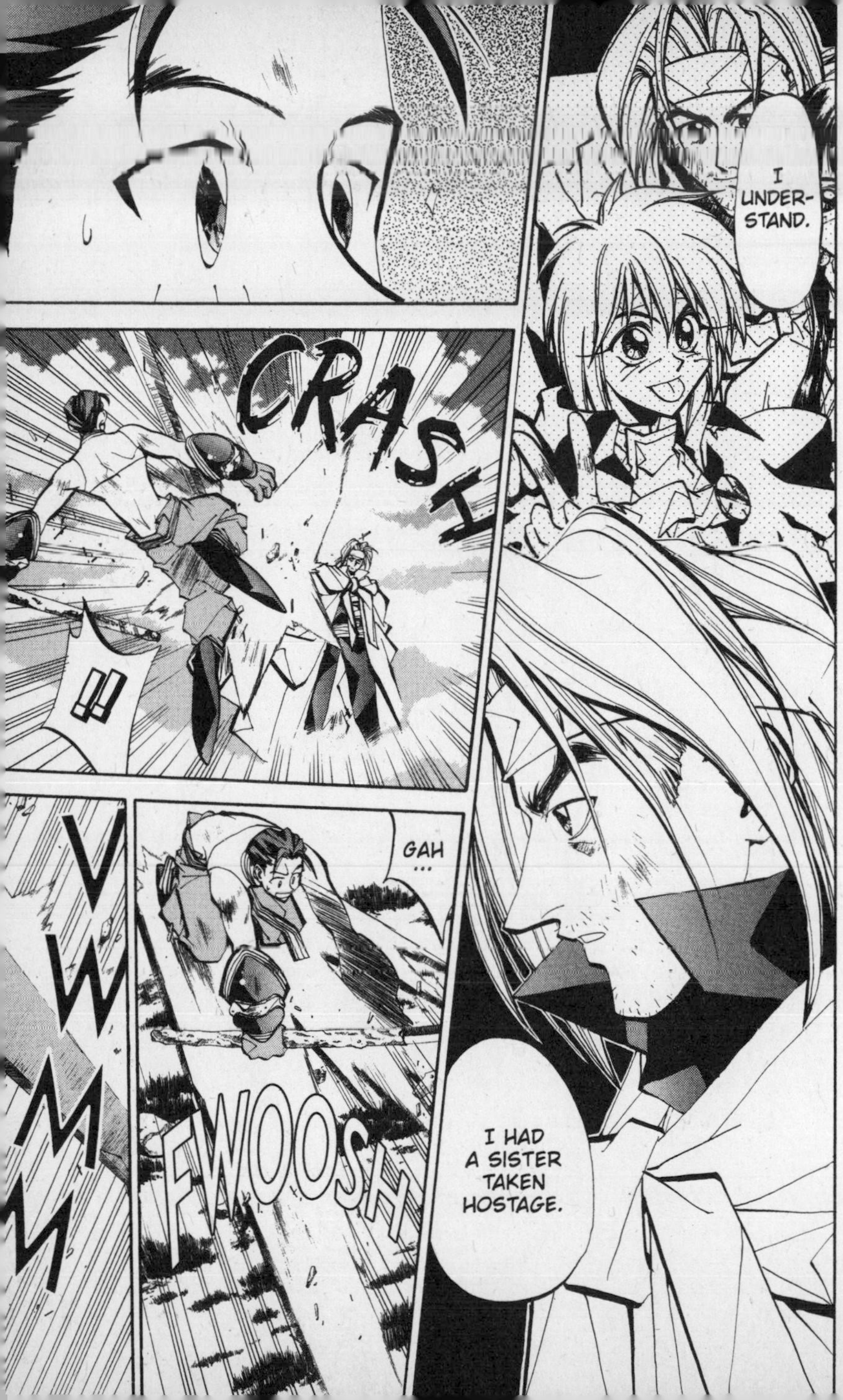
I UNDER-STAND.
I HAD A SISTER TAKEN HOSTAGE.
CRASH
!!
GAH ...
FWOOSH
VWMM

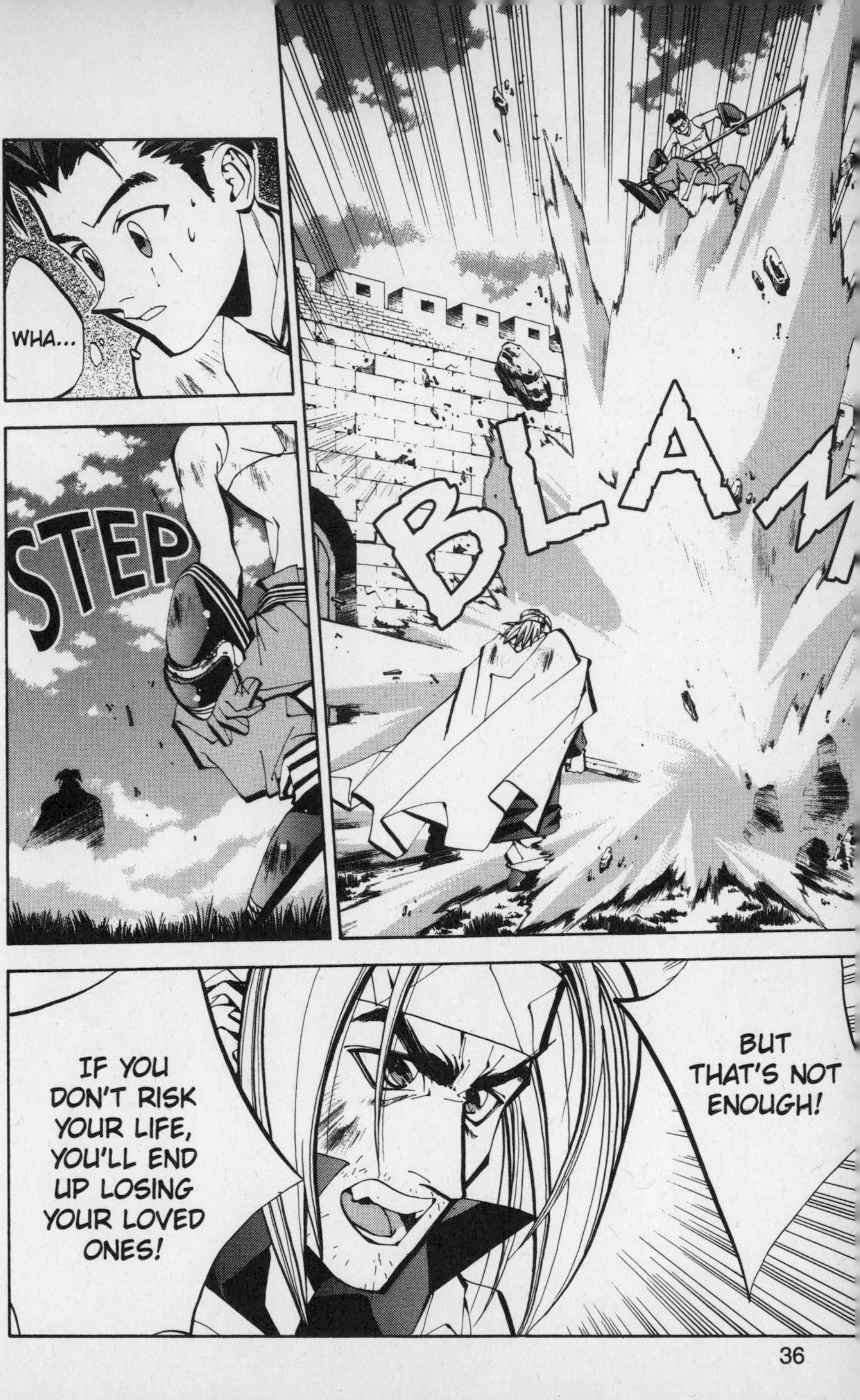
BLAM
WHA...
STEP
BUT THAT'S NOT ENOUGH!
IF YOU DON'T RISK YOUR LIFE, YOU'LL END UP LOSING YOUR LOVED ONES!

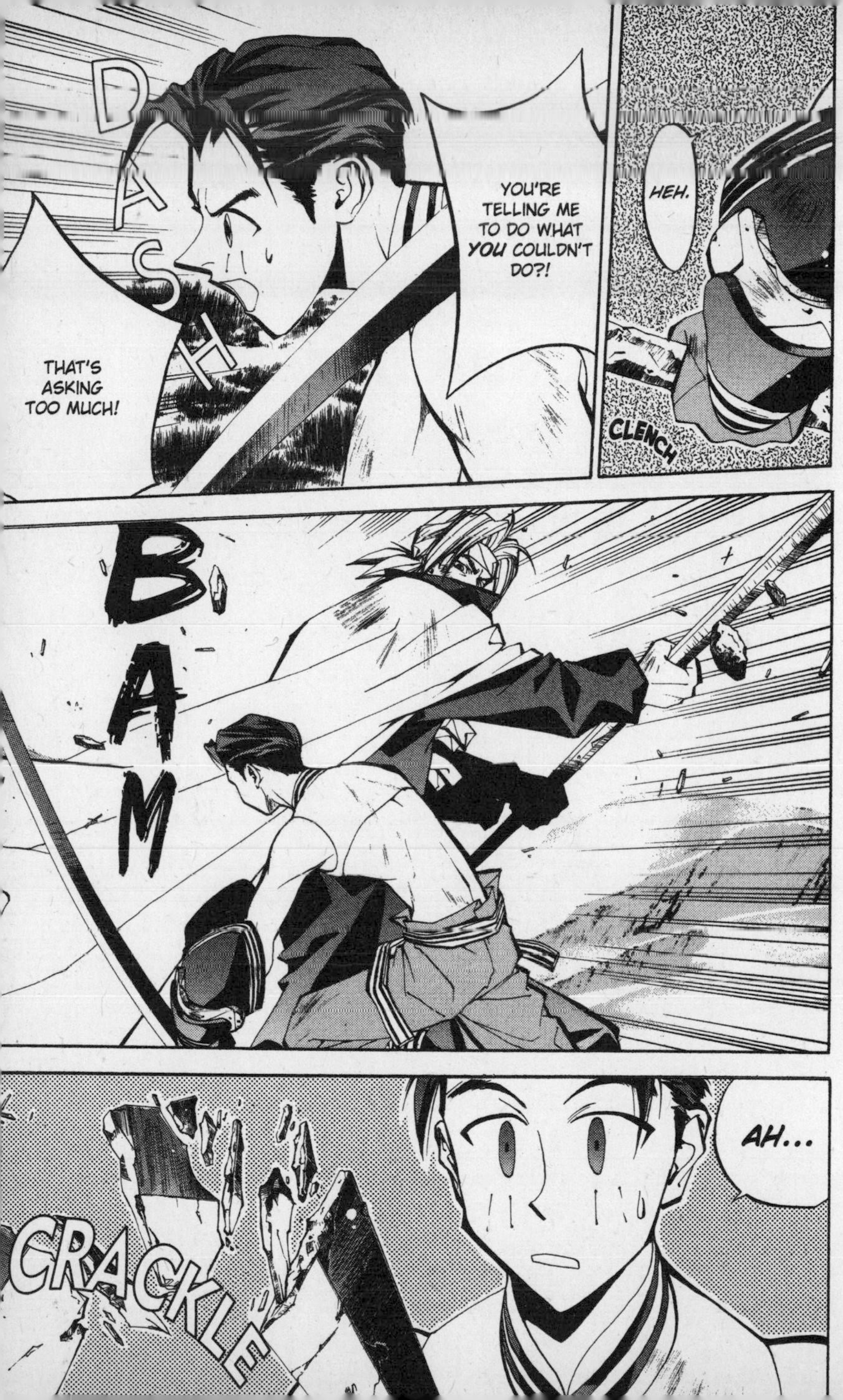
HEH.
CLENCH
YOU'RE TELLING ME TO DO WHAT YOU COULDN'T DO?!
DASH
THAT'S ASKING TOO MUCH!
BAM
AH...
CRACKLE

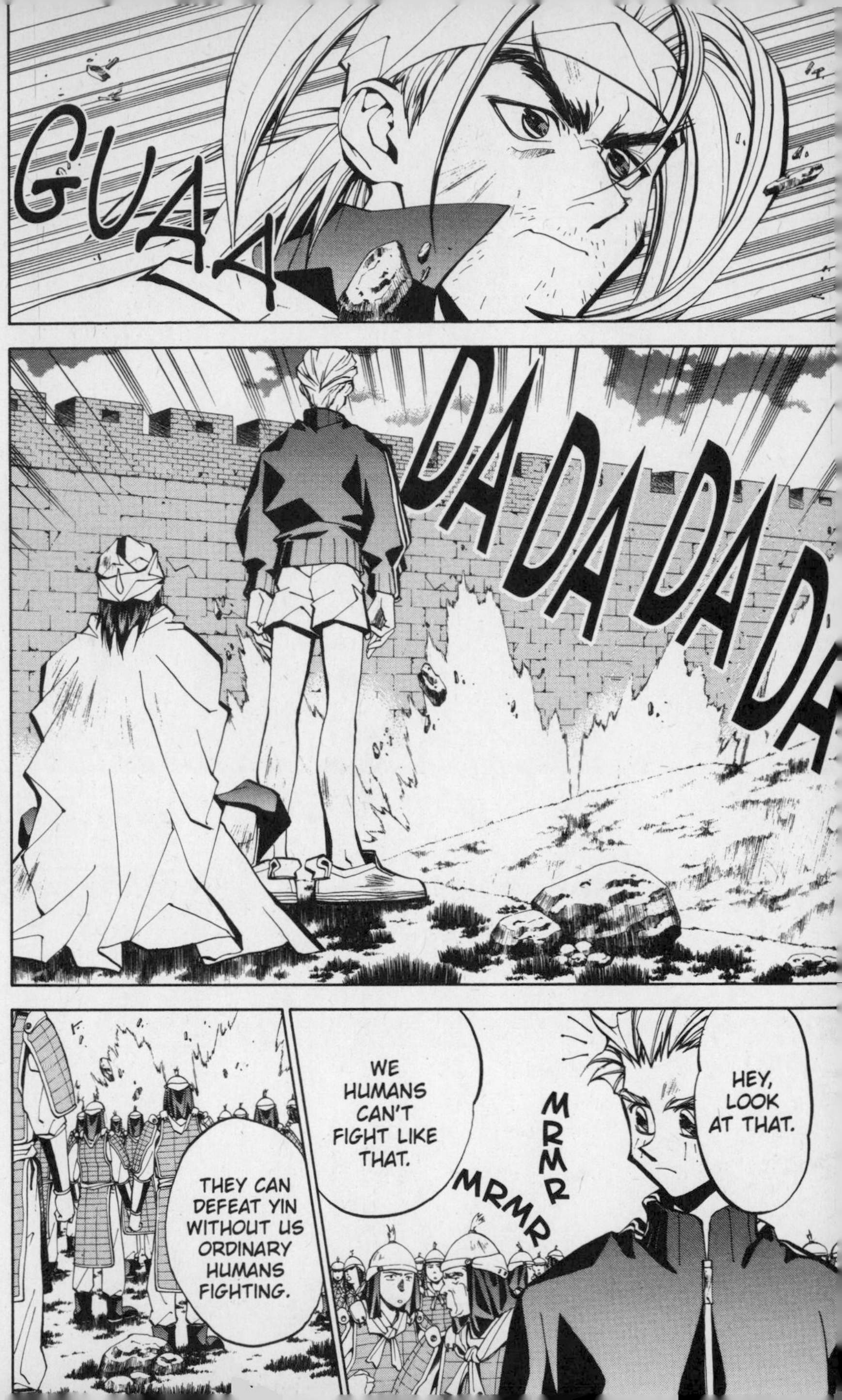
GUAA
DADADADA
HEY, LOOK AT THAT.
MRMR MRMR
WE HUMANS CAN'T FIGHT LIKE THAT.
THEY CAN DEFEAT YIN WITHOUT US ORDINARY HUMANS FIGHTING.

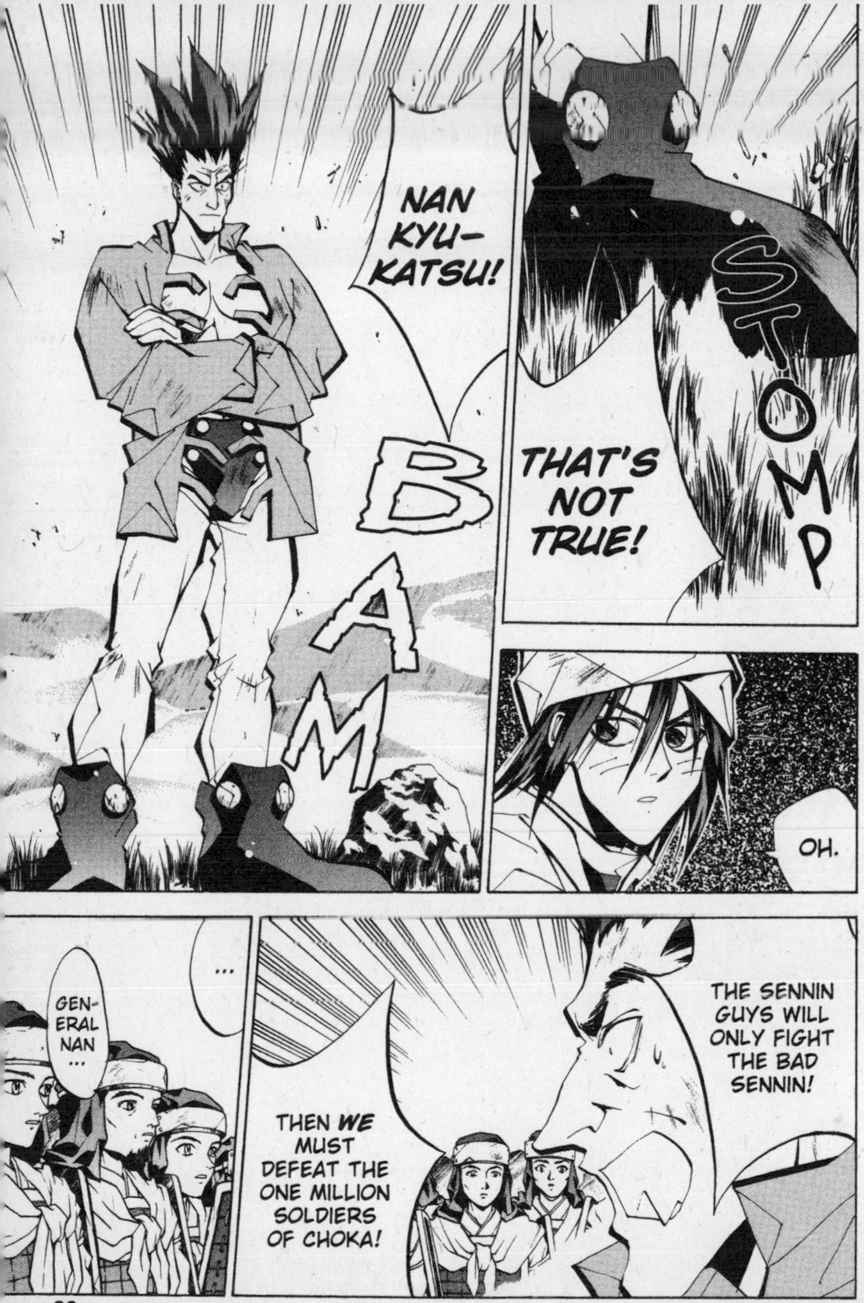
STOMP
THAT'S NOT TRUE!
OH.
NAN KYU-KATSU!
BAM
THE SENNIN GUYS WILL ONLY FIGHT THE BAD SENNIN!
THEN **WE** MUST DEFEAT THE ONE MILLION SOLDIERS OF CHOKA!
...
GEN-ERAL NAN ...

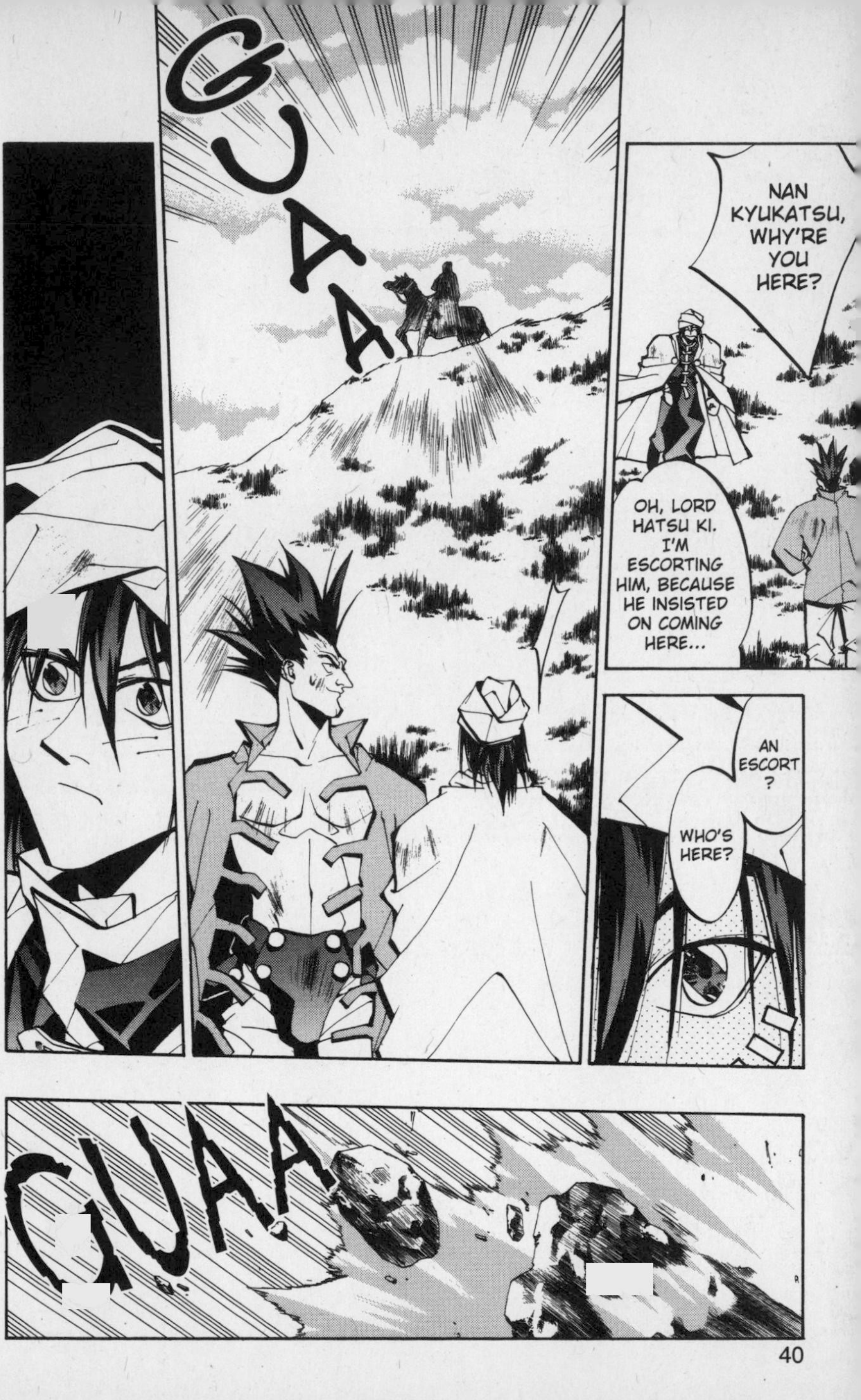
NAN KYUKATSU, WHY'RE YOU HERE?
OH, LORD HATSU KI. I'M ESCORTING HIM, BECAUSE HE INSISTED ON COMING HERE...
AN ESCORT?
WHO'S HERE?
GUAA
GUAA

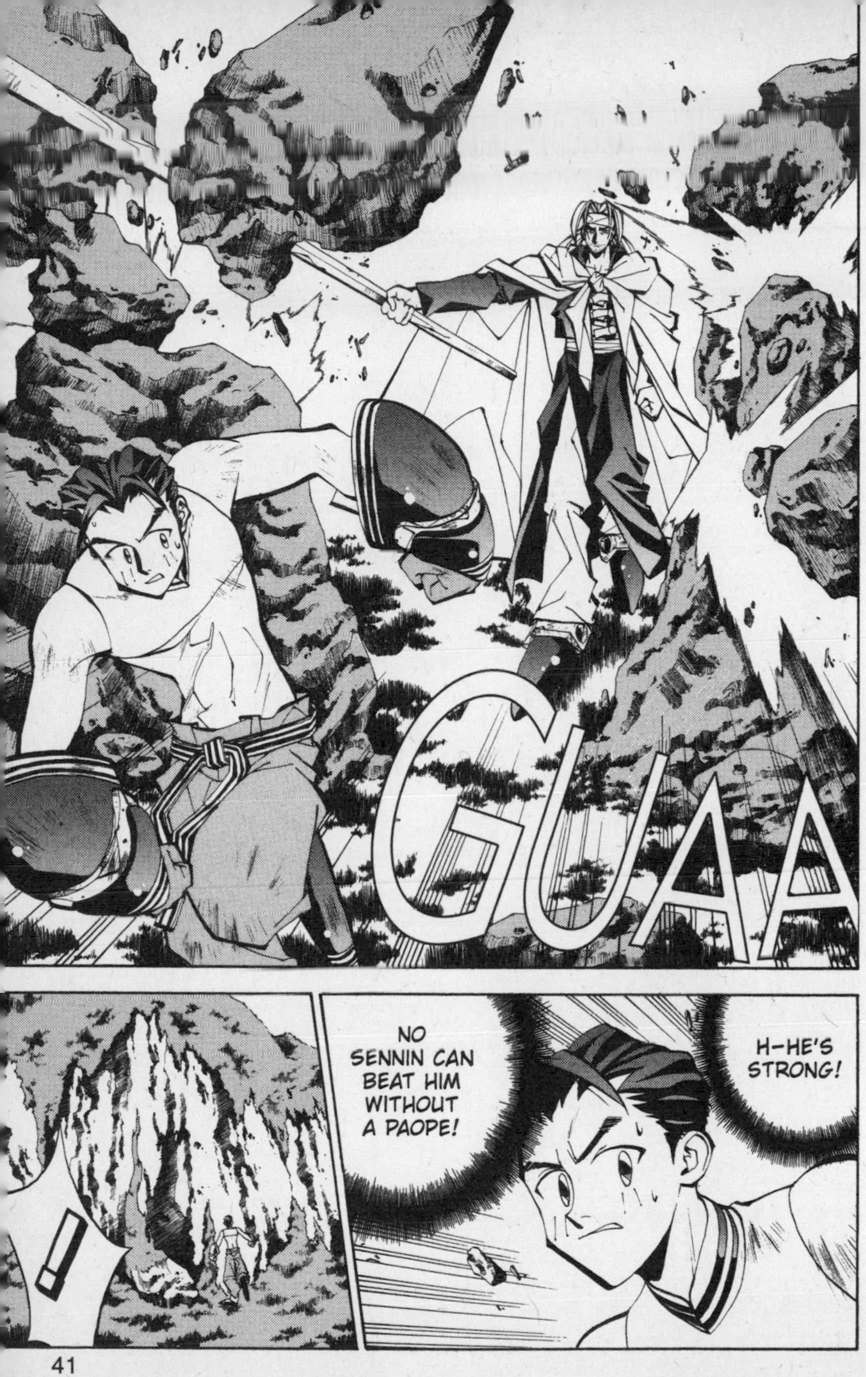
GUAA
H-HE'S STRONG!
NO SENNIN CAN BEAT HIM WITHOUT A PAOPE!
!

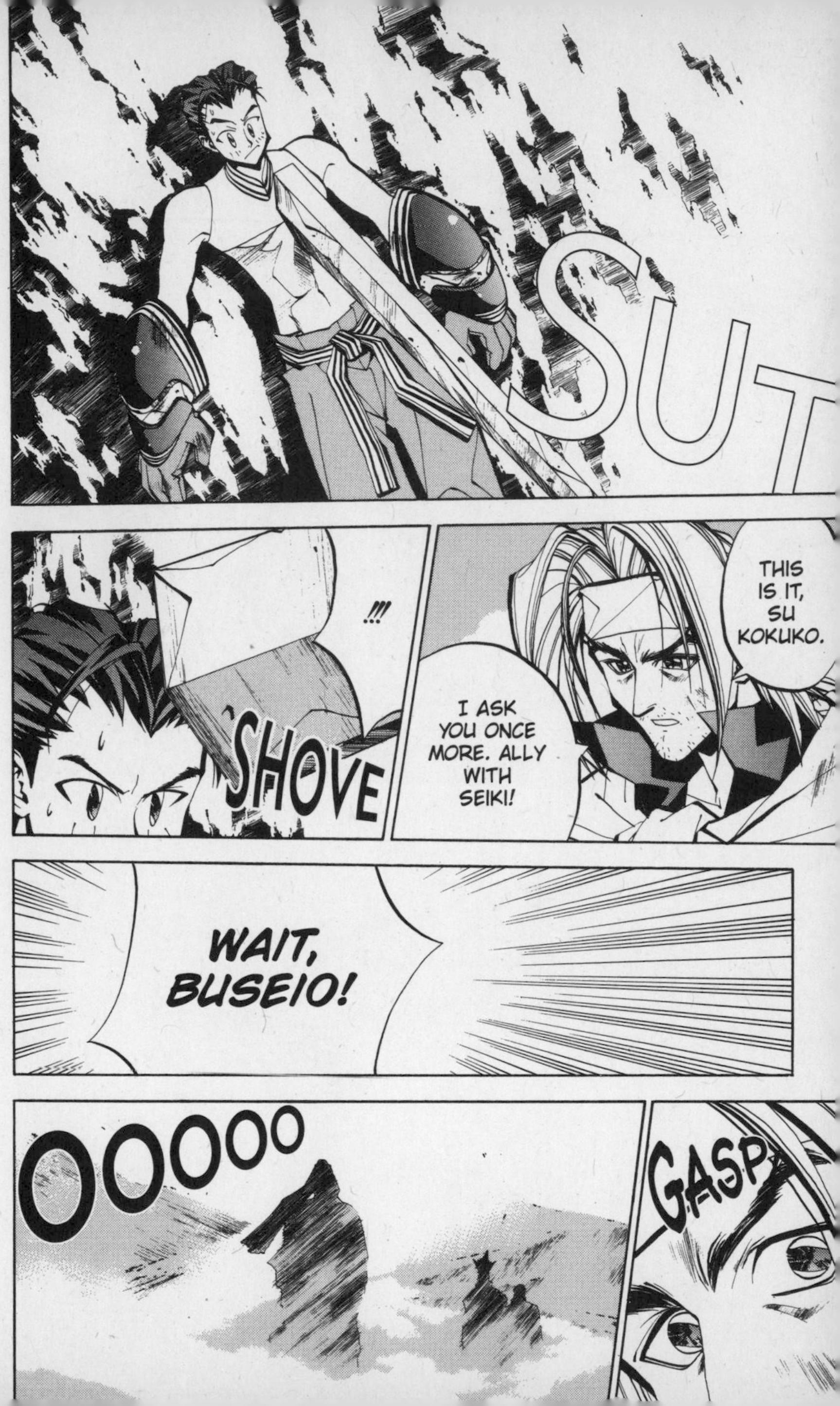
SUT
THIS IS IT, SU KOKUKO.
I ASK YOU ONCE MORE. ALLY WITH SEIKI!
!!!
SHOVE
WAIT, BUSEIO!
GASP
OOOOO

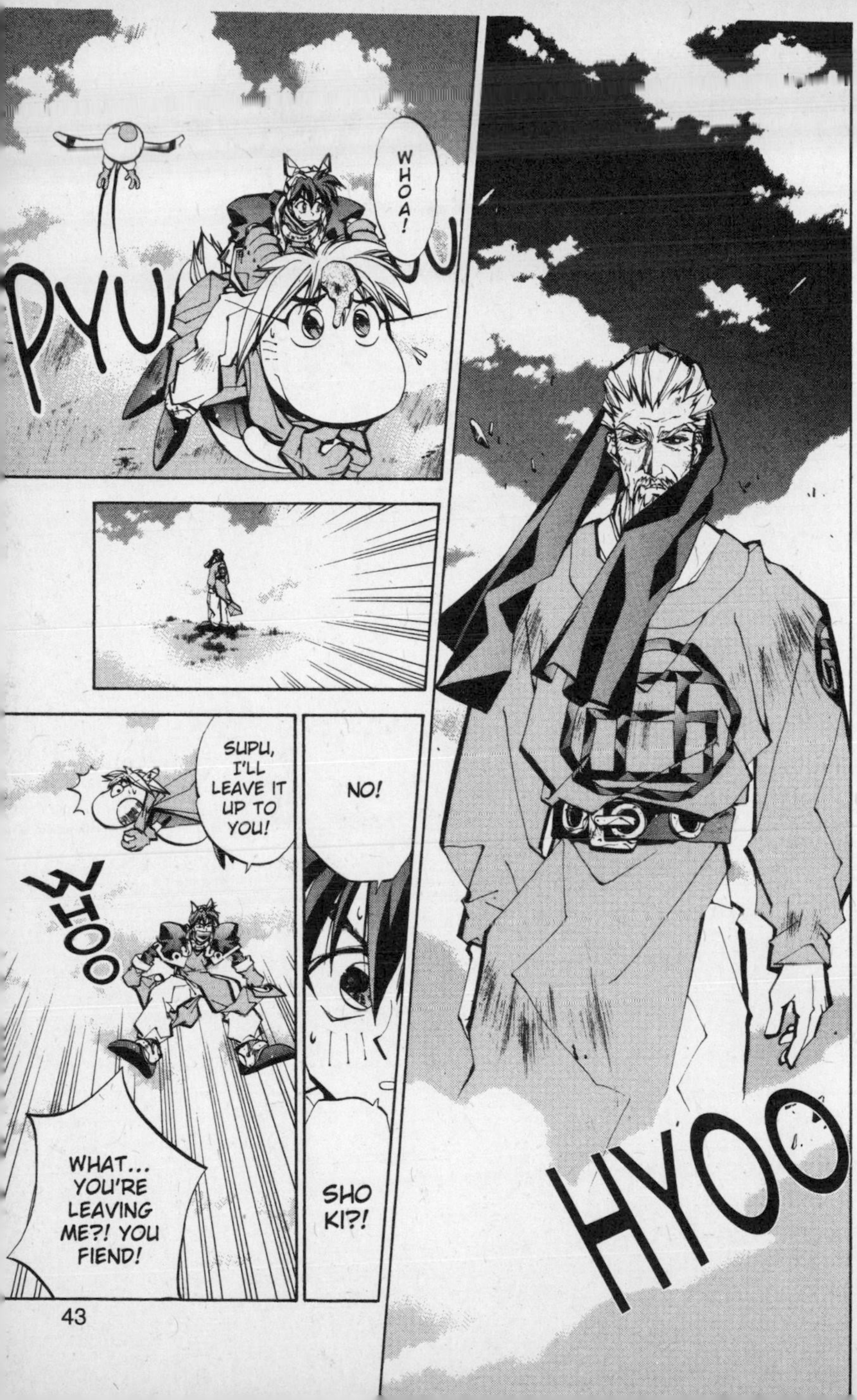
HYOO
WHOA!
PYU U
NO!
SHO KI?!
SUPU, I'LL LEAVE IT UP TO YOU!
WHOO
WHAT... YOU'RE LEAVING ME?! YOU FIEND!

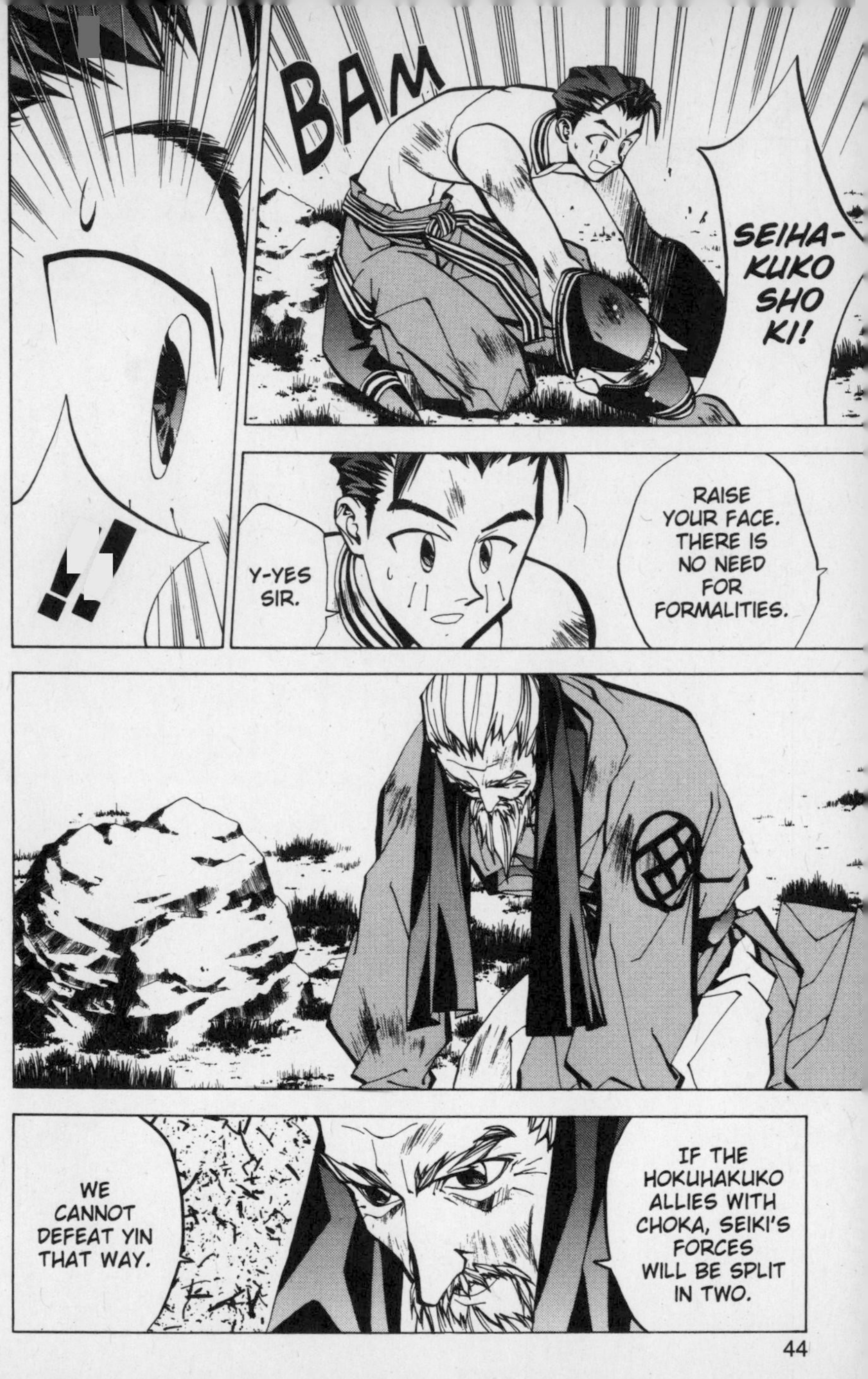
BAM
SEIHAKUKO SHO KI!
RAISE YOUR FACE. THERE IS NO NEED FOR FORMALITIES.
Y-YES SIR.
!!
IF THE HOKUHAKUKO ALLIES WITH CHOKA, SEIKI'S FORCES WILL BE SPLIT IN TWO.
WE CANNOT DEFEAT YIN THAT WAY.

READ THIS WAY

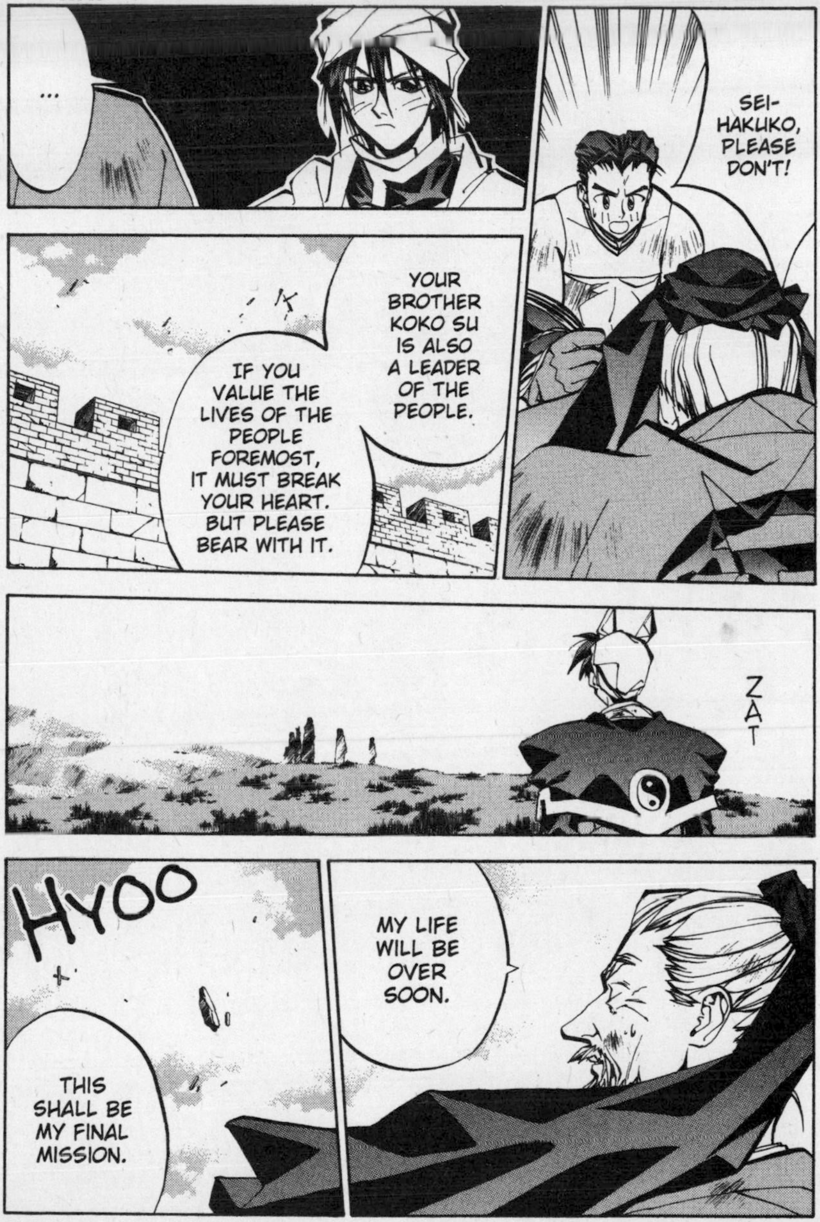

SEI-HAKUKO, PLEASE DON'T!
...
YOUR BROTHER KOKO SU IS ALSO A LEADER OF THE PEOPLE.
IF YOU VALUE THE LIVES OF THE PEOPLE FOREMOST, IT MUST BREAK YOUR HEART. BUT PLEASE BEAR WITH IT.
ZAT
MY LIFE WILL BE OVER SOON.
HYOO
THIS SHALL BE MY FINAL MISSION.

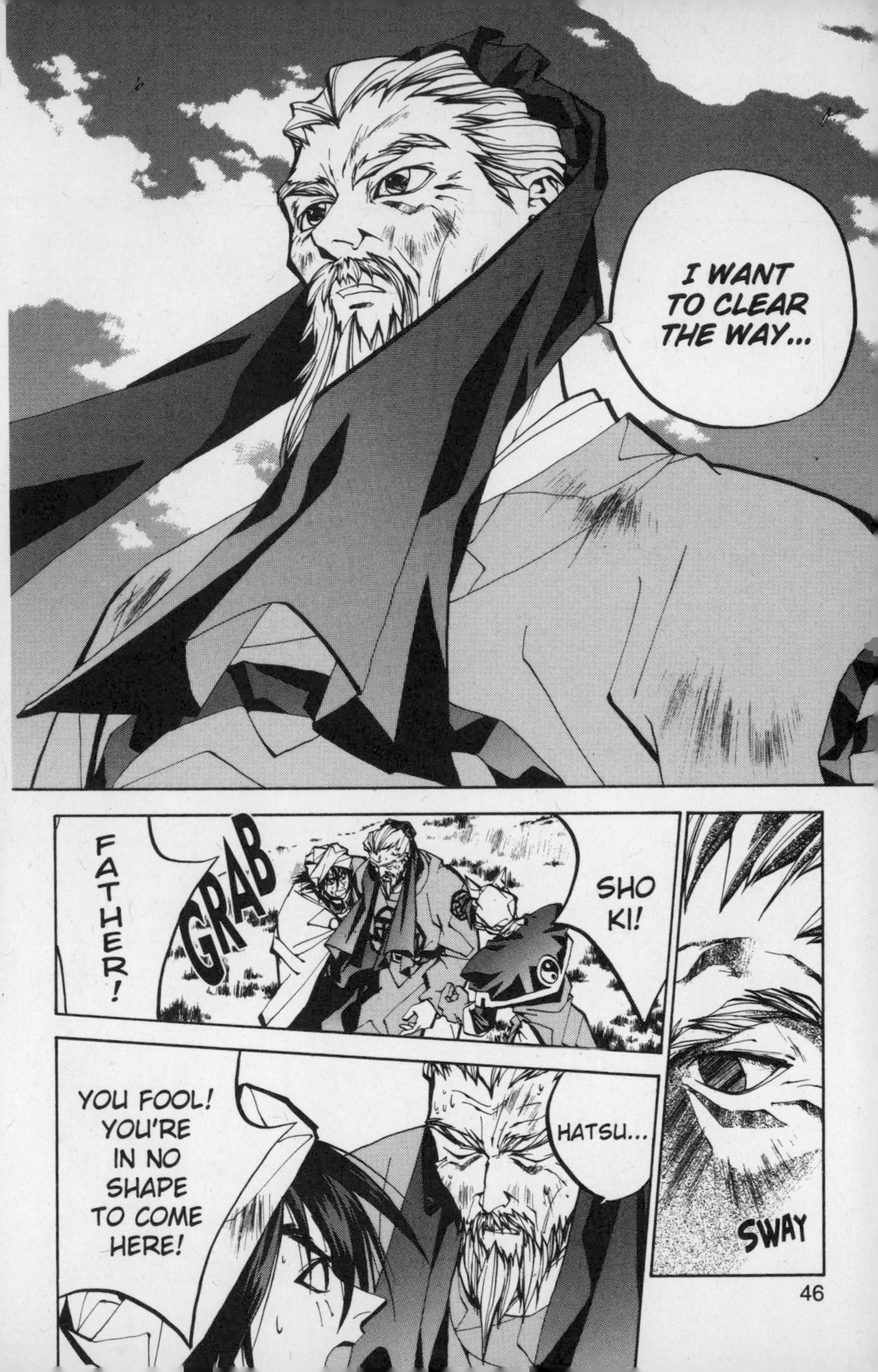
I WANT TO CLEAR THE WAY...
SWAY
SHO KI!
GRAB
FATHER!
HATSU...
YOU FOOL! YOU'RE IN NO SHAPE TO COME HERE!

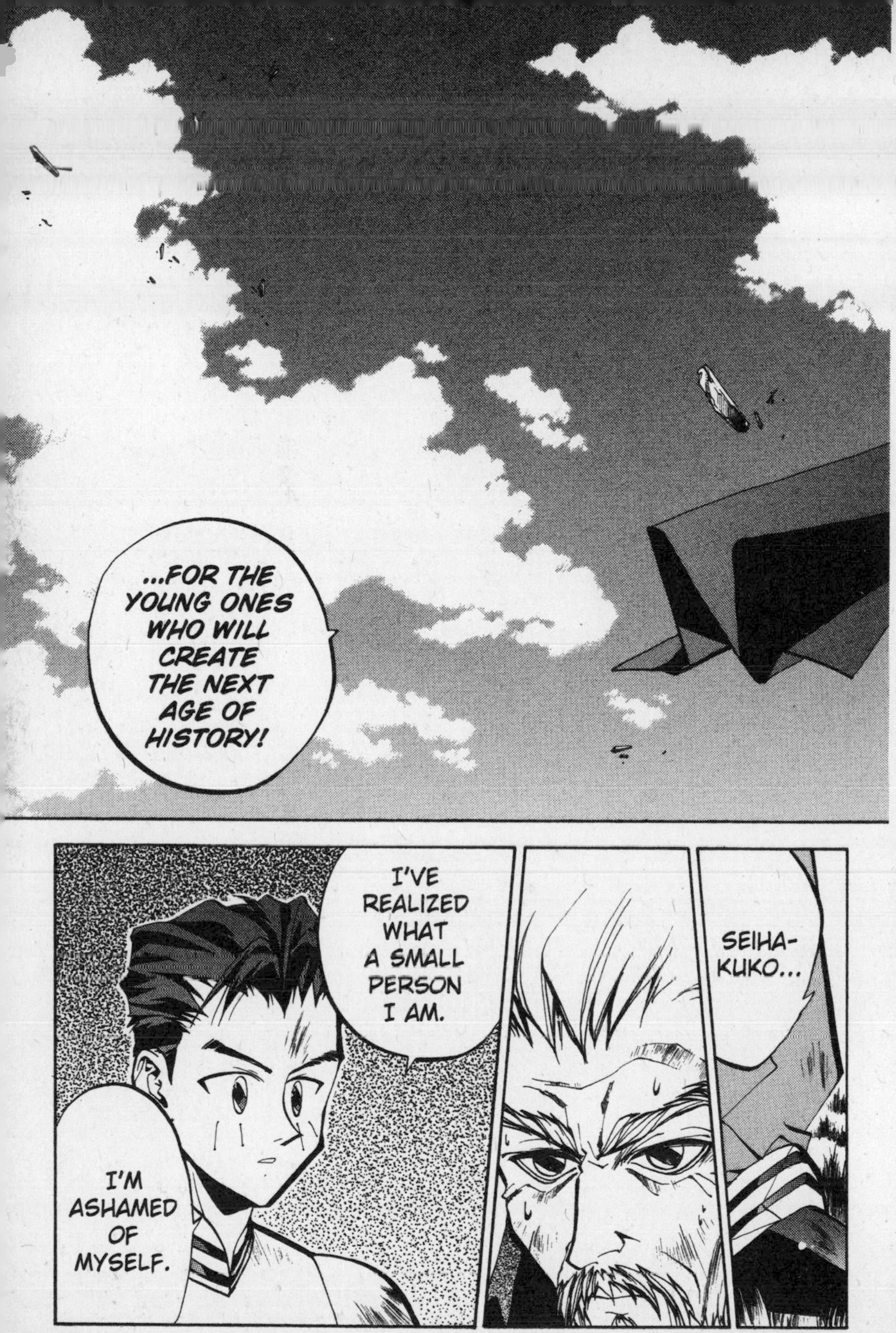
...FOR THE YOUNG ONES WHO WILL CREATE THE NEXT AGE OF HISTORY!
SEIHA-KUKO...
I'VE REALIZED WHAT A SMALL PERSON I AM.
I'M ASHAMED OF MYSELF.

封神演義

CHAPTER 54: THE CURTAIN FALLS, PART 2

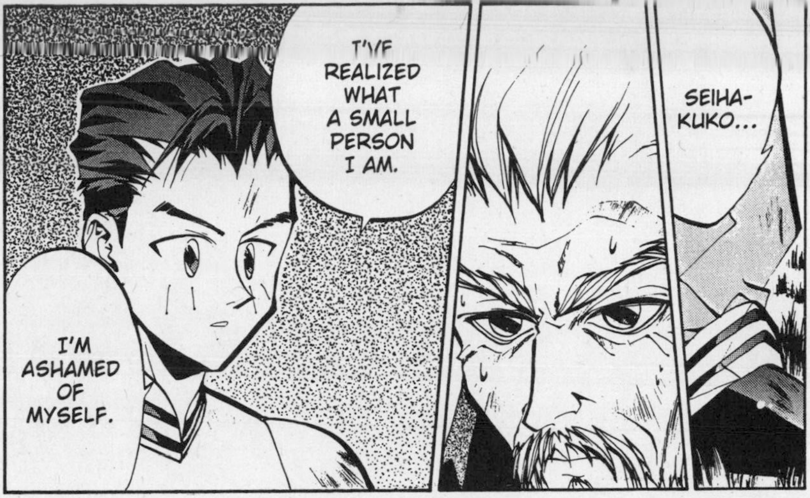
SEIHA-
KUKO...
I'VE REALIZED WHAT A SMALL PERSON I AM.
I'M ASHAMED OF MYSELF.

LORD SHO KI...

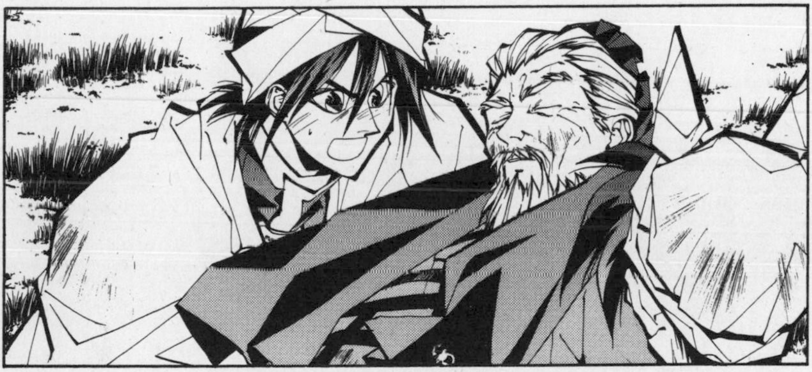

...FELL UNCONSCIOUS
AFTER THAT...

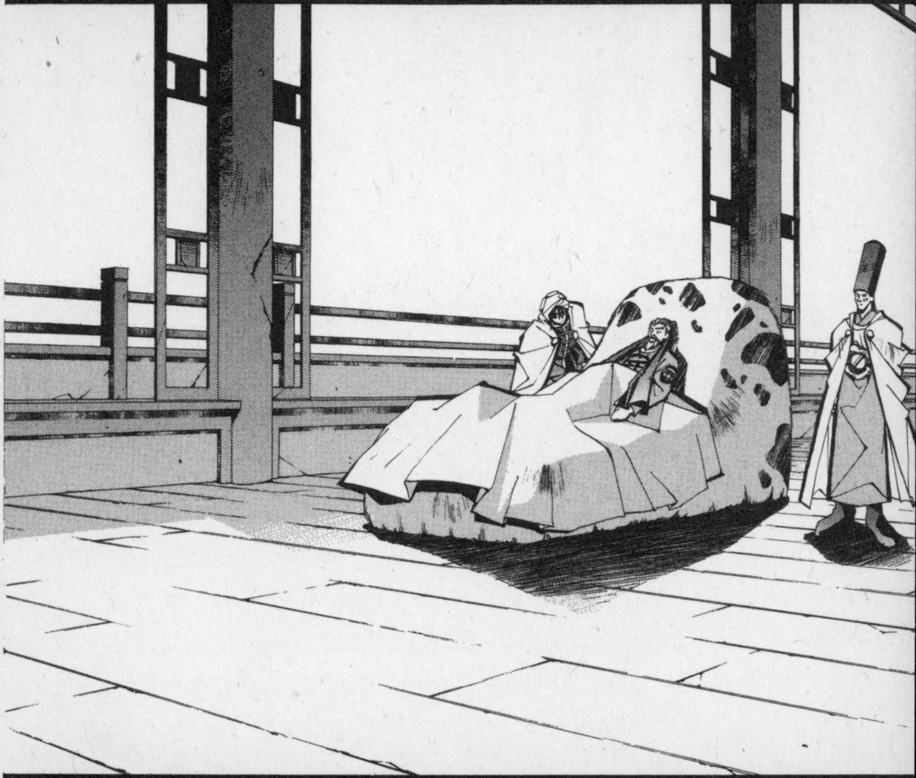

Part 2

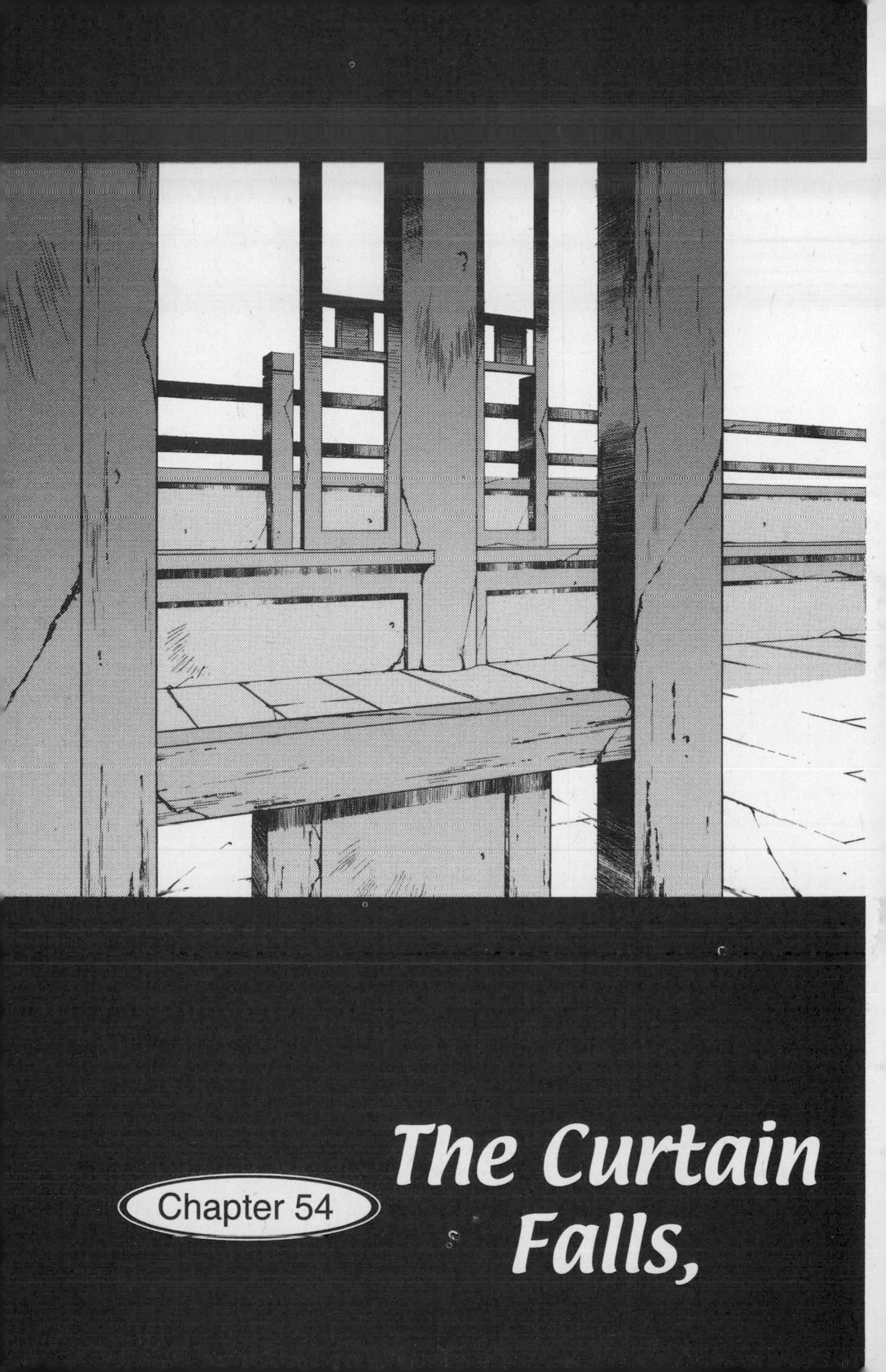

Chapter 54

The Curtain Falls,

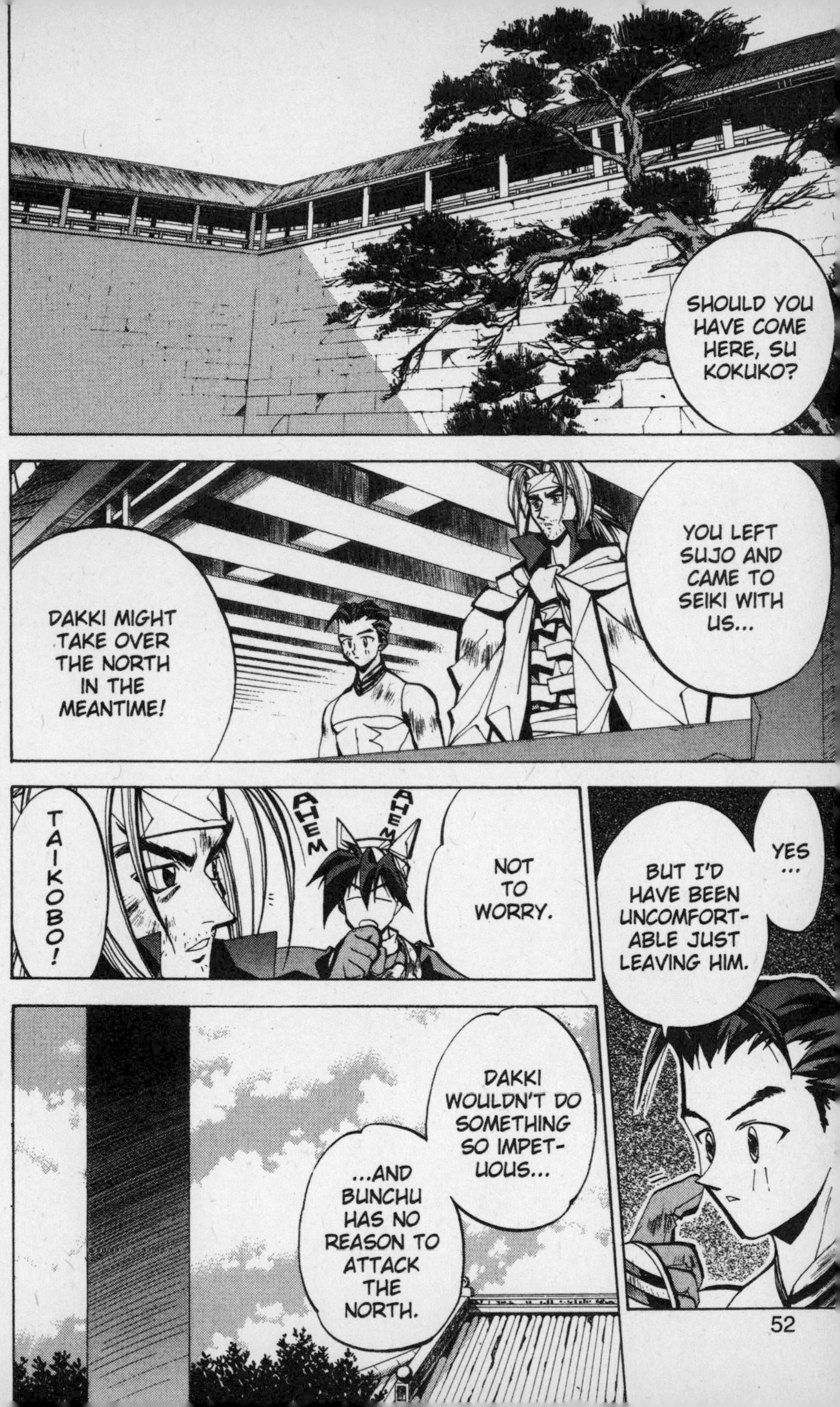
SHOULD YOU HAVE COME HERE, SU KOKUKO?
YOU LEFT SUJO AND CAME TO SEIKI WITH US...
DAKKI MIGHT TAKE OVER THE NORTH IN THE MEANTIME!
YES...
BUT I'D HAVE BEEN UNCOMFORT-ABLE JUST LEAVING HIM.
NOT TO WORRY.
AHEM
AHEM
TAIKOBO!
DAKKI WOULDN'T DO SOMETHING SO IMPET-UOUS...
...AND BUNCHU HAS NO REASON TO ATTACK THE NORTH.

READ THIS WAY

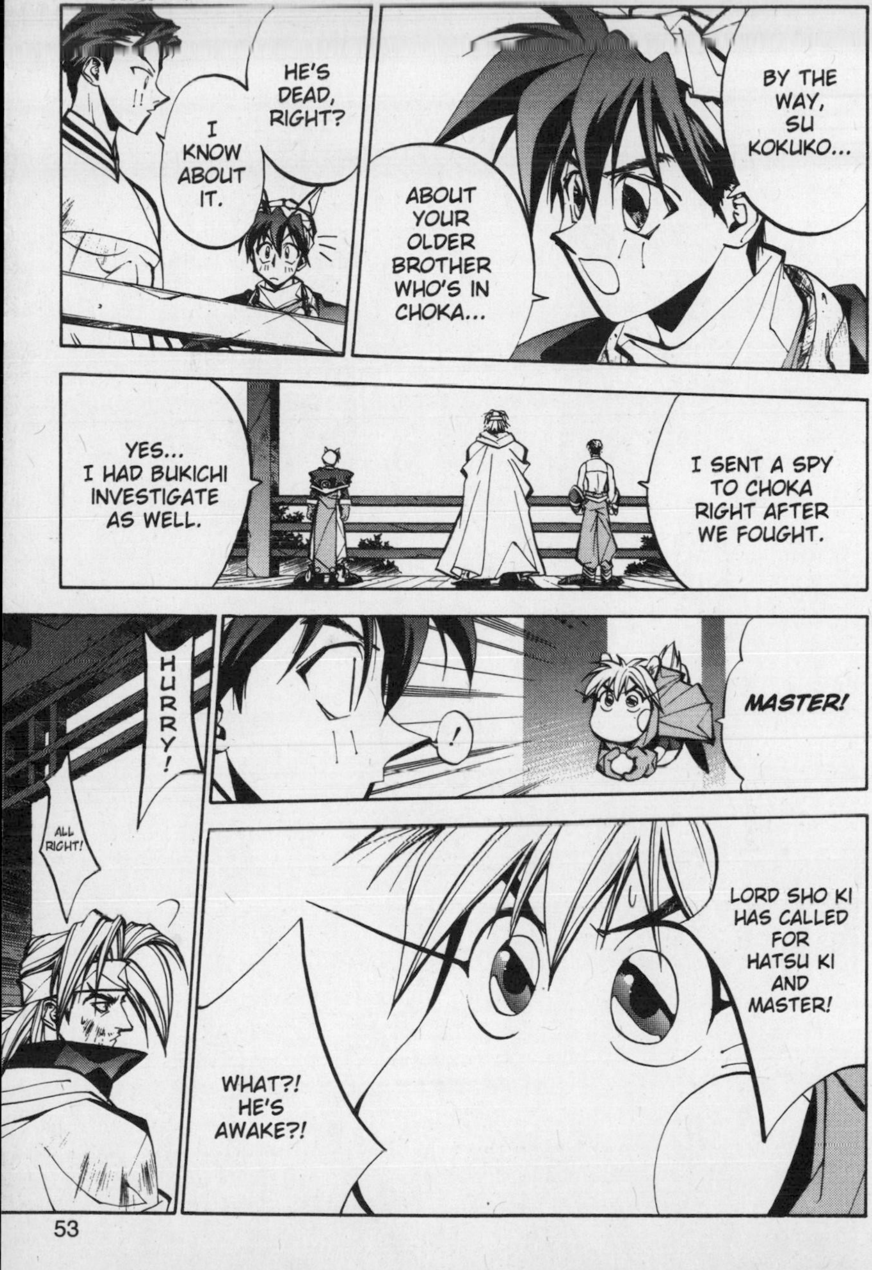
BY THE WAY, SU KOKUKO...
ABOUT YOUR OLDER BROTHER WHO'S IN CHOKA...
HE'S DEAD, RIGHT?
I KNOW ABOUT IT.
I SENT A SPY TO CHOKA RIGHT AFTER WE FOUGHT.
YES... I HAD BUKICHI INVESTIGATE AS WELL.
MASTER!
!
LORD SHO KI HAS CALLED FOR HATSU KI AND MASTER!
WHAT?! HE'S AWAKE?!
HURRY!
ALL RIGHT!

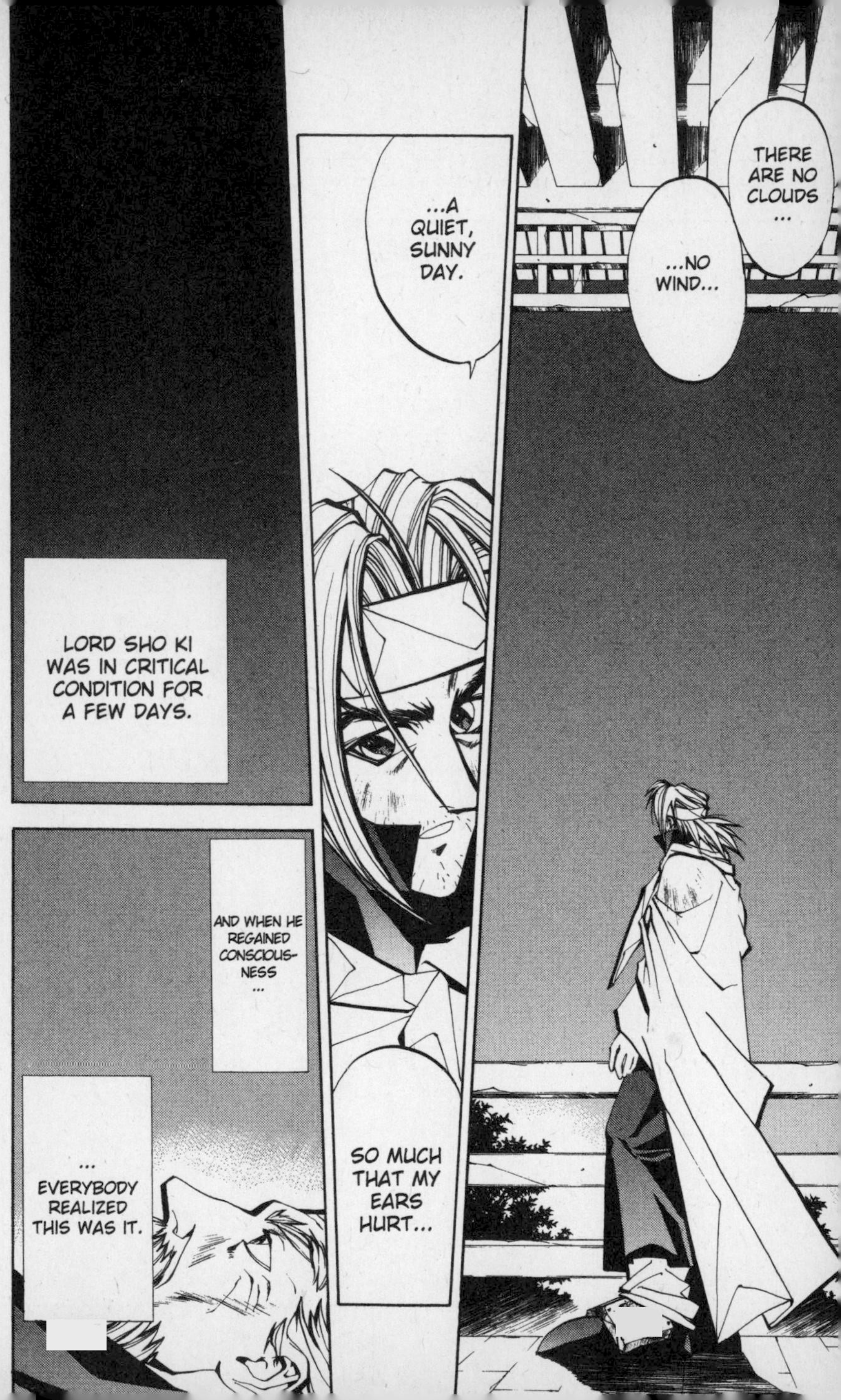
THERE ARE NO CLOUDS ...
...NO WIND...
...A QUIET, SUNNY DAY.
SO MUCH THAT MY EARS HURT...
LORD SHO KI WAS IN CRITICAL CONDITION FOR A FEW DAYS.
AND WHEN HE REGAINED CONSCIOUS-NESS ...
... EVERYBODY REALIZED THIS WAS IT.

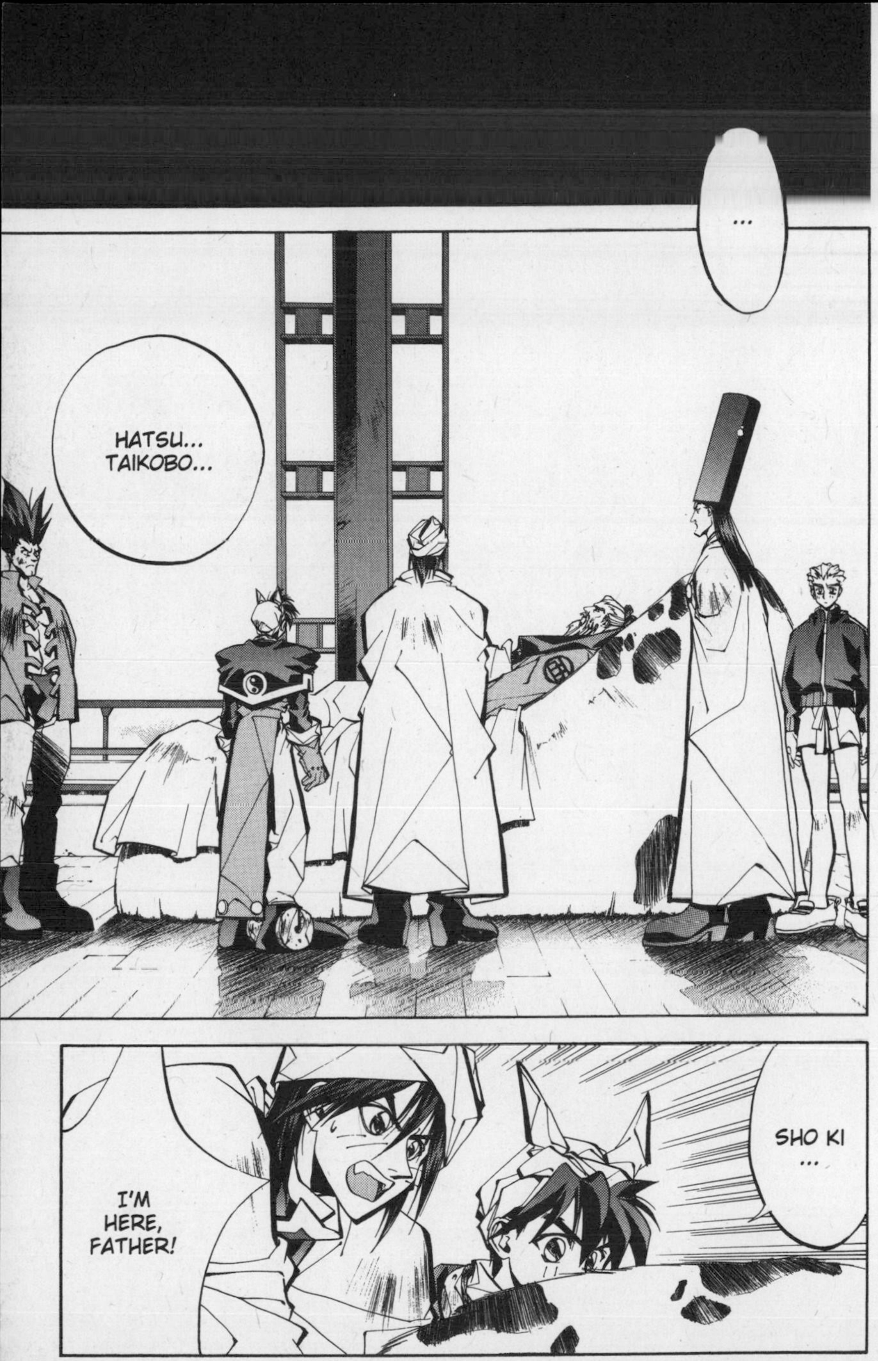
...
HATSU... TAIKOBO...
SHO KI ...
I'M HERE, FATHER!

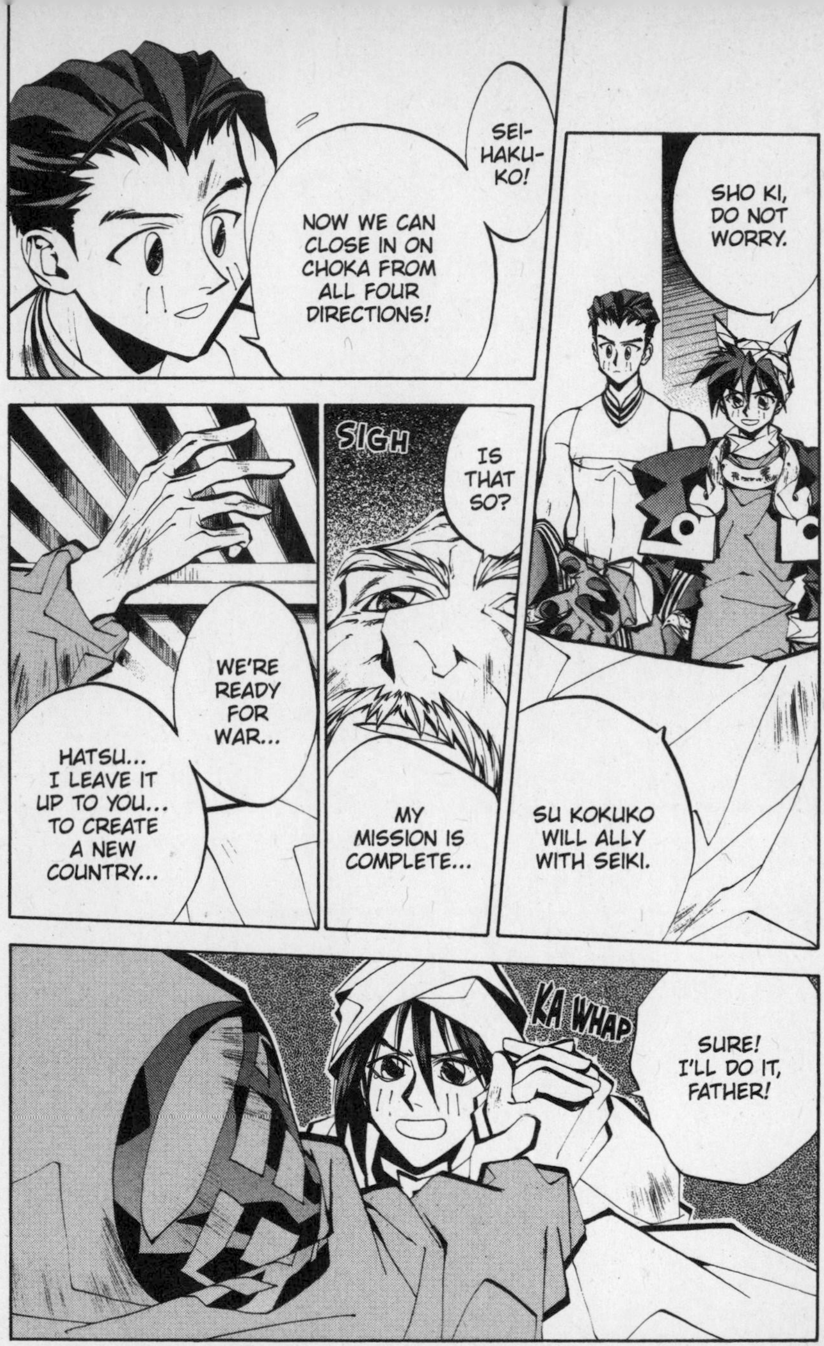
SHO KI, DO NOT WORRY.
SU KOKUKO WILL ALLY WITH SEIKI.
SEI-HAKU-KO!
NOW WE CAN CLOSE IN ON CHOKA FROM ALL FOUR DIRECTIONS!
SIGH
IS THAT SO?
MY MISSION IS COMPLETE...
WE'RE READY FOR WAR...
HATSU... I LEAVE IT UP TO YOU... TO CREATE A NEW COUNTRY...
KA WHAP
SURE! I'LL DO IT, FATHER!

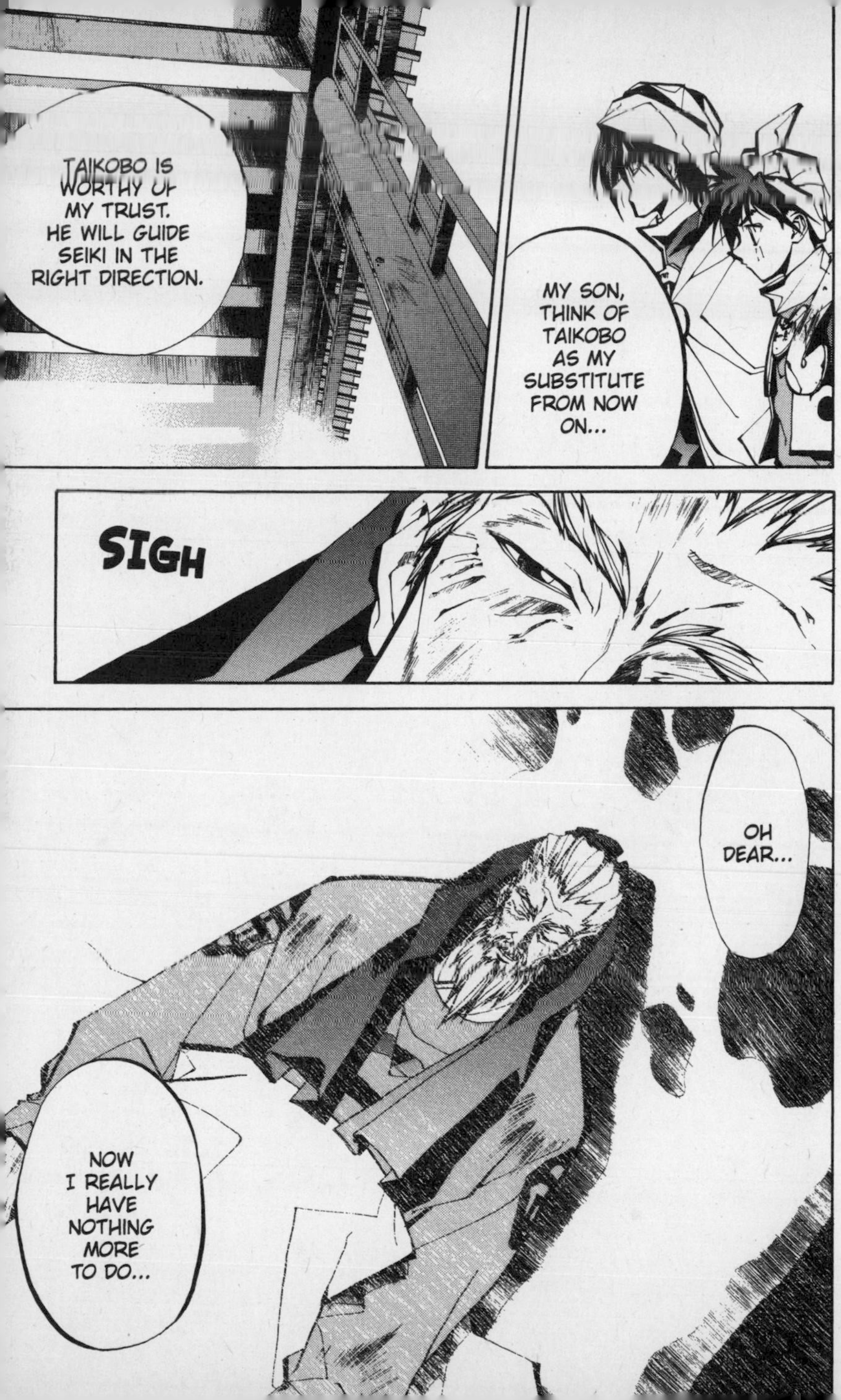
MY SON, THINK OF TAIKOBO AS MY SUBSTITUTE FROM NOW ON...
TAIKOBO IS WORTHY OF MY TRUST. HE WILL GUIDE SEIKI IN THE RIGHT DIRECTION.
SIGH
OH DEAR...
NOW I REALLY HAVE NOTHING MORE TO DO...

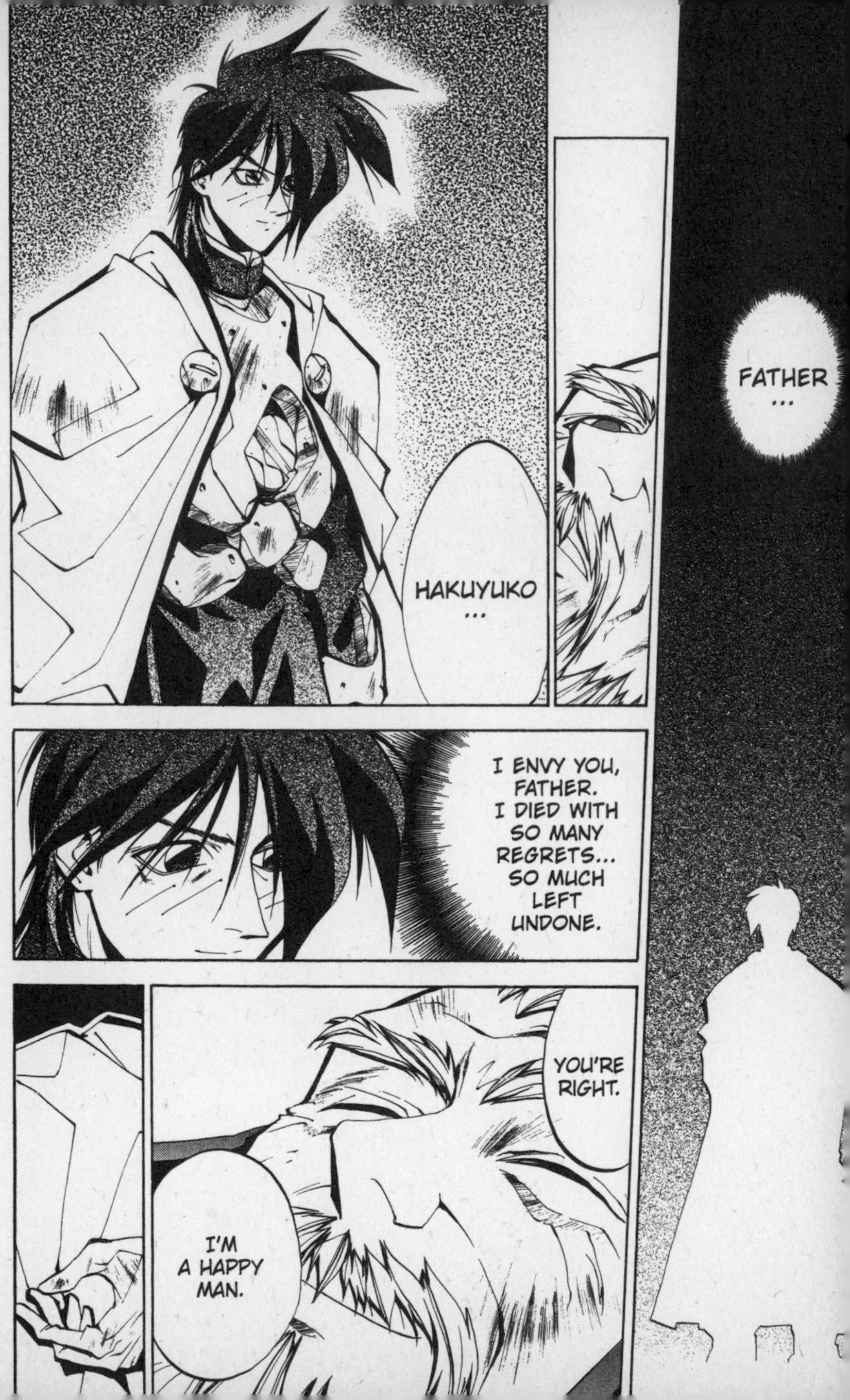
FATHER ...
HAKUYUKO ...
I ENVY YOU, FATHER. I DIED WITH SO MANY REGRETS... SO MUCH LEFT UNDONE.
YOU'RE RIGHT.
I'M A HAPPY MAN.

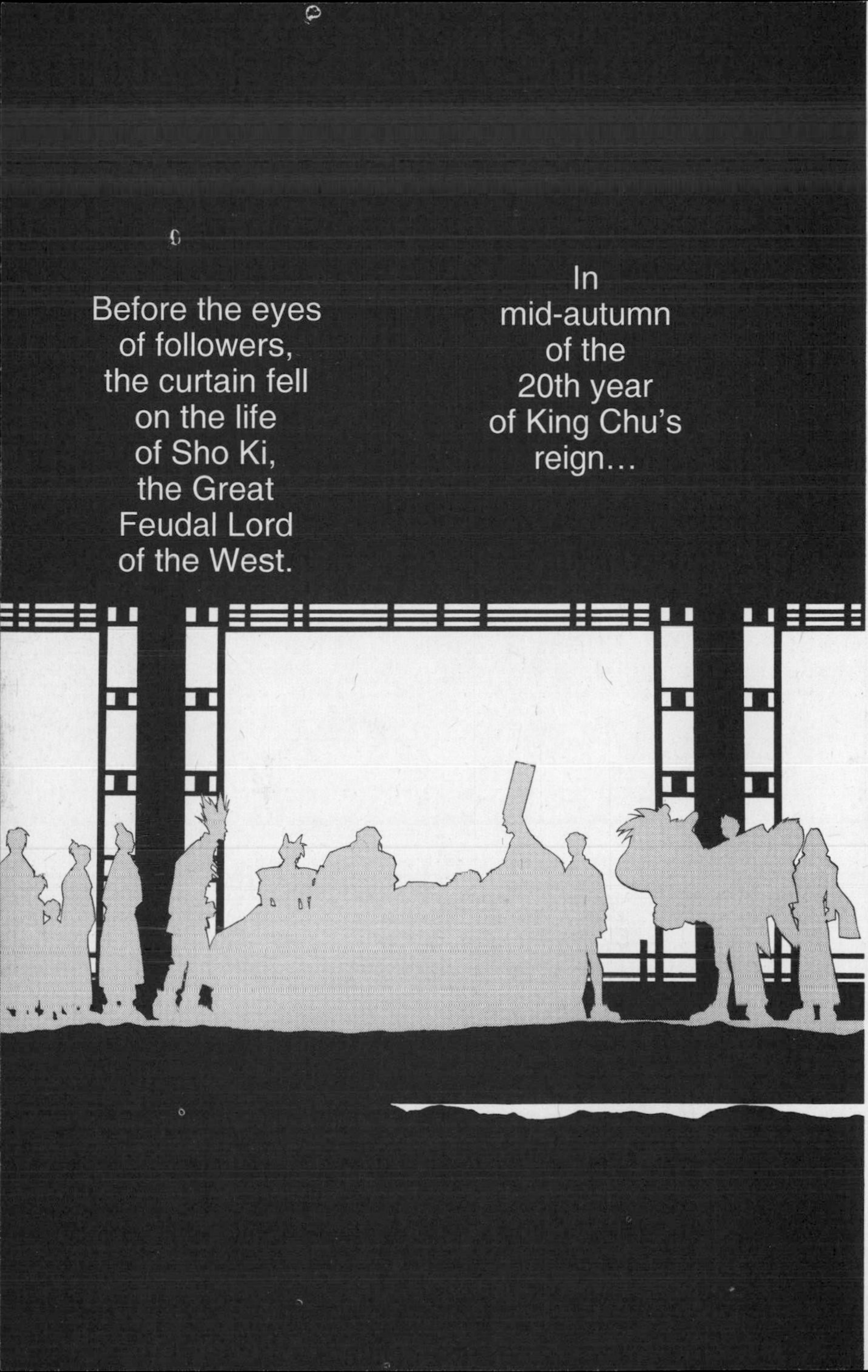
In mid-autumn of the 20th year of King Chu's reign...
Before the eyes of followers, the curtain fell on the life of Sho Ki, the Great Feudal Lord of the West.

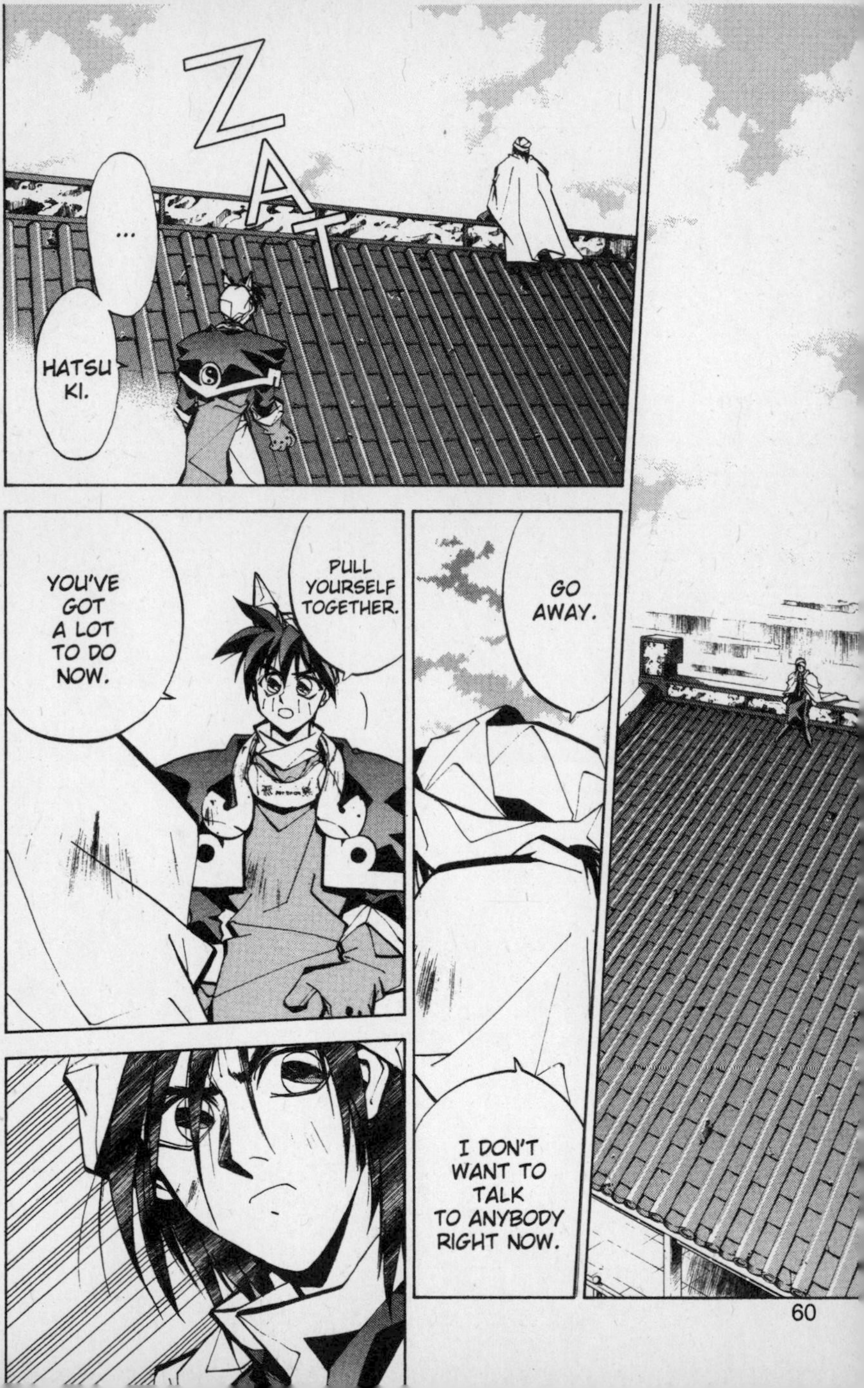
ZAT
...
HATSUKI.
GO AWAY.
I DON'T WANT TO TALK TO ANYBODY RIGHT NOW.
PULL YOURSELF TOGETHER.
YOU'VE GOT A LOT TO DO NOW.

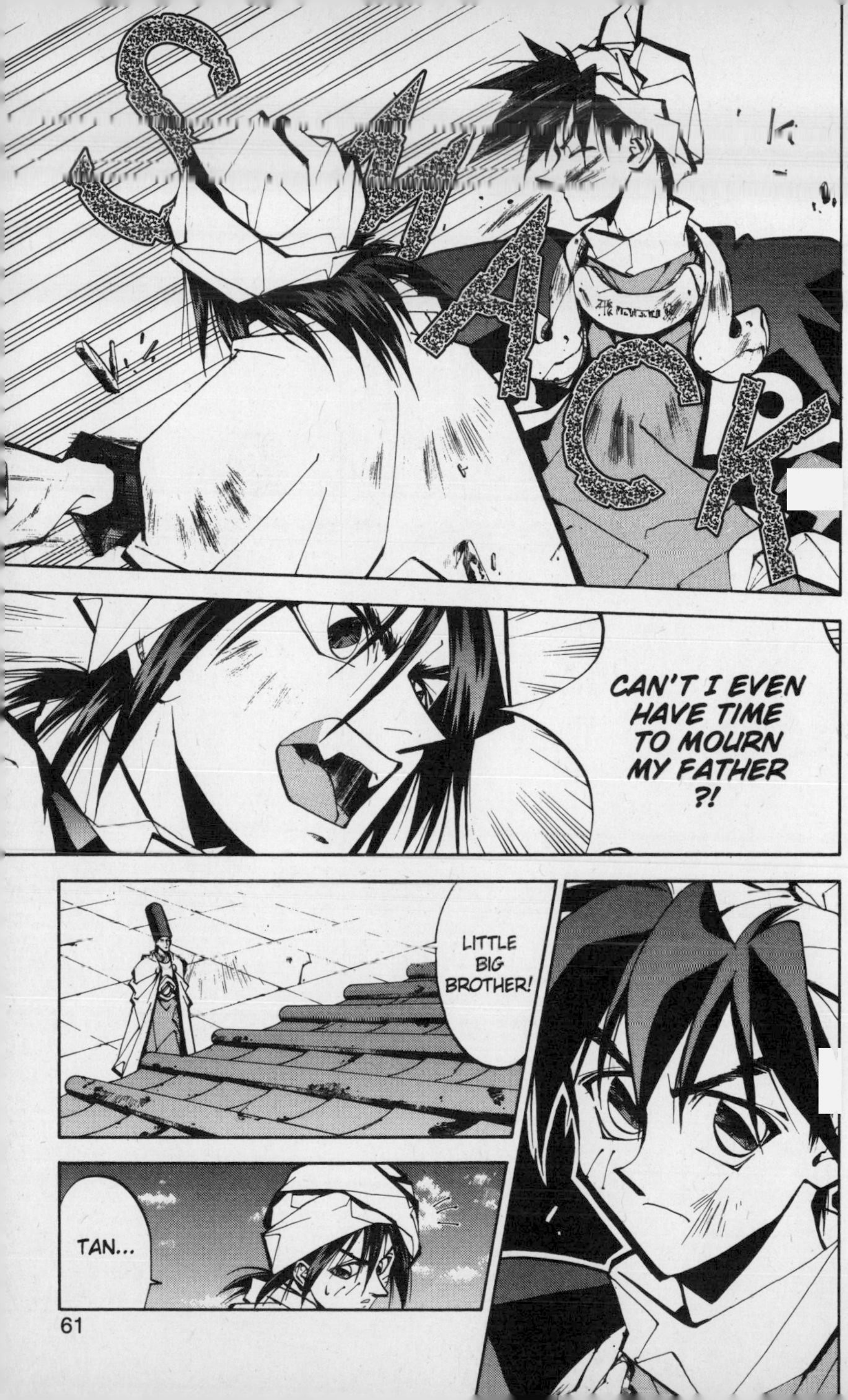
SMACK
CAN'T I EVEN HAVE TIME TO MOURN MY FATHER ?!
LITTLE BIG BROTHER!
TAN...

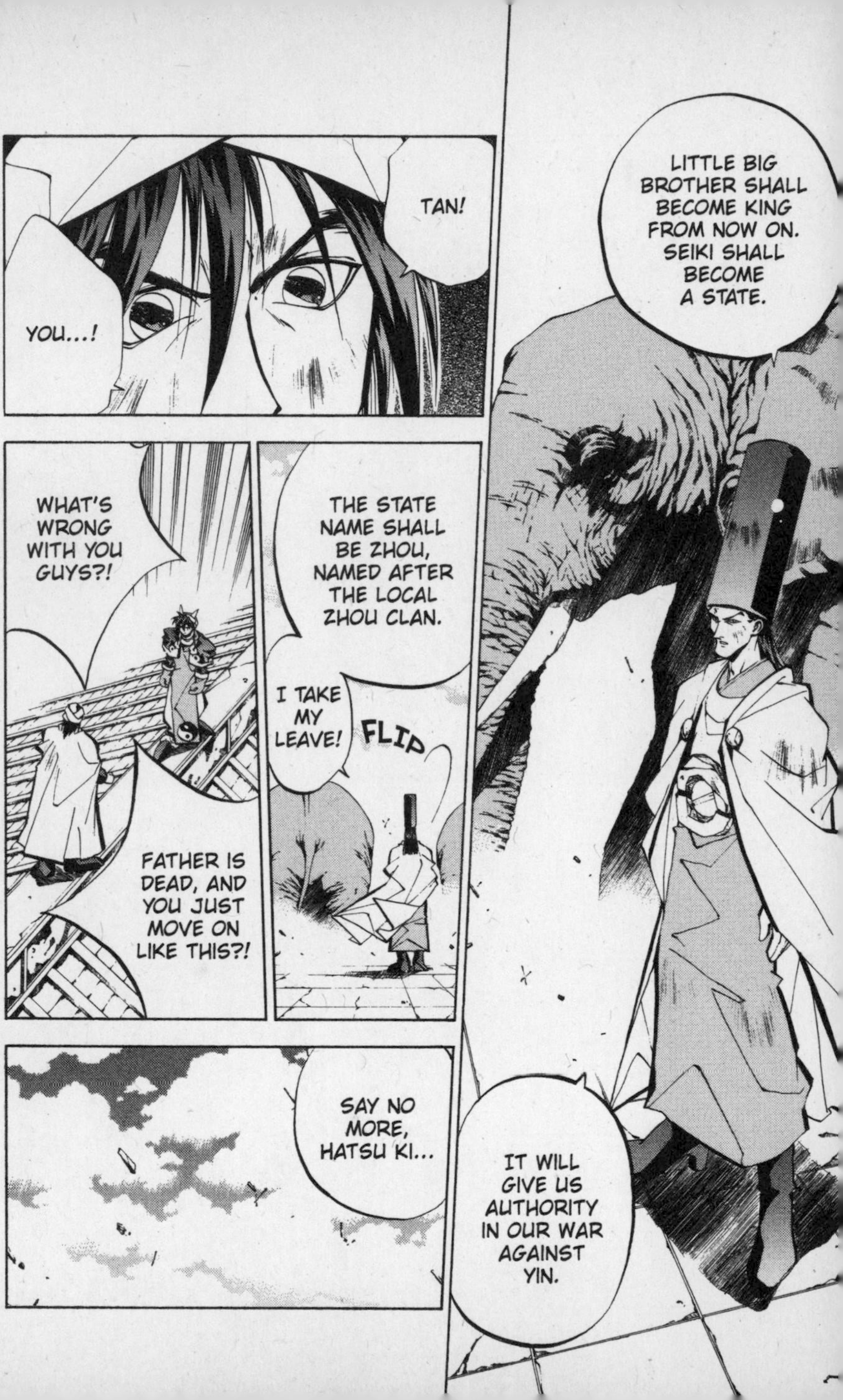
LITTLE BIG BROTHER SHALL BECOME KING FROM NOW ON. SEIKI SHALL BECOME A STATE.
IT WILL GIVE US AUTHORITY IN OUR WAR AGAINST YIN.
TAN!
YOU...!
THE STATE NAME SHALL BE ZHOU, NAMED AFTER THE LOCAL ZHOU CLAN.
I TAKE MY LEAVE!
FLIP
WHAT'S WRONG WITH YOU GUYS?!
FATHER IS DEAD, AND YOU JUST MOVE ON LIKE THIS?!
SAY NO MORE, HATSU KI...

READ THIS WAY

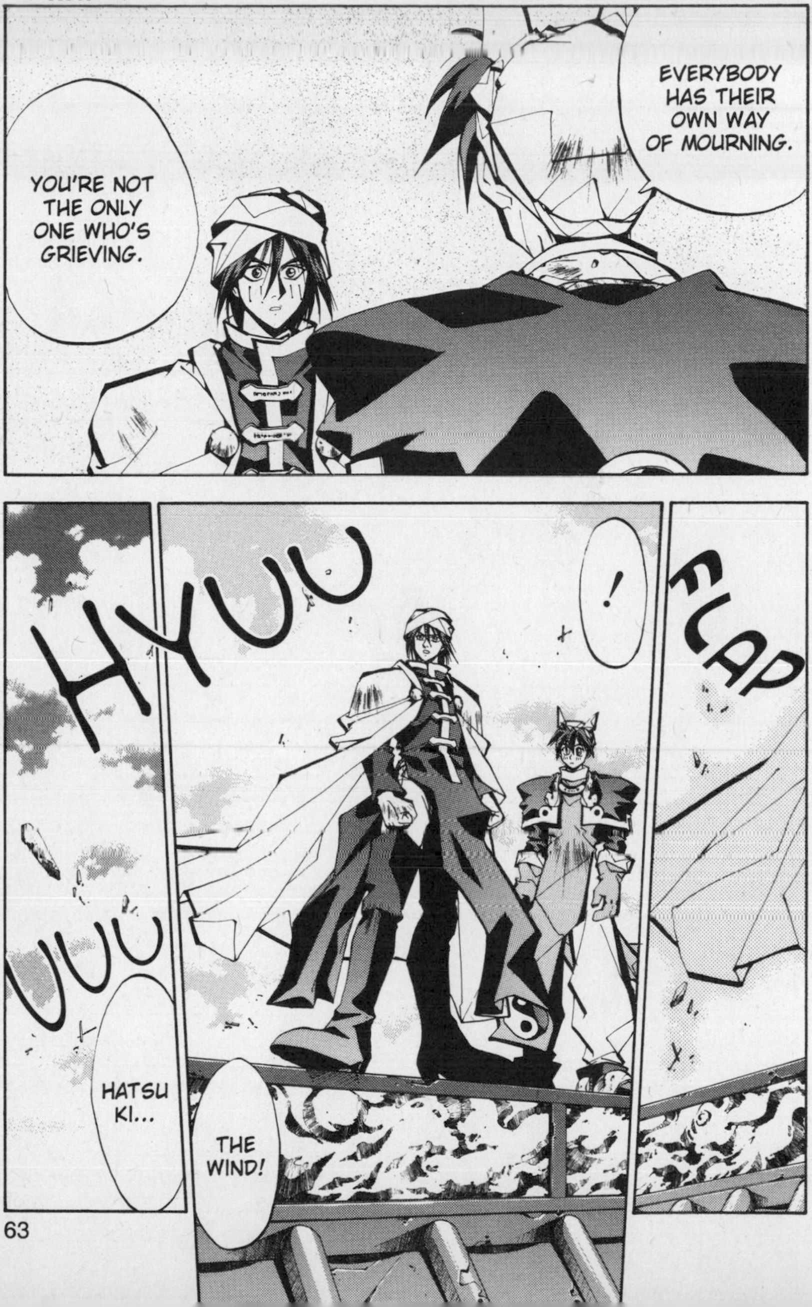
EVERYBODY HAS THEIR OWN WAY OF MOURNING.
YOU'RE NOT THE ONLY ONE WHO'S GRIEVING.
FLAP
!
HYUU
THE WIND!
UUU
HATSU KI...

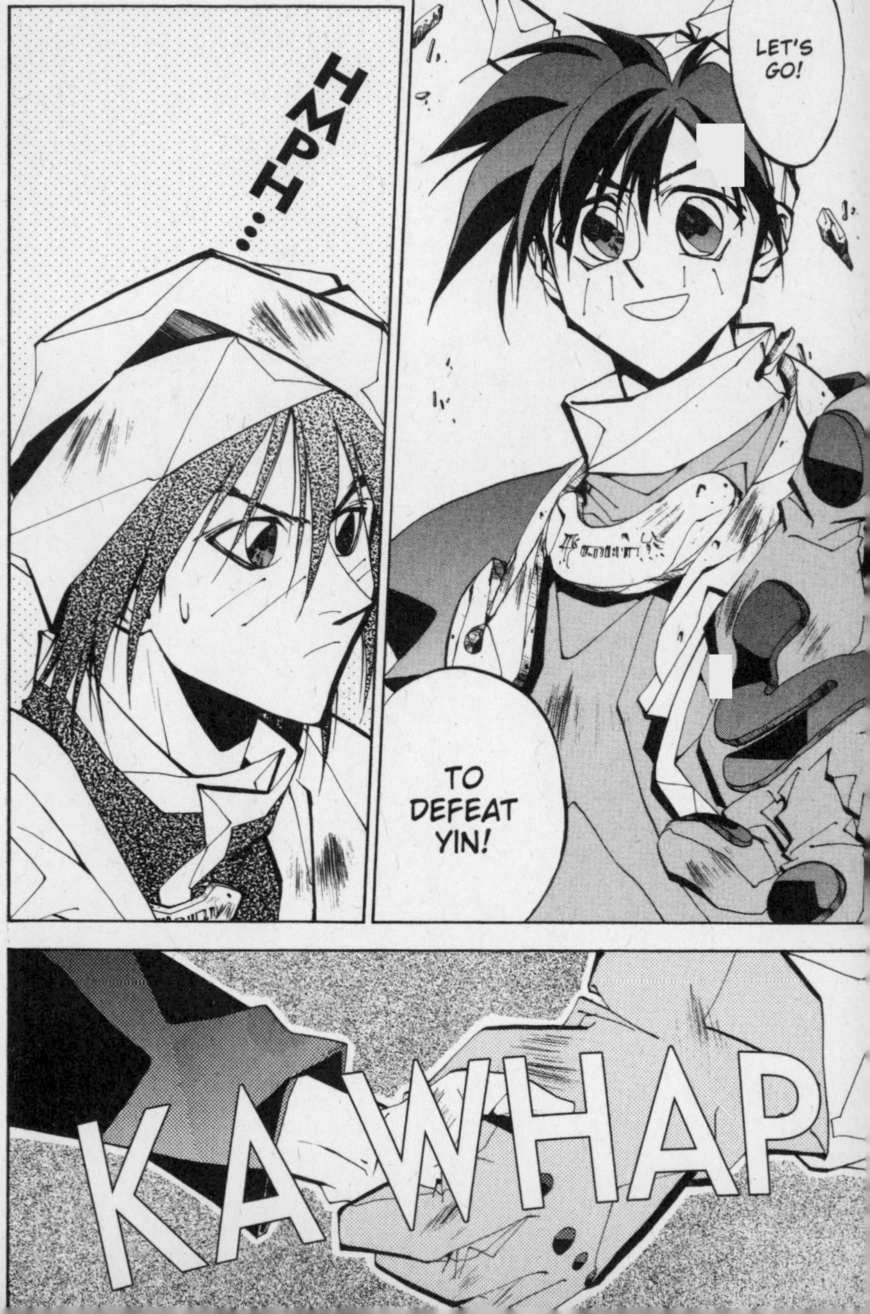
LET'S GO!
TO DEFEAT YIN!
HMPH...
KAWHAP

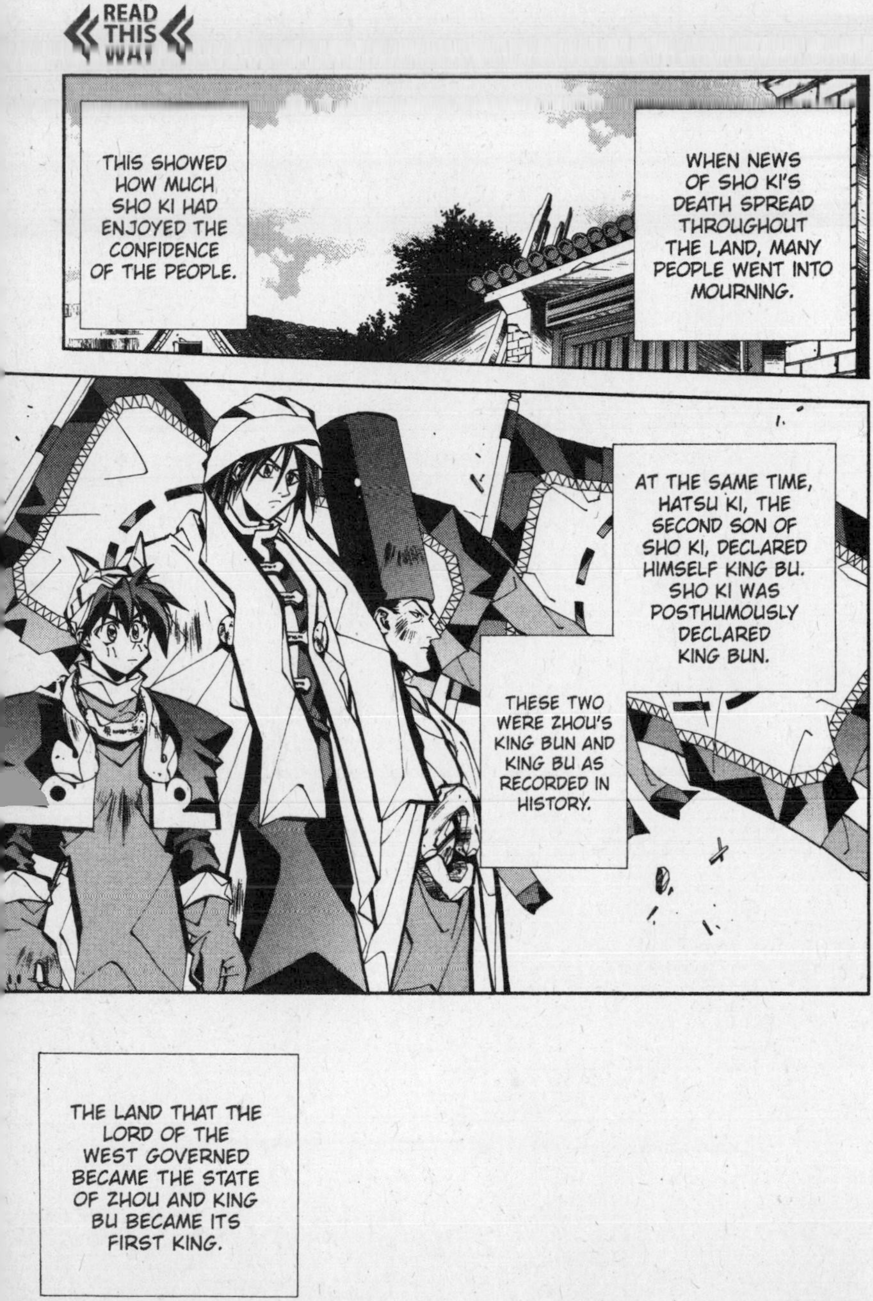
READ THIS WAY
WHEN NEWS OF SHO KI'S DEATH SPREAD THROUGHOUT THE LAND, MANY PEOPLE WENT INTO MOURNING.
THIS SHOWED HOW MUCH SHO KI HAD ENJOYED THE CONFIDENCE OF THE PEOPLE.
AT THE SAME TIME, HATSU KI, THE SECOND SON OF SHO KI, DECLARED HIMSELF KING BU. SHO KI WAS POSTHUMOUSLY DECLARED KING BUN.
THESE TWO WERE ZHOU'S KING BUN AND KING BU AS RECORDED IN HISTORY.
THE LAND THAT THE LORD OF THE WEST GOVERNED BECAME THE STATE OF ZHOU AND KING BU BECAME ITS FIRST KING.

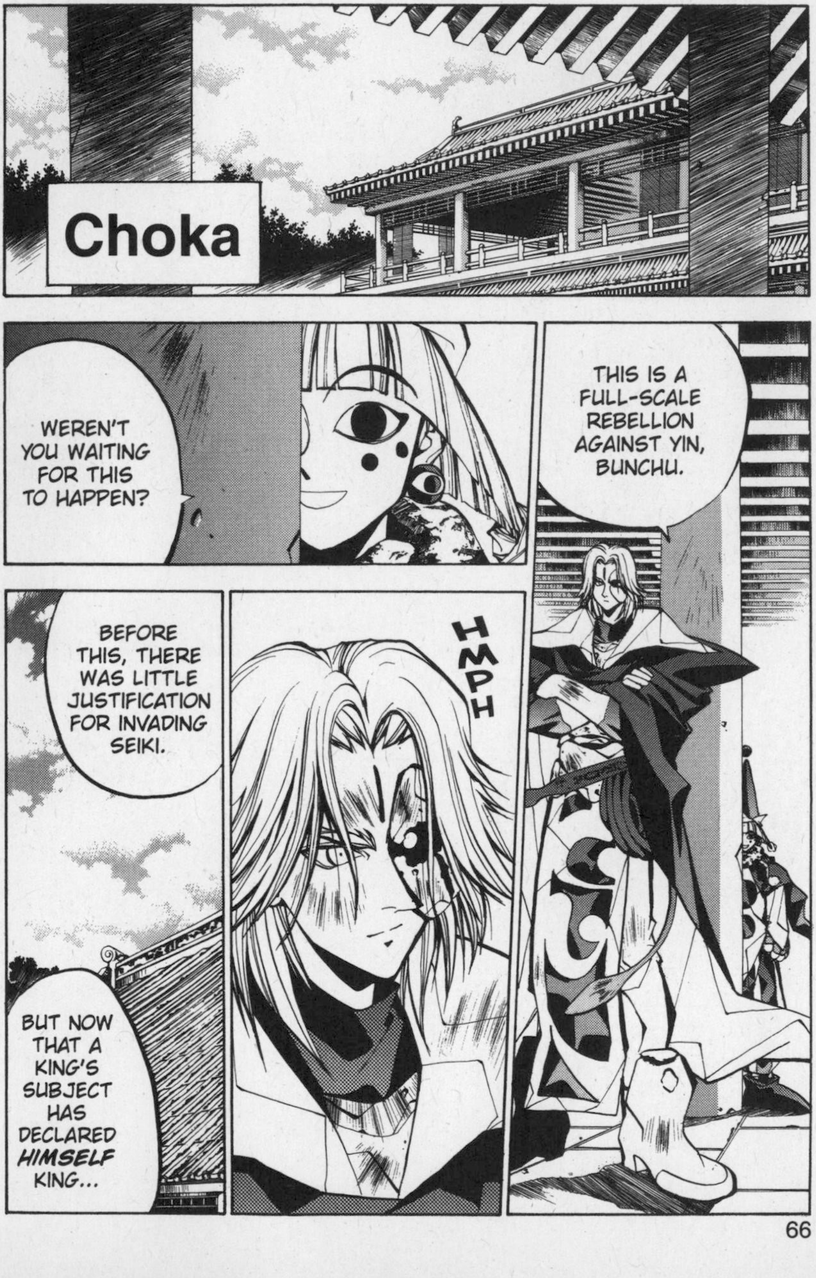

Choka
THIS IS A FULL-SCALE REBELLION AGAINST YIN, BUNCHU.
WEREN'T YOU WAITING FOR THIS TO HAPPEN?
HMPH
BEFORE THIS, THERE WAS LITTLE JUSTIFICATION FOR INVADING SEIKI.
BUT NOW THAT A KING'S SUBJECT HAS DECLARED *HIMSELF* KING...

READ THIS WAY

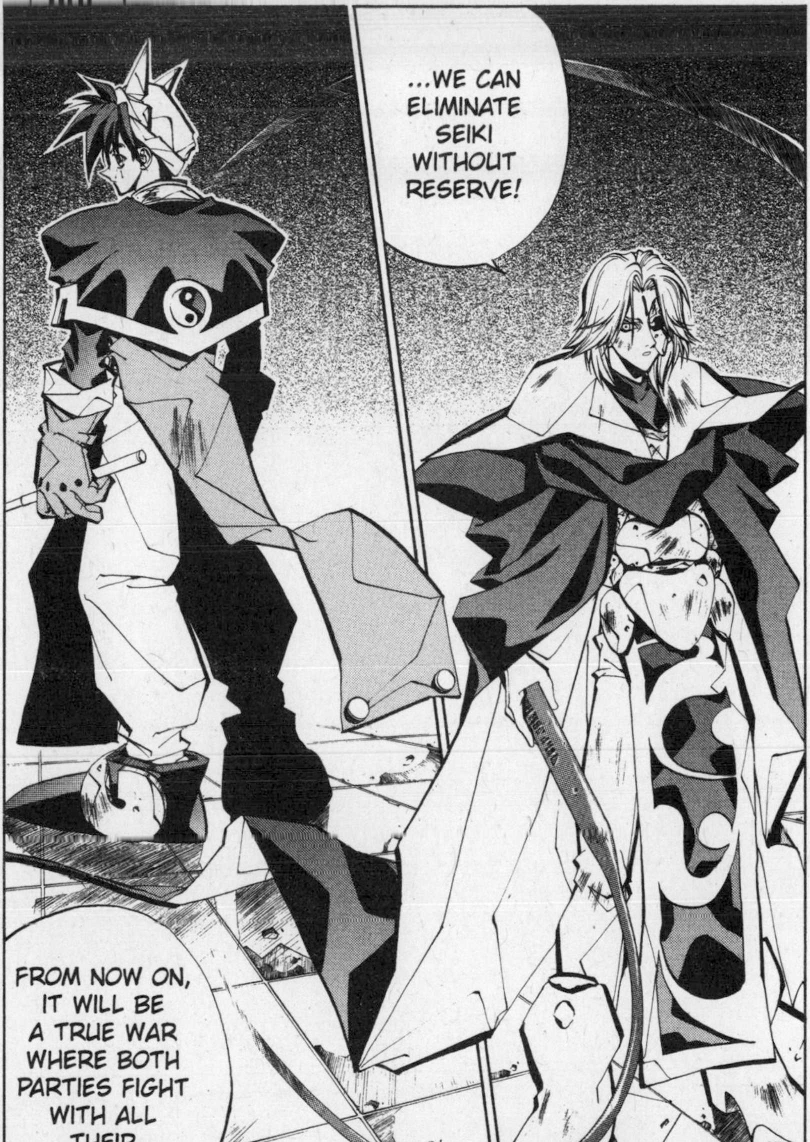
...WE CAN ELIMINATE SEIKI WITHOUT RESERVE!
FROM NOW ON, IT WILL BE A TRUE WAR WHERE BOTH PARTIES FIGHT WITH ALL THEIR STRENGTH!

封神演義

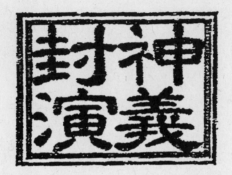

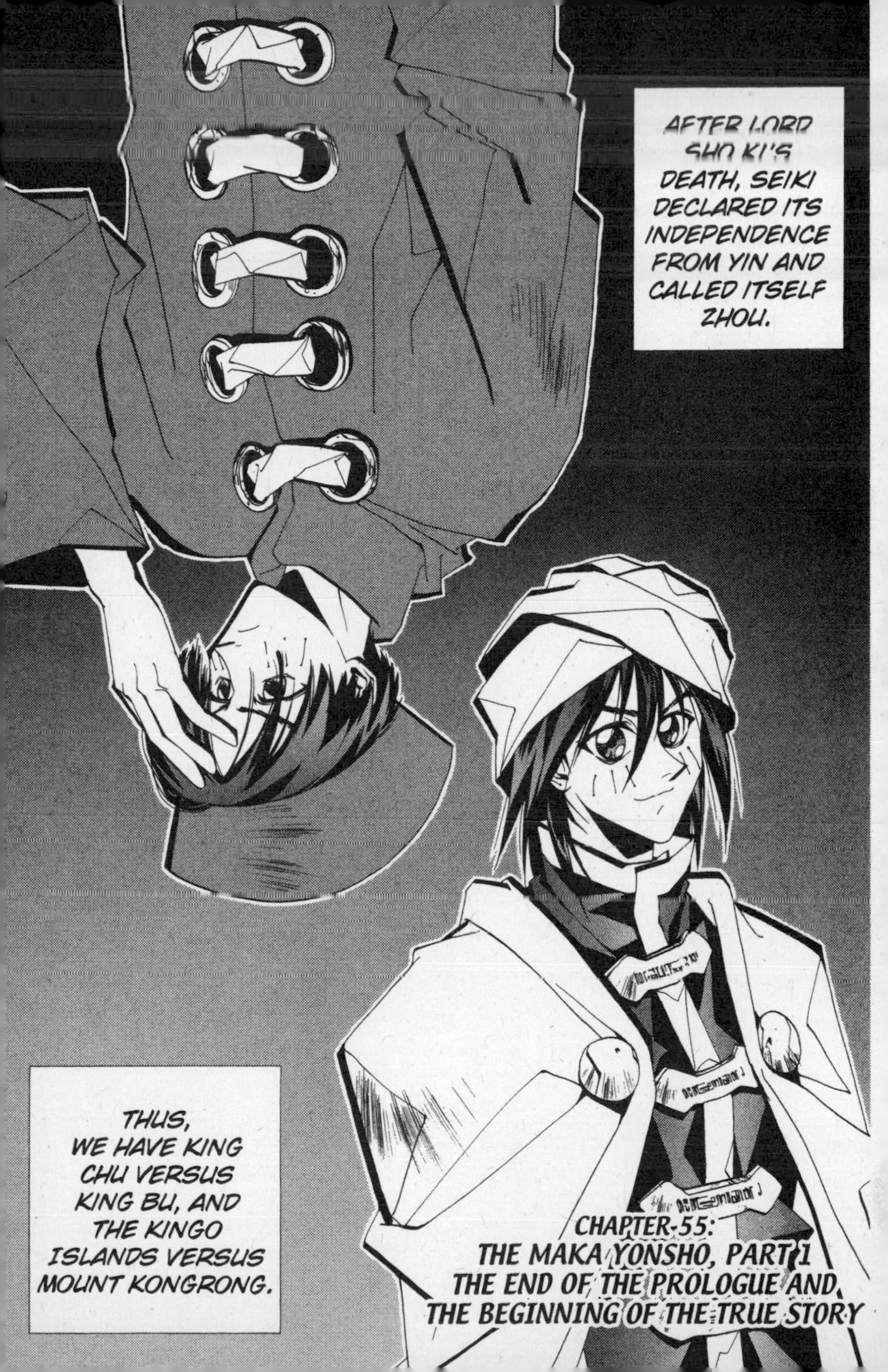
AFTER LORD SHO KI'S DEATH, SEIKI DECLARED ITS INDEPENDENCE FROM YIN AND CALLED ITSELF ZHOU.
THUS, WE HAVE KING CHU VERSUS KING BU, AND THE KINGO ISLANDS VERSUS MOUNT KONGRONG.
CHAPTER 55:
THE MAKA YONSHO, PART 1
THE END OF THE PROLOGUE AND THE BEGINNING OF THE TRUE STORY

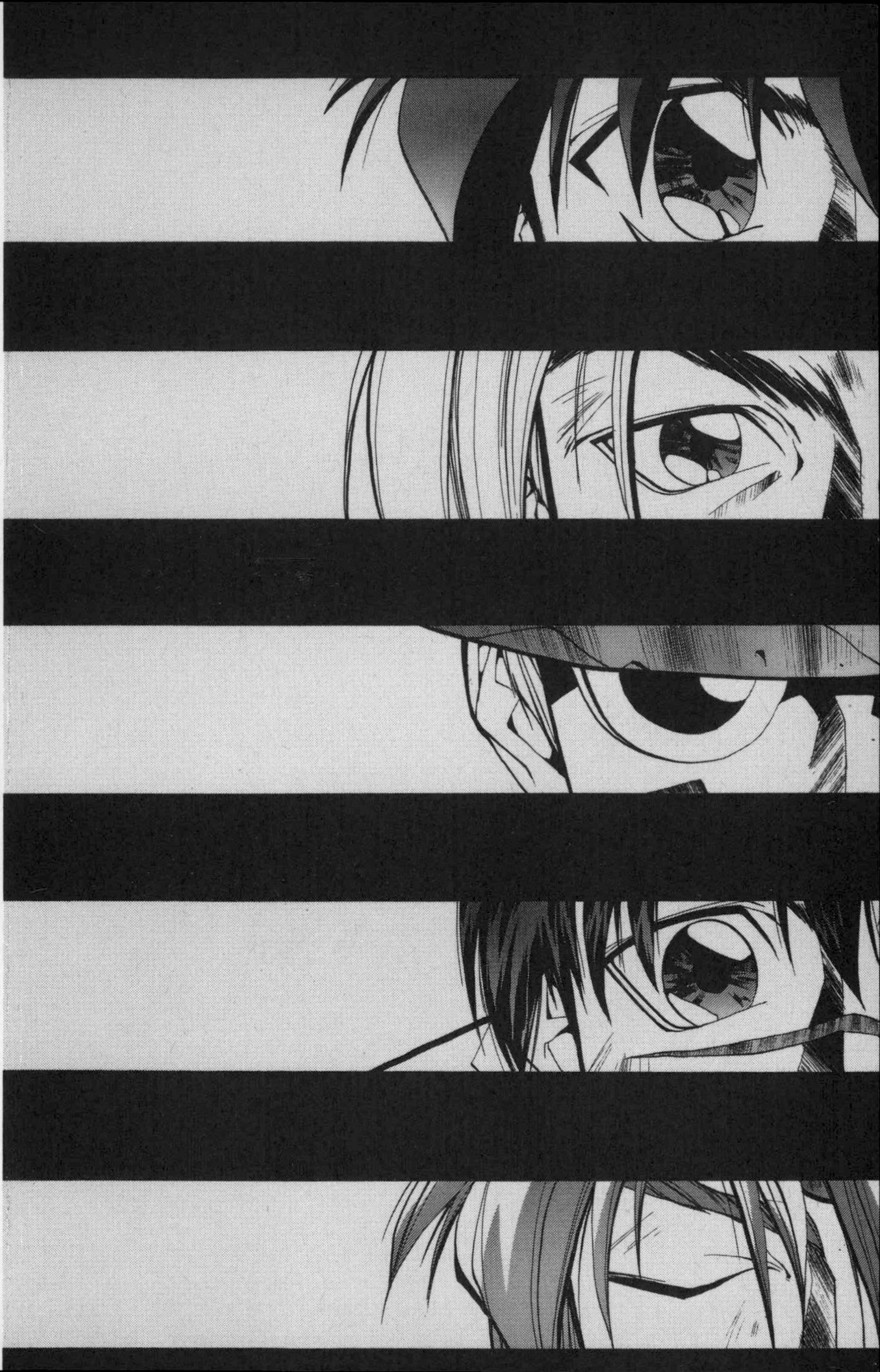

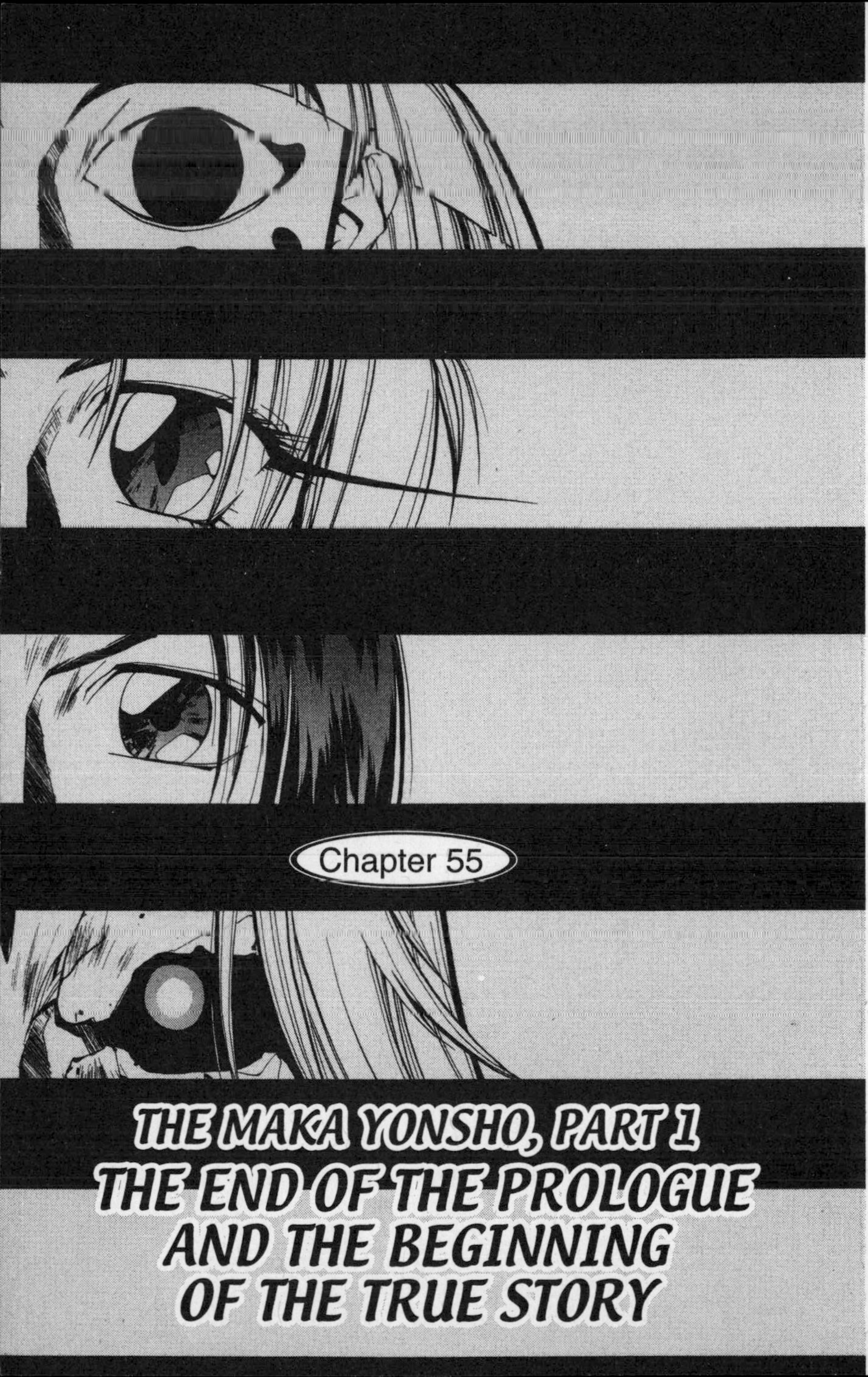
Chapter 55
THE MAKA YONSHO, PART 1
THE END OF THE PROLOGUE AND THE BEGINNING OF THE TRUE STORY

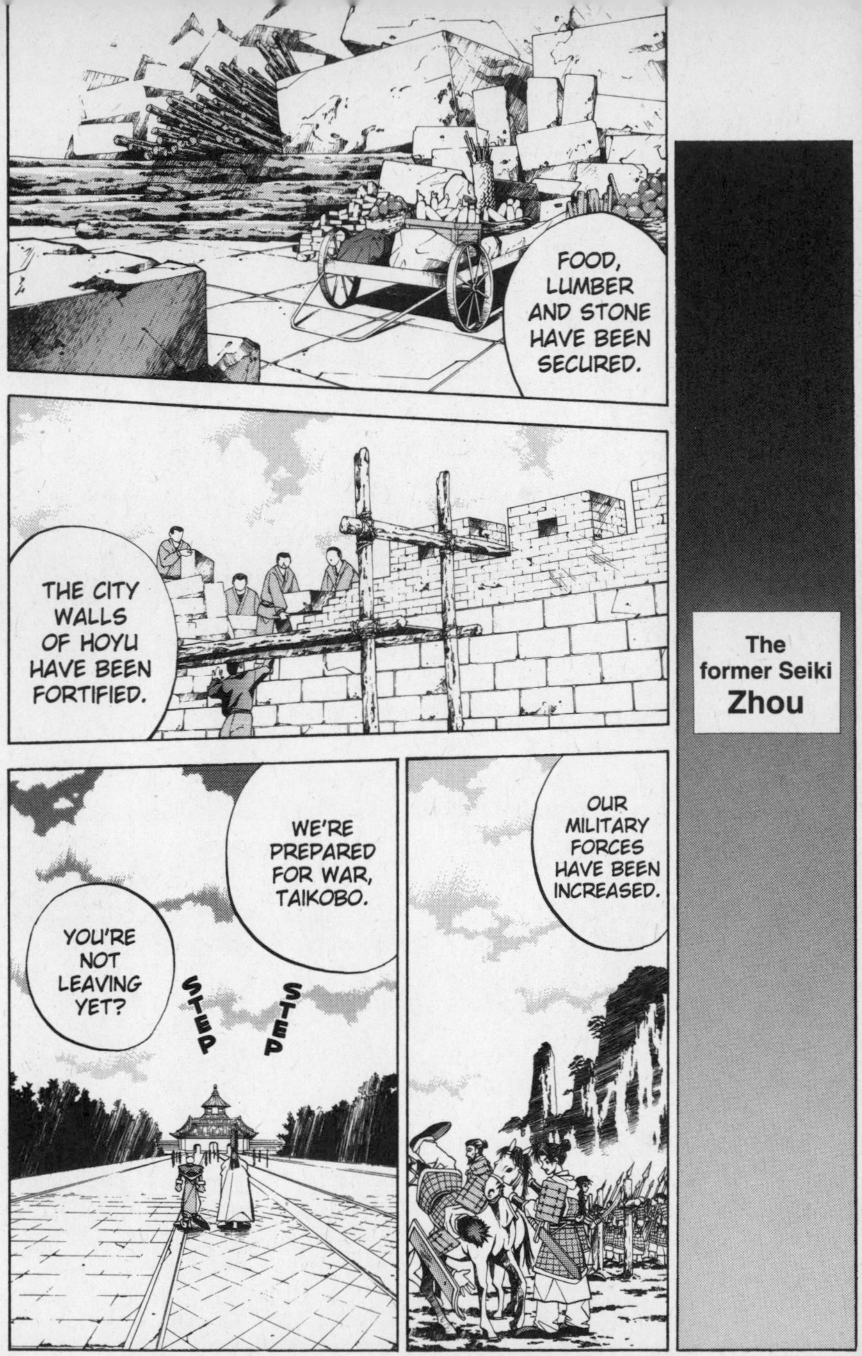
The former Seiki Zhou
FOOD, LUMBER AND STONE HAVE BEEN SECURED.
THE CITY WALLS OF HOYU HAVE BEEN FORTIFIED.
OUR MILITARY FORCES HAVE BEEN INCREASED.
WE'RE PREPARED FOR WAR, TAIKOBO.
STEP
STEP
YOU'RE NOT LEAVING YET?

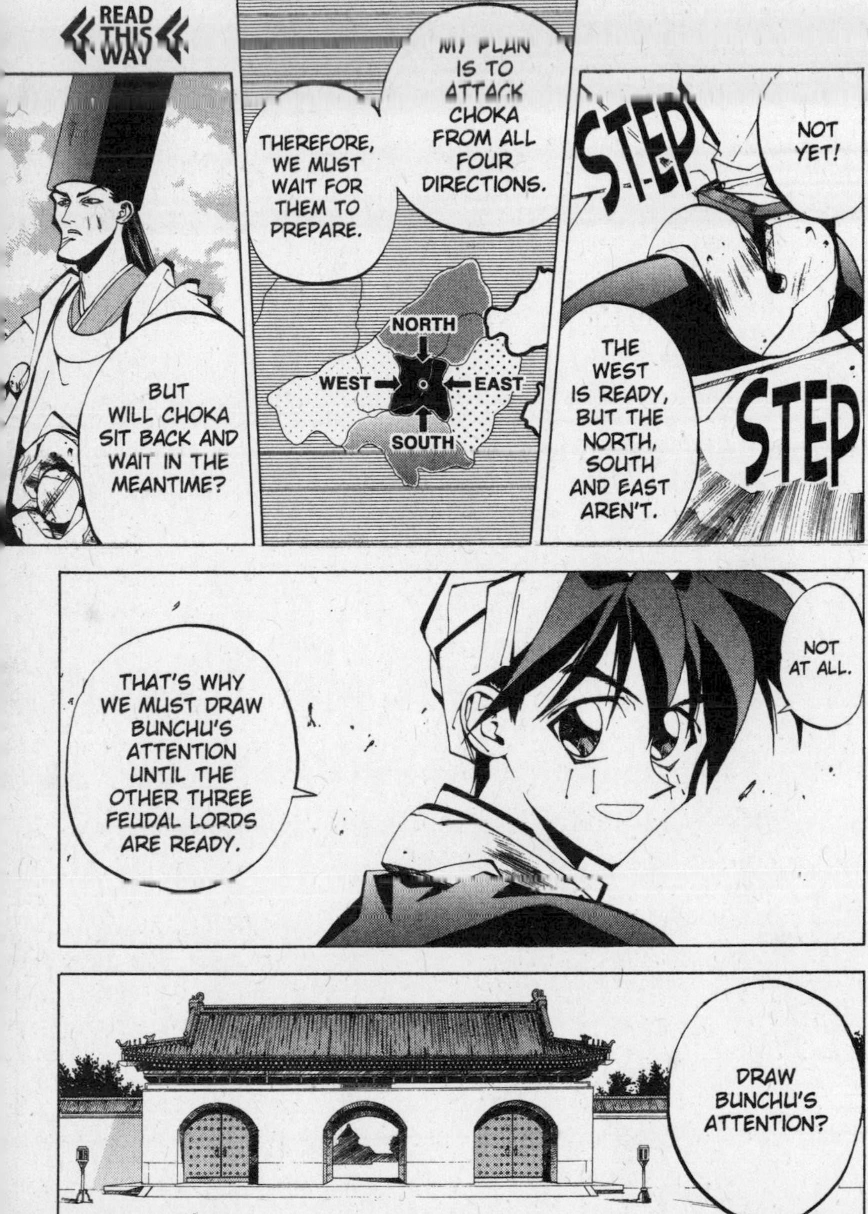
READ THIS WAY
STEP!
NOT YET!
THE WEST IS READY, BUT THE NORTH, SOUTH AND EAST AREN'T.
STEP
MY PLAN IS TO ATTACK CHOKA FROM ALL FOUR DIRECTIONS.
THEREFORE, WE MUST WAIT FOR THEM TO PREPARE.
NORTH
WEST
EAST
SOUTH
BUT WILL CHOKA SIT BACK AND WAIT IN THE MEANTIME?
NOT AT ALL.
THAT'S WHY WE MUST DRAW BUNCHU'S ATTENTION UNTIL THE OTHER THREE FEUDAL LORDS ARE READY.
DRAW BUNCHU'S ATTENTION?

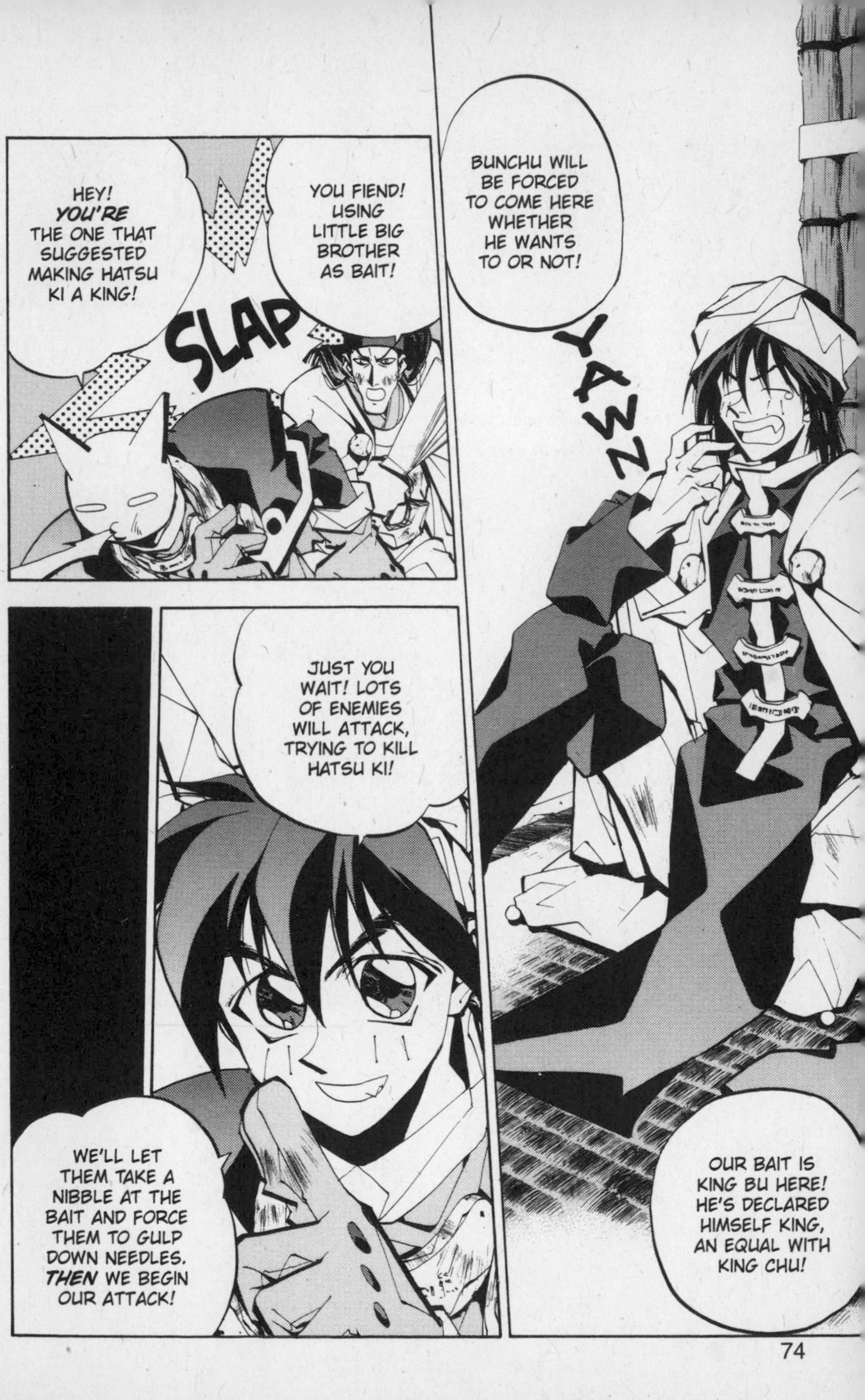
BUNCHU WILL BE FORCED TO COME HERE WHETHER HE WANTS TO OR NOT!
YAWN
OUR BAIT IS KING BU HERE! HE'S DECLARED HIMSELF KING, AN EQUAL WITH KING CHU!
YOU FIEND! USING LITTLE BIG BROTHER AS BAIT!
SLAP
HEY! ***YOU'RE*** THE ONE THAT SUGGESTED MAKING HATSU KI A KING!
JUST YOU WAIT! LOTS OF ENEMIES WILL ATTACK, TRYING TO KILL HATSU KI!
WE'LL LET THEM TAKE A NIBBLE AT THE BAIT AND FORCE THEM TO GULP DOWN NEEDLES. ***THEN*** WE BEGIN OUR ATTACK!

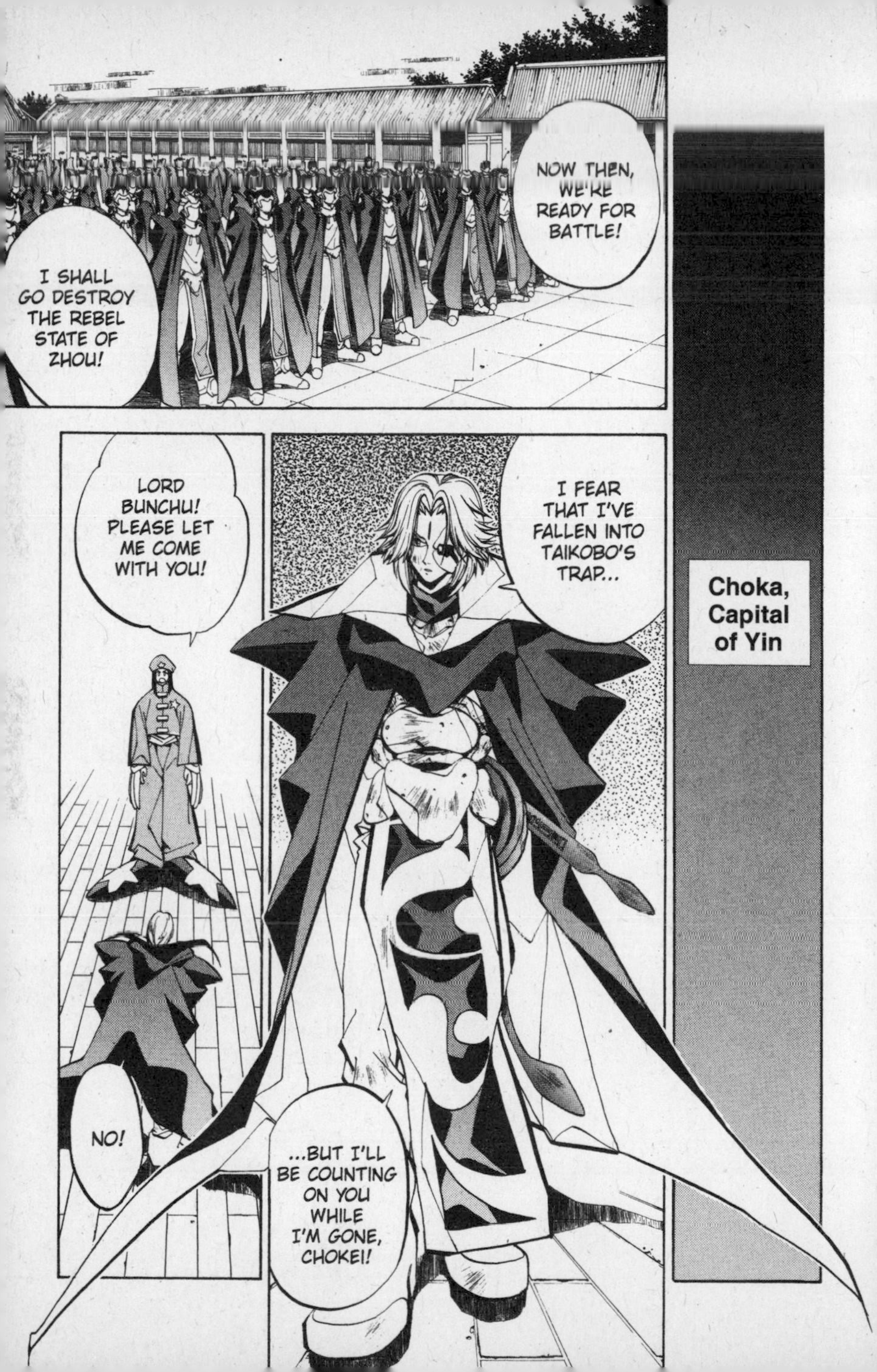
Choka, Capital of Yin
NOW THEN, WE'RE READY FOR BATTLE!
I SHALL GO DESTROY THE REBEL STATE OF ZHOU!
I FEAR THAT I'VE FALLEN INTO TAIKOBO'S TRAP...
LORD BUNCHU! PLEASE LET ME COME WITH YOU!
NO!
...BUT I'LL BE COUNTING ON YOU WHILE I'M GONE, CHOKEI!

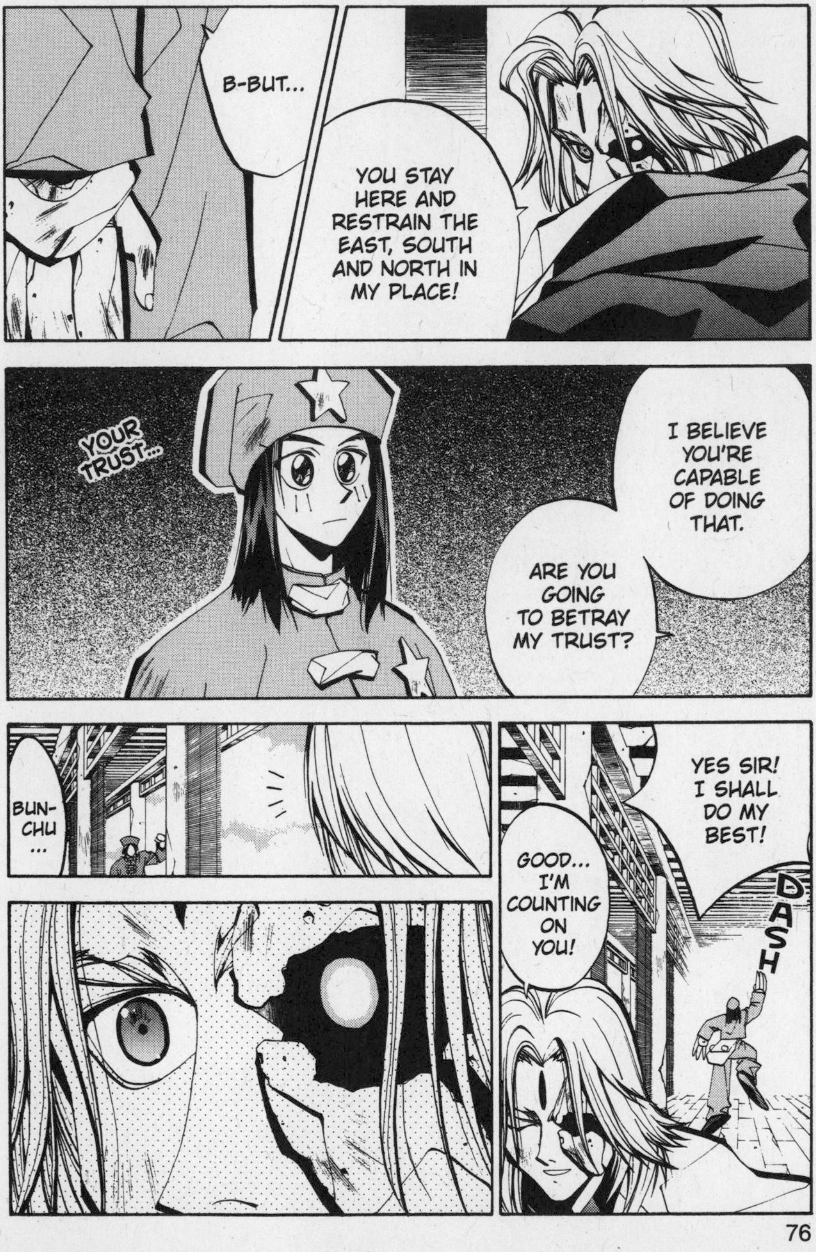
YOU STAY HERE AND RESTRAIN THE EAST, SOUTH AND NORTH IN MY PLACE!
B-BUT...
I BELIEVE YOU'RE CAPABLE OF DOING THAT.
ARE YOU GOING TO BETRAY MY TRUST?
YOUR TRUST...
YES SIR! I SHALL DO MY BEST!
DASH
GOOD... I'M COUNTING ON YOU!
BUN-CHU...

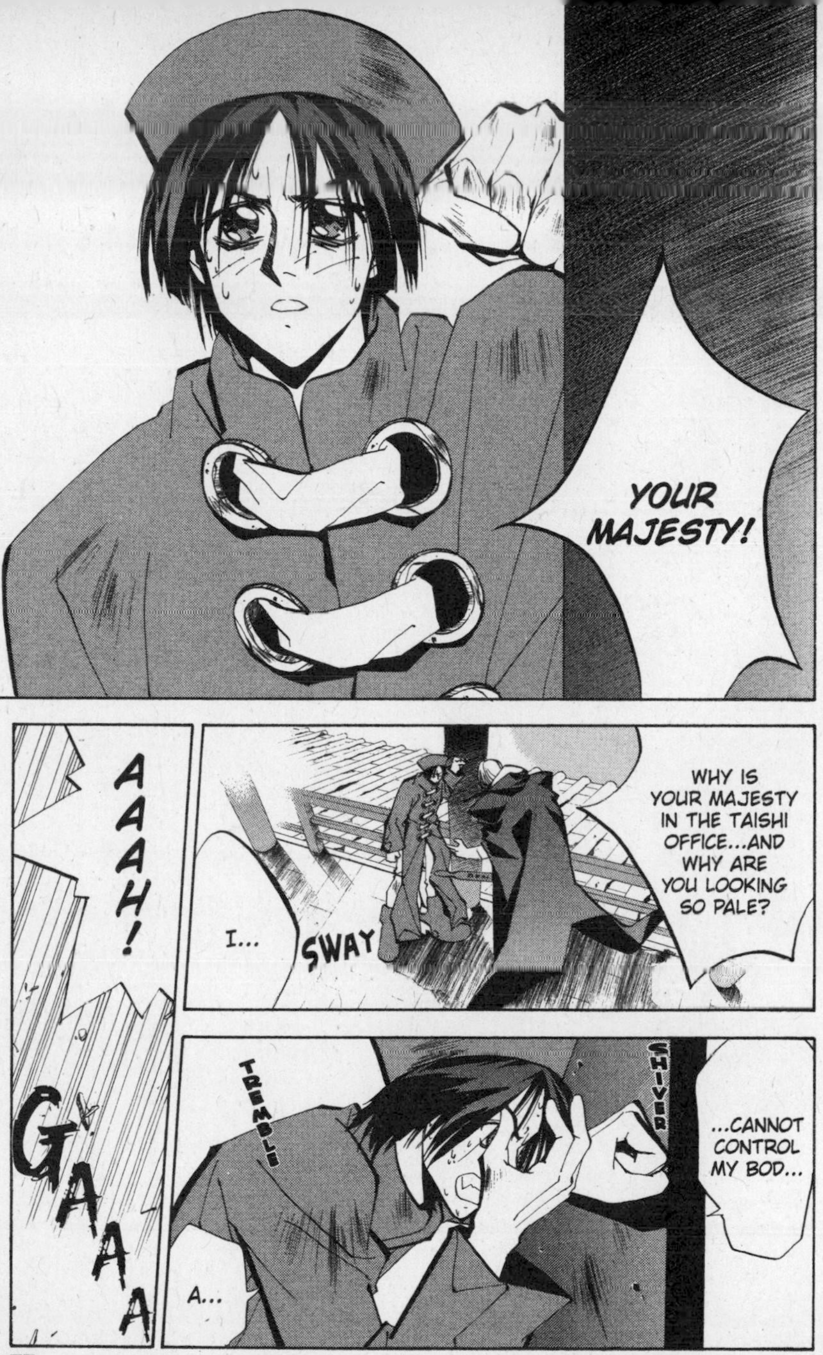
YOUR MAJESTY!
WHY IS YOUR MAJESTY IN THE TAISHI OFFICE...AND WHY ARE YOU LOOKING SO PALE?
SWAY
I...
SHIVER
TREMBLE
...CANNOT CONTROL MY BOD...
A...
AAAAH!
GAAAA

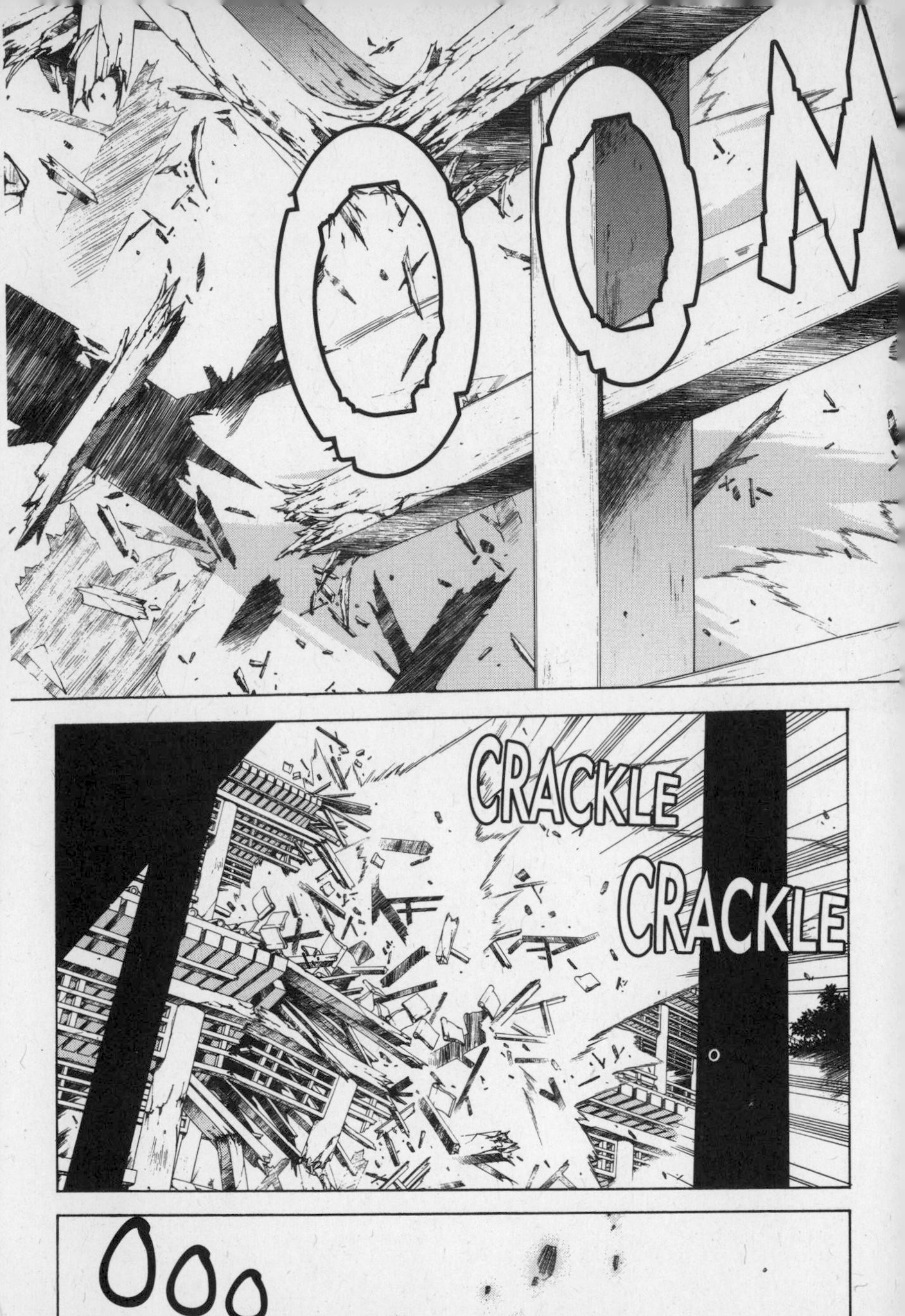
OOM
CRACKLE
CRACKLE
OOo

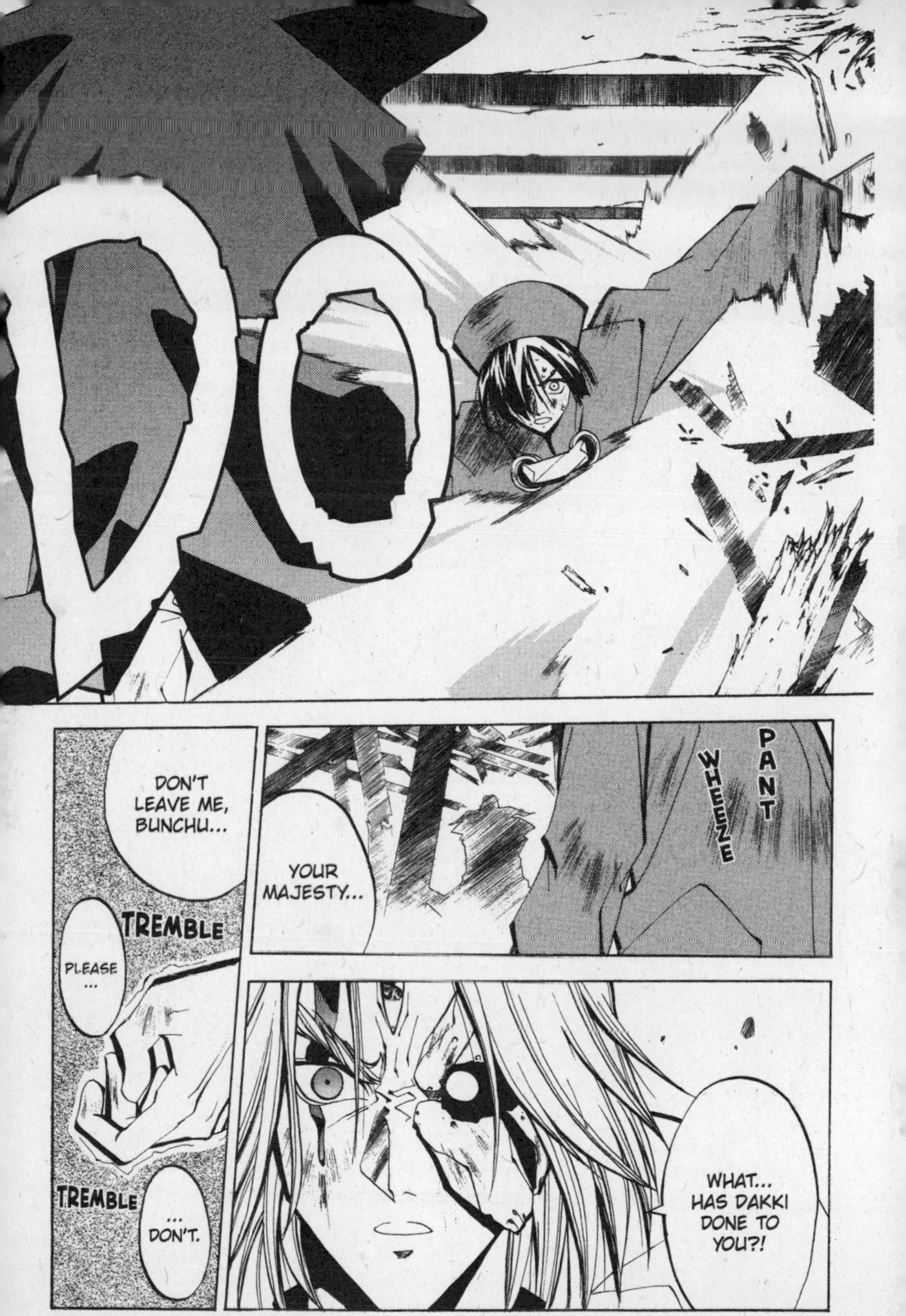
PANT
WHEEZE
YOUR MAJESTY...
WHAT... HAS DAKKI DONE TO YOU?!
DON'T LEAVE ME, BUNCHU...
TREMBLE
PLEASE ...
TREMBLE
... DON'T.

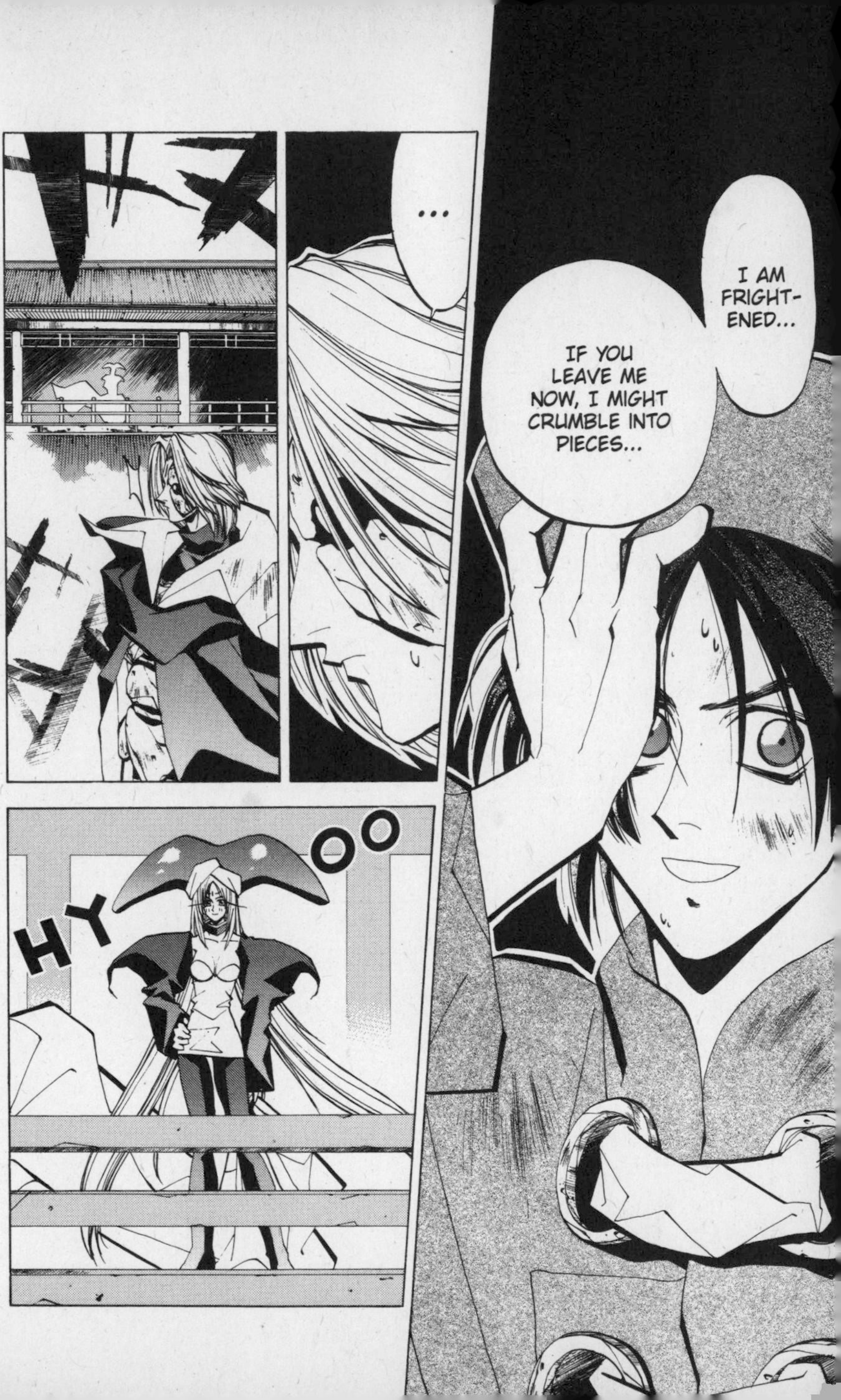
I AM FRIGHT-ENED...
IF YOU LEAVE ME NOW, I MIGHT CRUMBLE INTO PIECES...
...
HYOO

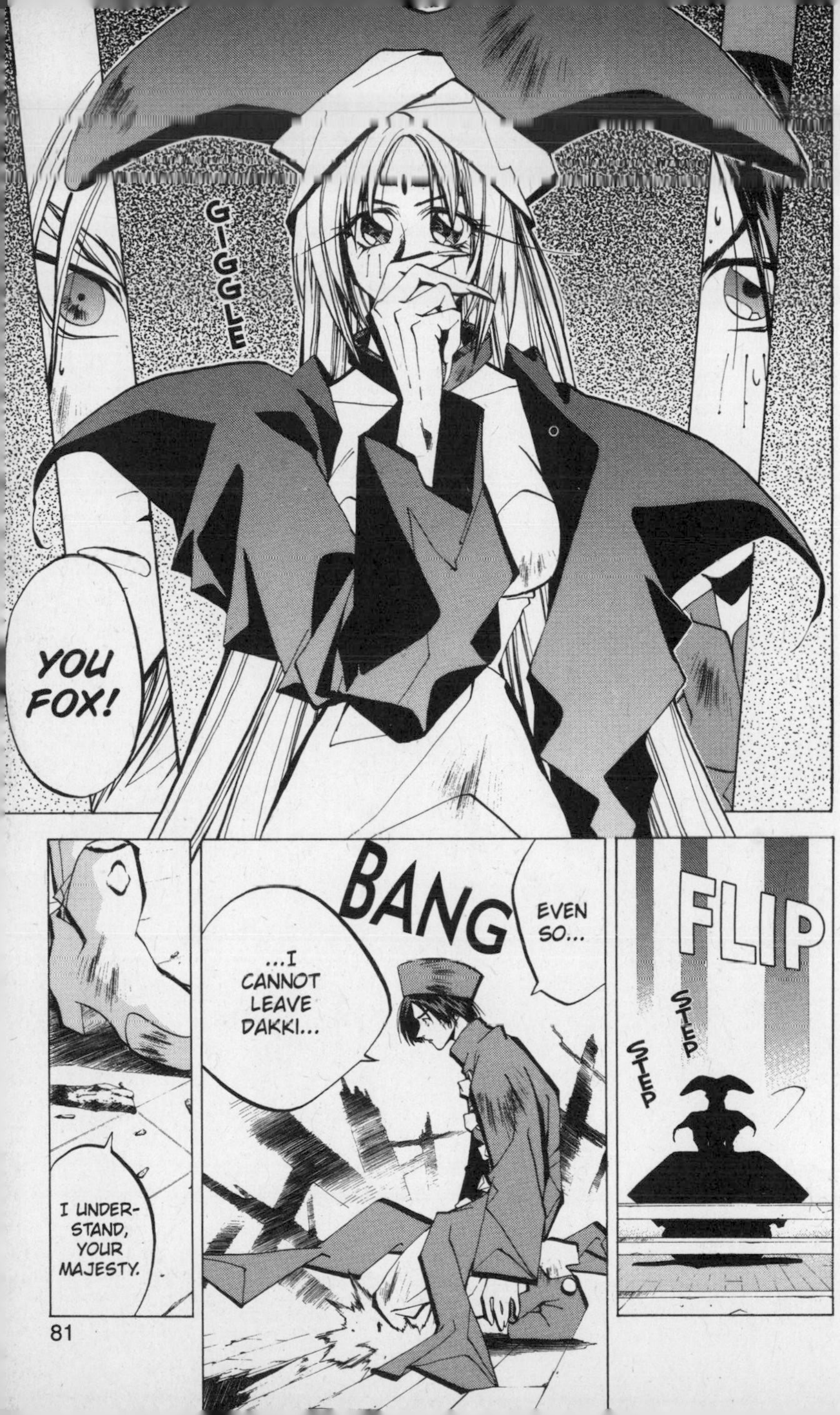
GIGGLE
YOU FOX!
FLIP
STEP
STEP
BANG
EVEN SO...
...I CANNOT LEAVE DAKKI...
I UNDER-STAND, YOUR MAJESTY.

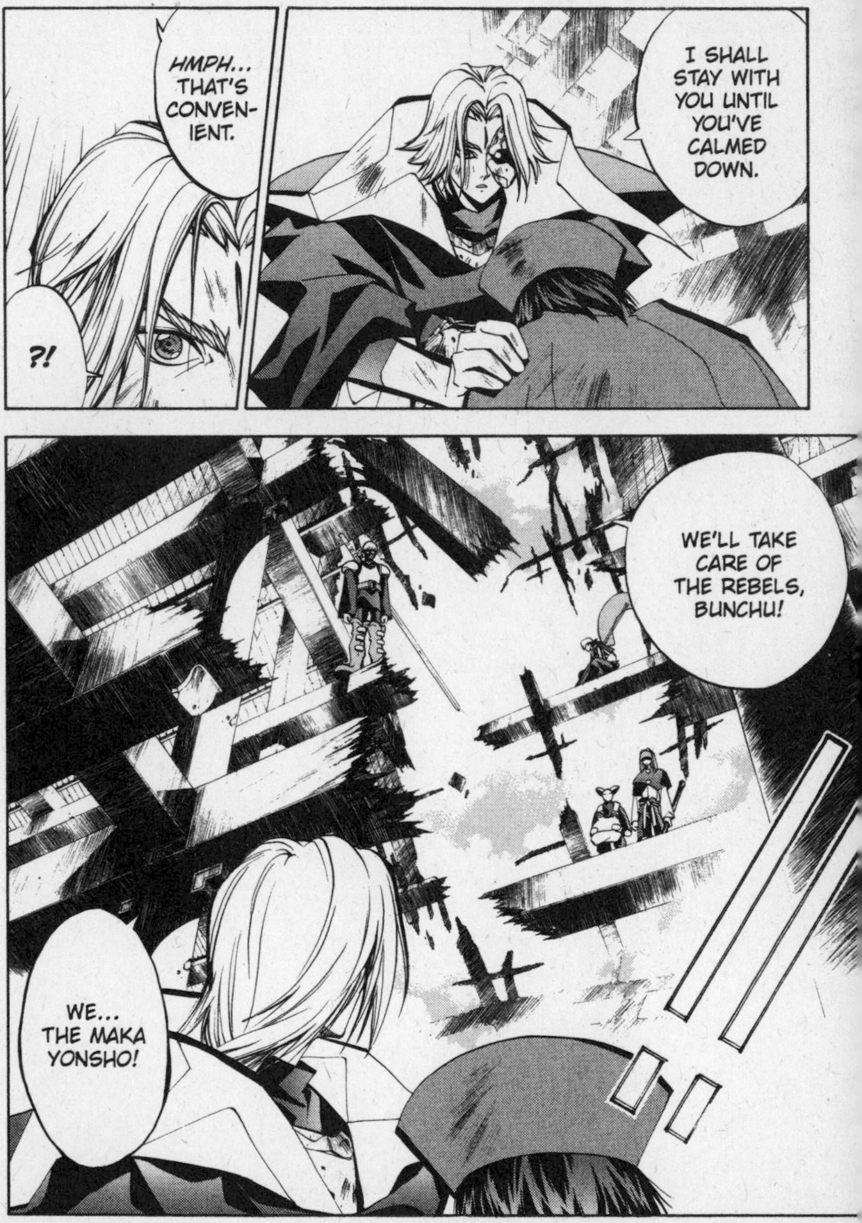
I SHALL STAY WITH YOU UNTIL YOU'VE CALMED DOWN.
HMPH... THAT'S CONVEN-IENT.
?!
WE'LL TAKE CARE OF THE REBELS, BUNCHU!
WE... THE MAKA YONSHO!

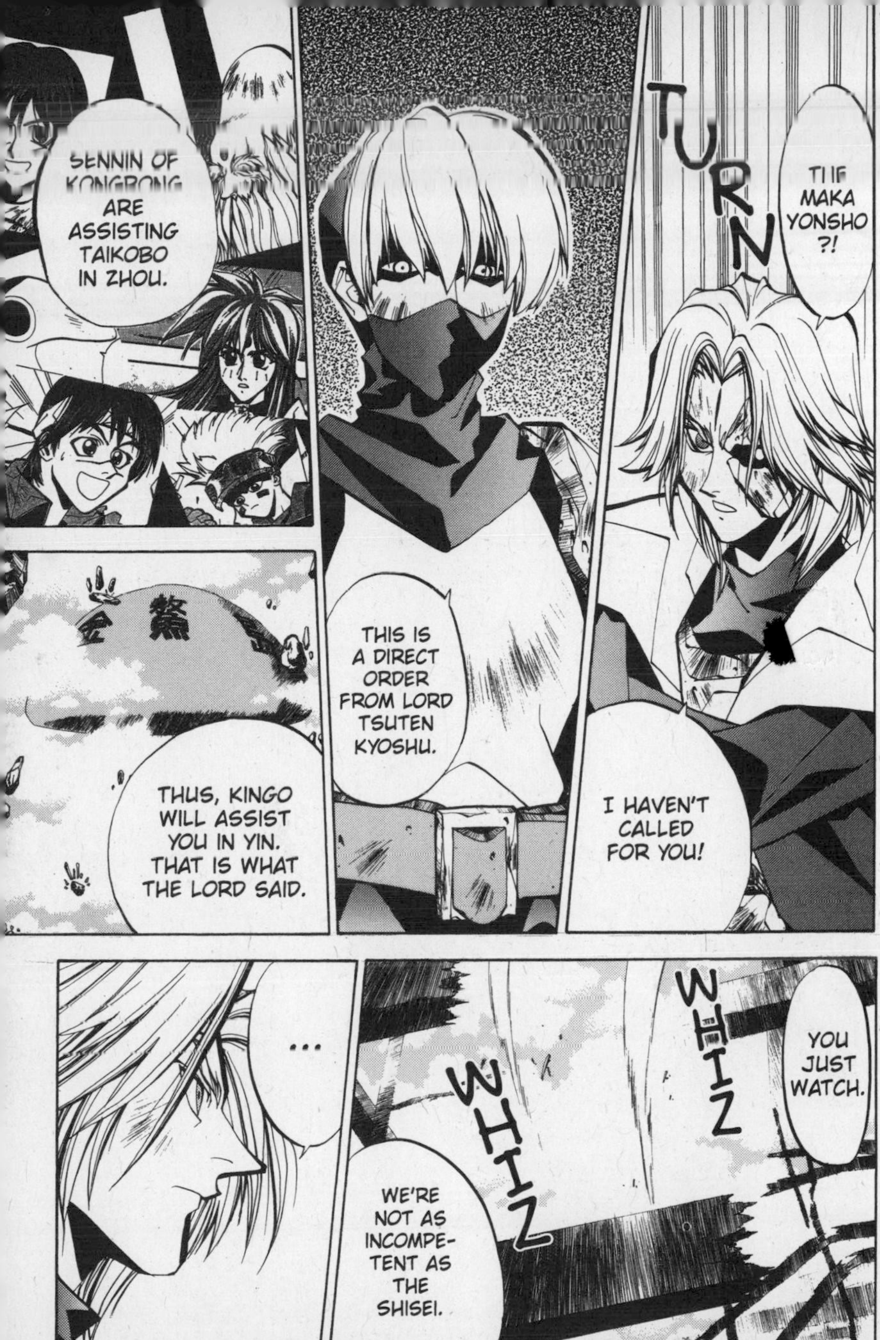
TURN
THE MAKA YONSHO ?!
I HAVEN'T CALLED FOR YOU!
THIS IS A DIRECT ORDER FROM LORD TSUTEN KYOSHU.
SENNIN OF KONGRONG ARE ASSISTING TAIKOBO IN ZHOU.
金 鰲
THUS, KINGO WILL ASSIST YOU IN YIN. THAT IS WHAT THE LORD SAID.
WHIZ
YOU JUST WATCH.
WHIZ
WE'RE NOT AS INCOMPETENT AS THE SHISEI.
...

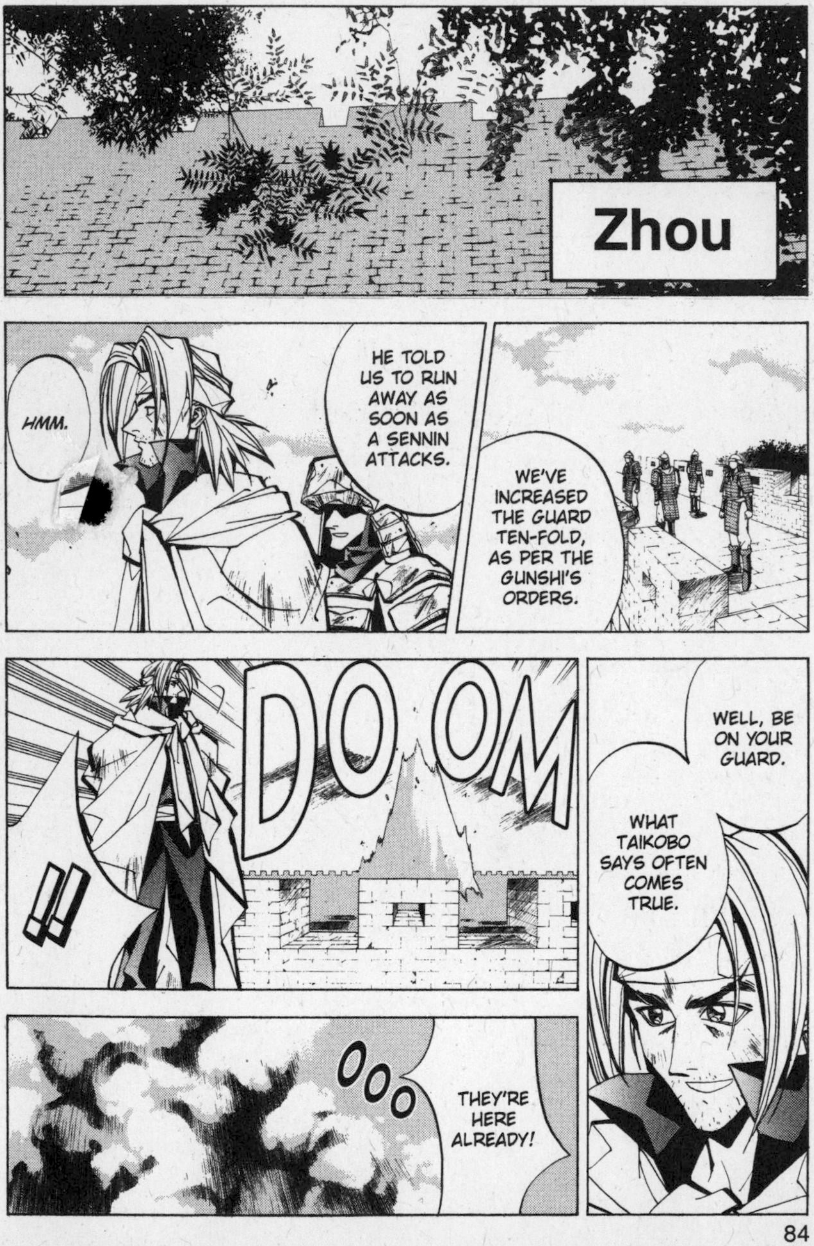
Zhou
WE'VE INCREASED THE GUARD TEN-FOLD, AS PER THE GUNSHI'S ORDERS.
HE TOLD US TO RUN AWAY AS SOON AS A SENNIN ATTACKS.
HMM.
WELL, BE ON YOUR GUARD.
WHAT TAIKOBO SAYS OFTEN COMES TRUE.
DOOM
!!
OOO
THEY'RE HERE ALREADY!

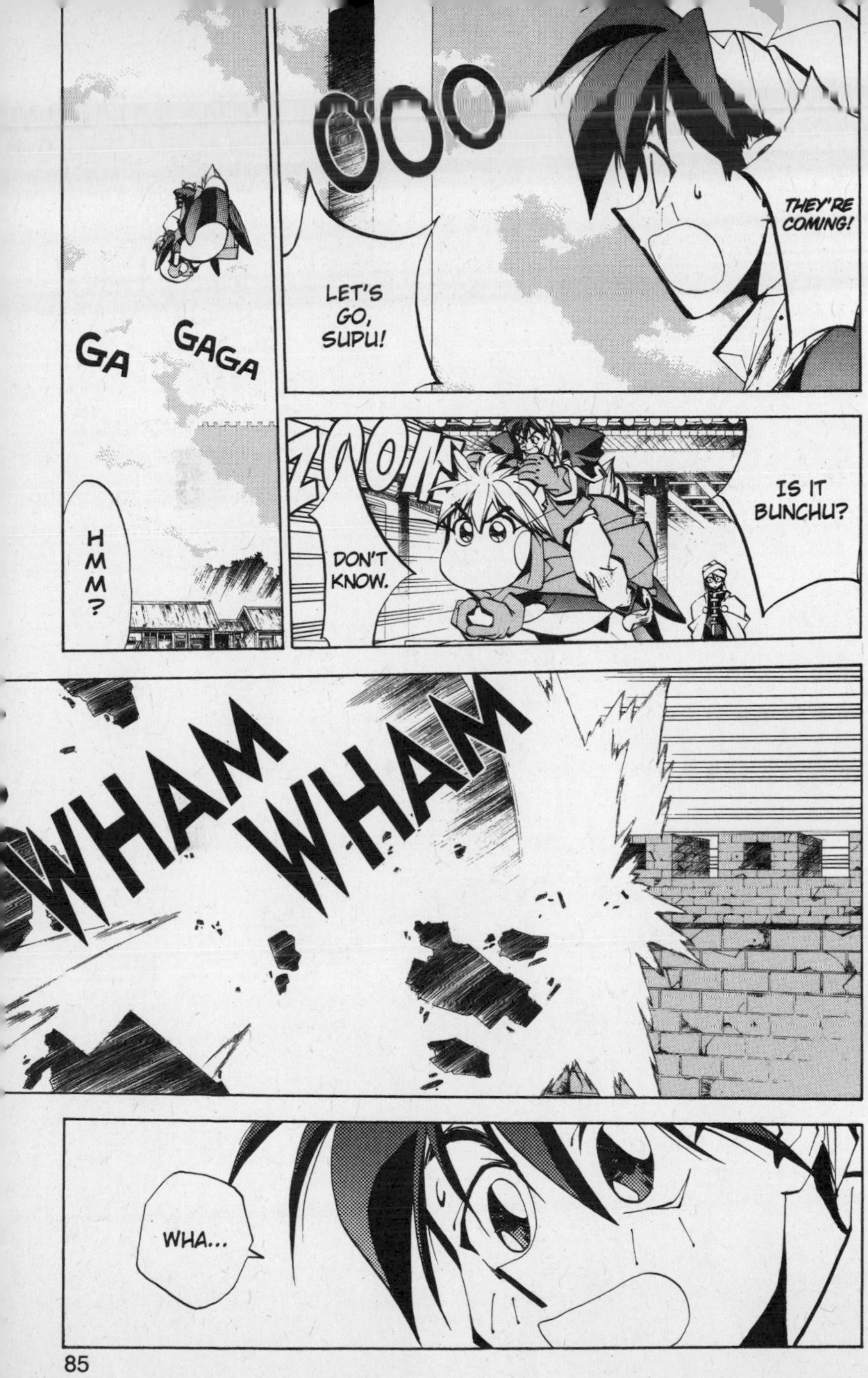
THEY'RE COMING!
OOO
LET'S GO, SUPU!
IS IT BUNCHU?
ZOOM
DON'T KNOW.
GAGA
GA
HMM?
WHAM WHAM
WHA...

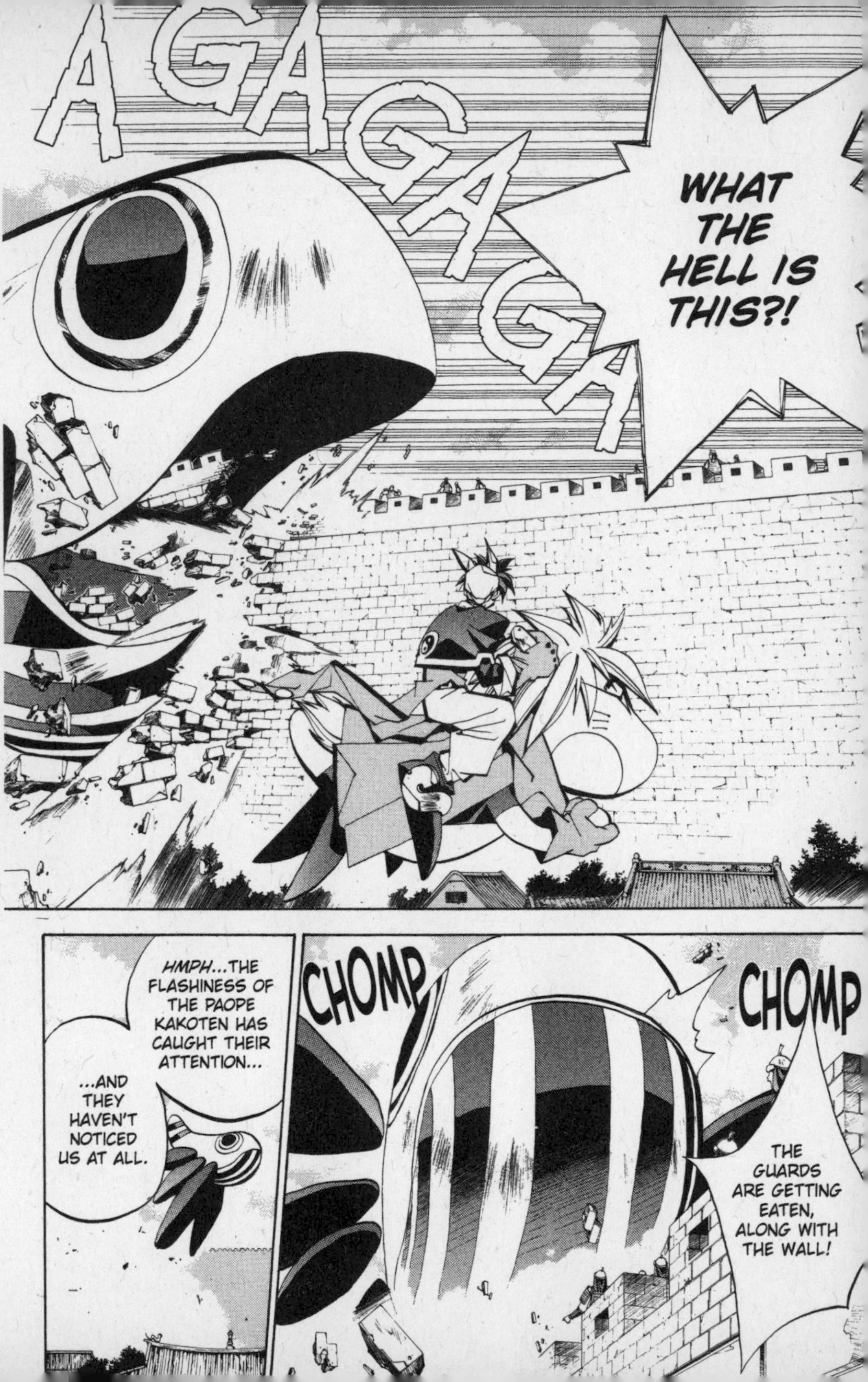
WHAT THE HELL IS THIS?!
AGAGAGAGA
CHOMP
CHOMP
THE GUARDS ARE GETTING EATEN, ALONG WITH THE WALL!
HMPH...THE FLASHINESS OF THE PAOPE KAKOTEN HAS CAUGHT THEIR ATTENTION...
...AND THEY HAVEN'T NOTICED US AT ALL.

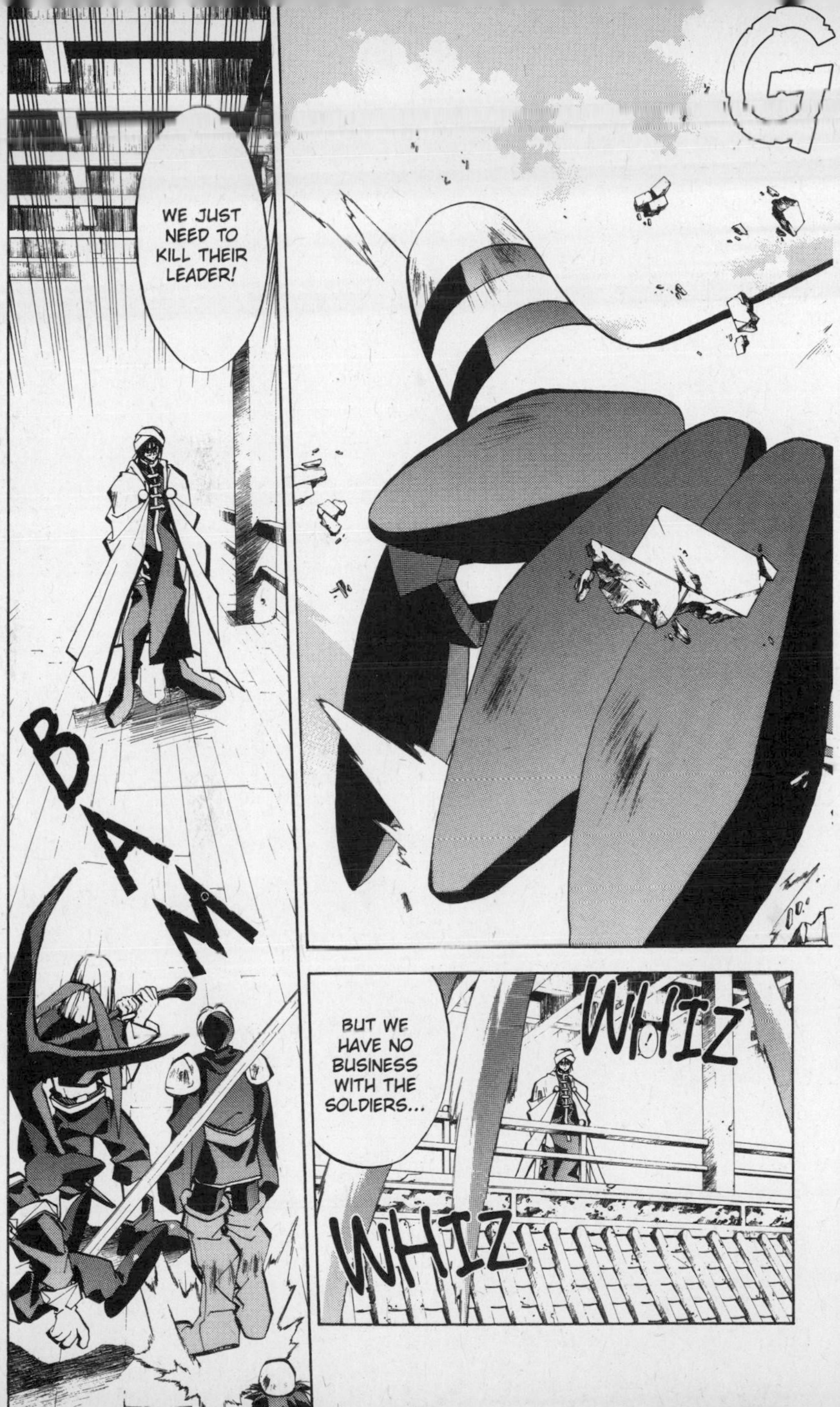
G
BUT WE HAVE NO BUSINESS WITH THE SOLDIERS...
WHIZ
WHIZ
WE JUST NEED TO KILL THEIR LEADER!
BAM

封神演義

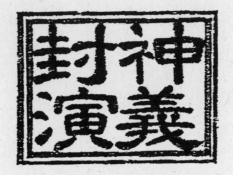

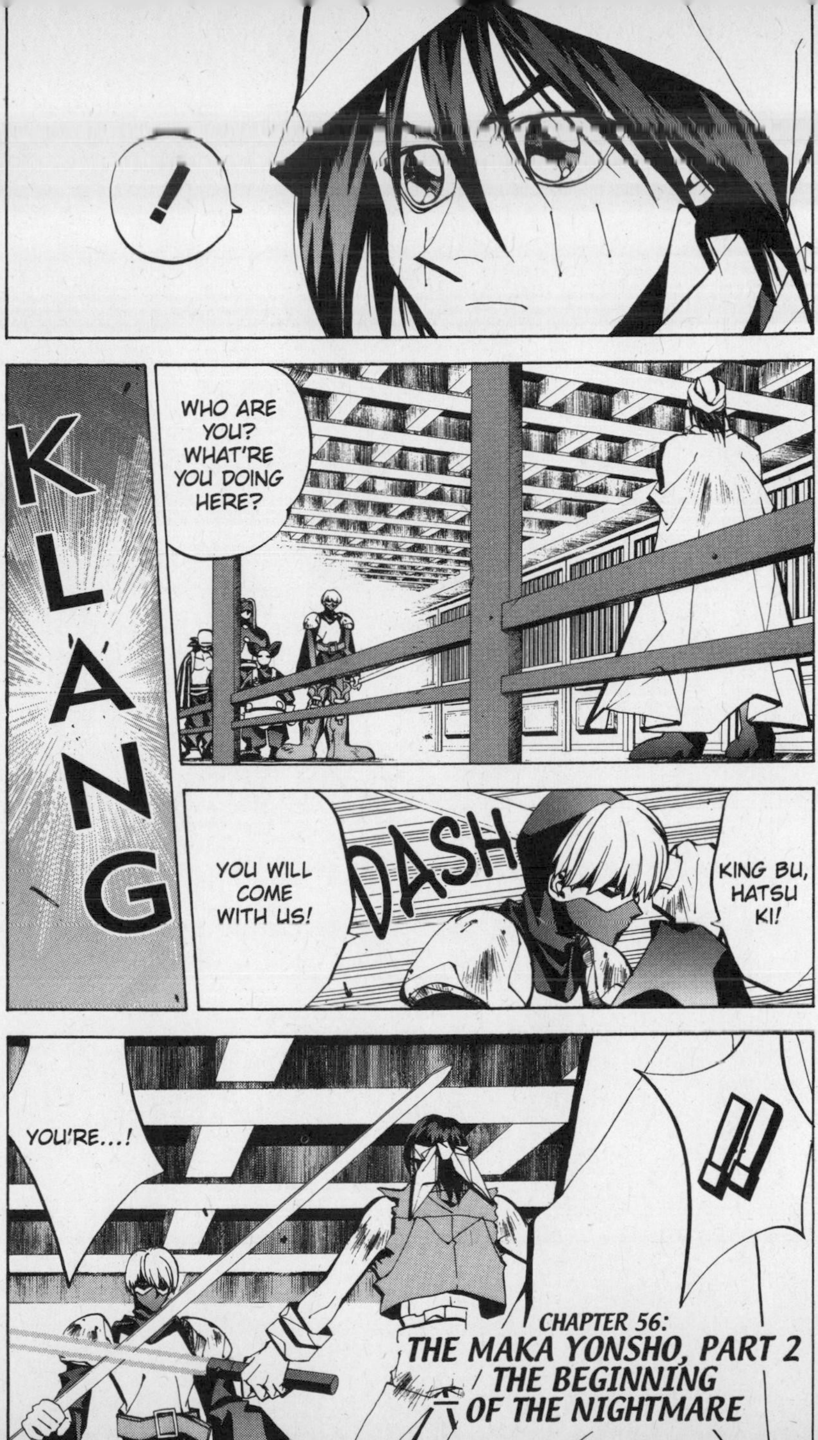
!
WHO ARE YOU? WHAT'RE YOU DOING HERE?
KING BU, HATSU KI!
DASH
YOU WILL COME WITH US!
KLANG
!!
YOU'RE...!
CHAPTER 56:
THE MAKA YONSHO, PART 2 / THE BEGINNING OF THE NIGHTMARE

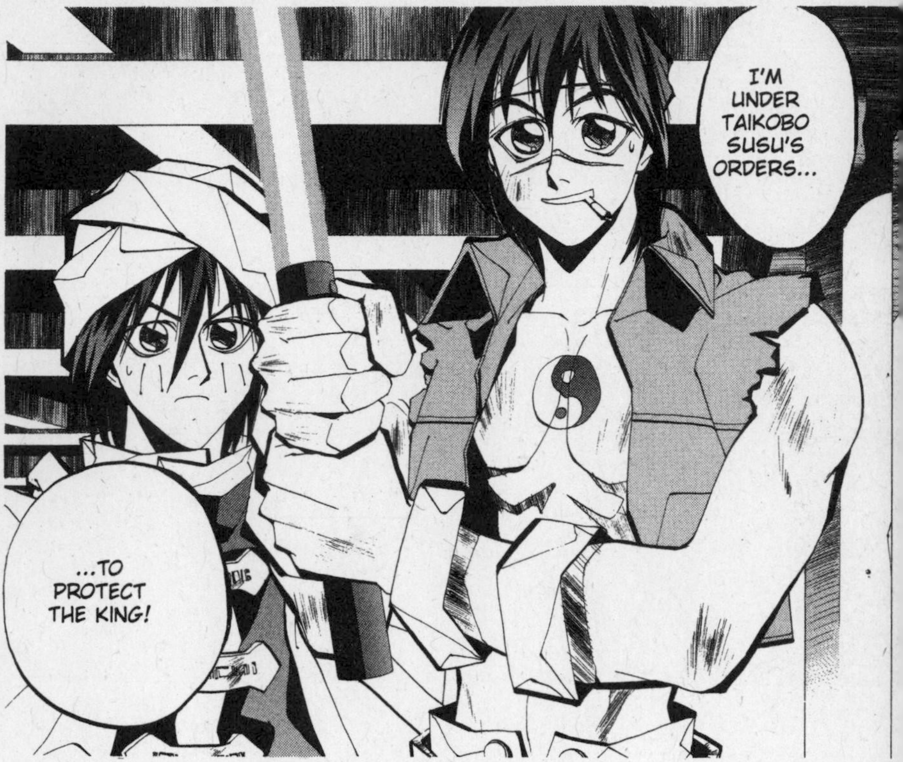
I'M UNDER TAIKOBO SUSU'S ORDERS...
...TO PROTECT THE KING!

Chapter 56

THE MAKA YONSHO, PART 2 THE BEGINNING OF THE NIGHTMARE

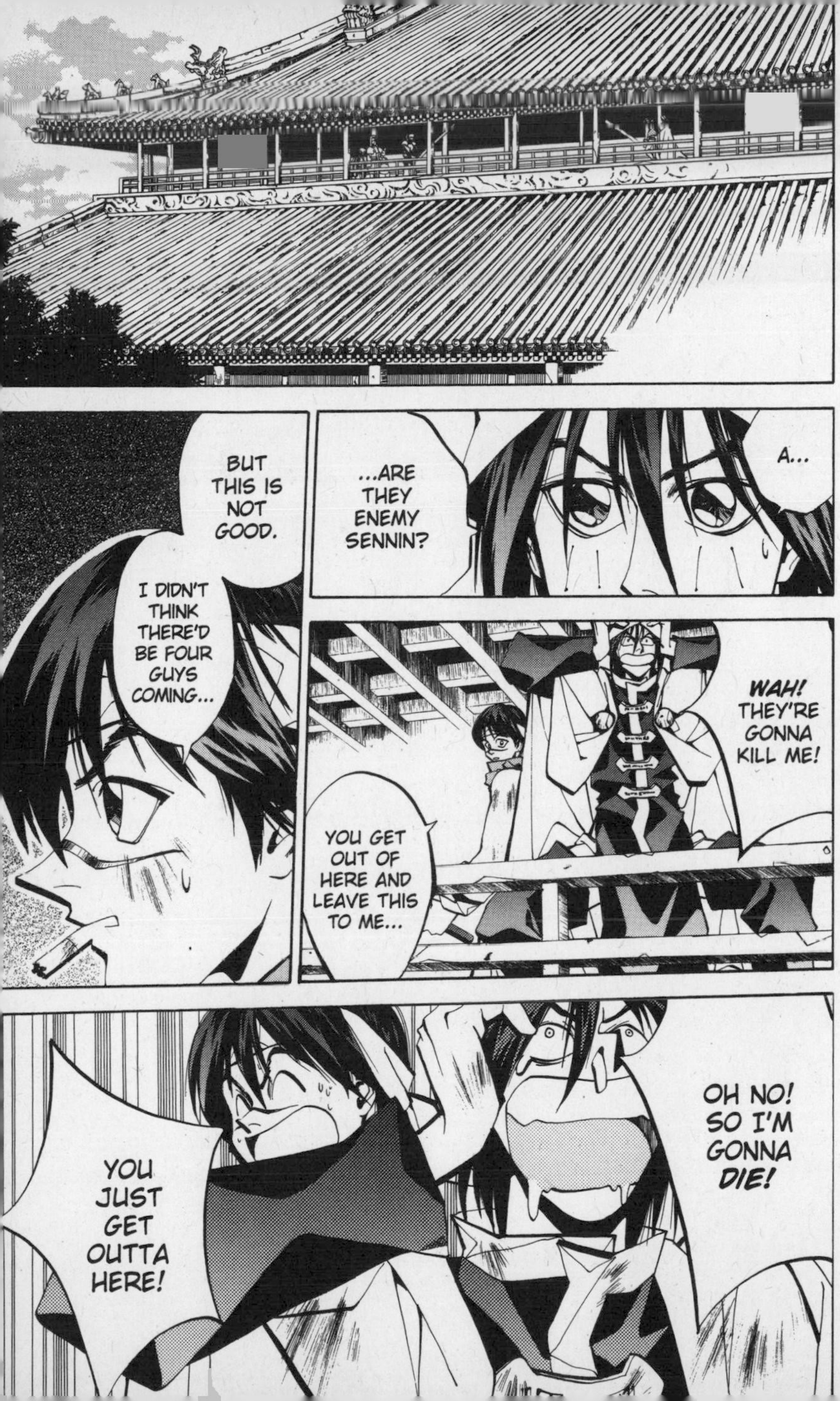
A...
...ARE THEY ENEMY SENNIN?
WAH! THEY'RE GONNA KILL ME!
YOU GET OUT OF HERE AND LEAVE THIS TO ME...
BUT THIS IS NOT GOOD.
I DIDN'T THINK THERE'D BE FOUR GUYS COMING...
OH NO! SO I'M GONNA *DIE!*
YOU JUST GET OUTTA HERE!

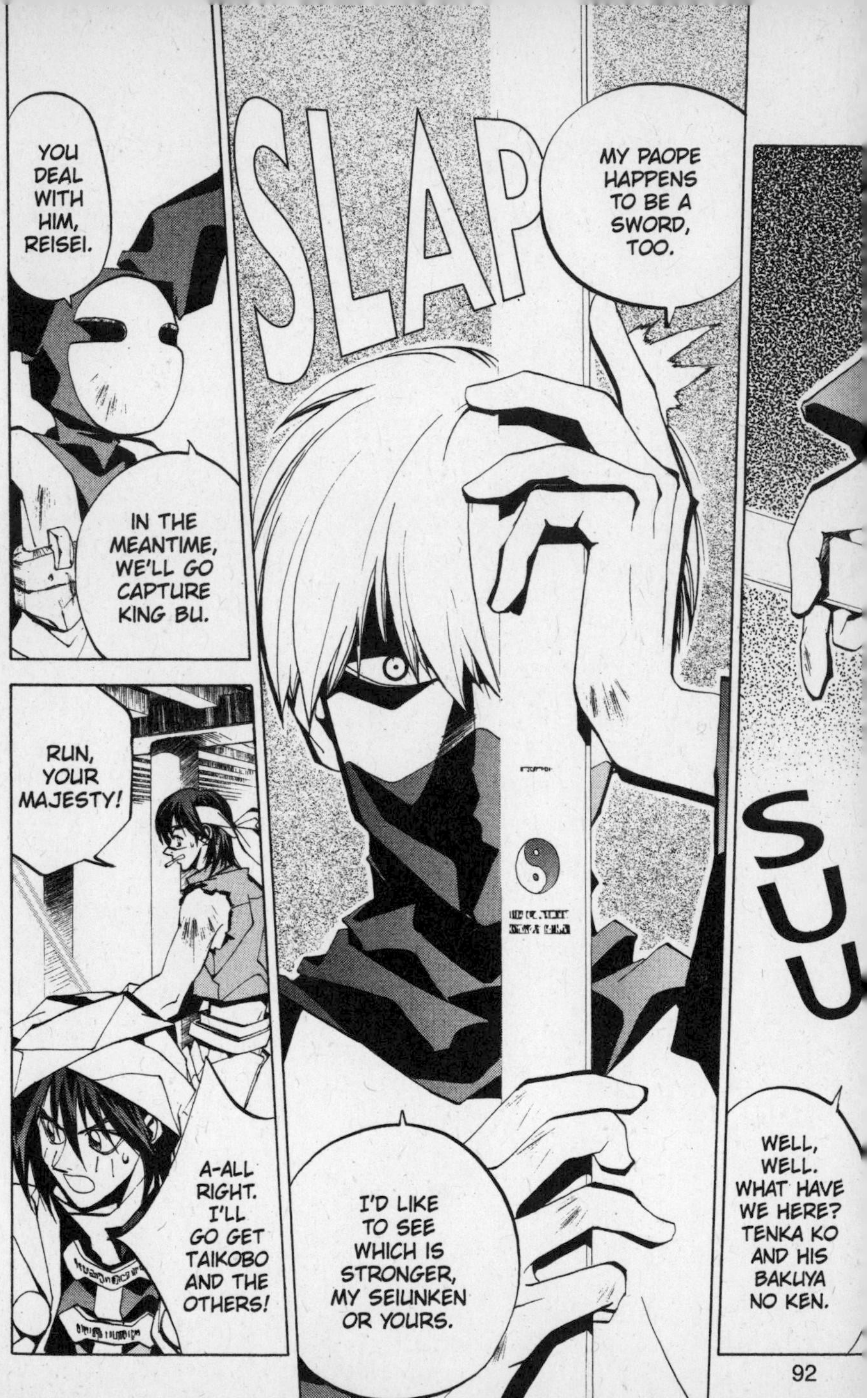
SUU
WELL, WELL. WHAT HAVE WE HERE? TENKA KO AND HIS BAKUYA NO KEN.
MY PAOPE HAPPENS TO BE A SWORD, TOO.
SLAP
I'D LIKE TO SEE WHICH IS STRONGER, MY SEIUNKEN OR YOURS.
YOU DEAL WITH HIM, REISEI.
IN THE MEANTIME, WE'LL GO CAPTURE KING BU.
RUN, YOUR MAJESTY!
A-ALL RIGHT. I'LL GO GET TAIKOBO AND THE OTHERS!

READ THIS WAY

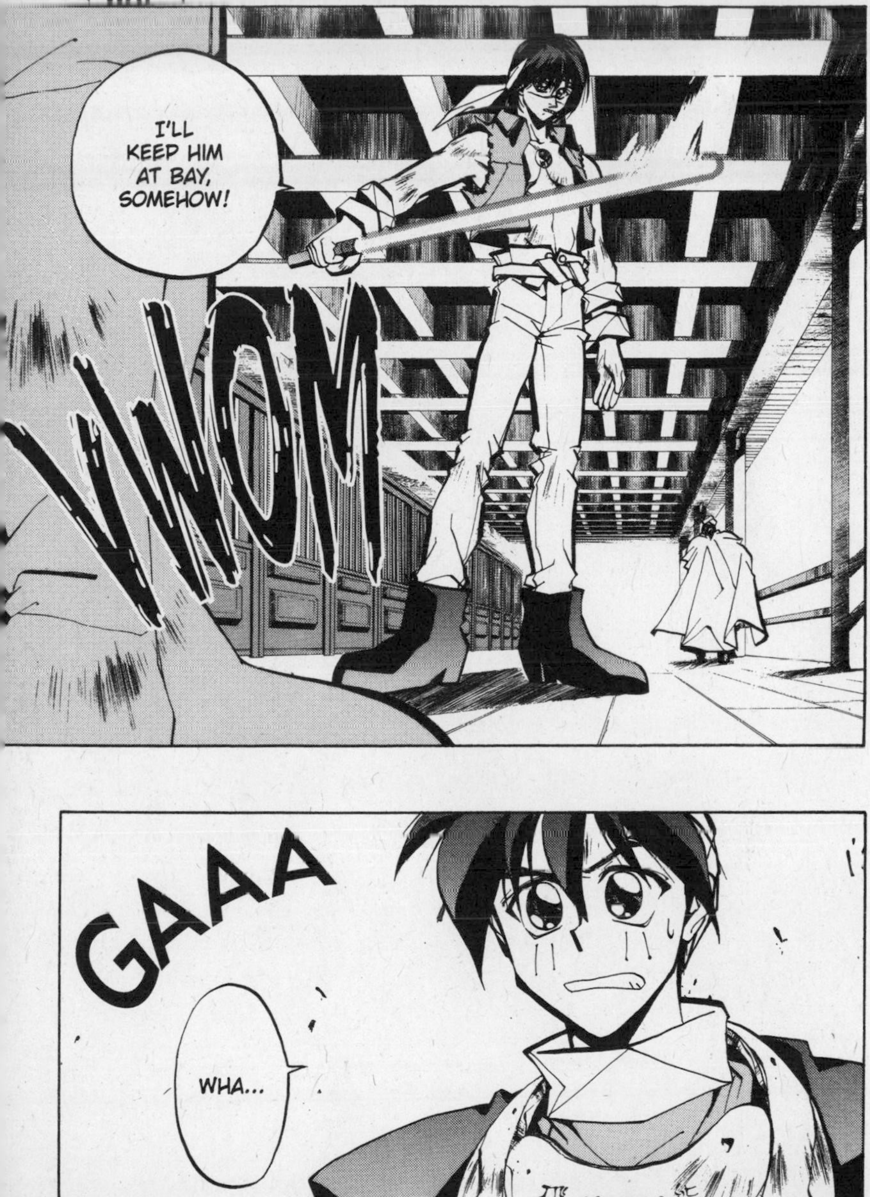
I'LL KEEP HIM AT BAY, SOMEHOW!
VWOM
GAAA
WHA...

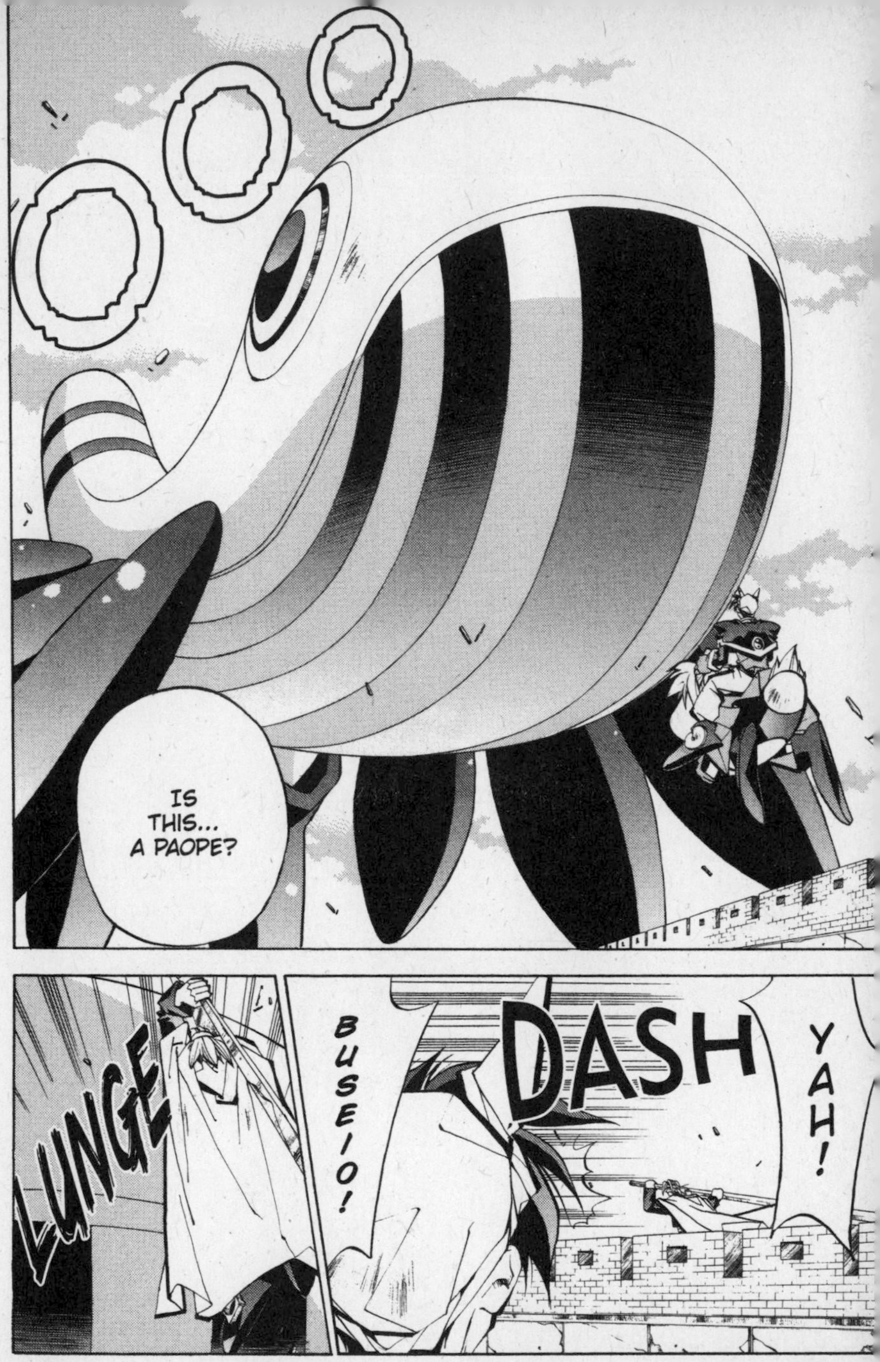
IS THIS... A PAOPE?
YAH!
DASH
BUSEIO!
LUNGE

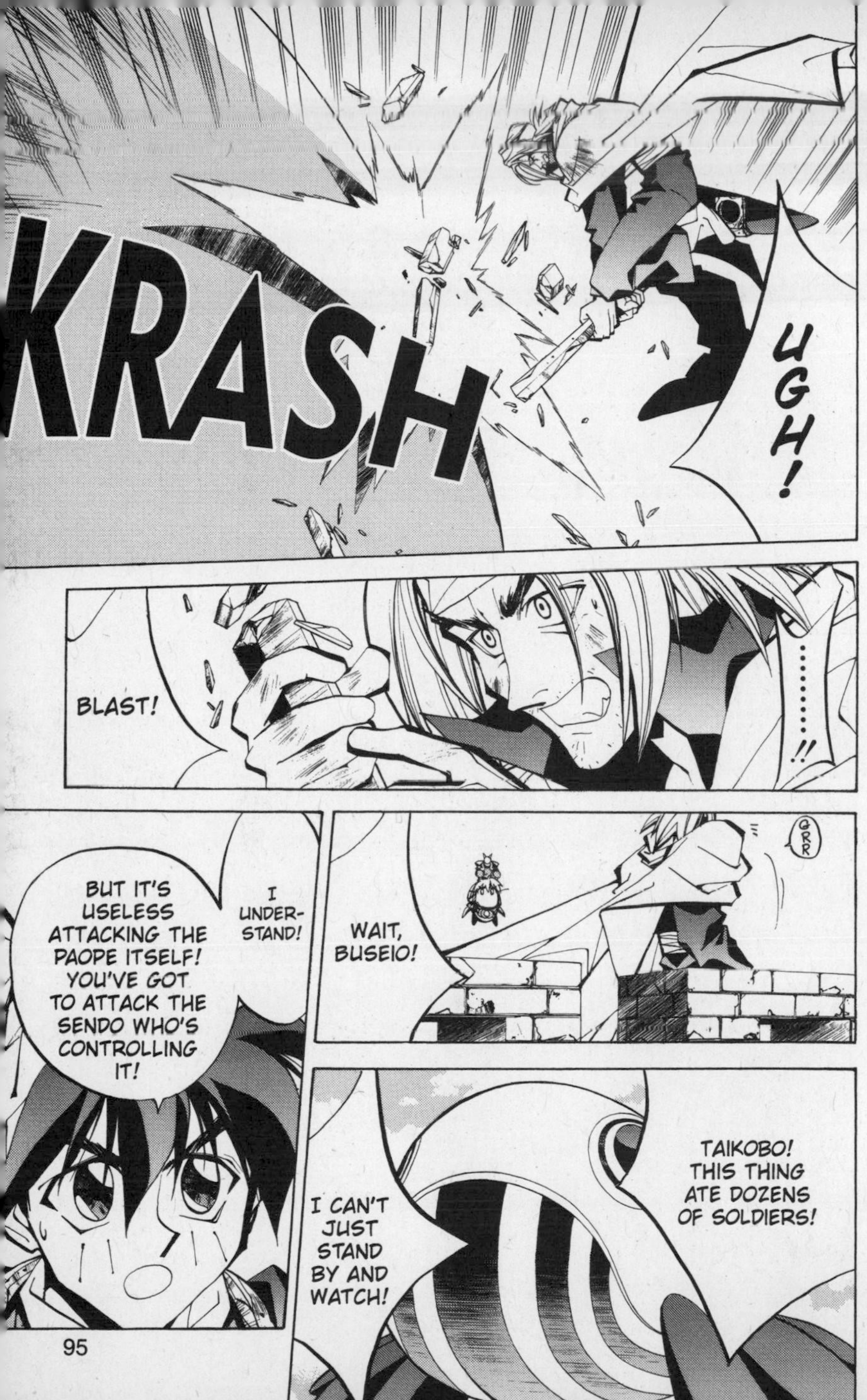
KRASH
UGH!
......!!
BLAST!
GRR
WAIT, BUSEIO!
TAIKOBO! THIS THING ATE DOZENS OF SOLDIERS!
I CAN'T JUST STAND BY AND WATCH!
I UNDER-STAND!
BUT IT'S USELESS ATTACKING THE PAOPE ITSELF! YOU'VE GOT TO ATTACK THE SENDO WHO'S CONTROLLING IT!

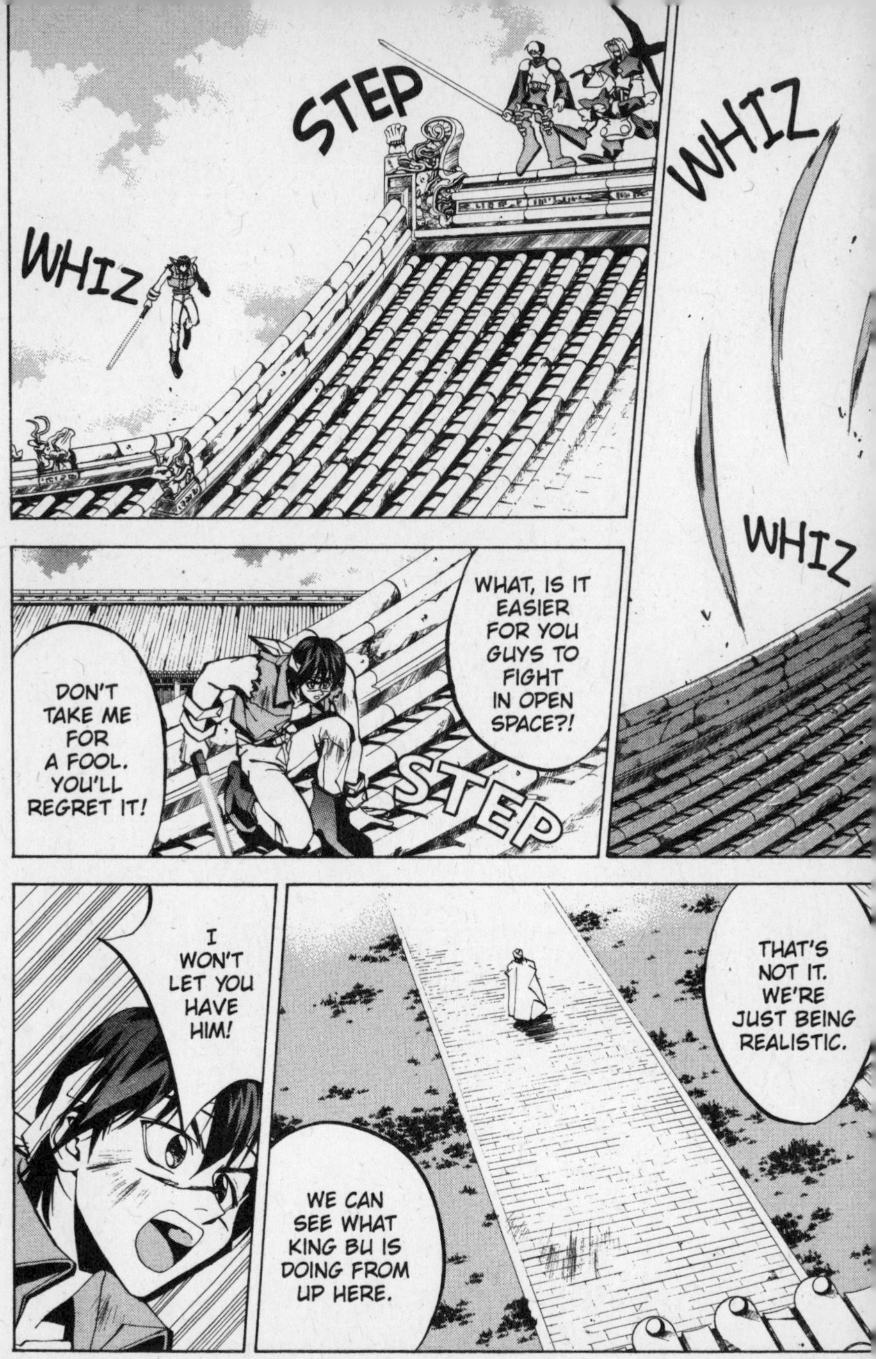
WHIZ
WHIZ
STEP
WHIZ
WHAT, IS IT EASIER FOR YOU GUYS TO FIGHT IN OPEN SPACE?!
STEP
DON'T TAKE ME FOR A FOOL. YOU'LL REGRET IT!
THAT'S NOT IT. WE'RE JUST BEING REALISTIC.
WE CAN SEE WHAT KING BU IS DOING FROM UP HERE.
I WON'T LET YOU HAVE HIM!

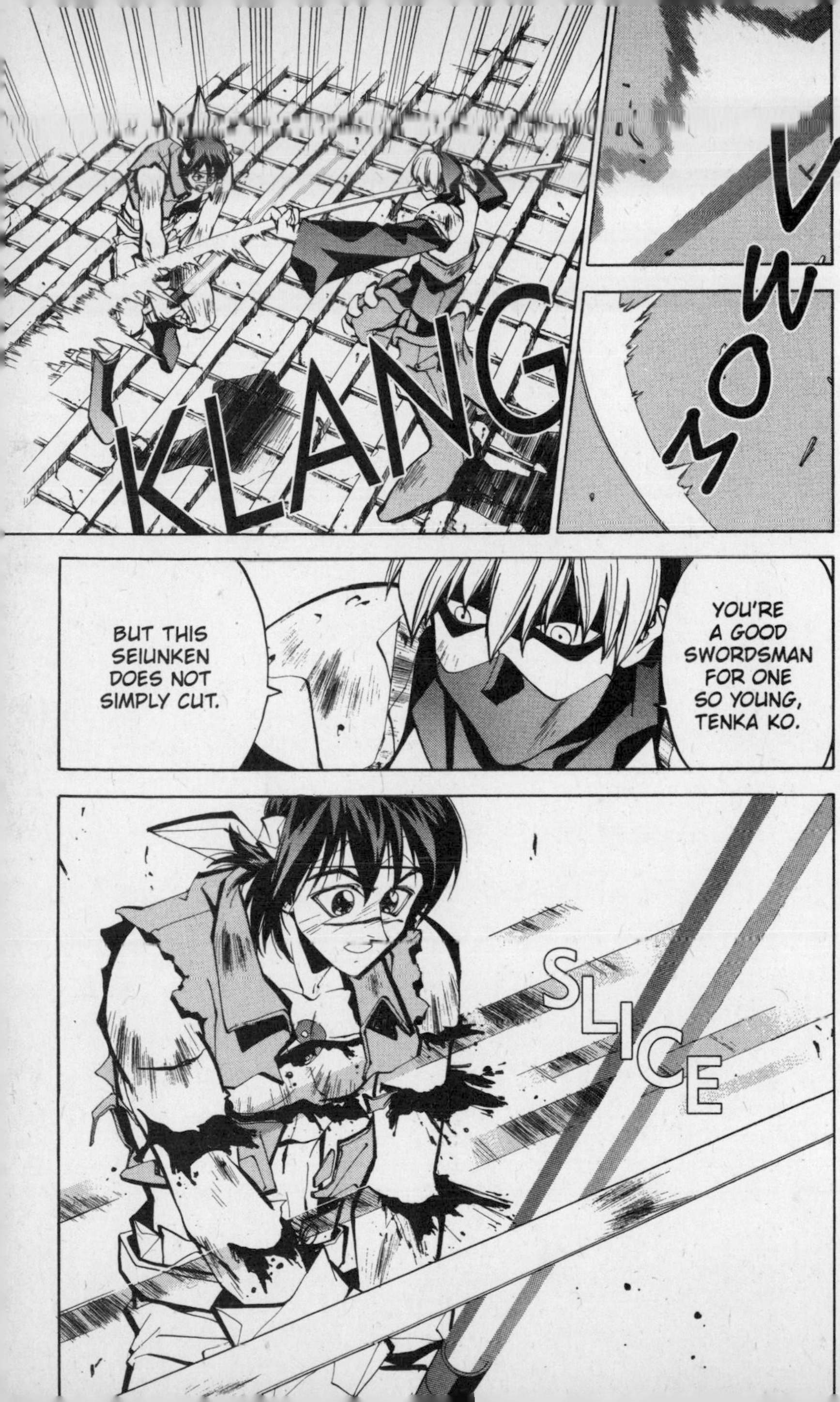
VWOM
KLANG
YOU'RE A GOOD SWORDSMAN FOR ONE SO YOUNG, TENKA KO.
BUT THIS SEIUNKEN DOES NOT SIMPLY CUT.
SLICE

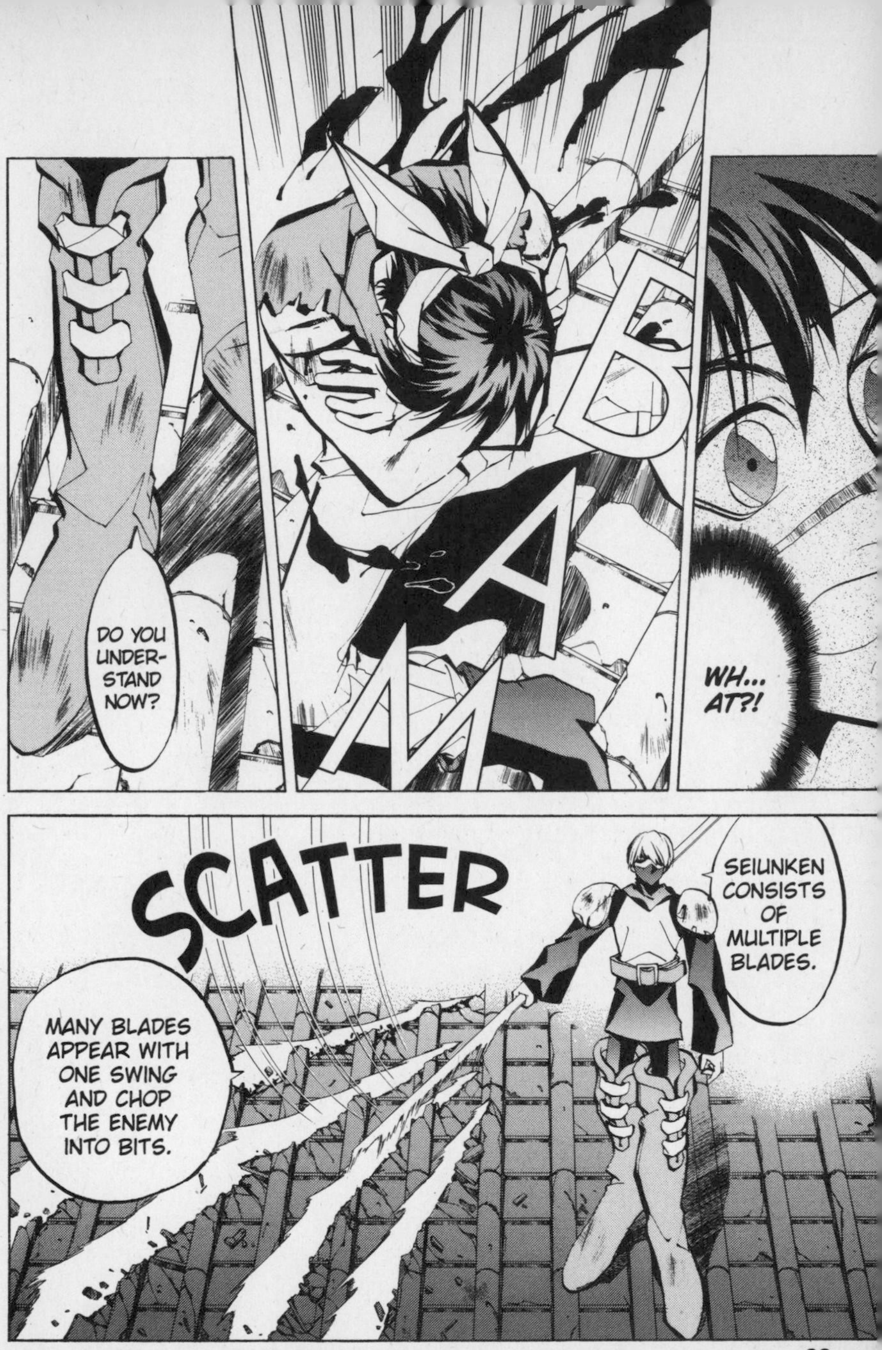
WH... AT?!
BAM
DO YOU UNDER-STAND NOW?
SEIUNKEN CONSISTS OF MULTIPLE BLADES.
SCATTER
MANY BLADES APPEAR WITH ONE SWING AND CHOP THE ENEMY INTO BITS.

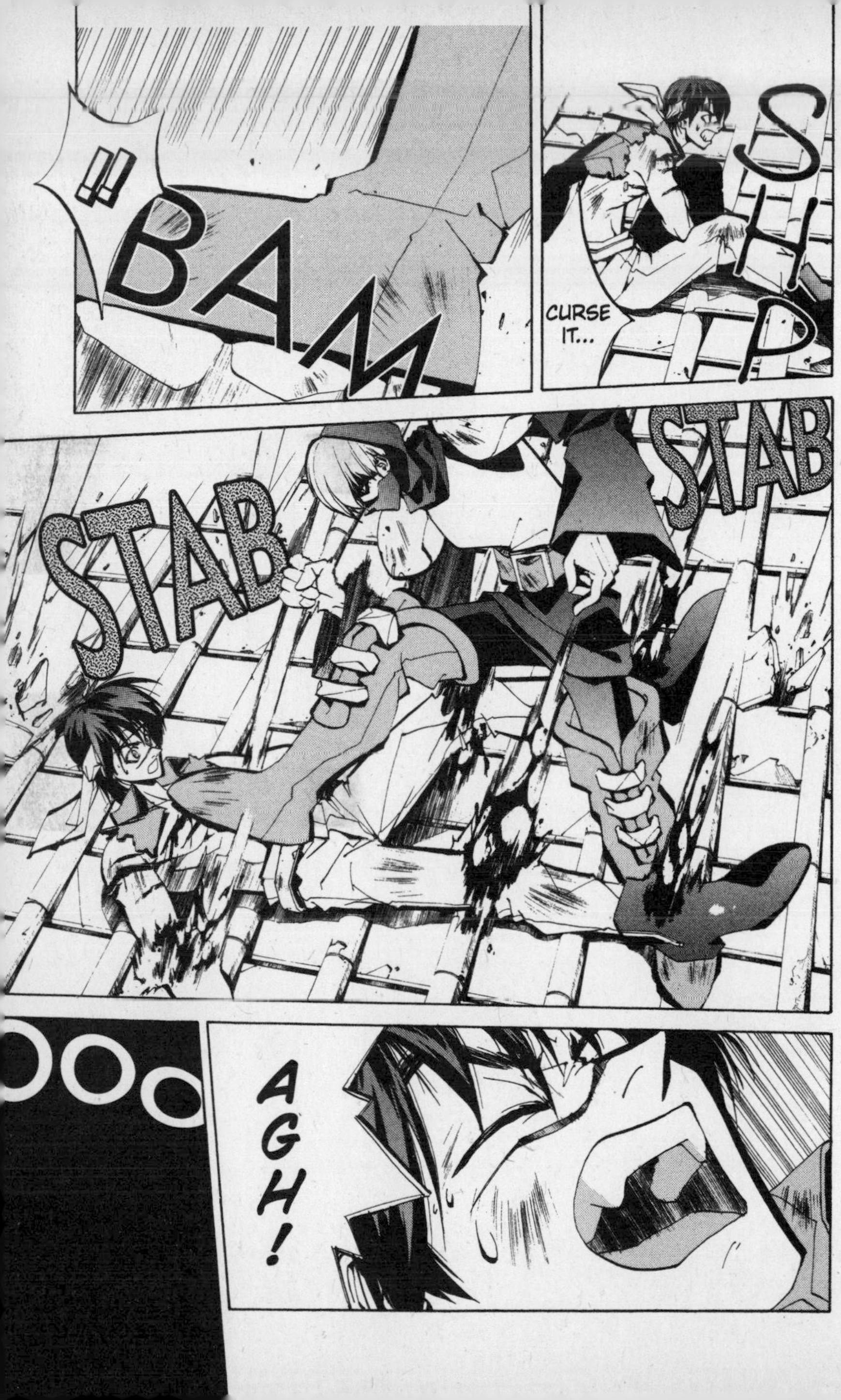
SHP
CURSE IT...
!!
BAM
STAB
STAB
AGH!

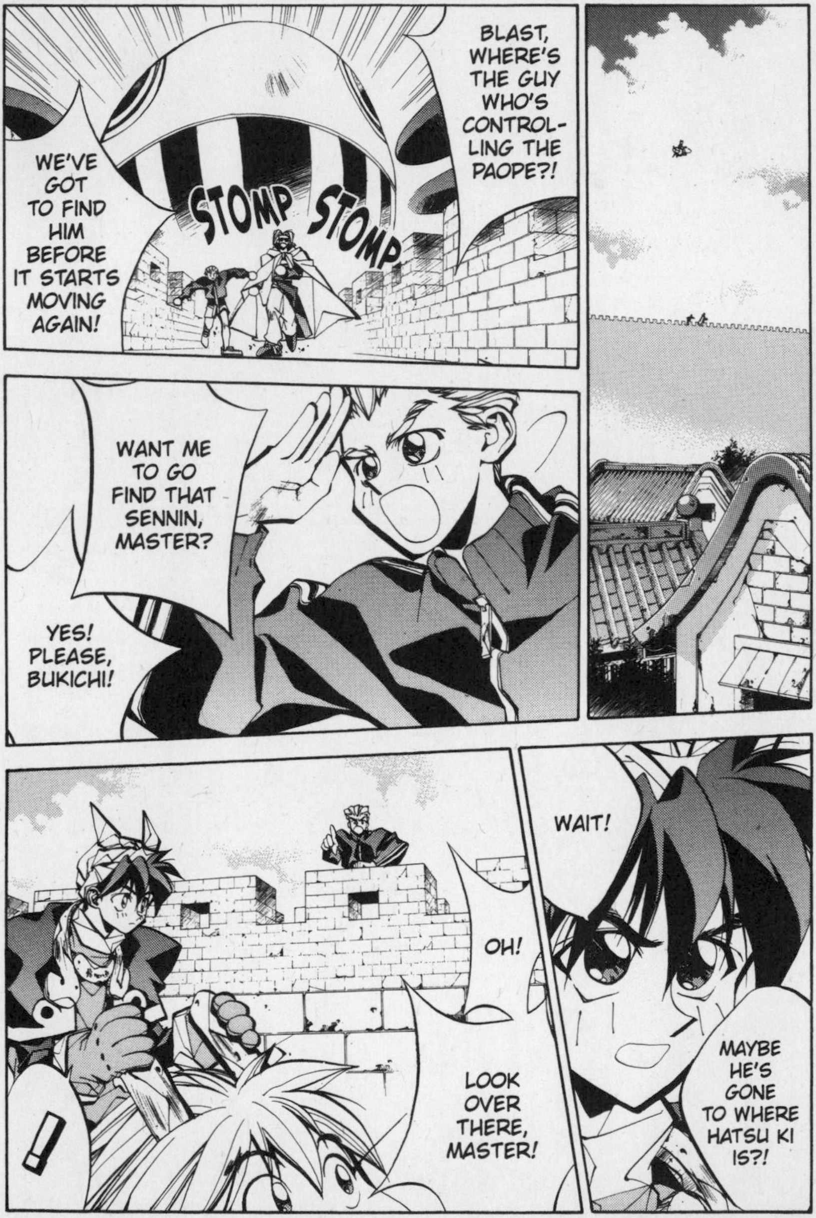
BLAST, WHERE'S THE GUY WHO'S CONTROL-LING THE PAOPE?!
STOMP STOMP
WE'VE GOT TO FIND HIM BEFORE IT STARTS MOVING AGAIN!
WANT ME TO GO FIND THAT SENNIN, MASTER?
YES! PLEASE, BUKICHI!
WAIT!
MAYBE HE'S GONE TO WHERE HATSU KI IS?!
OH!
LOOK OVER THERE, MASTER!
!

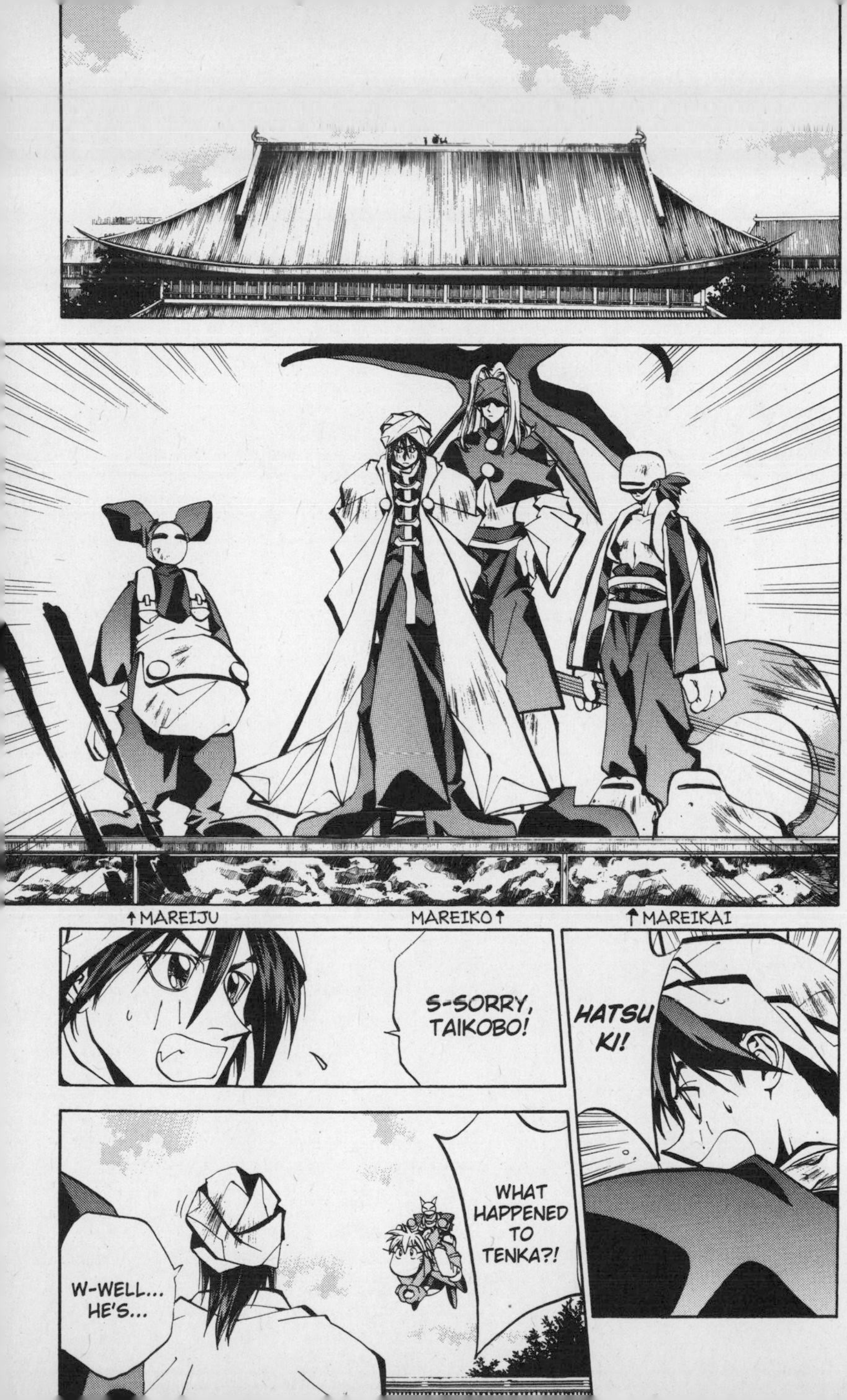

↑MAREIKAI
MAREIKO↑
↑MAREIJU
HATSU KI!
S-SORRY, TAIKOBO!
WHAT HAPPENED TO TENKA?!
W-WELL... HE'S...

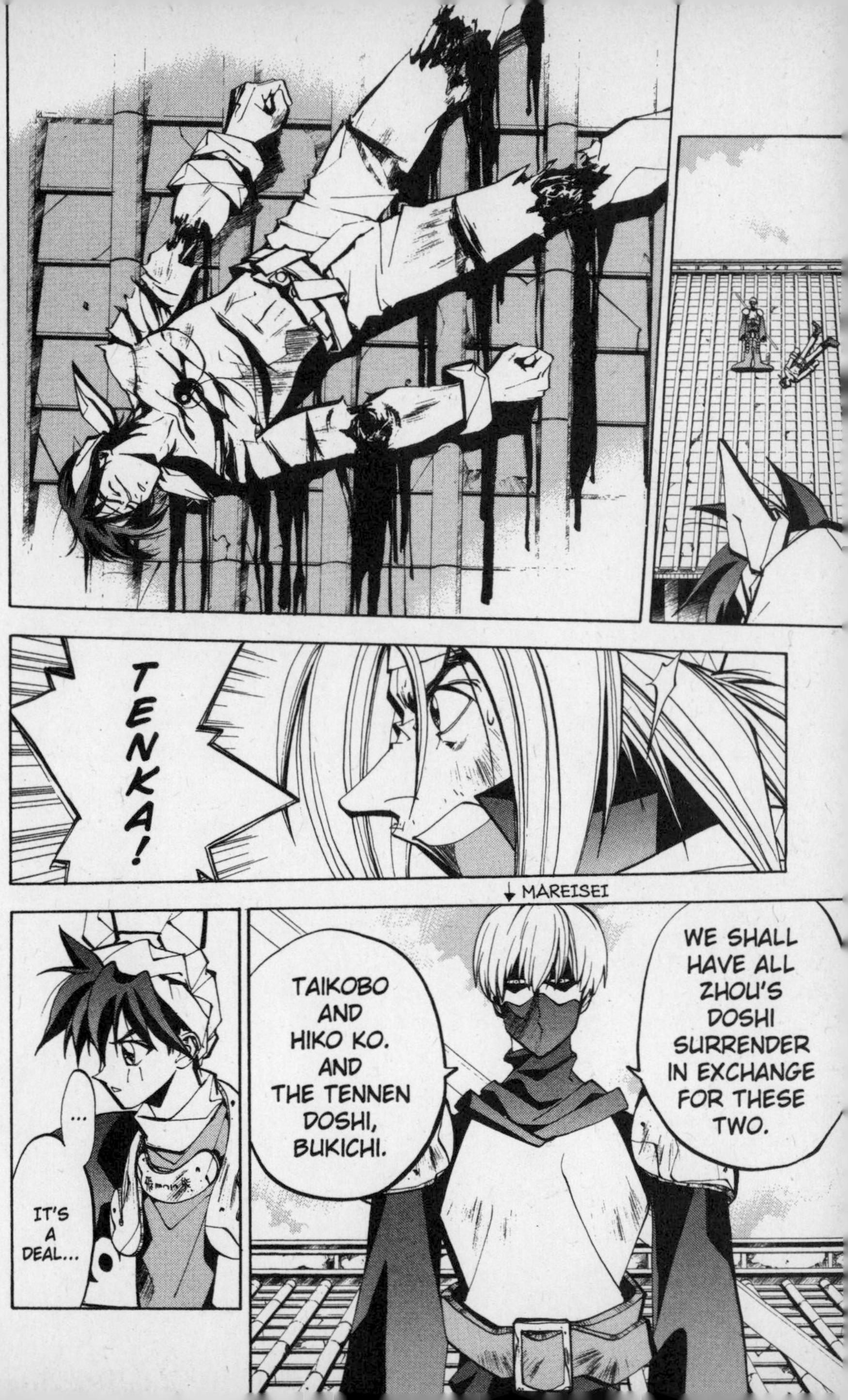
TENKA!
MAREISEI
WE SHALL HAVE ALL ZHOU'S DOSHI SURRENDER IN EXCHANGE FOR THESE TWO.
TAIKOBO AND HIKO KO. AND THE TENNEN DOSHI, BUKICHI.
...
IT'S A DEAL...

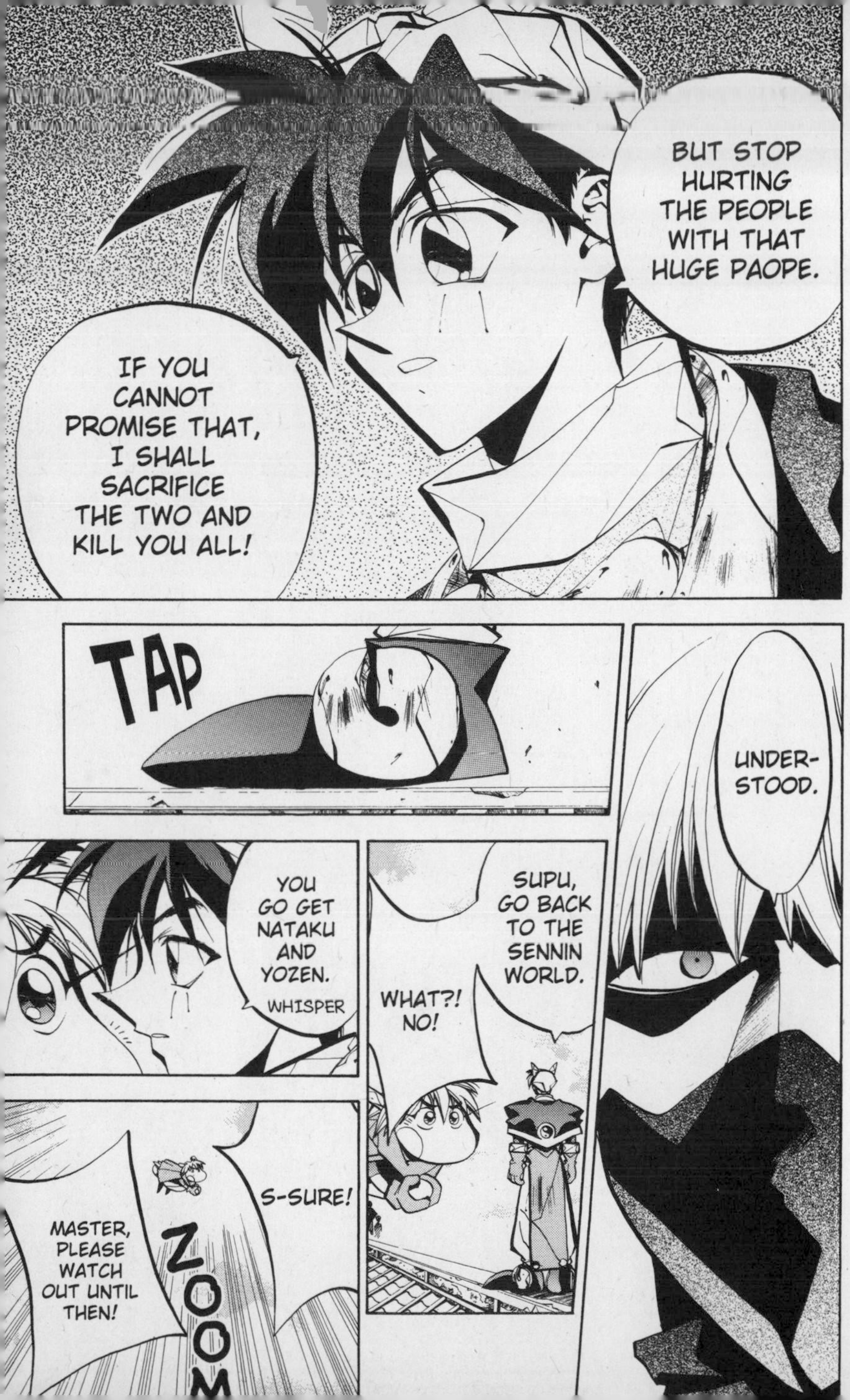
BUT STOP HURTING THE PEOPLE WITH THAT HUGE PAOPE.
IF YOU CANNOT PROMISE THAT, I SHALL SACRIFICE THE TWO AND KILL YOU ALL!
UNDER-STOOD.
TAP
SUPU, GO BACK TO THE SENNIN WORLD.
WHAT?! NO!
YOU GO GET NATAKU AND YOZEN.
WHISPER
S-SURE!
MASTER, PLEASE WATCH OUT UNTIL THEN!
ZOOM

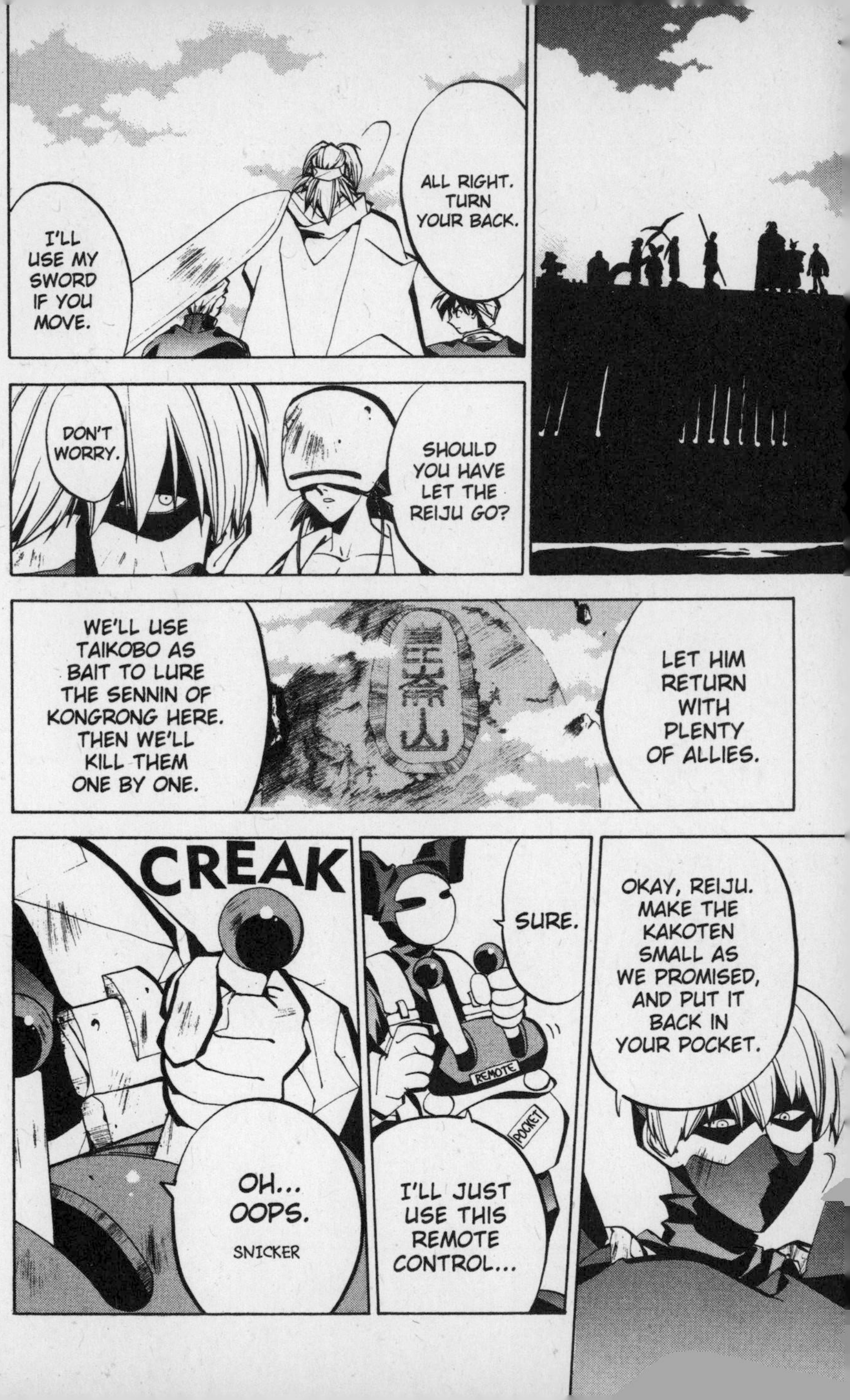
ALL RIGHT. TURN YOUR BACK.
I'LL USE MY SWORD IF YOU MOVE.
SHOULD YOU HAVE LET THE REIJU GO?
DON'T WORRY.
LET HIM RETURN WITH PLENTY OF ALLIES.
WE'LL USE TAIKOBO AS BAIT TO LURE THE SENNIN OF KONGRONG HERE. THEN WE'LL KILL THEM ONE BY ONE.
OKAY, REIJU. MAKE THE KAKOTEN SMALL AS WE PROMISED, AND PUT IT BACK IN YOUR POCKET.
SURE.
REMOTE
POCKET
I'LL JUST USE THIS REMOTE CONTROL...
CREAK
OH... OOPS.
SNICKER

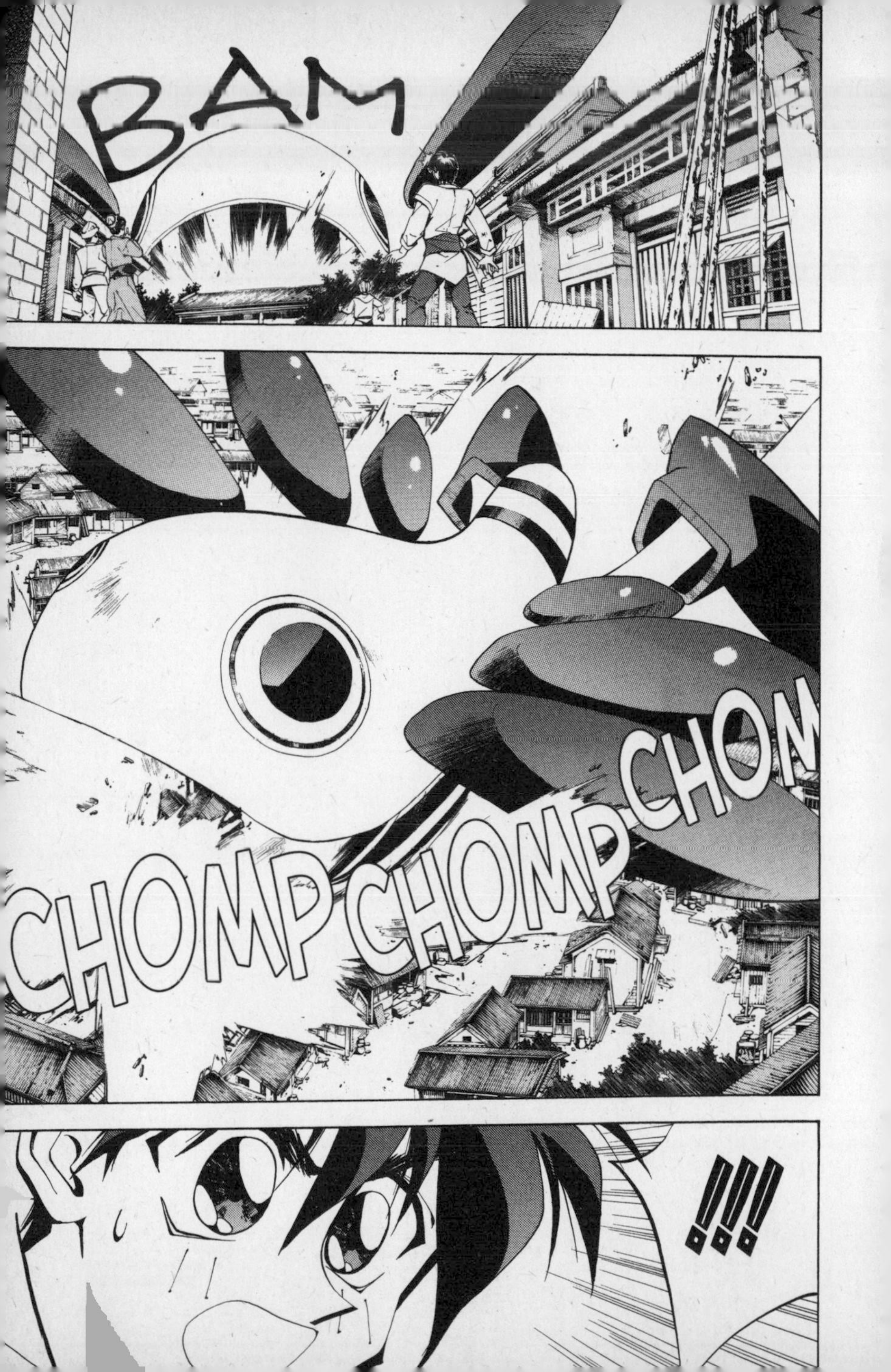
BAM
CHOMP CHOMP CHOM
!!!!

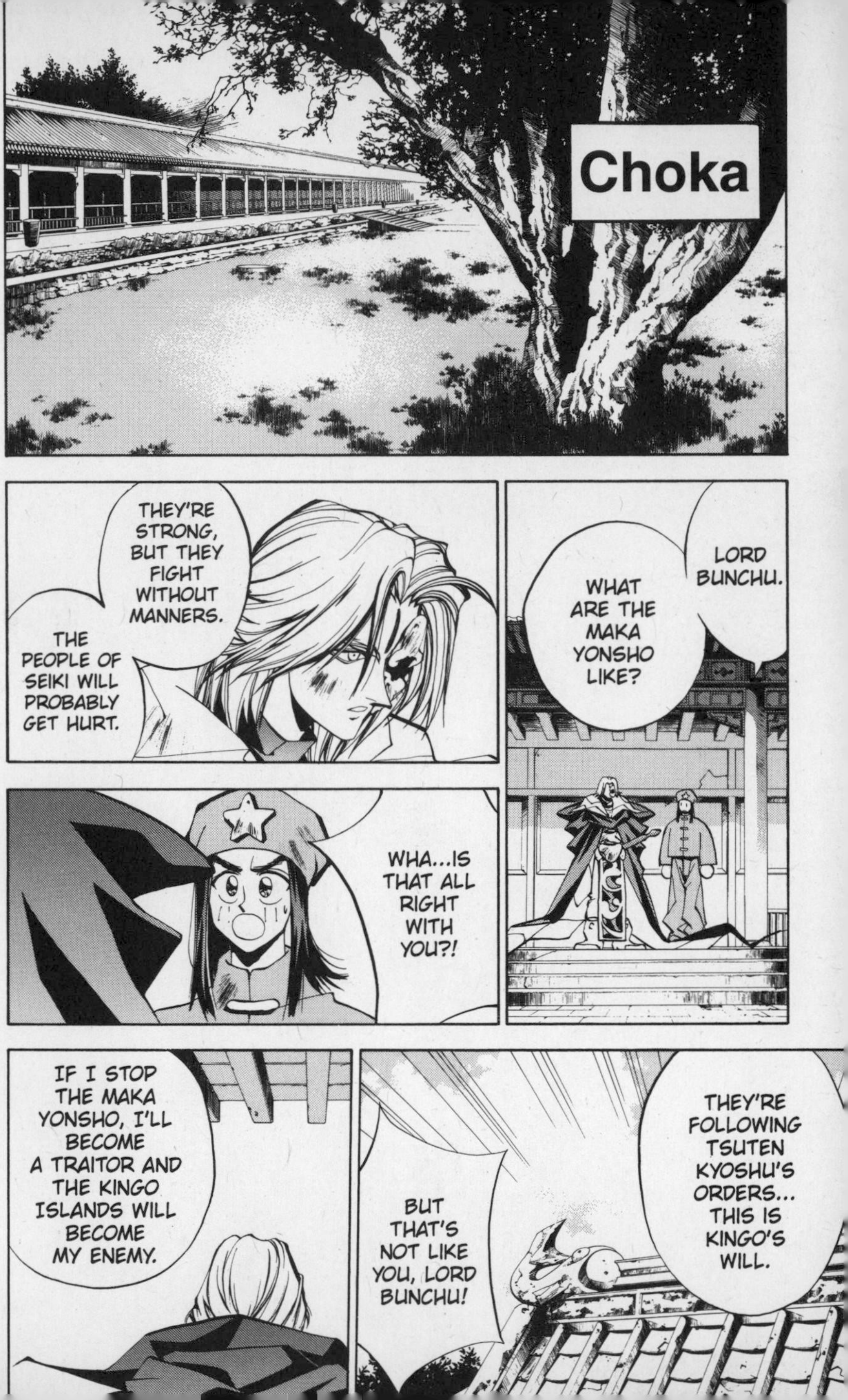
Choka
LORD BUNCHU.
WHAT ARE THE MAKA YONSHO LIKE?
THEY'RE STRONG, BUT THEY FIGHT WITHOUT MANNERS.
THE PEOPLE OF SEIKI WILL PROBABLY GET HURT.
WHA...IS THAT ALL RIGHT WITH YOU?!
THEY'RE FOLLOWING TSUTEN KYOSHU'S ORDERS... THIS IS KINGO'S WILL.
BUT THAT'S NOT LIKE YOU, LORD BUNCHU!
IF I STOP THE MAKA YONSHO, I'LL BECOME A TRAITOR AND THE KINGO ISLANDS WILL BECOME MY ENEMY.

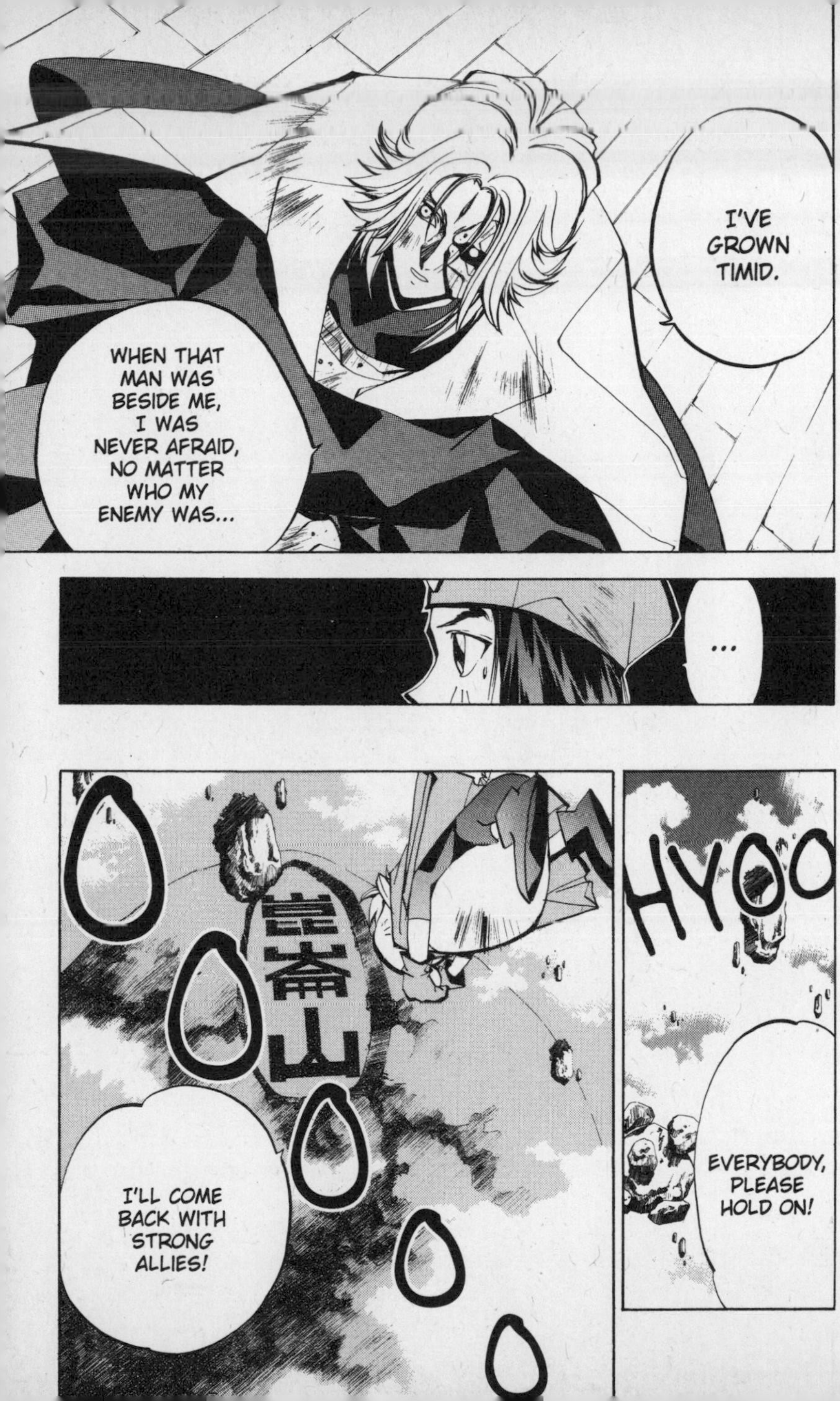
I'VE GROWN TIMID.
WHEN THAT MAN WAS BESIDE ME, I WAS NEVER AFRAID, NO MATTER WHO MY ENEMY WAS...
...
HYOO
EVERYBODY, PLEASE HOLD ON!
崑崙山
I'LL COME BACK WITH STRONG ALLIES!

封神演義

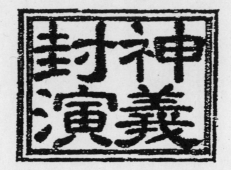

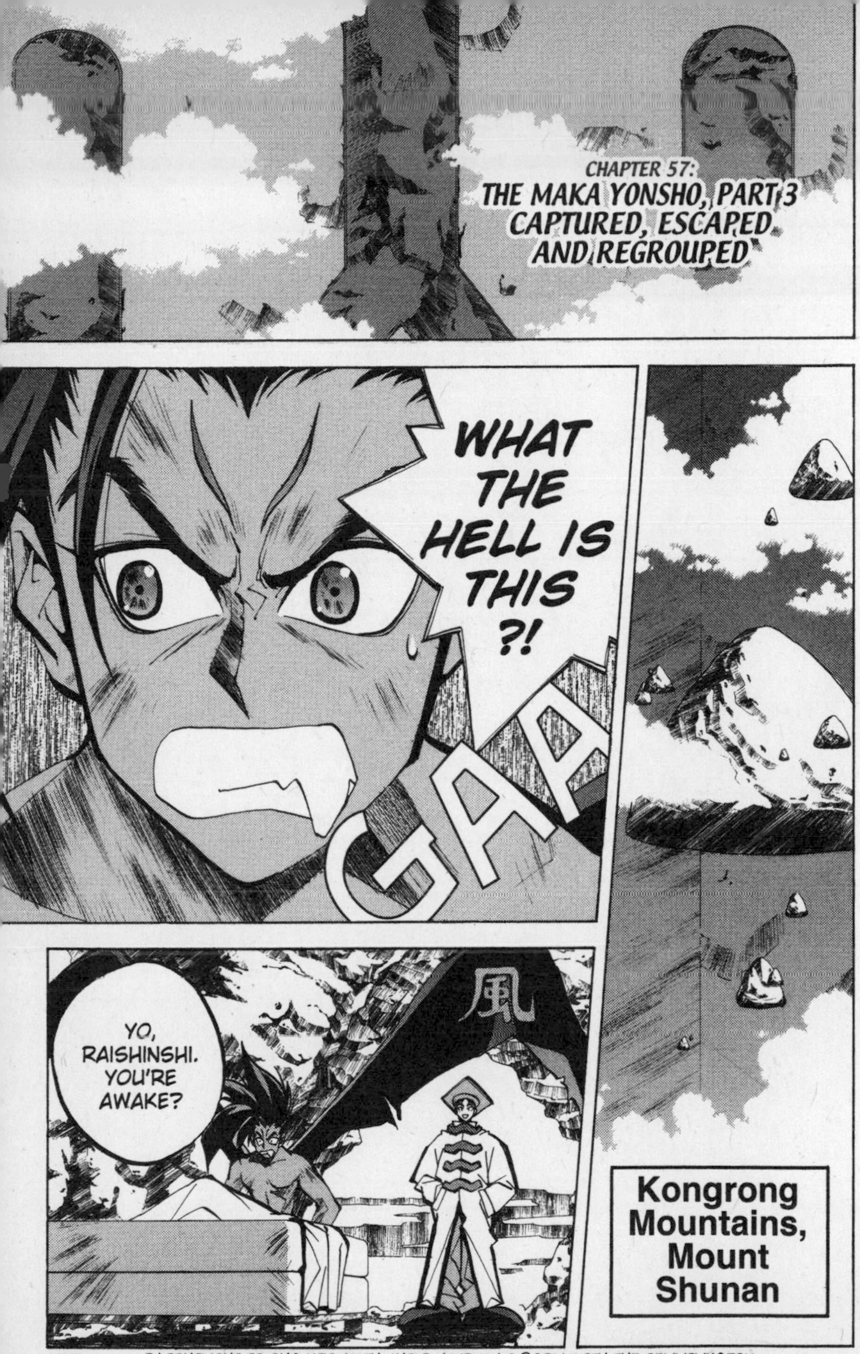
CHAPTER 57:
THE MAKA YONSHO, PART 3
CAPTURED, ESCAPED AND REGROUPED
Kongrong Mountains, Mount Shunan
WHAT THE HELL IS THIS ?!
GAA
YO, RAISHINSHI. YOU'RE AWAKE?
風

RAISHINSHI IS SHO KI'S 100TH CHILD AND WAS BORN WITH THE SENNINKOTSU.
HE TRAINED UNDER UNCHUSHI, A SENNIN LIVING IN THE KONGRONG MOUNTAINS.

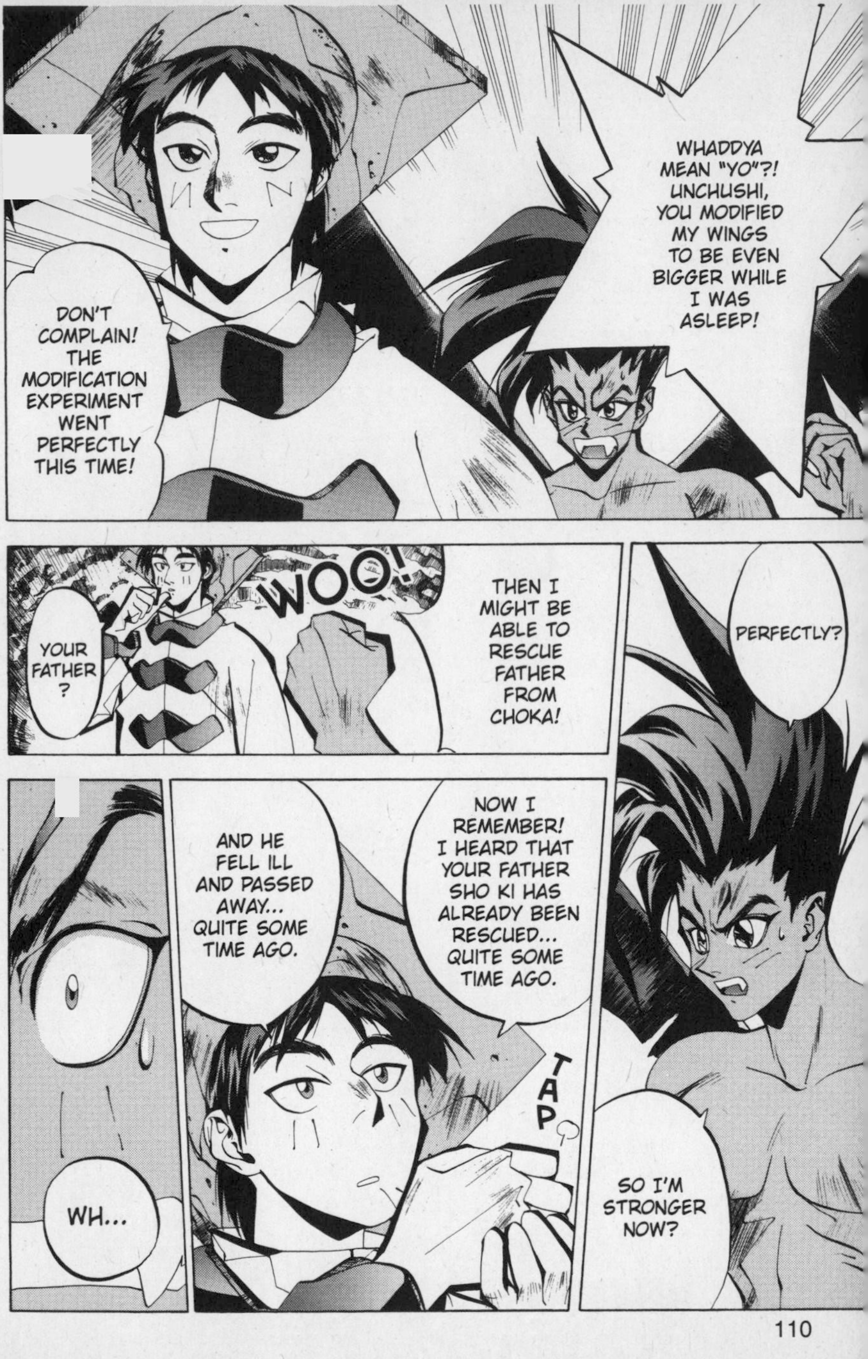
WHADDYA MEAN "YO"?! UNCHUSHI, YOU MODIFIED MY WINGS TO BE EVEN BIGGER WHILE I WAS ASLEEP!
DON'T COMPLAIN! THE MODIFICATION EXPERIMENT WENT PERFECTLY THIS TIME!
PERFECTLY?
SO I'M STRONGER NOW?
THEN I MIGHT BE ABLE TO RESCUE FATHER FROM CHOKA!
WOO!
YOUR FATHER ?
NOW I REMEMBER! I HEARD THAT YOUR FATHER SHO KI HAS ALREADY BEEN RESCUED... QUITE SOME TIME AGO.
AND HE FELL ILL AND PASSED AWAY... QUITE SOME TIME AGO.
TAP
WH...

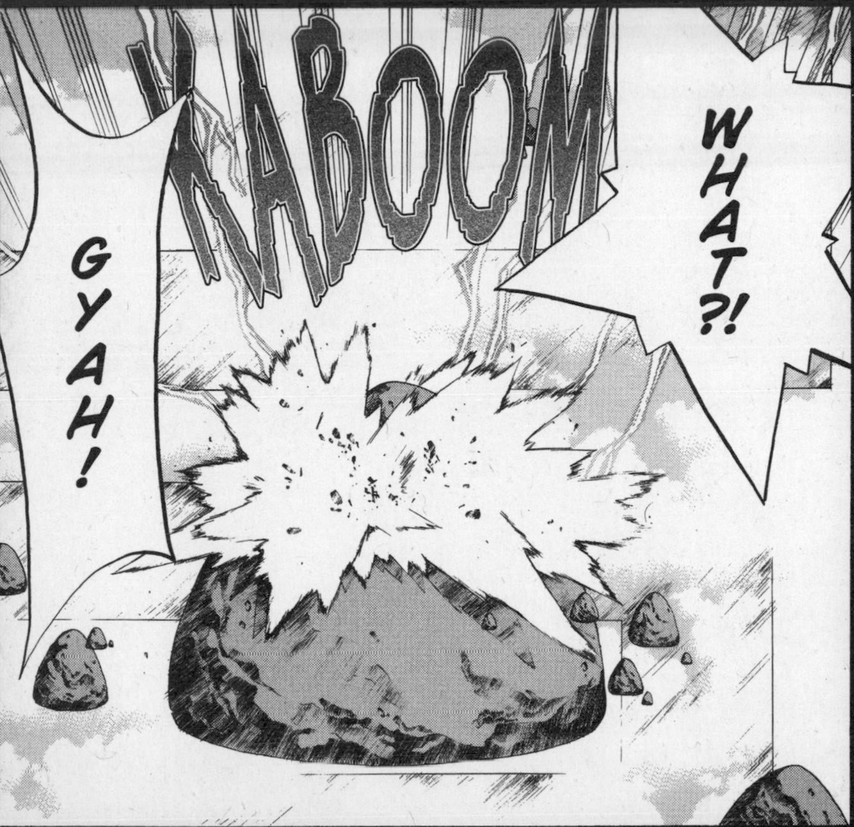
KABOOM
WHAT?!
GYAH!

Chapter 57

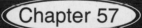

THE MAKA YONSHO, PART 3 CAPTURED, ESCAPED AND REGROUPED

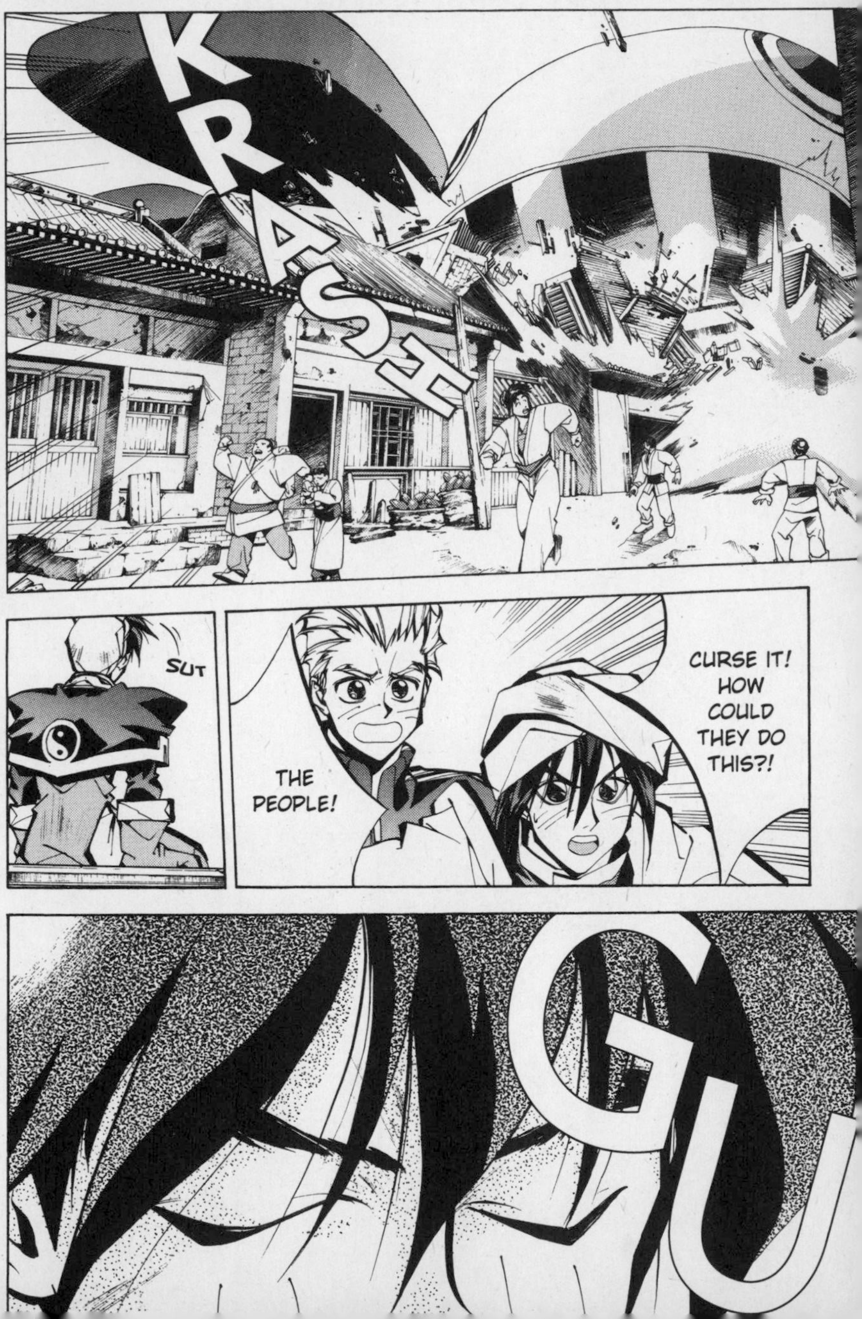
KRASH
CURSE IT! HOW COULD THEY DO THIS?!
THE PEOPLE!
SUT
GU

READ THIS WAY

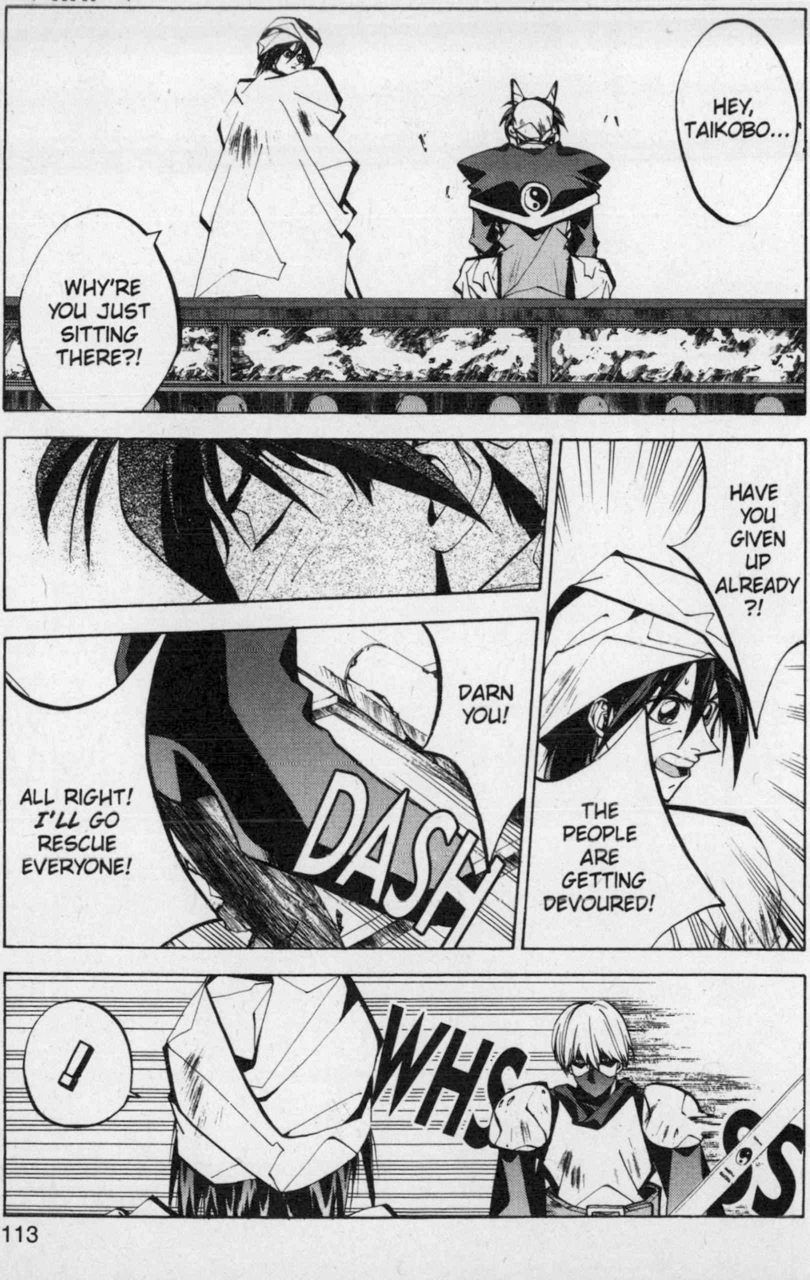

HEY, TAIKOBO...
WHY'RE YOU JUST SITTING THERE?!
HAVE YOU GIVEN UP ALREADY ?!
THE PEOPLE ARE GETTING DEVOURED!
DARN YOU!
DASH
ALL RIGHT! *I'LL* GO RESCUE EVERYONE!
WHSSS
!

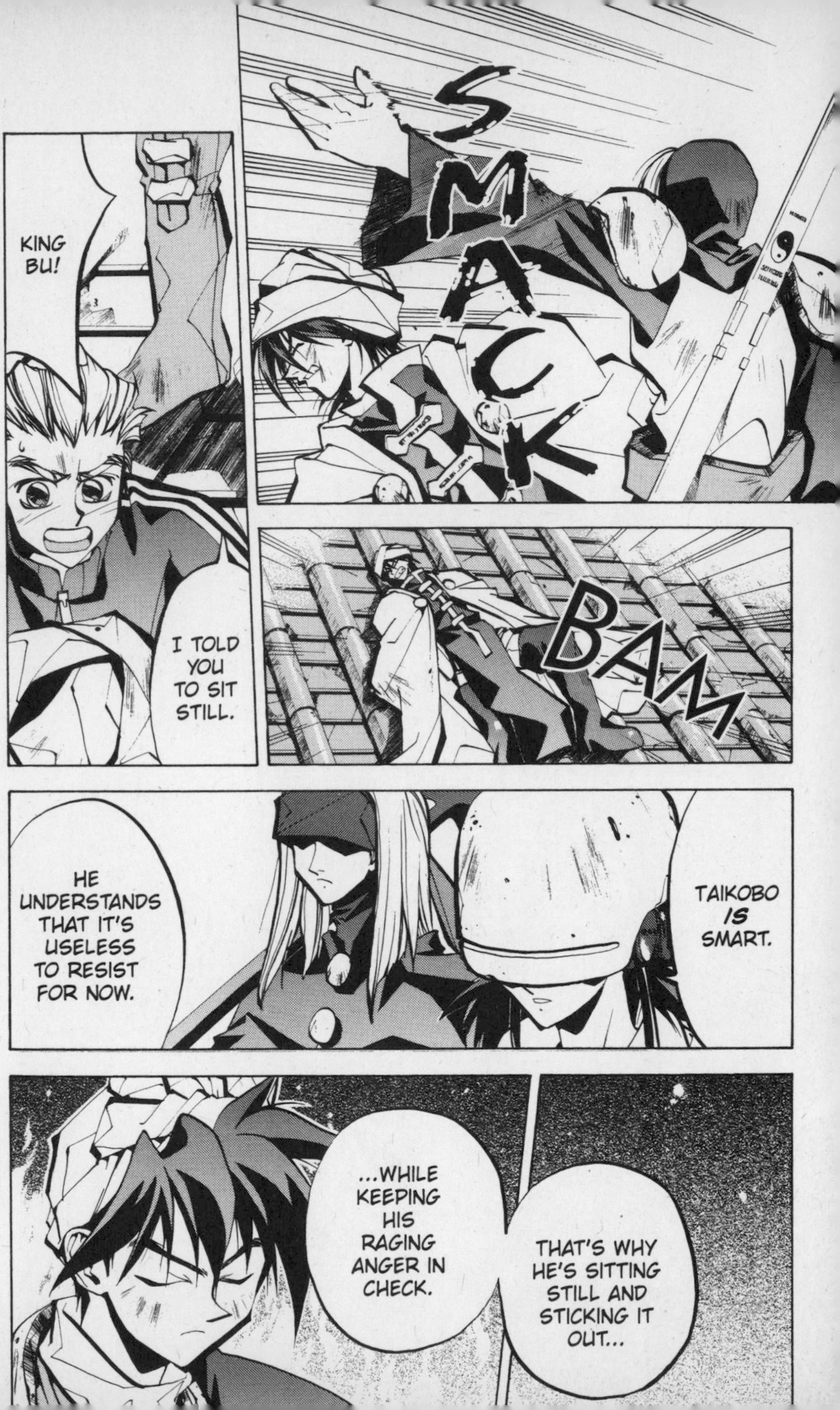
SMACK
BAM
KING BU!
I TOLD YOU TO SIT STILL.
TAIKOBO *IS* SMART.
HE UNDERSTANDS THAT IT'S USELESS TO RESIST FOR NOW.
THAT'S WHY HE'S SITTING STILL AND STICKING IT OUT...
...WHILE KEEPING HIS RAGING ANGER IN CHECK.

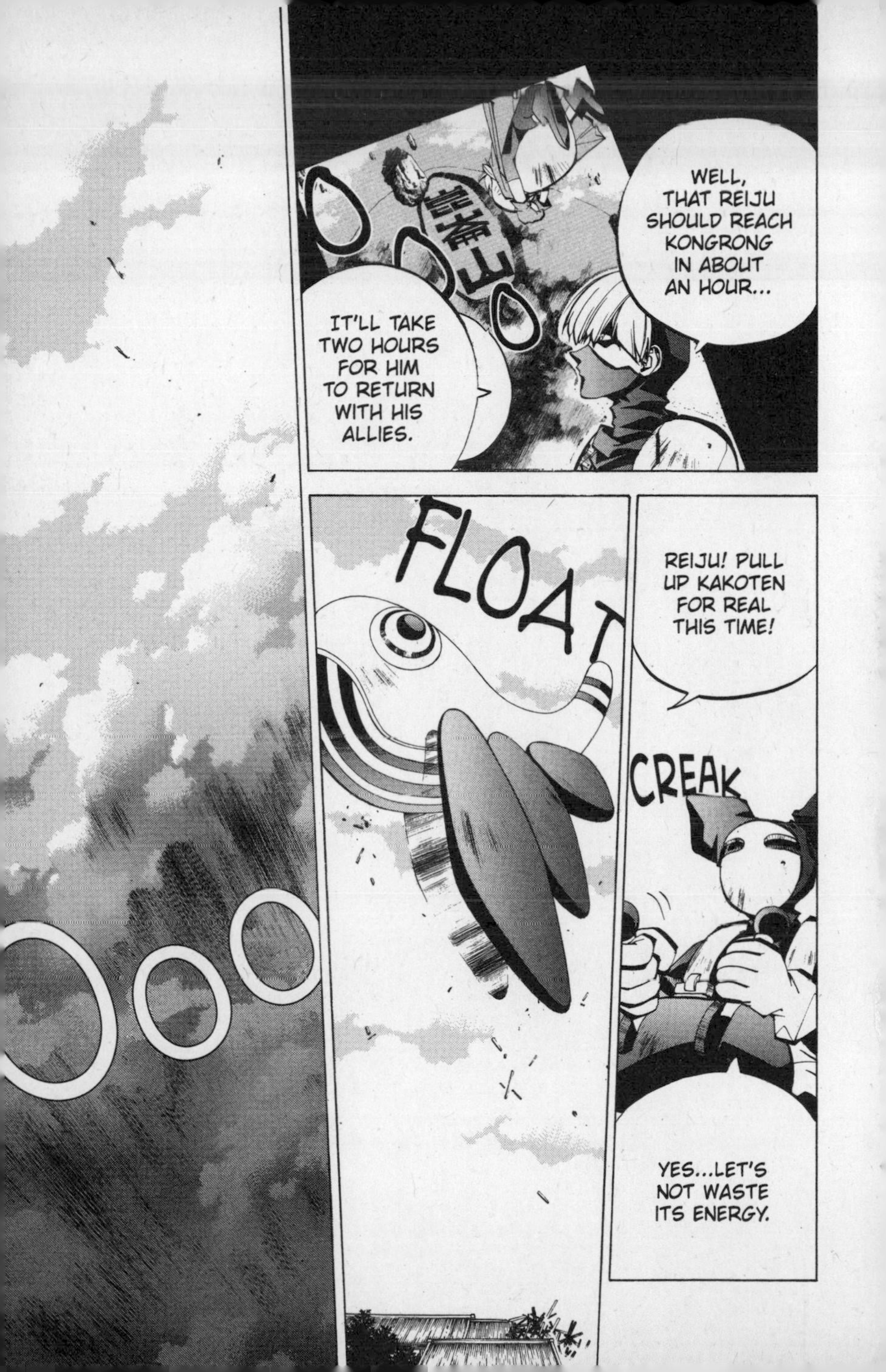
WELL, THAT REIJU SHOULD REACH KONGRONG IN ABOUT AN HOUR...
IT'LL TAKE TWO HOURS FOR HIM TO RETURN WITH HIS ALLIES.
REIJU! PULL UP KAKOTEN FOR REAL THIS TIME!
CREAK
YES...LET'S NOT WASTE ITS ENERGY.
FLOAT

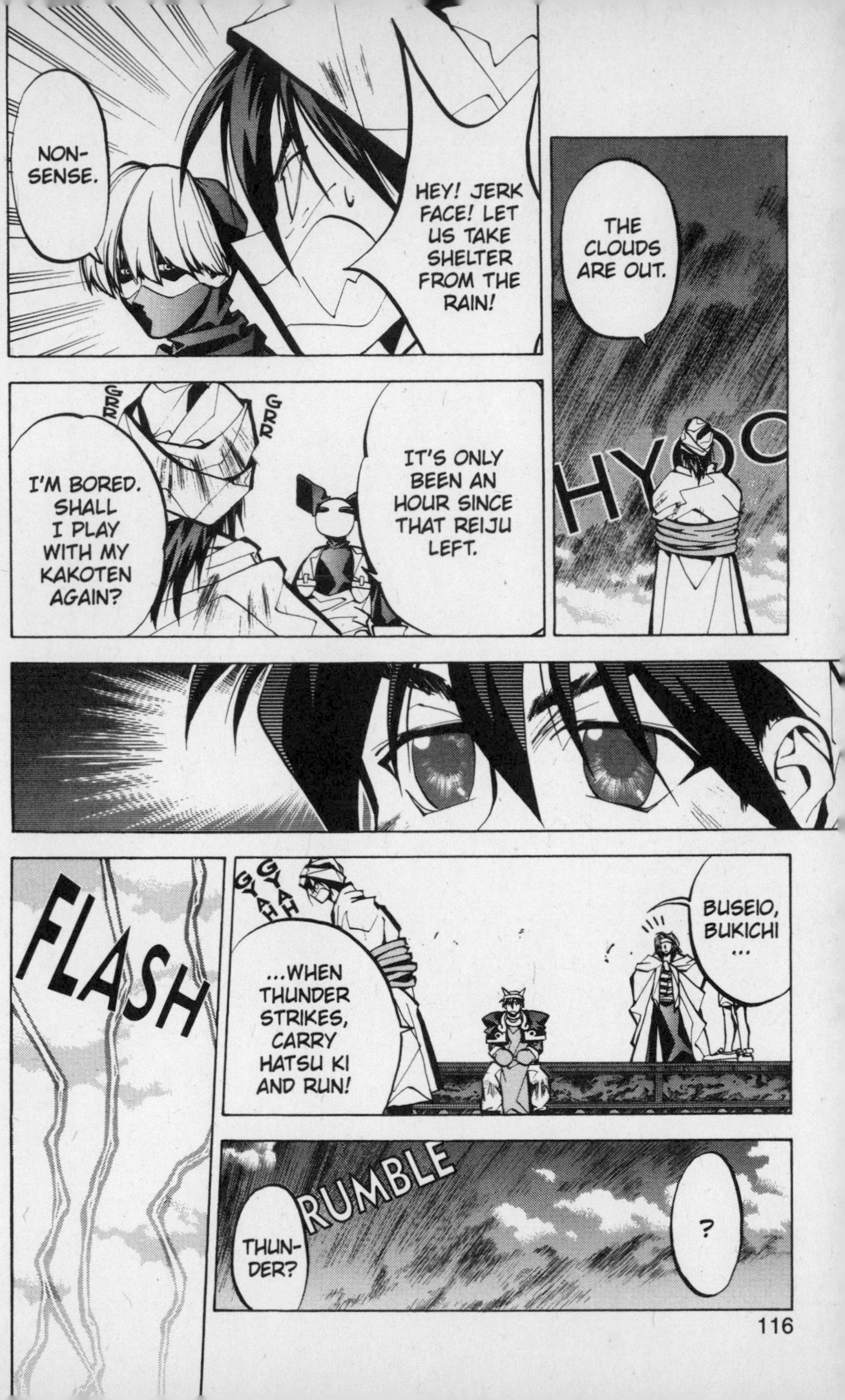
THE CLOUDS ARE OUT.
HYOO
HEY! JERK FACE! LET US TAKE SHELTER FROM THE RAIN!
NON-SENSE.
GRR GRR
IT'S ONLY BEEN AN HOUR SINCE THAT REIJU LEFT.
I'M BORED. SHALL I PLAY WITH MY KAKOTEN AGAIN?
BUSEIO, BUKICHI...
GYAH GYAH
...WHEN THUNDER STRIKES, CARRY HATSU KI AND RUN!
?
RUMBLE
THUN-DER?
FLASH

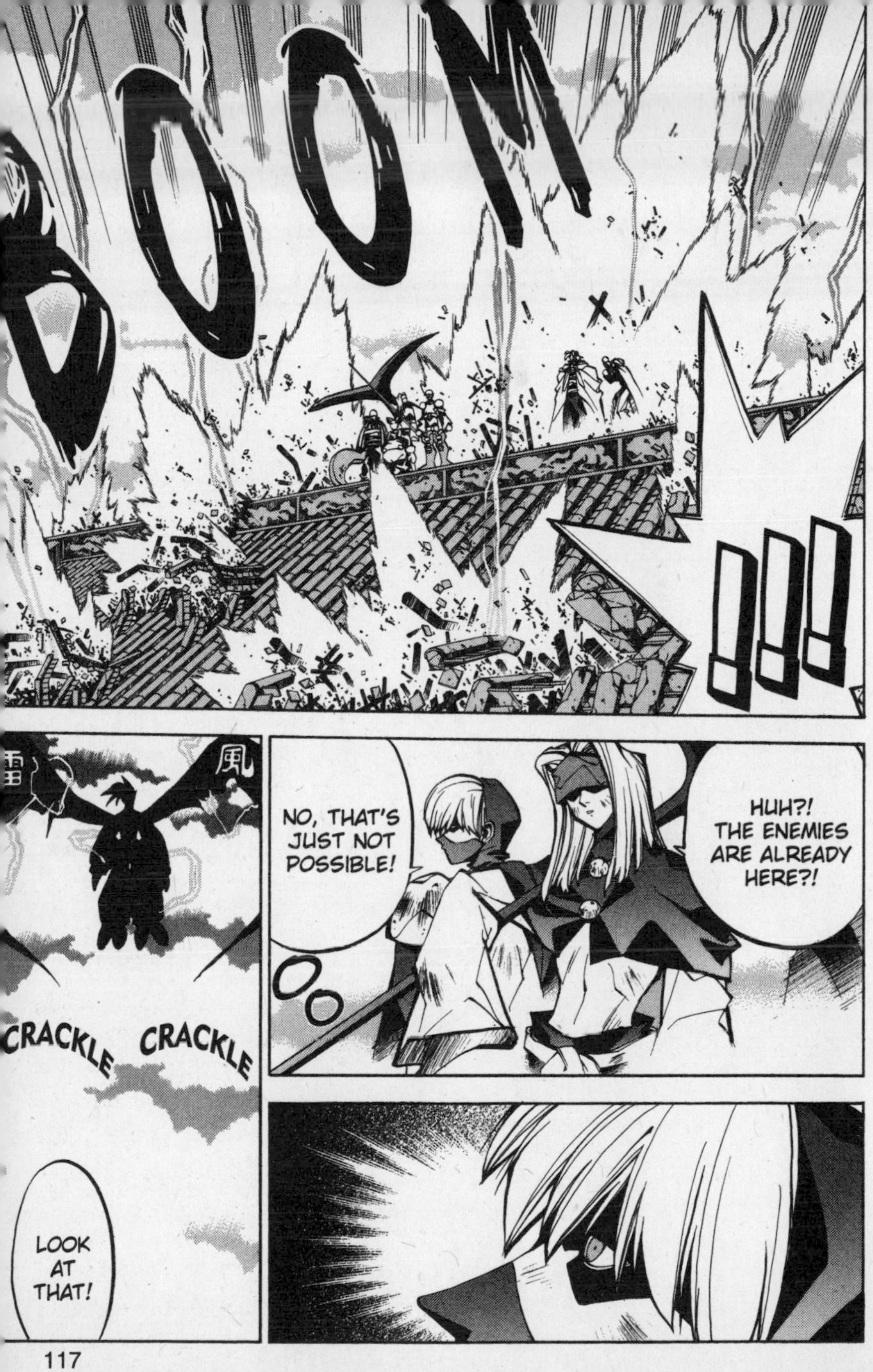
DOOM
!!!
HUH?! THE ENEMIES ARE ALREADY HERE?!
NO, THAT'S JUST NOT POSSIBLE!
雷
風
CRACKLE CRACKLE
LOOK AT THAT!

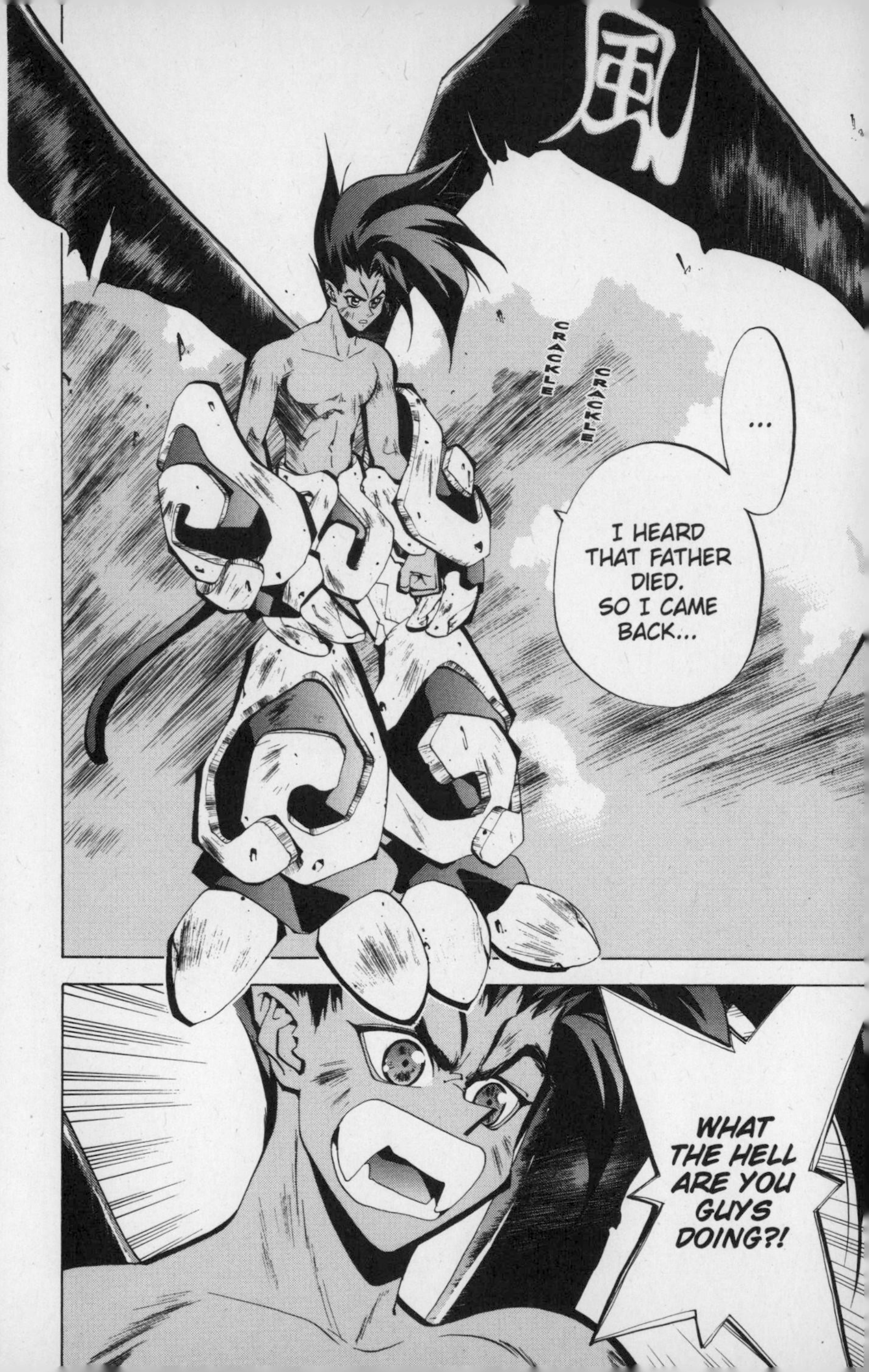

風
CRACKLE
CRACKLE
...
I HEARD THAT FATHER DIED. SO I CAME BACK...
WHAT THE HELL ARE YOU GUYS DOING?!

READ THIS WAY

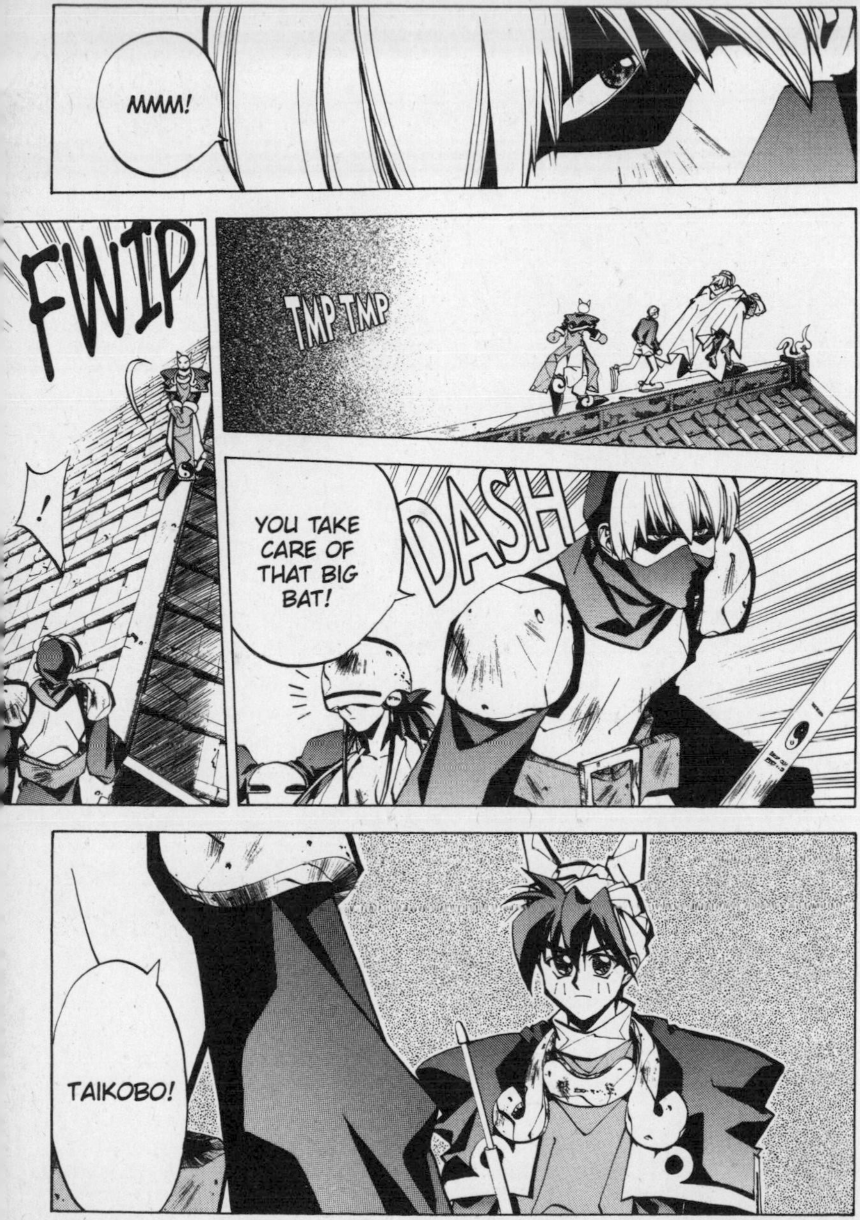

MMM!
TMP TMP
DASH
YOU TAKE CARE OF THAT BIG BAT!
FWIP
!
TAIKOBO!

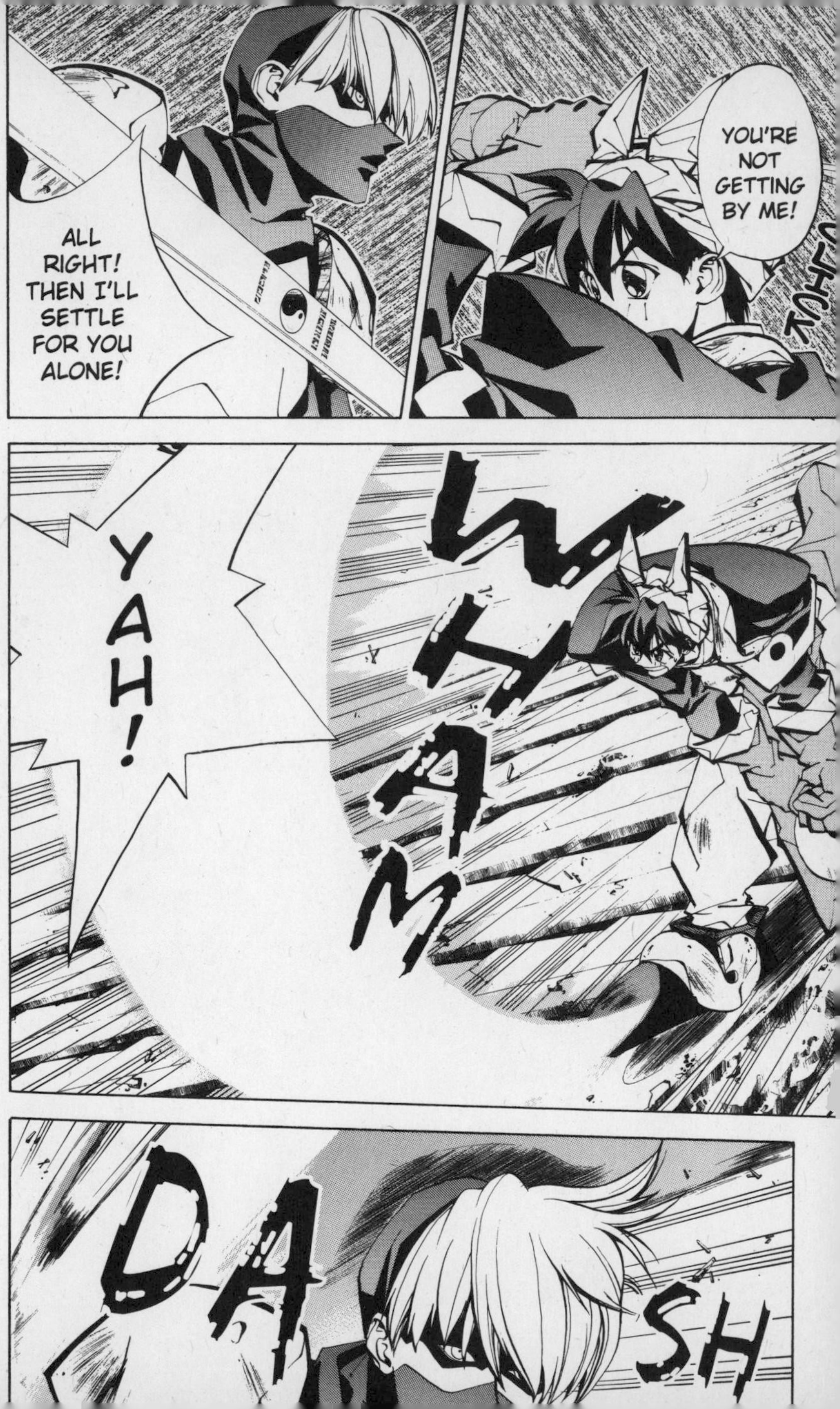
YOU'RE NOT GETTING BY ME!
CLICK
ALL RIGHT! THEN I'LL SETTLE FOR YOU ALONE!
WHAM
YAH!
DASH

READ THIS WAY

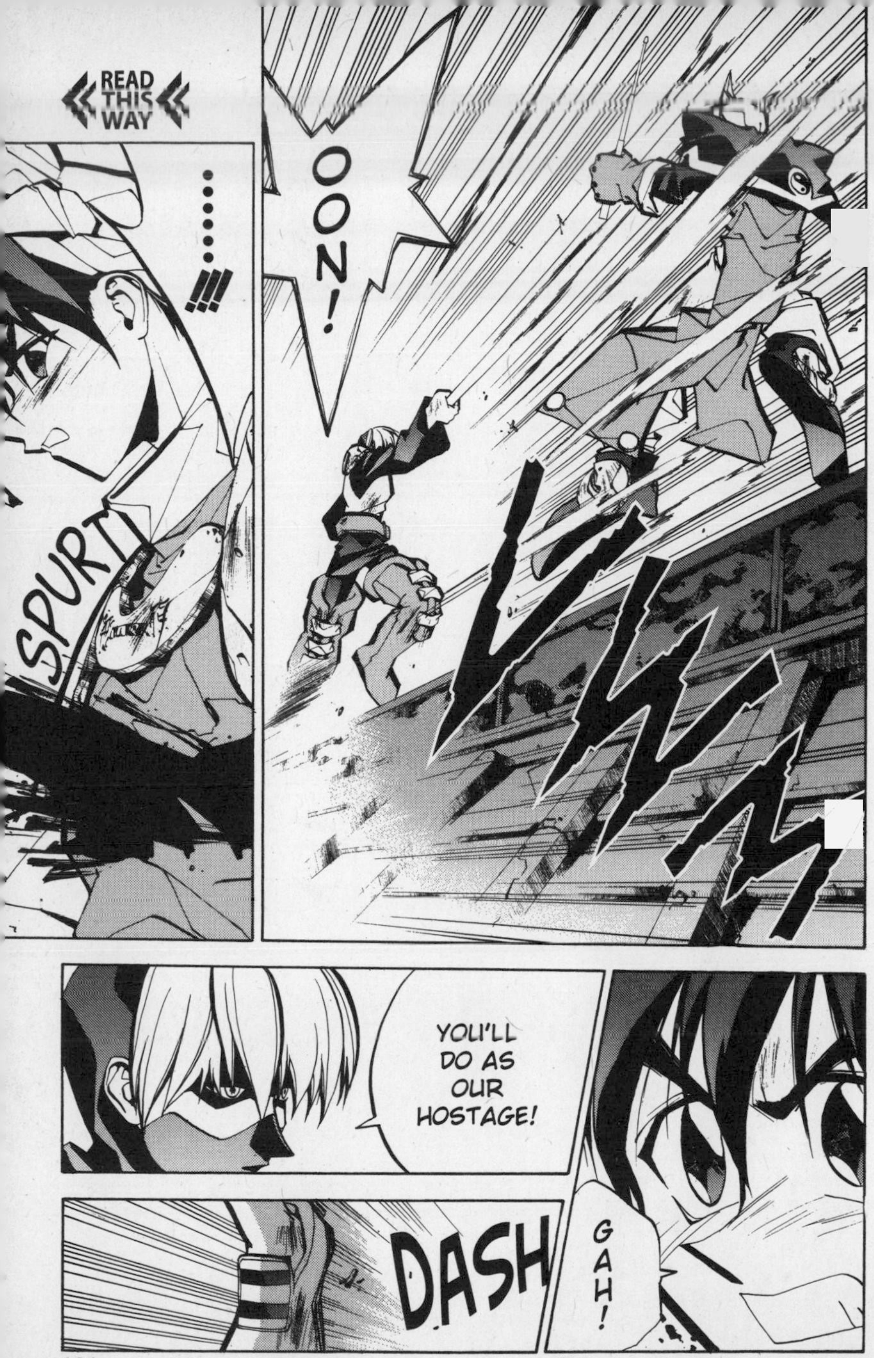
OON!
......!!!
SPURT
GAH!
YOU'LL DO AS OUR HOSTAGE!
DASH

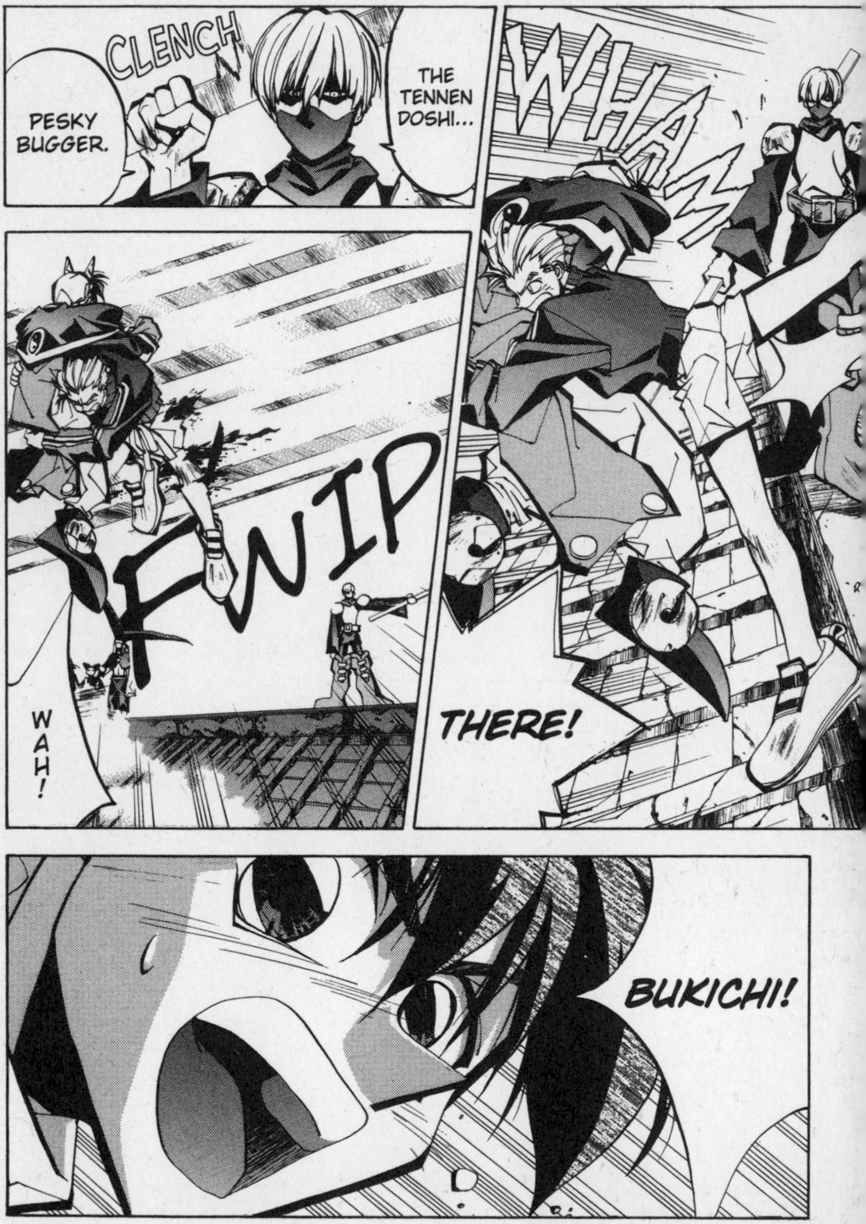
WHAM
THERE!
THE TENNEN DOSHI...
CLENCH
PESKY BUGGER.
FWIP
WAH!
BUKICHI!

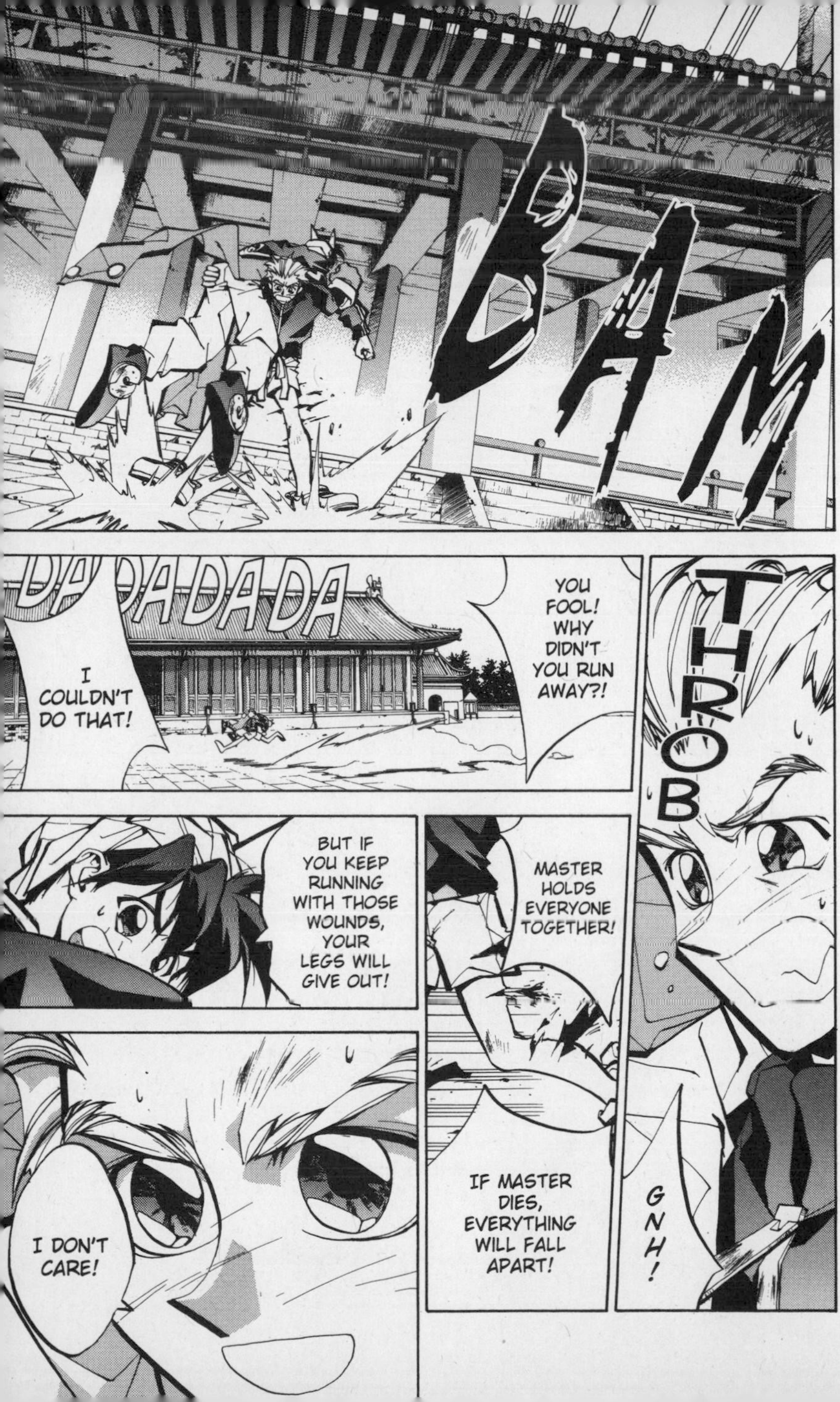
BAM
THROB
GNH!
YOU FOOL! WHY DIDN'T YOU RUN AWAY?!
I COULDN'T DO THAT!
DA DADADA
MASTER HOLDS EVERYONE TOGETHER!
IF MASTER DIES, EVERYTHING WILL FALL APART!
BUT IF YOU KEEP RUNNING WITH THOSE WOUNDS, YOUR LEGS WILL GIVE OUT!
I DON'T CARE!

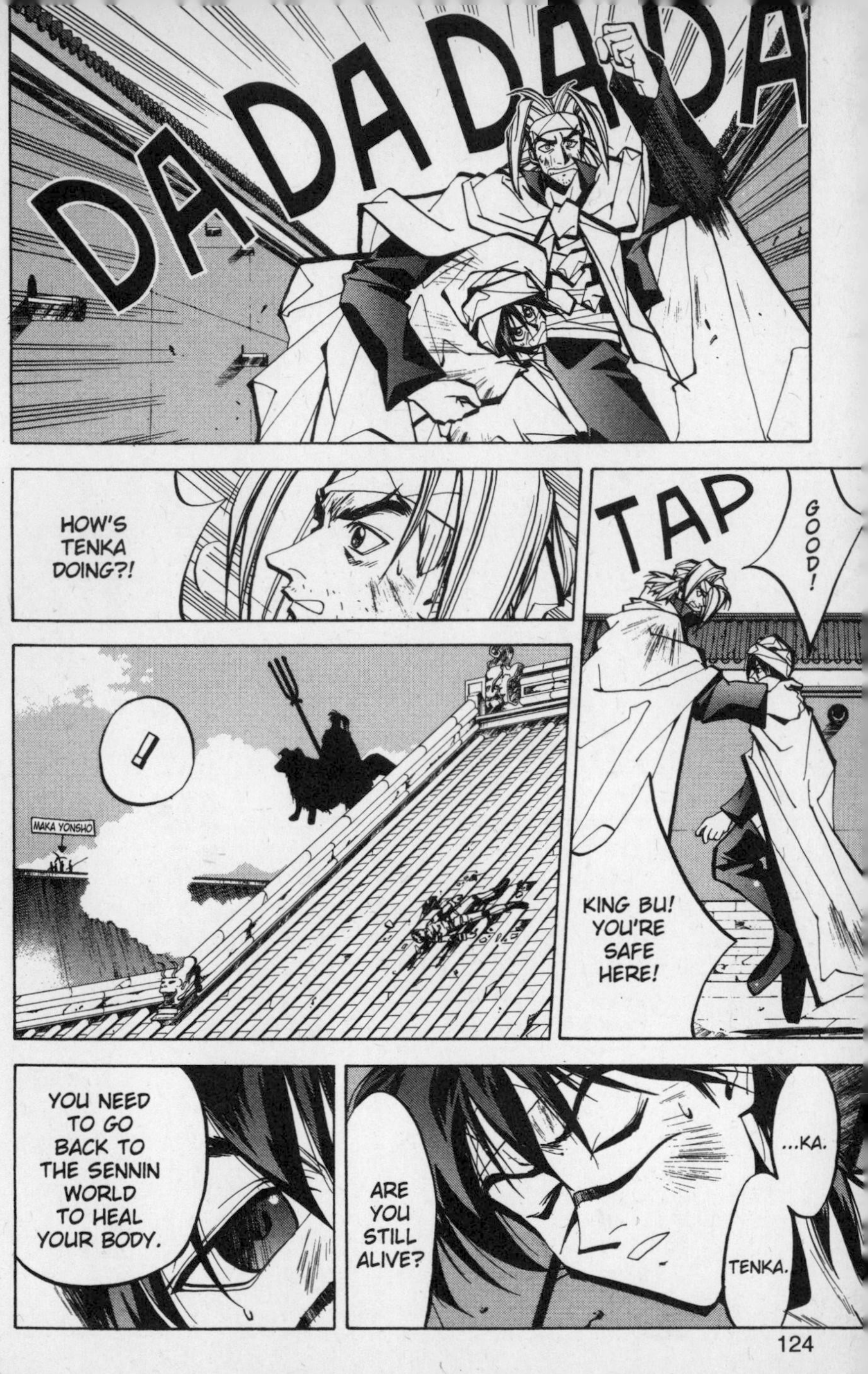
DA DA DA DA DA
TAP
GOOD!
KING BU! YOU'RE SAFE HERE!
HOW'S TENKA DOING?!
!
MAKA YONSHO
...KA.
TENKA.
ARE YOU STILL ALIVE?
YOU NEED TO GO BACK TO THE SENNIN WORLD TO HEAL YOUR BODY.

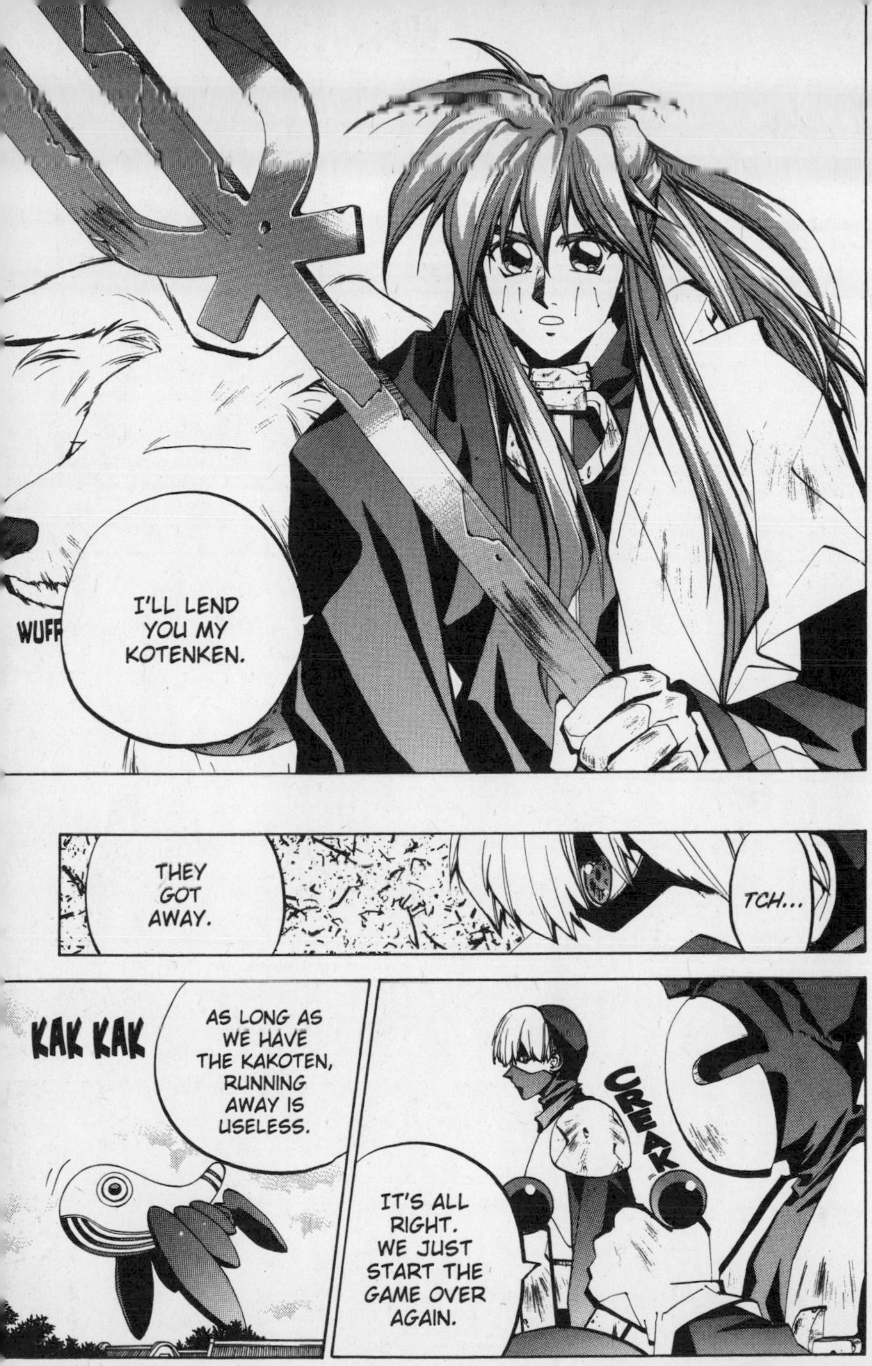
I'LL LEND YOU MY KOTENKEN.
WUFF
TCH...
THEY GOT AWAY.
CREAK
IT'S ALL RIGHT. WE JUST START THE GAME OVER AGAIN.
AS LONG AS WE HAVE THE KAKOTEN, RUNNING AWAY IS USELESS.
KAK KAK

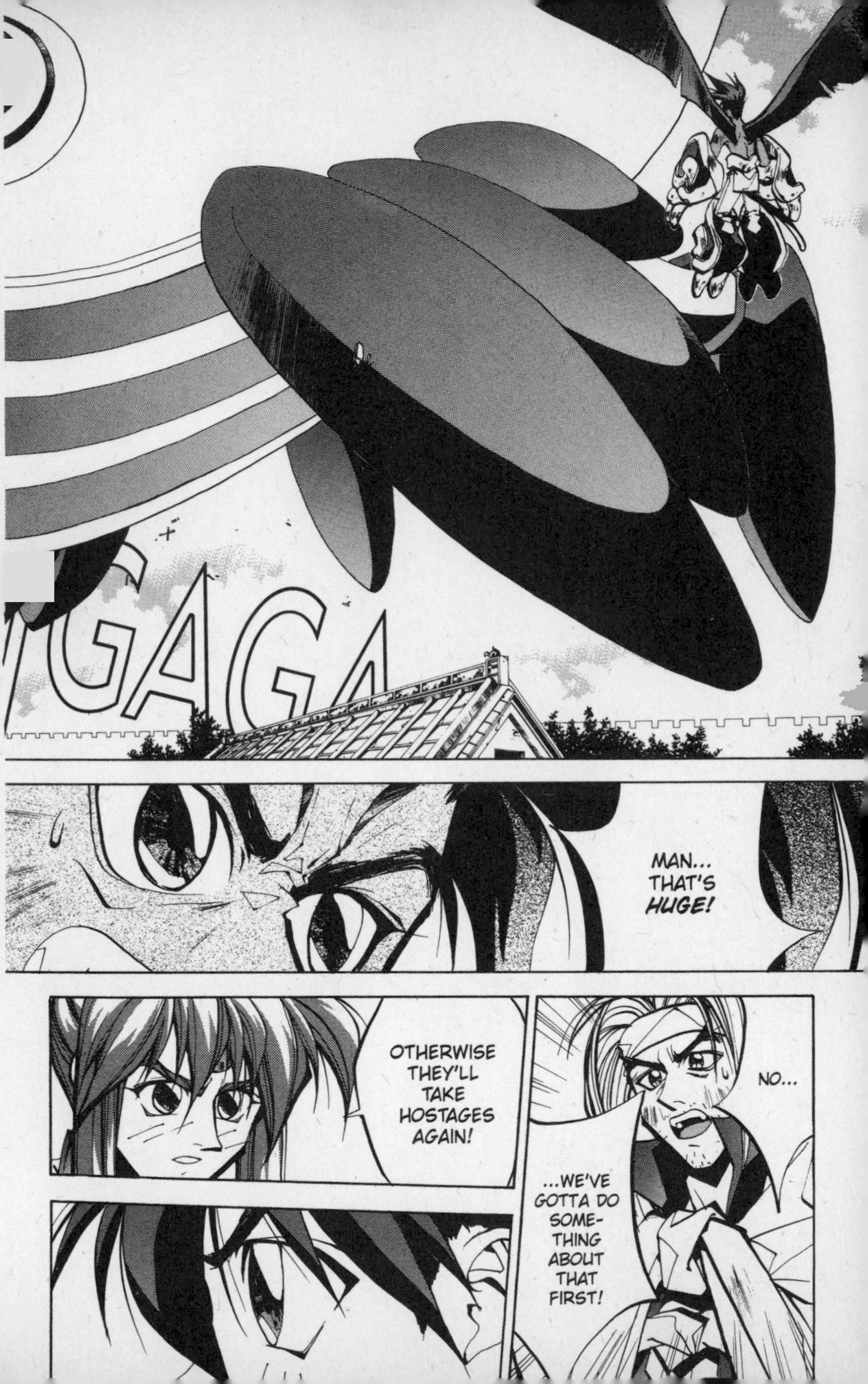
GAGA
MAN... THAT'S HUGE!
NO...
...WE'VE GOTTA DO SOME-THING ABOUT THAT FIRST!
OTHERWISE THEY'LL TAKE HOSTAGES AGAIN!

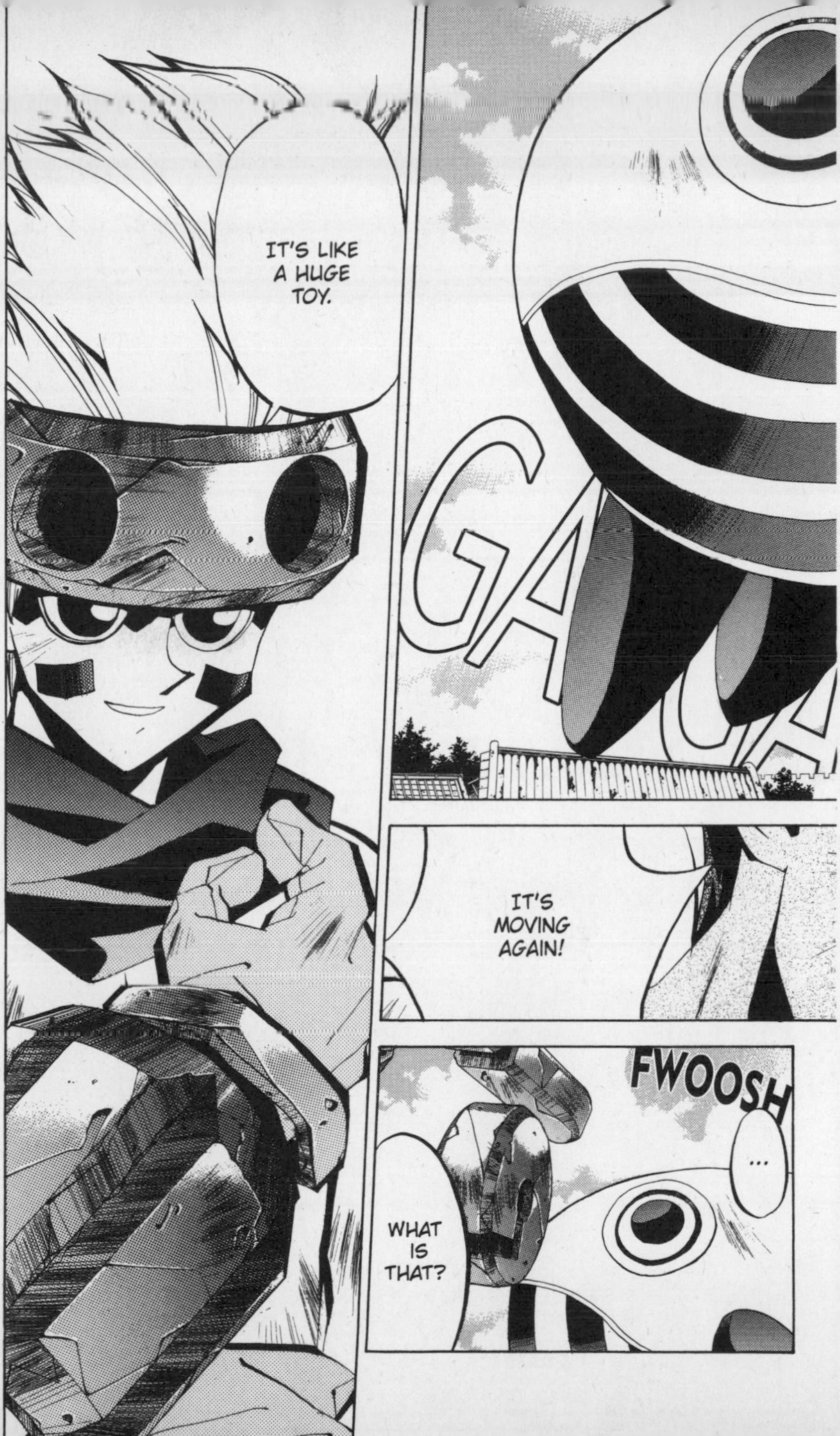
GACHA
IT'S MOVING AGAIN!
FWOOSH
...
WHAT IS THAT?
IT'S LIKE A HUGE TOY.

封神演義

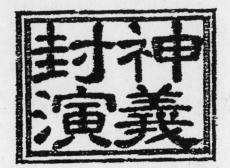

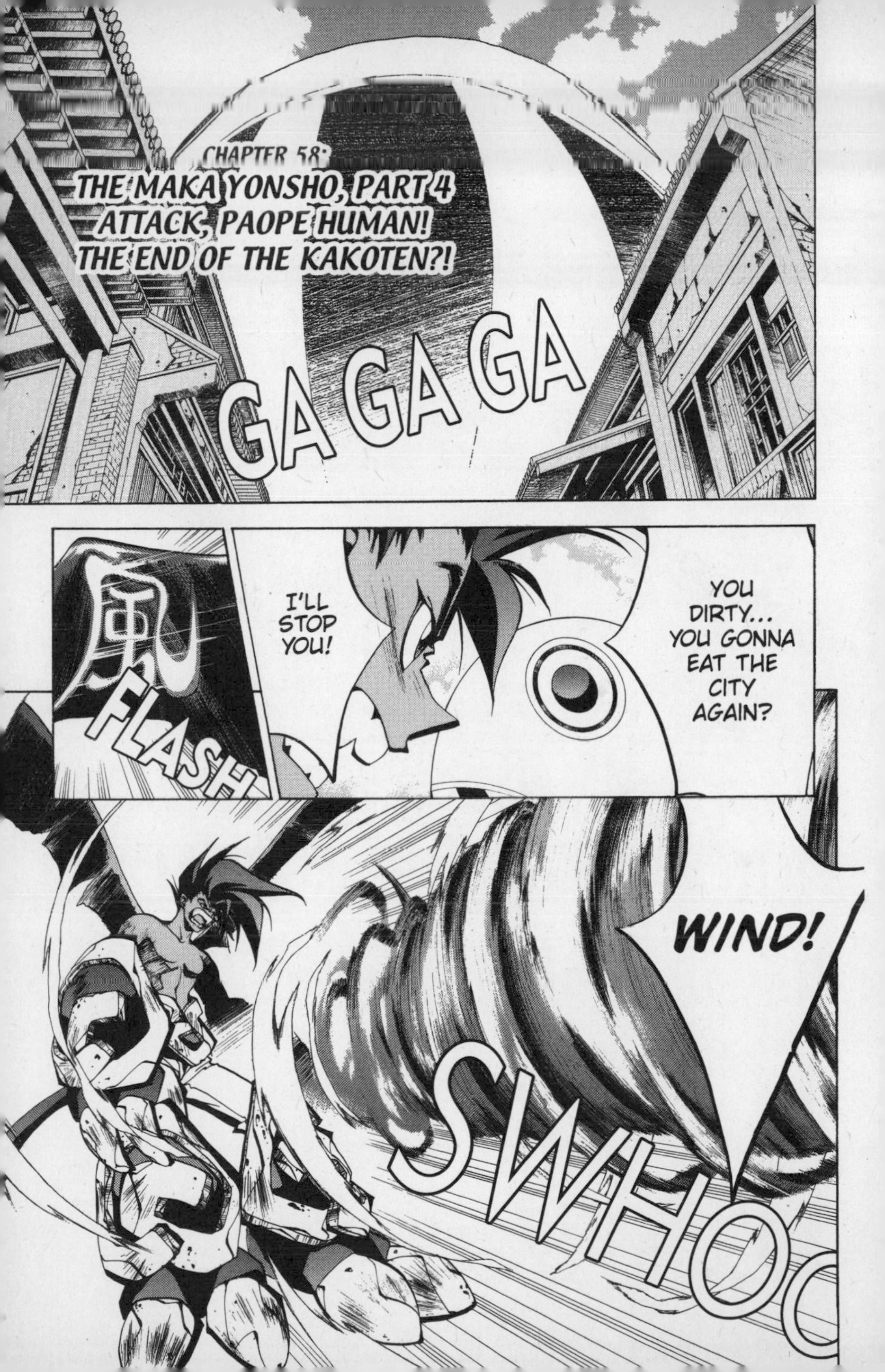
CHAPTER 58:
THE MAKA YONSHO, PART 4
ATTACK, PAOPE HUMAN!
THE END OF THE KAKOTEN?!
GA GA GA
YOU DIRTY... YOU GONNA EAT THE CITY AGAIN?
I'LL STOP YOU!
風
FLASH
WIND!
SWHOO

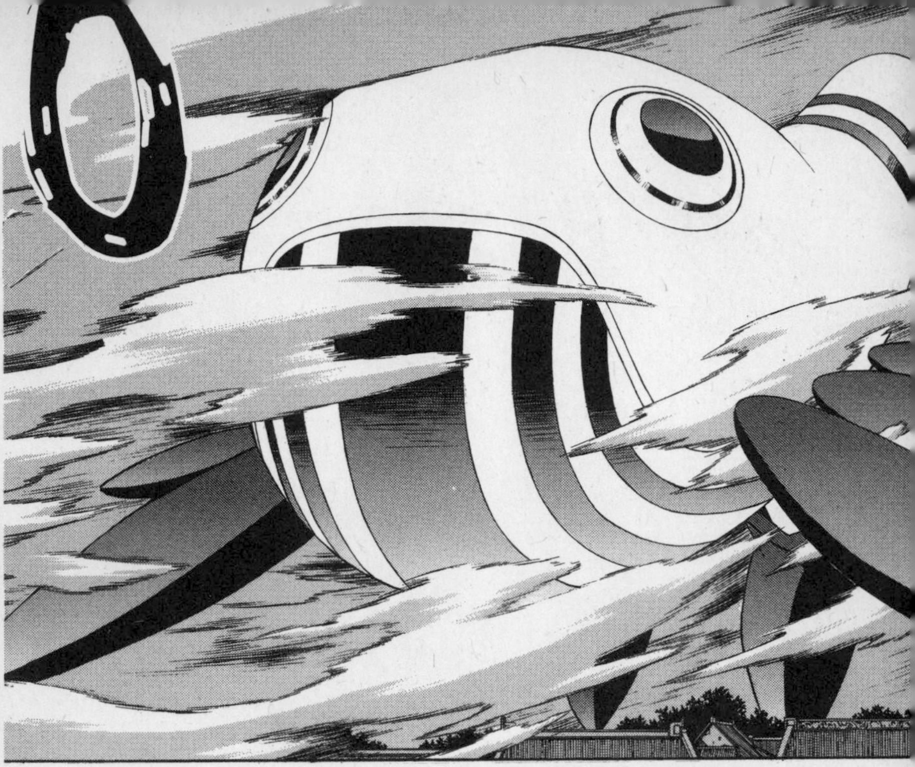

ATTACK, PAOPE HUMAN! THE END OF THE KAKOTEN?!

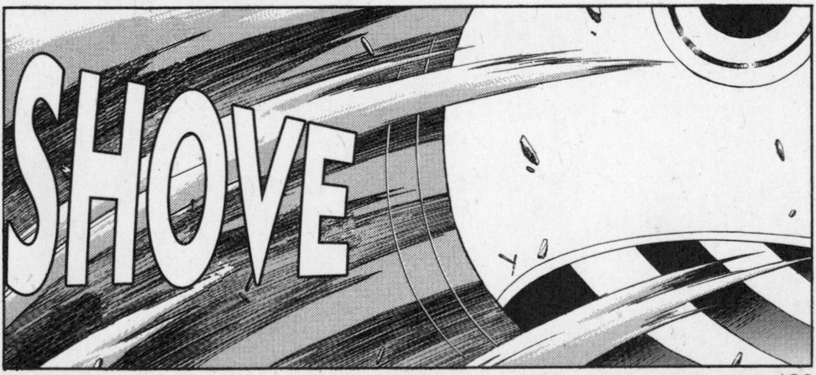
SHOVE

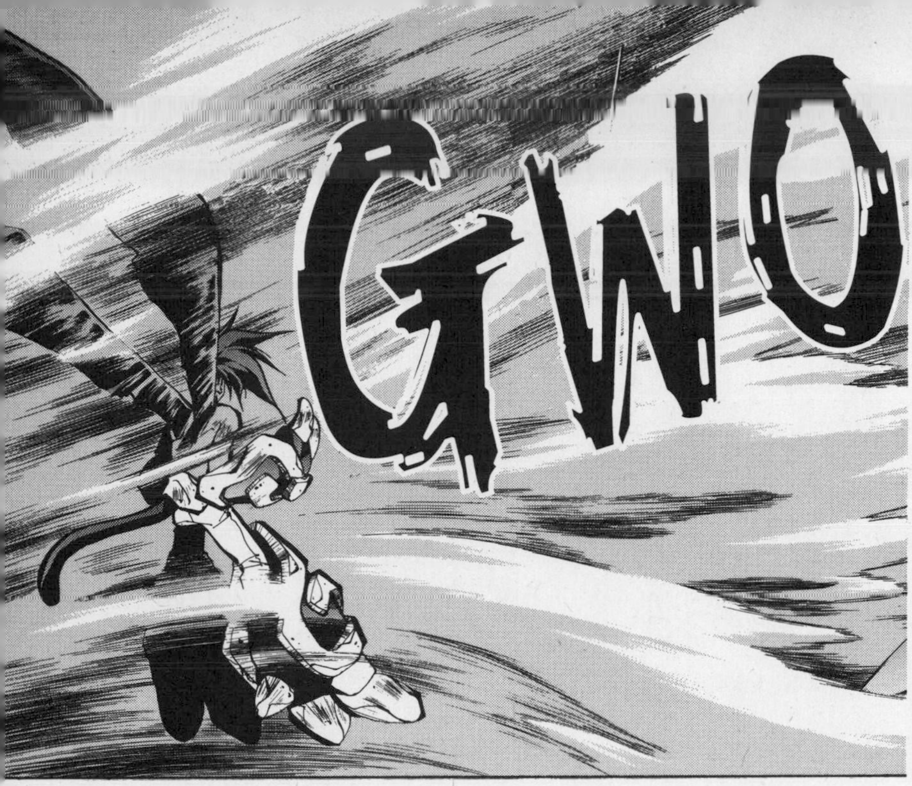
GWO

Chapter 58

THE MAKA YONSHO, PART 4

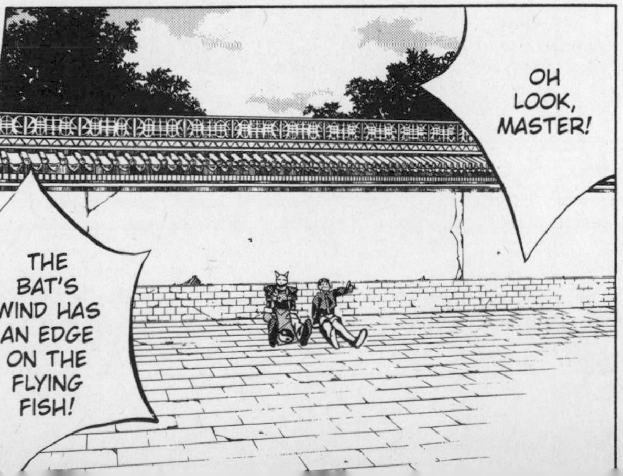
OH LOOK, MASTER!
THE BAT'S WIND HAS AN EDGE ON THE FLYING FISH!

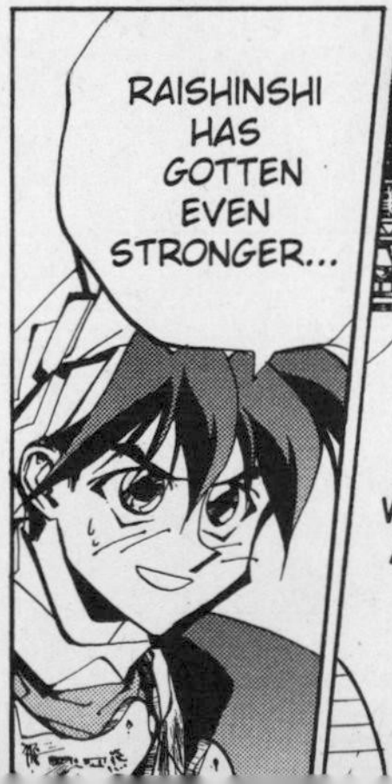
RAISHINSHI HAS GOTTEN EVEN STRONGER...

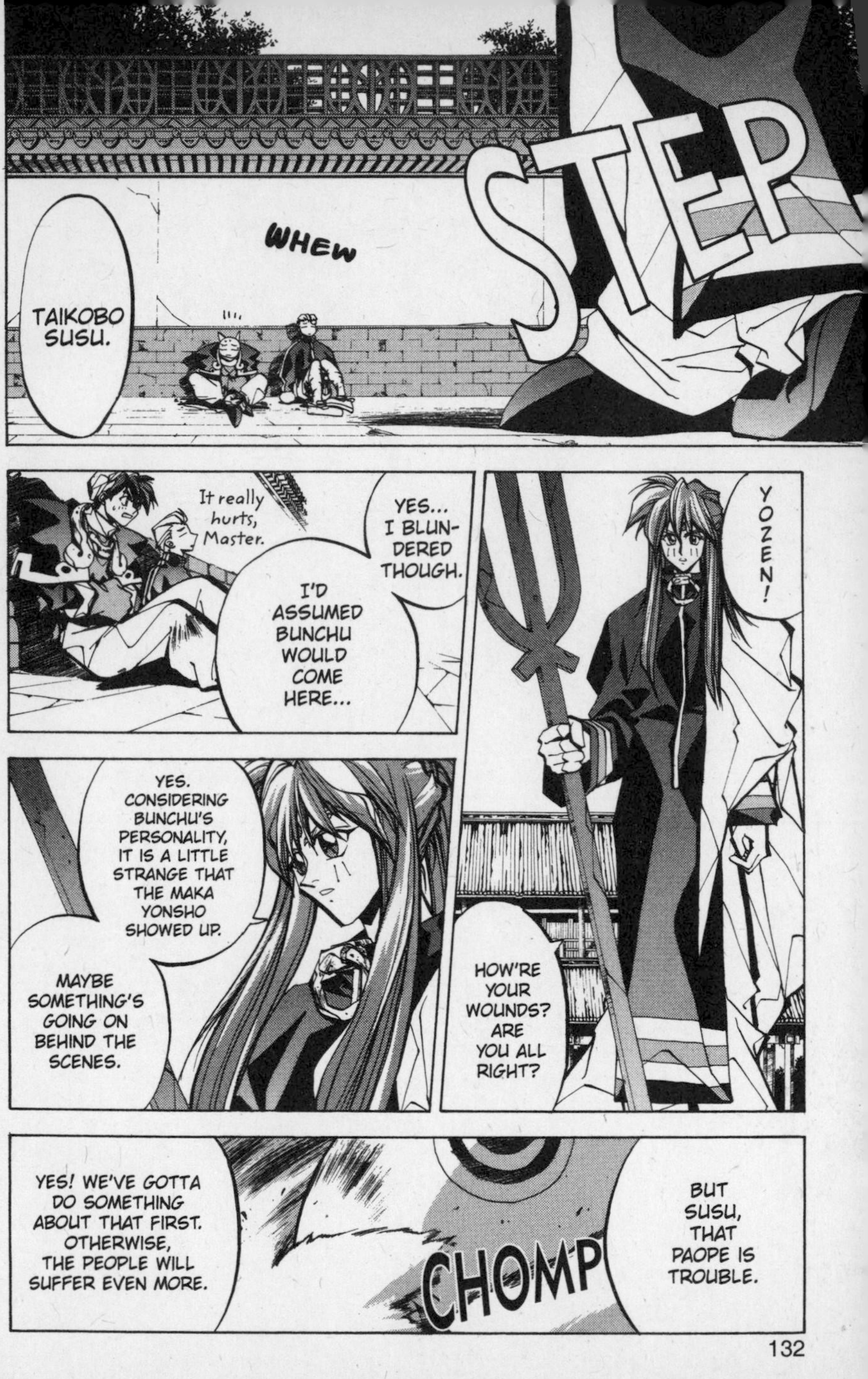
STEP
WHEW
TAIKOBO SUSU.
YOZEN!
HOW'RE YOUR WOUNDS? ARE YOU ALL RIGHT?
YES... I BLUN-DERED THOUGH.
It really hurts, Master.
I'D ASSUMED BUNCHU WOULD COME HERE...
YES. CONSIDERING BUNCHU'S PERSONALITY, IT IS A LITTLE STRANGE THAT THE MAKA YONSHO SHOWED UP.
MAYBE SOMETHING'S GOING ON BEHIND THE SCENES.
BUT SUSU, THAT PAOPE IS TROUBLE.
CHOMP
YES! WE'VE GOTTA DO SOMETHING ABOUT THAT FIRST. OTHERWISE, THE PEOPLE WILL SUFFER EVEN MORE.

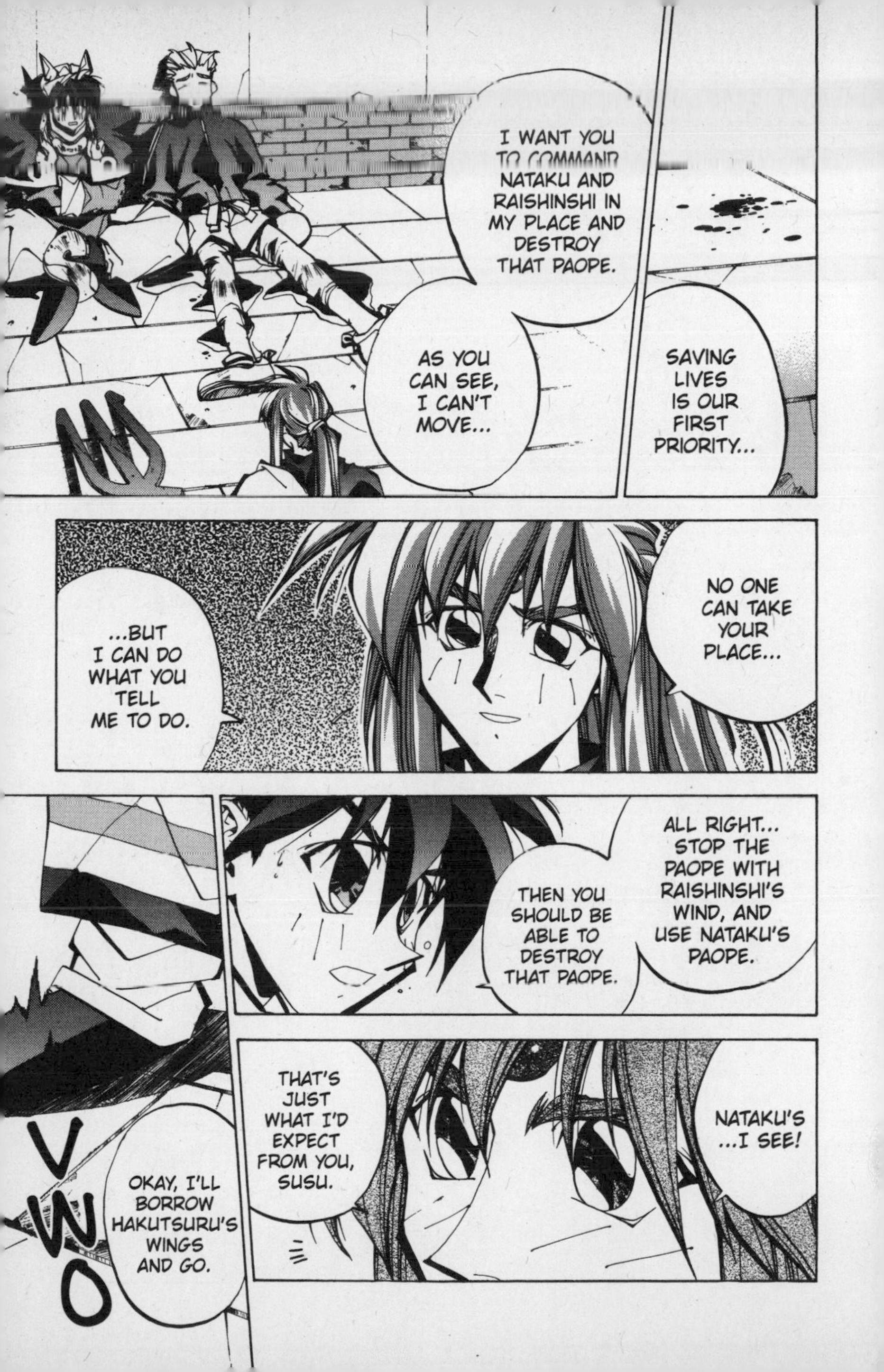
SAVING LIVES IS OUR FIRST PRIORITY...
I WANT YOU TO COMMAND NATAKU AND RAISHINSHI IN MY PLACE AND DESTROY THAT PAOPE.
AS YOU CAN SEE, I CAN'T MOVE...
NO ONE CAN TAKE YOUR PLACE...
...BUT I CAN DO WHAT YOU TELL ME TO DO.
ALL RIGHT... STOP THE PAOPE WITH RAISHINSHI'S WIND, AND USE NATAKU'S PAOPE.
THEN YOU SHOULD BE ABLE TO DESTROY THAT PAOPE.
NATAKU'S ...I SEE!
THAT'S JUST WHAT I'D EXPECT FROM YOU, SUSU.
OKAY, I'LL BORROW HAKUTSURU'S WINGS AND GO.
VWOO

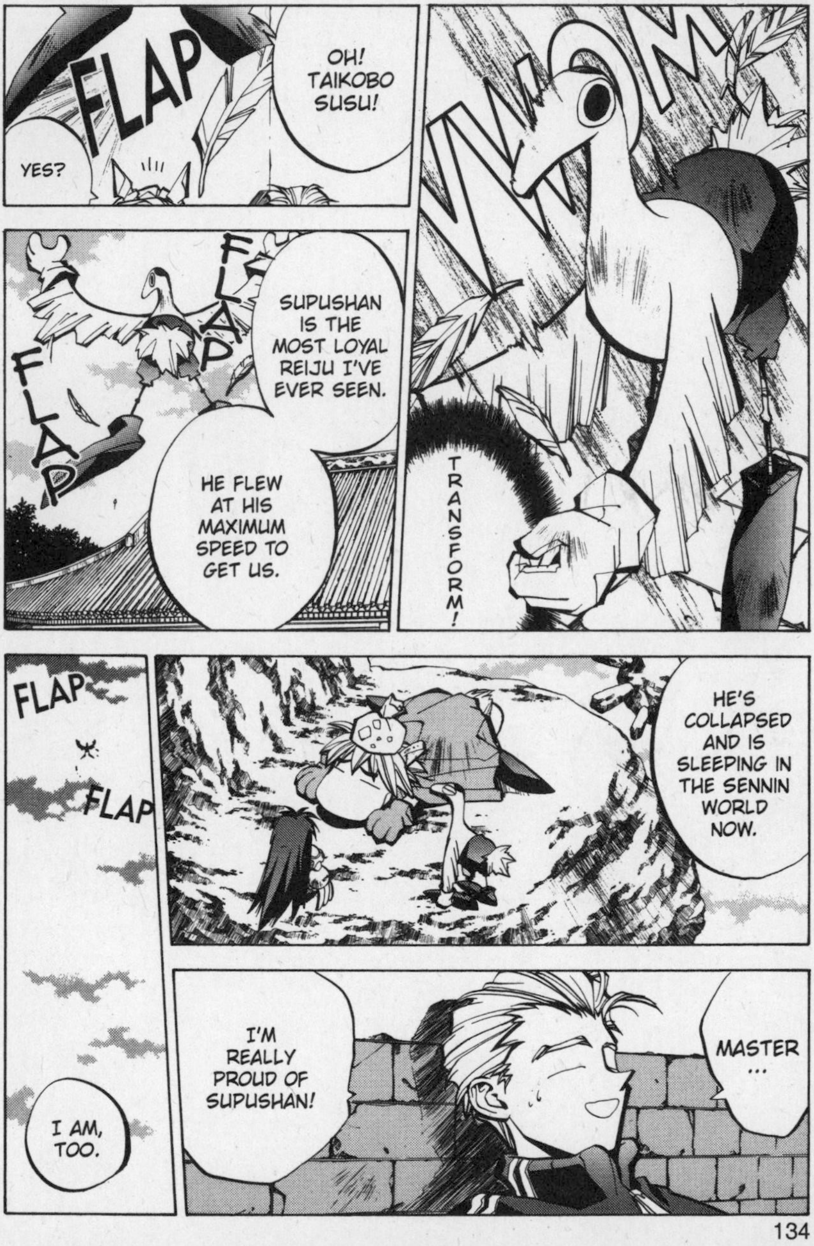
TRANSFORM!
OH! TAIKOBO SUSU!
FLAP
YES?
FLAP
SUPUSHAN IS THE MOST LOYAL REIJU I'VE EVER SEEN.
HE FLEW AT HIS MAXIMUM SPEED TO GET US.
FLAP
HE'S COLLAPSED AND IS SLEEPING IN THE SENNIN WORLD NOW.
MASTER ...
I'M REALLY PROUD OF SUPUSHAN!
FLAP
FLAP
I AM, TOO.

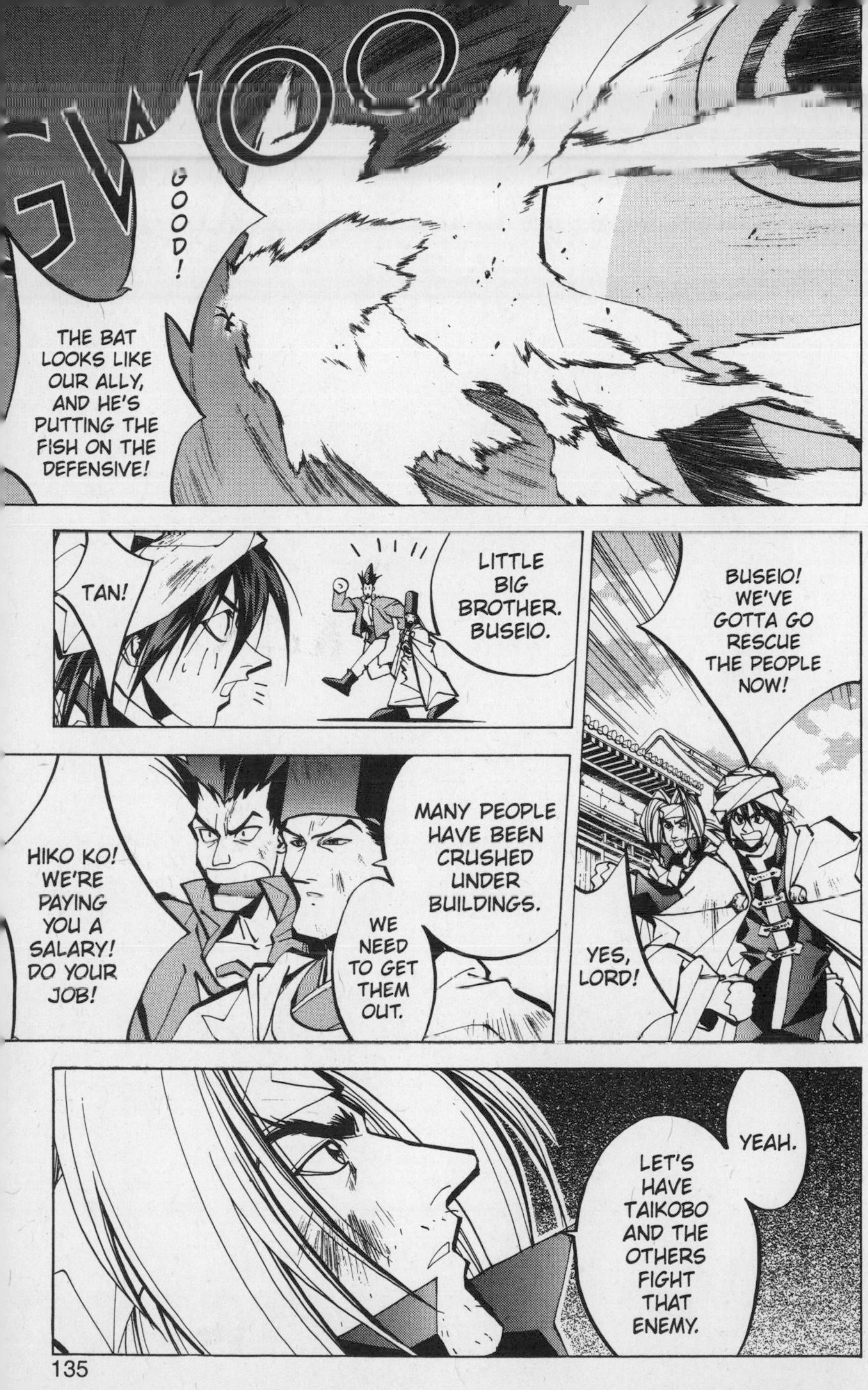
GOOD!
THE BAT LOOKS LIKE OUR ALLY, AND HE'S PUTTING THE FISH ON THE DEFENSIVE!
BUSEIO! WE'VE GOTTA GO RESCUE THE PEOPLE NOW!
YES, LORD!
LITTLE BIG BROTHER. BUSEIO.
TAN!
MANY PEOPLE HAVE BEEN CRUSHED UNDER BUILDINGS.
WE NEED TO GET THEM OUT.
HIKO KO! WE'RE PAYING YOU A SALARY! DO YOUR JOB!
YEAH.
LET'S HAVE TAIKOBO AND THE OTHERS FIGHT THAT ENEMY.

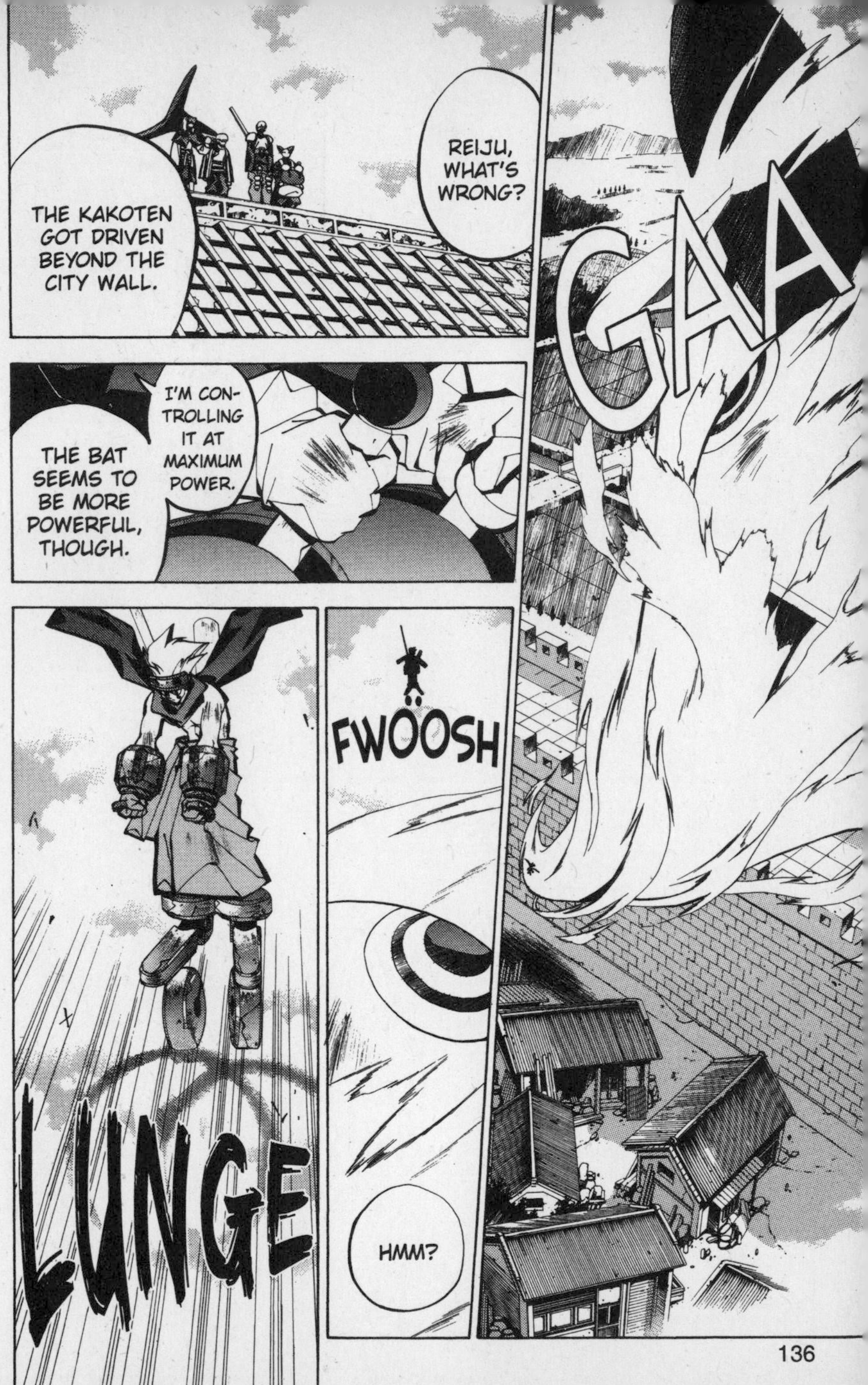
GAA
REIJU, WHAT'S WRONG?
THE KAKOTEN GOT DRIVEN BEYOND THE CITY WALL.
I'M CONTROLLING IT AT MAXIMUM POWER.
THE BAT SEEMS TO BE MORE POWERFUL, THOUGH.
FWOOSH
HMM?
LUNGE

READ THIS WAY

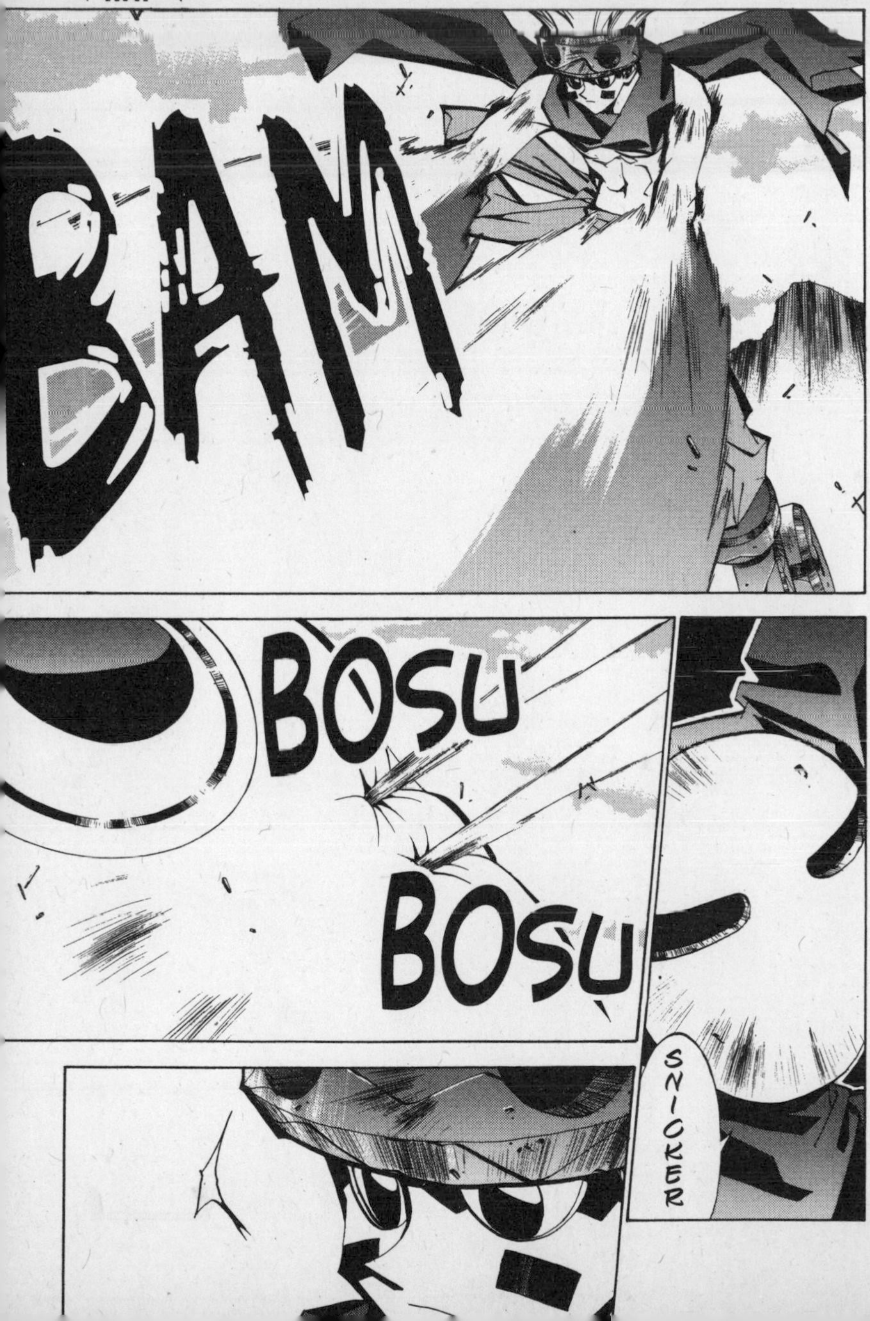
BAM
SNICKER
BOSU
BOSU

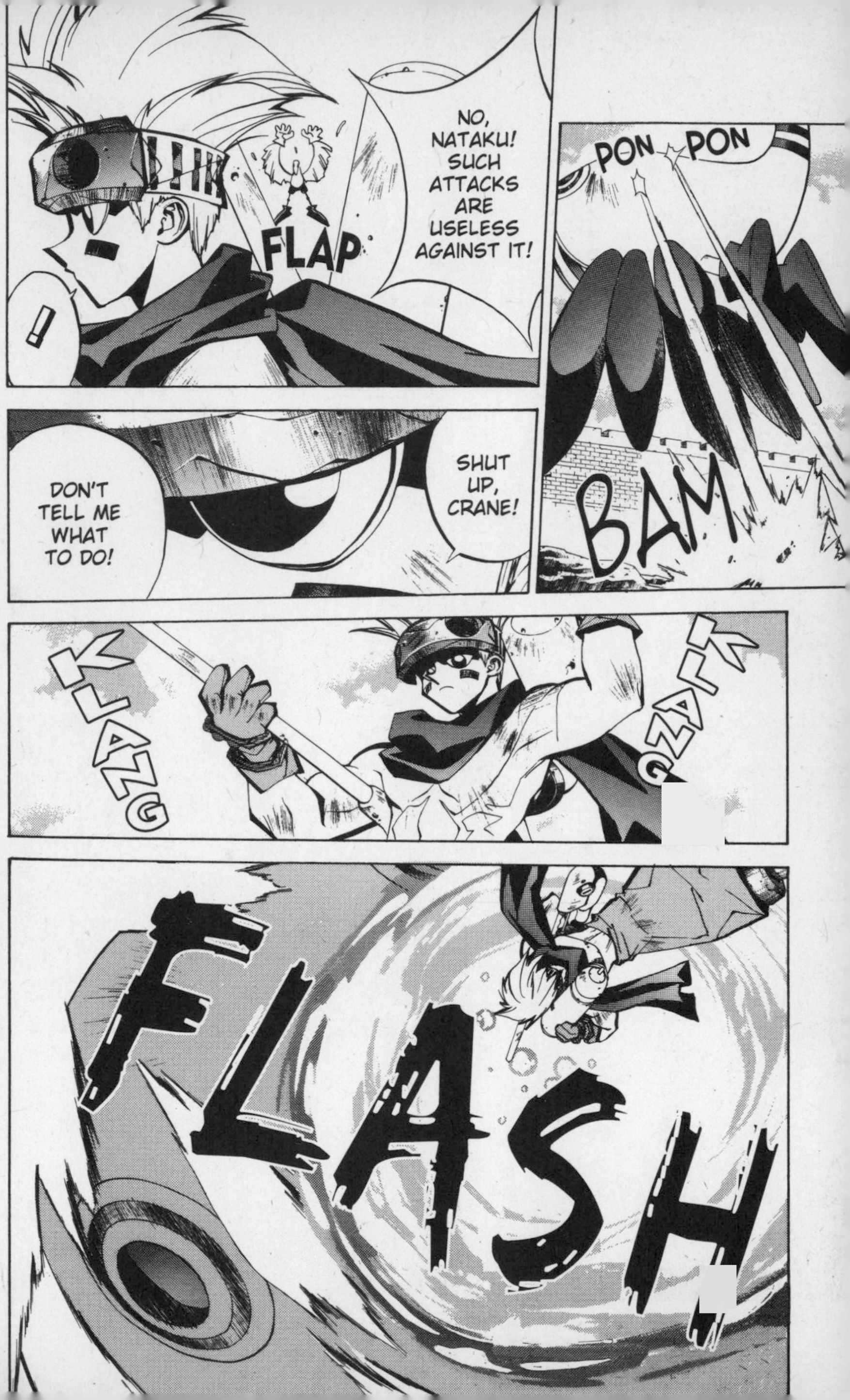
PON PON
BAM
NO, NATAKU! SUCH ATTACKS ARE USELESS AGAINST IT!
FLAP
!
SHUT UP, CRANE!
DON'T TELL ME WHAT TO DO!
KLANG
KLANG
FLASH

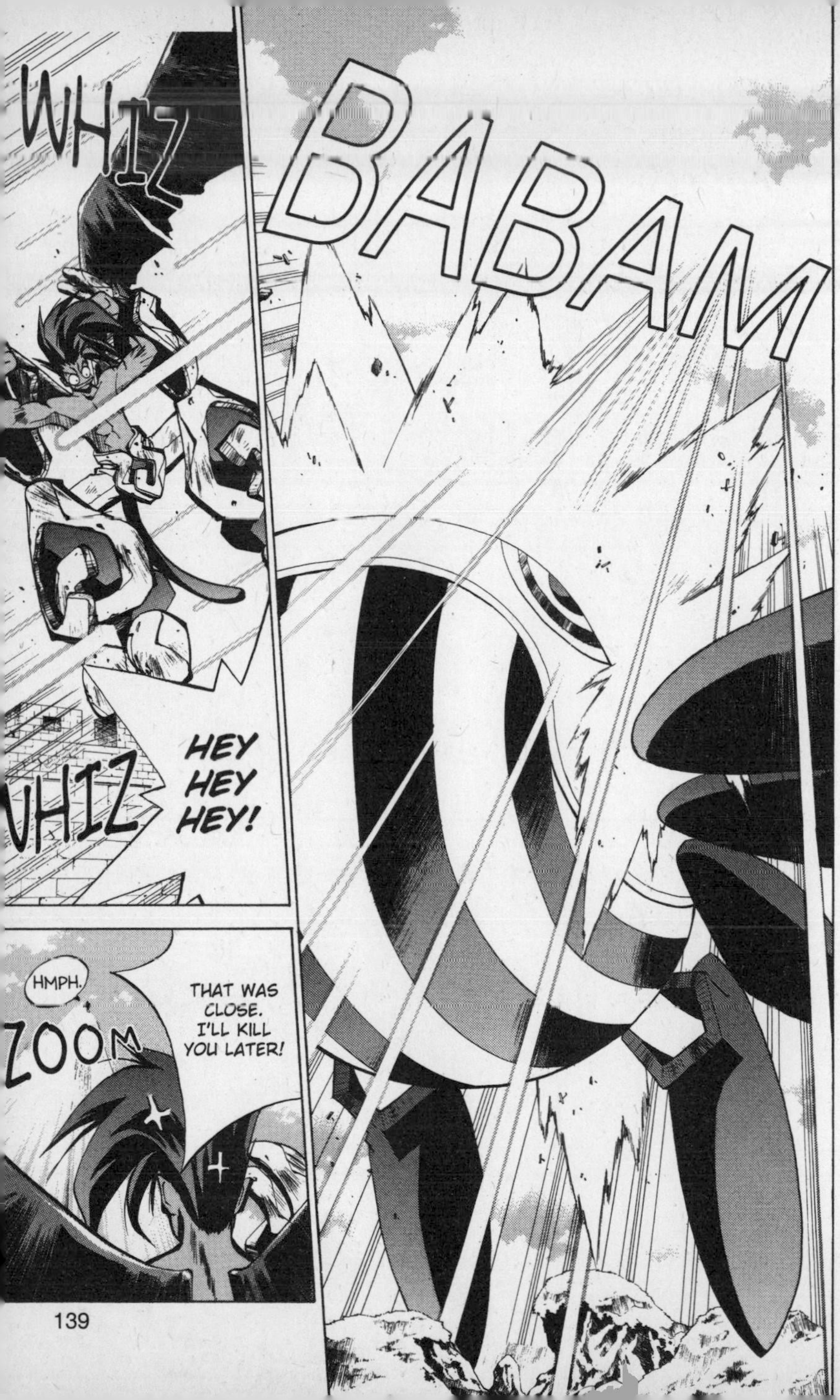
BABAM
WHIZ
HEY HEY HEY!
WHIZ
HMPH.
THAT WAS CLOSE. I'LL KILL YOU LATER!
ZOOM

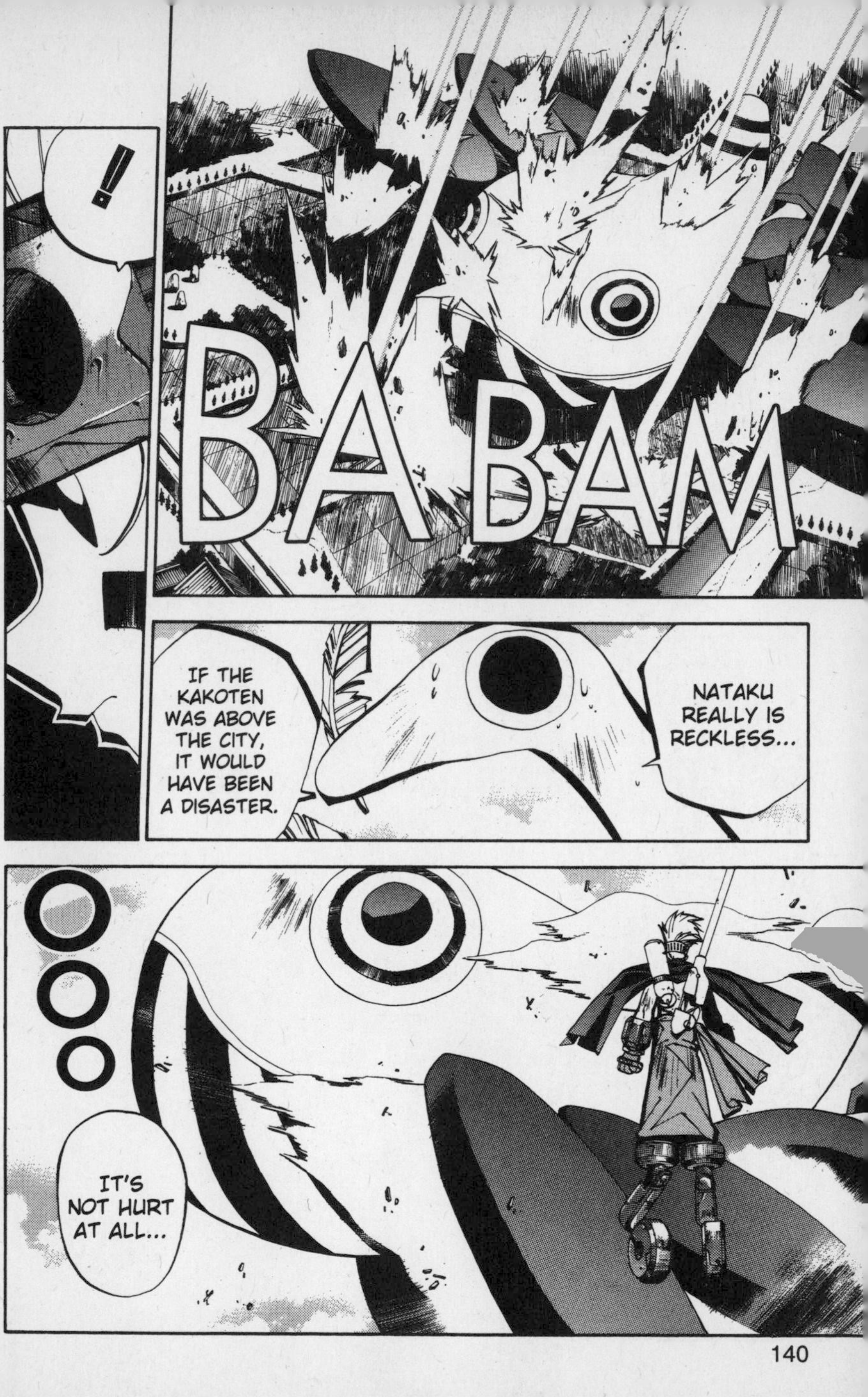
BA BAM
NATAKU REALLY IS RECKLESS...
IF THE KAKOTEN WAS ABOVE THE CITY, IT WOULD HAVE BEEN A DISASTER.
!
IT'S NOT HURT AT ALL...

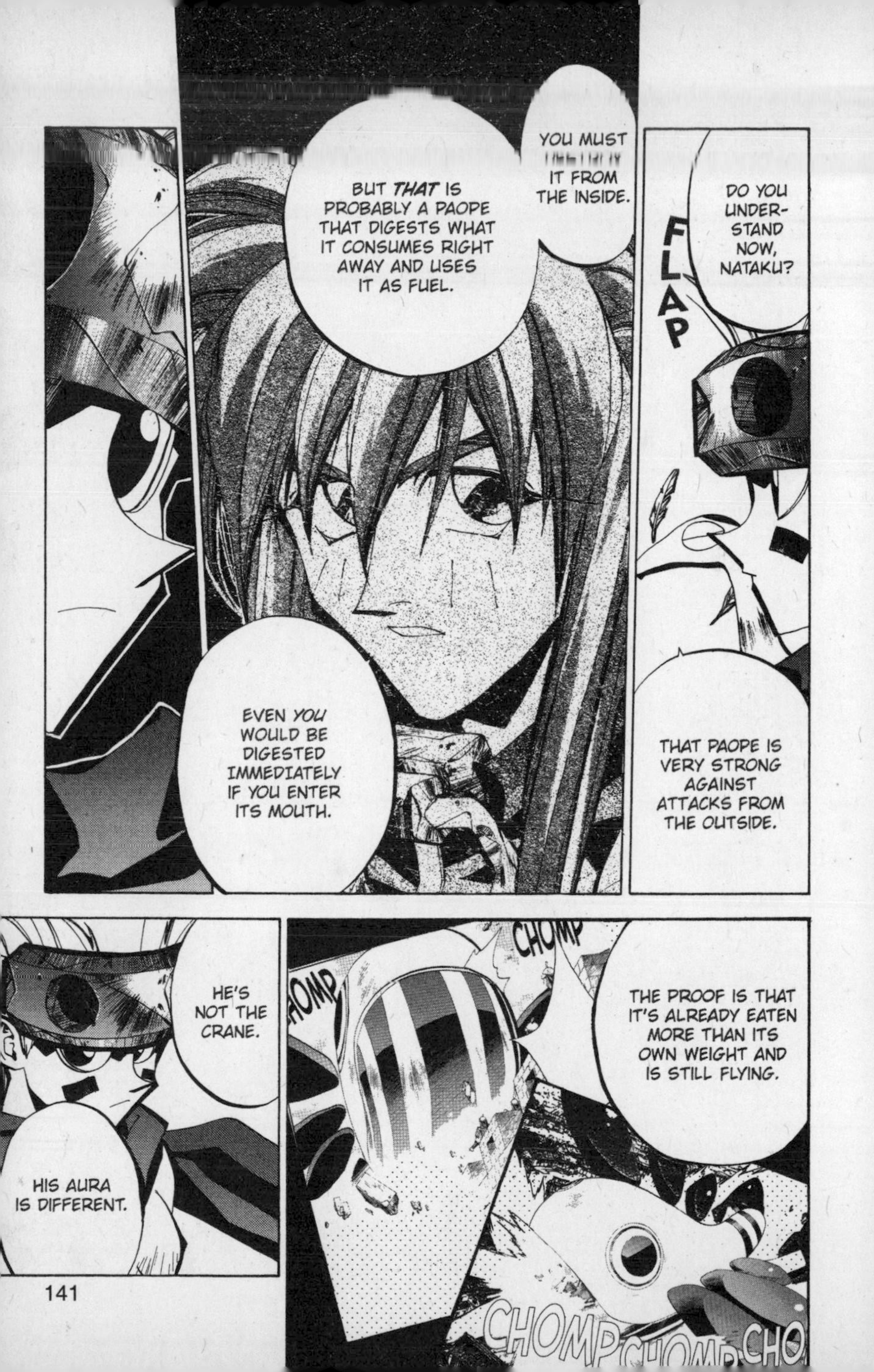
DO YOU UNDERSTAND NOW, NATAKU?
FLAP
THAT PAOPE IS VERY STRONG AGAINST ATTACKS FROM THE OUTSIDE.
YOU MUST
IT FROM THE INSIDE.
BUT *THAT* IS PROBABLY A PAOPE THAT DIGESTS WHAT IT CONSUMES RIGHT AWAY AND USES IT AS FUEL.
EVEN *YOU* WOULD BE DIGESTED IMMEDIATELY IF YOU ENTER ITS MOUTH.
CHOMP
THE PROOF IS THAT IT'S ALREADY EATEN MORE THAN ITS OWN WEIGHT AND IS STILL FLYING.
CHOMP
CHOMP CHOMP CHO
HE'S NOT THE CRANE.
HIS AURA IS DIFFERENT.

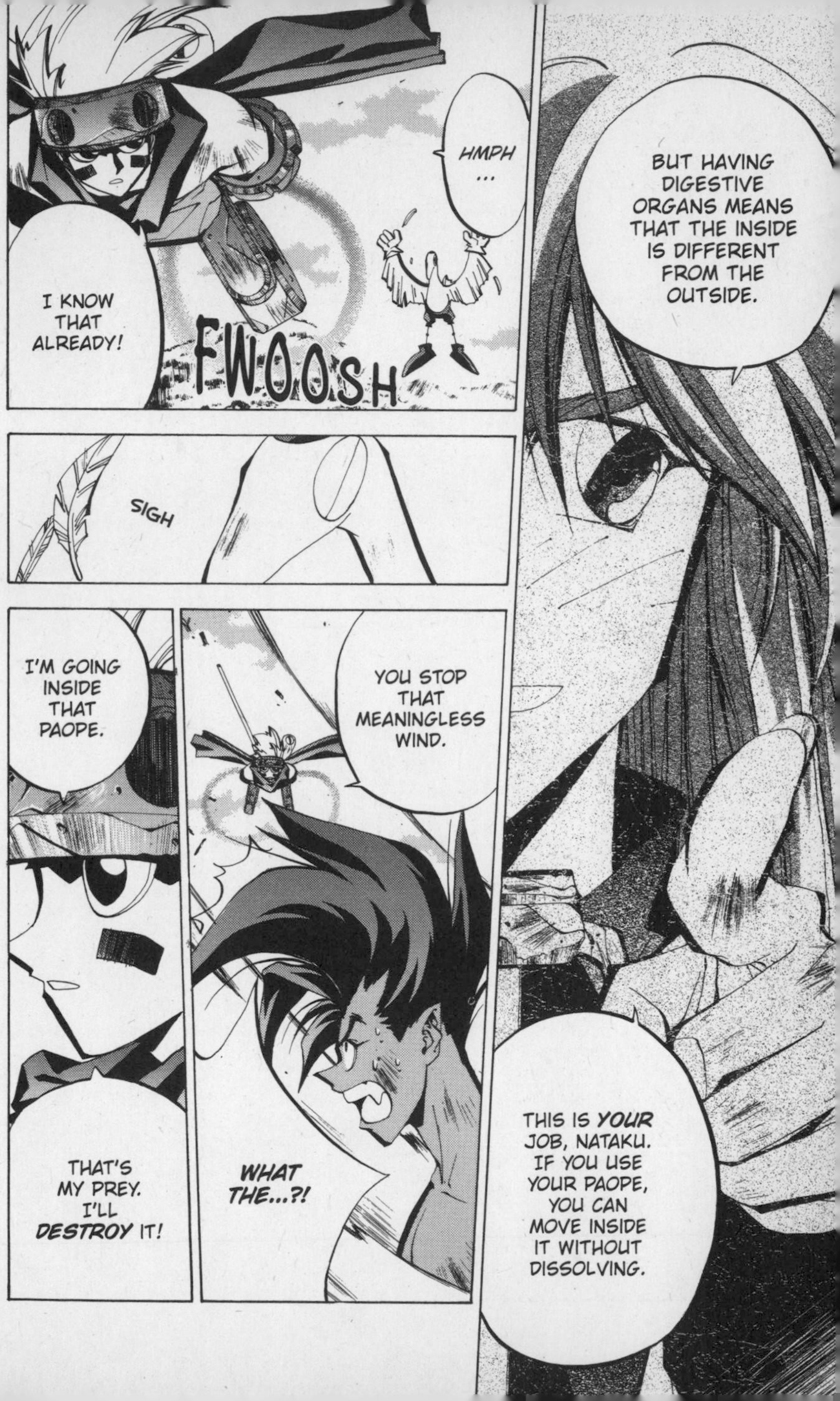
BUT HAVING DIGESTIVE ORGANS MEANS THAT THE INSIDE IS DIFFERENT FROM THE OUTSIDE.
THIS IS *YOUR* JOB, NATAKU. IF YOU USE YOUR PAOPE, YOU CAN MOVE INSIDE IT WITHOUT DISSOLVING.
HMPH ...
I KNOW THAT ALREADY!
FWOOSH
SIGH
YOU STOP THAT MEANINGLESS WIND.
WHAT THE...?!
I'M GOING INSIDE THAT PAOPE.
THAT'S MY PREY. I'LL ***DESTROY*** IT!

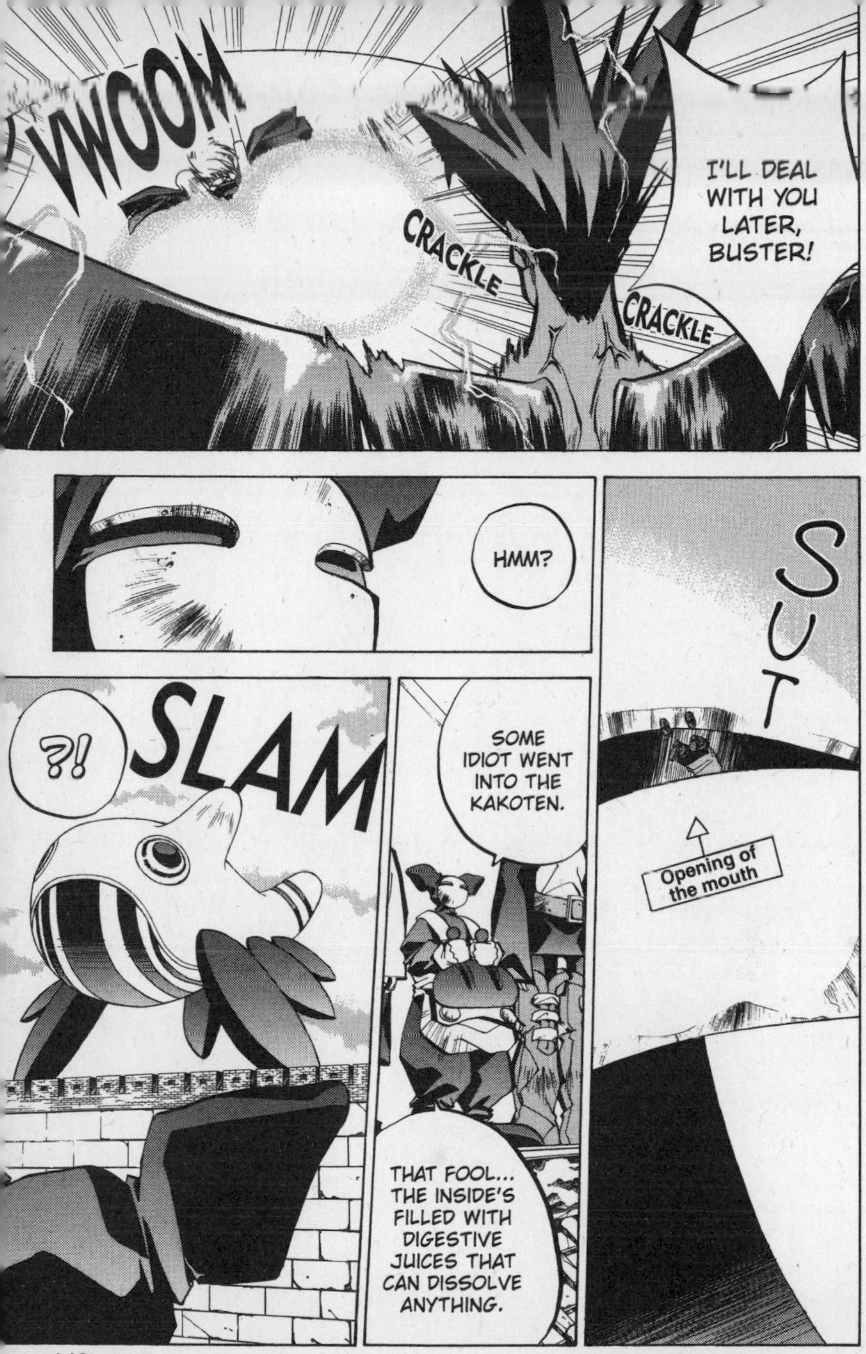
I'LL DEAL WITH YOU LATER, BUSTER!
VWOOM
CRACKLE
CRACKLE
SUT
Opening of the mouth
HMM?
SOME IDIOT WENT INTO THE KAKOTEN.
THAT FOOL... THE INSIDE'S FILLED WITH DIGESTIVE JUICES THAT CAN DISSOLVE ANYTHING.
?!
SLAM

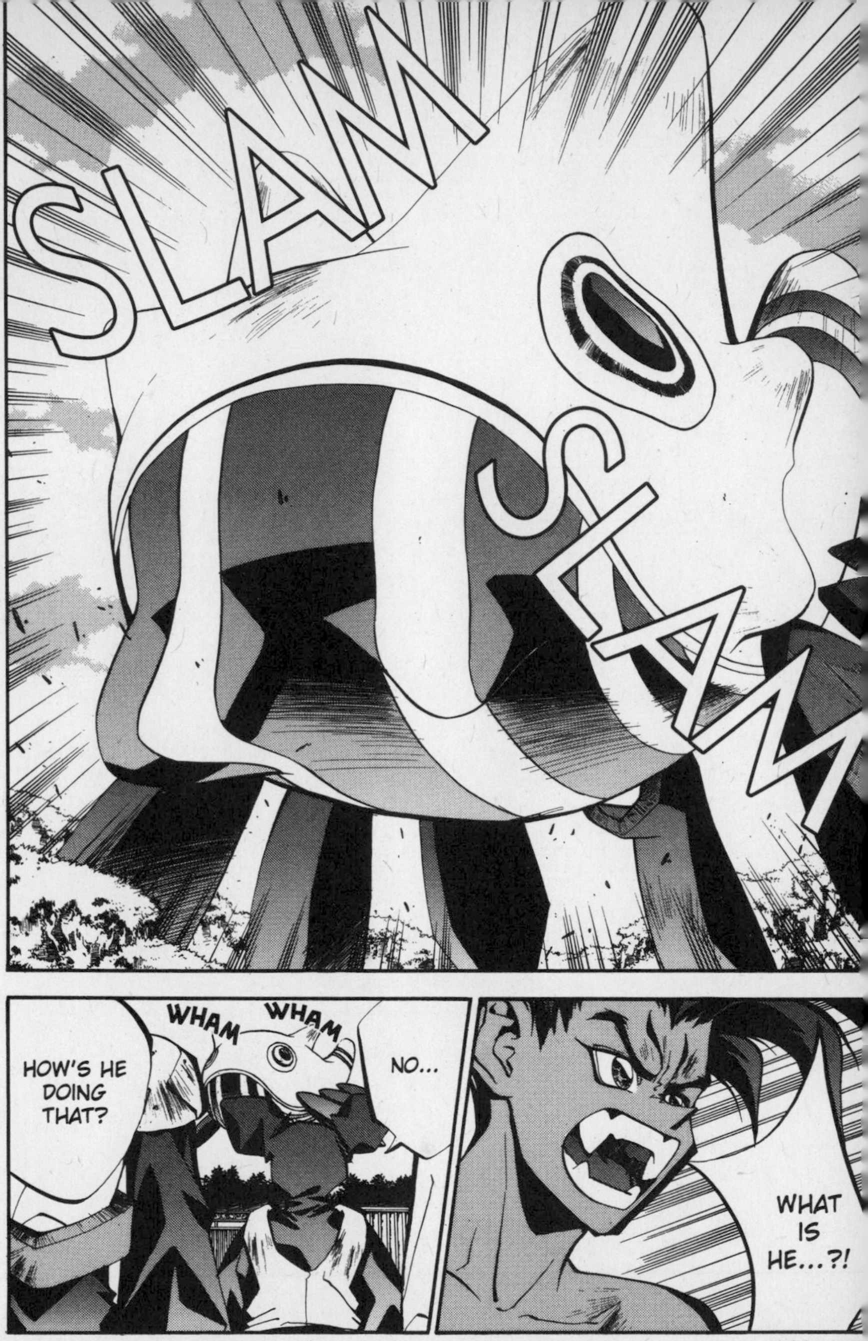
SLAM
SLAM
WHAT IS HE...?!
WHAM
WHAM
NO...
HOW'S HE DOING THAT?

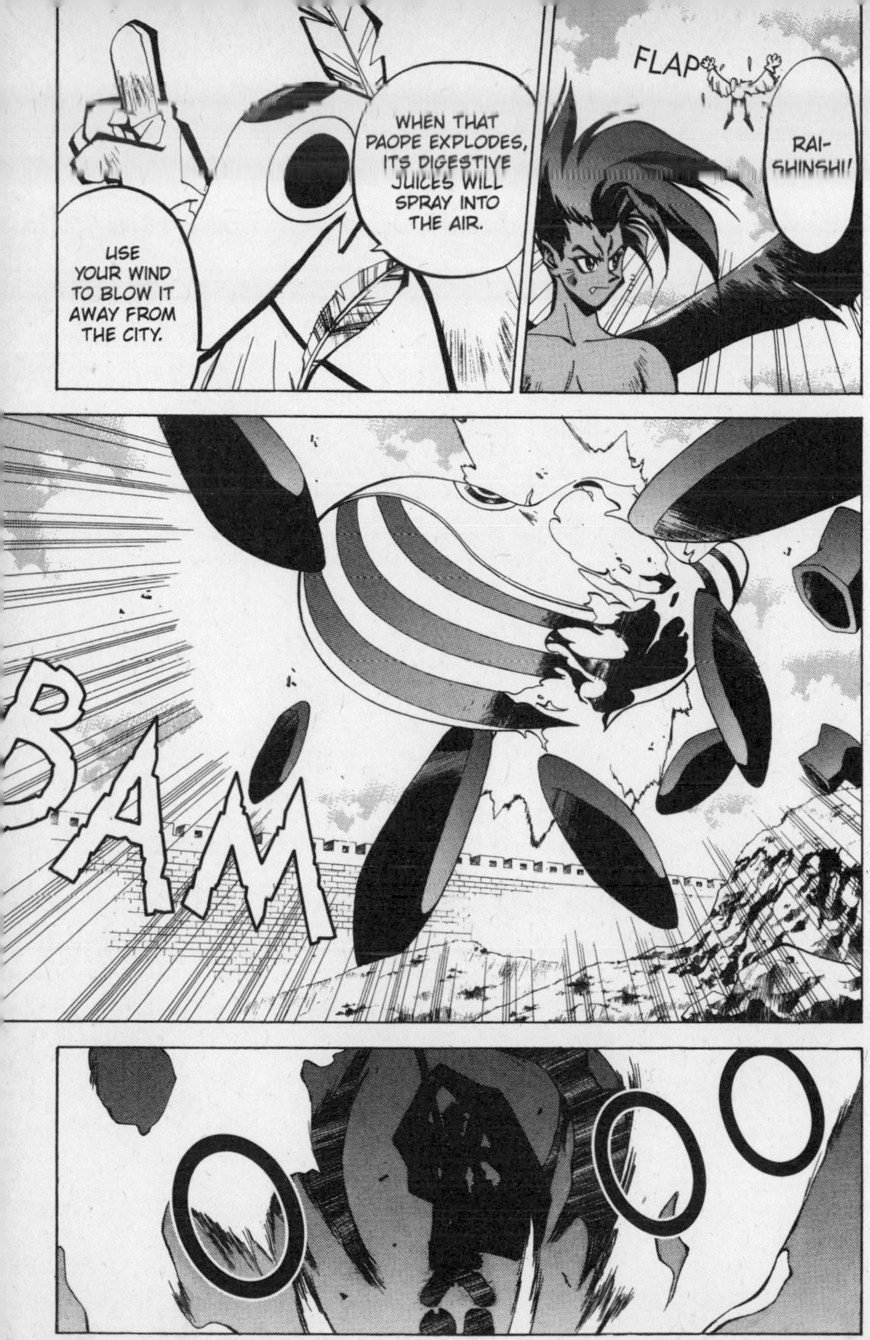
FLAP
RAI-SHINSHI!
WHEN THAT PAOPE EXPLODES, ITS DIGESTIVE JUICES WILL SPRAY INTO THE AIR.
USE YOUR WIND TO BLOW IT AWAY FROM THE CITY.
BAM

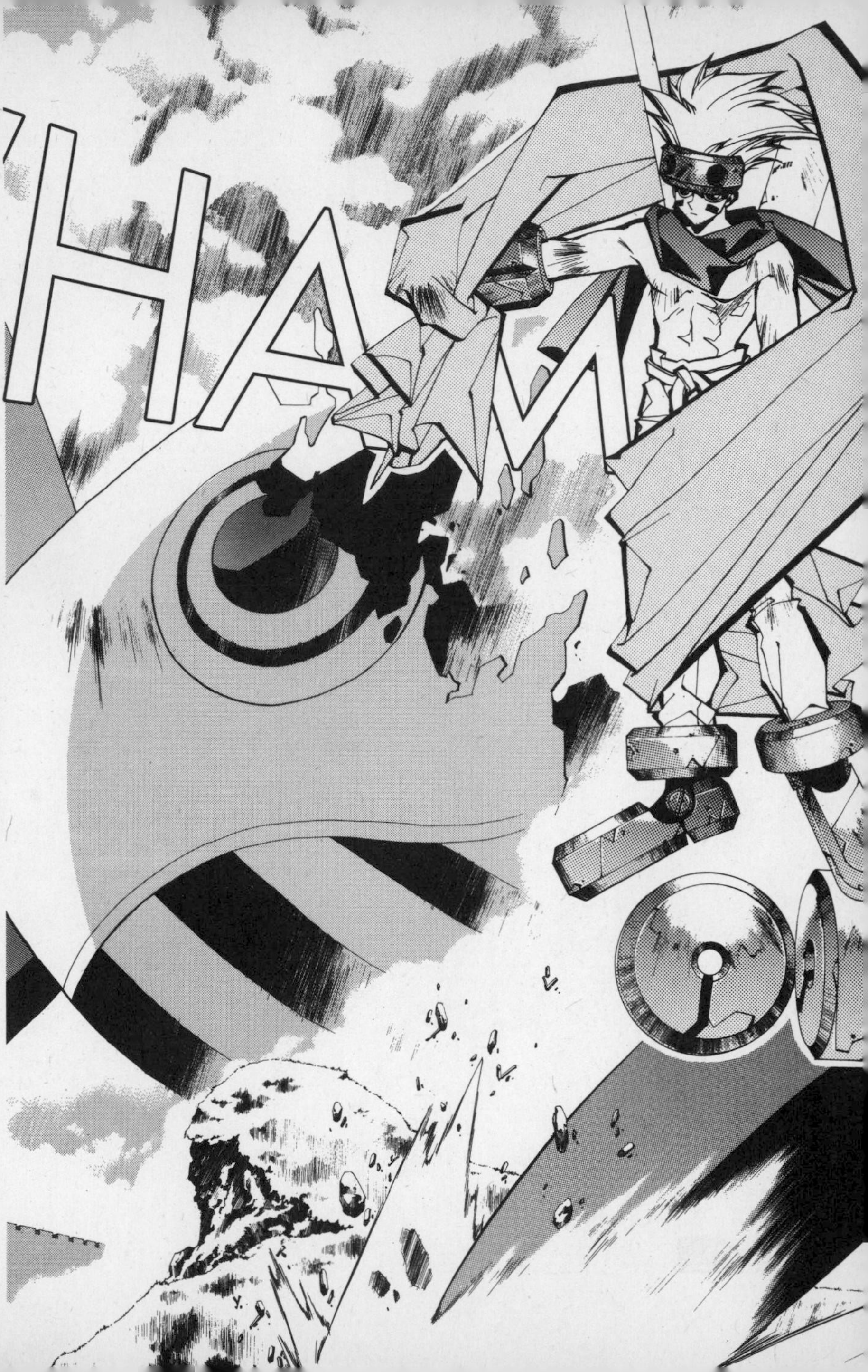
HAM

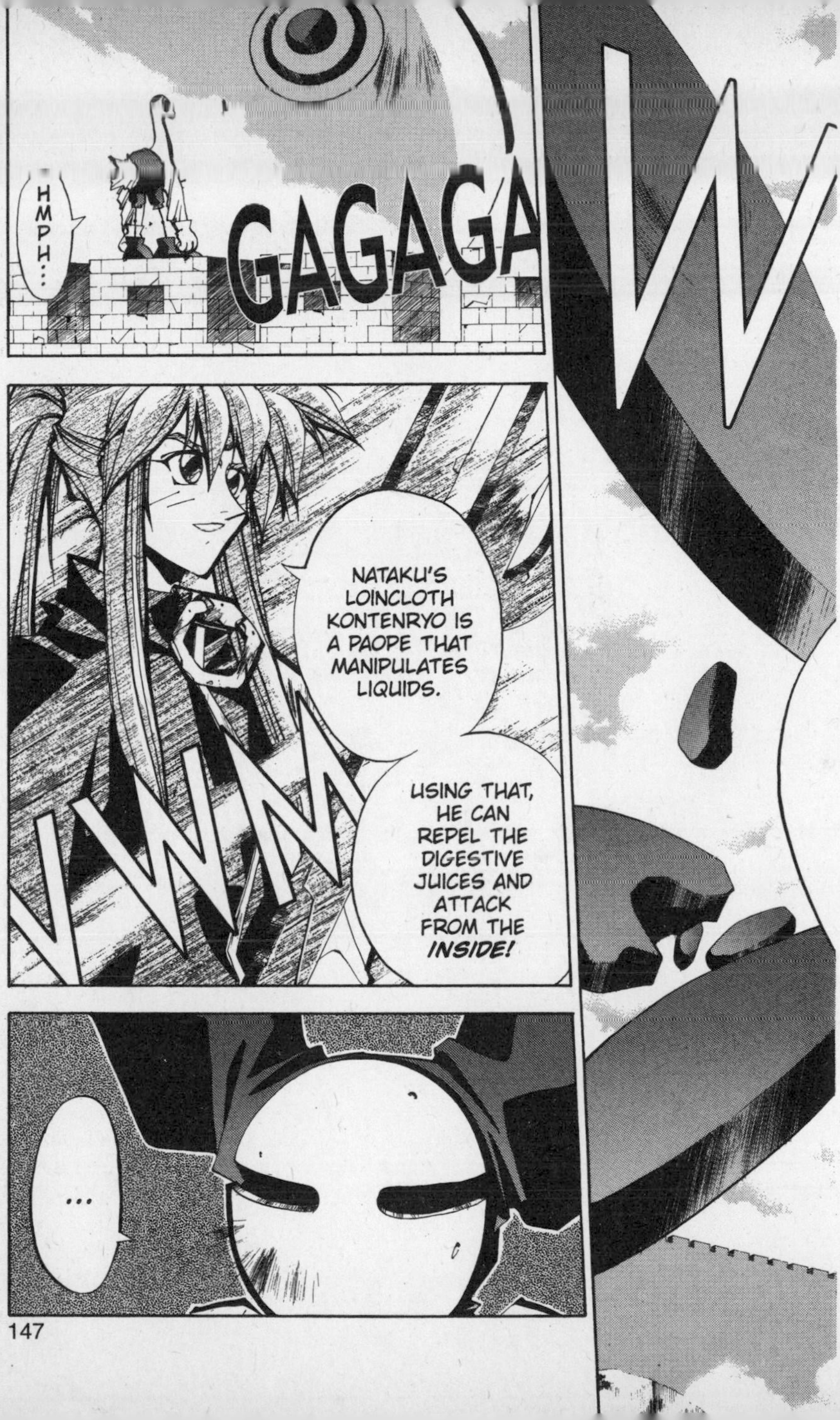
GAGAGA
HMPH...
NATAKU'S LOINCLOTH KONTENRYO IS A PAOPE THAT MANIPULATES LIQUIDS.
USING THAT, HE CAN REPEL THE DIGESTIVE JUICES AND ATTACK FROM THE *INSIDE!*
...

封神演義

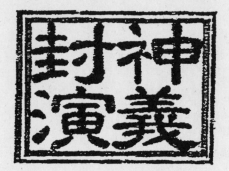

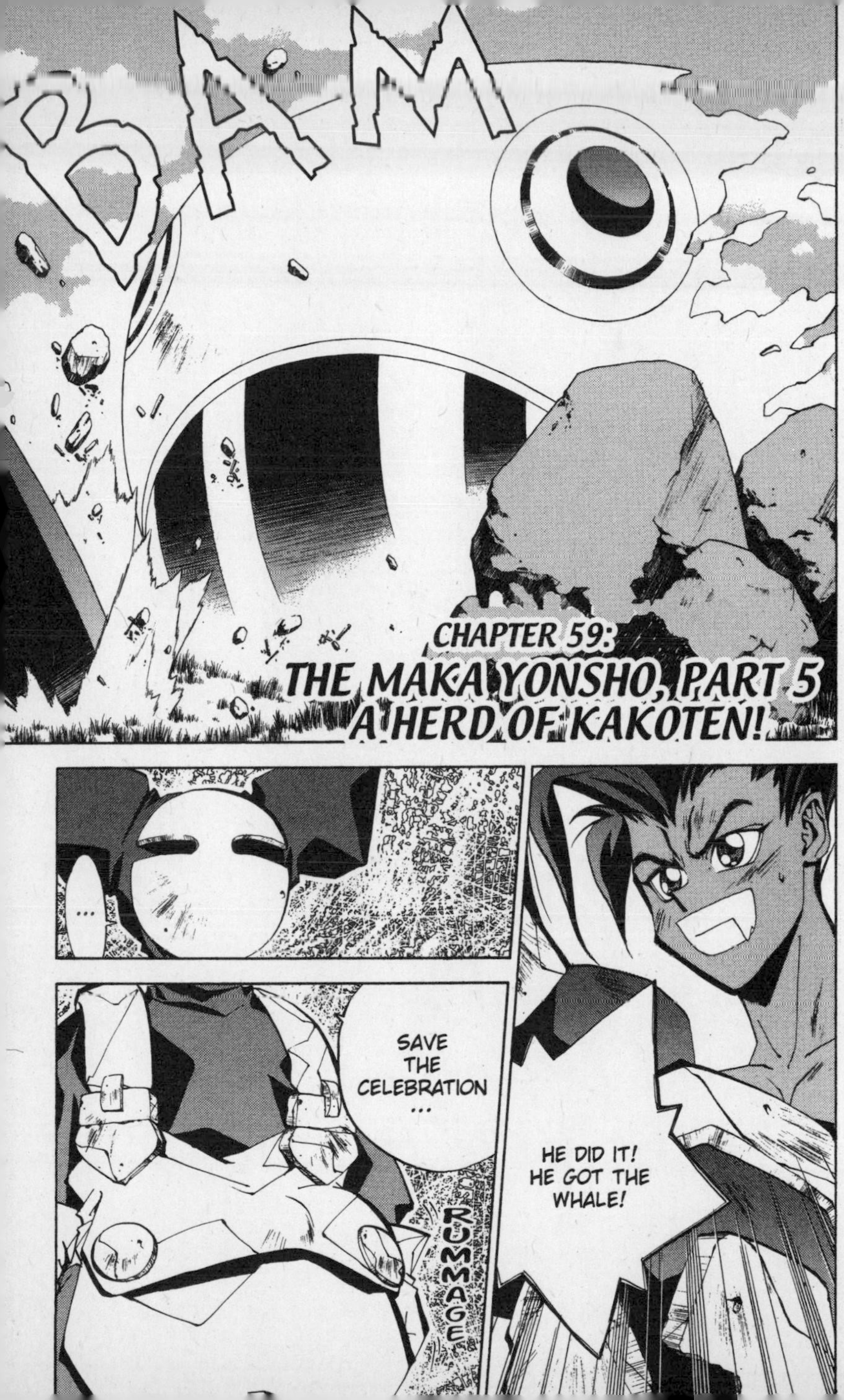
BAMO
CHAPTER 59:
THE MAKA YONSHO, PART 5
A HERD OF KAKOTEN!
HE DID IT! HE GOT THE WHALE!
...
SAVE THE CELEBRATION ...
RUMMAGE

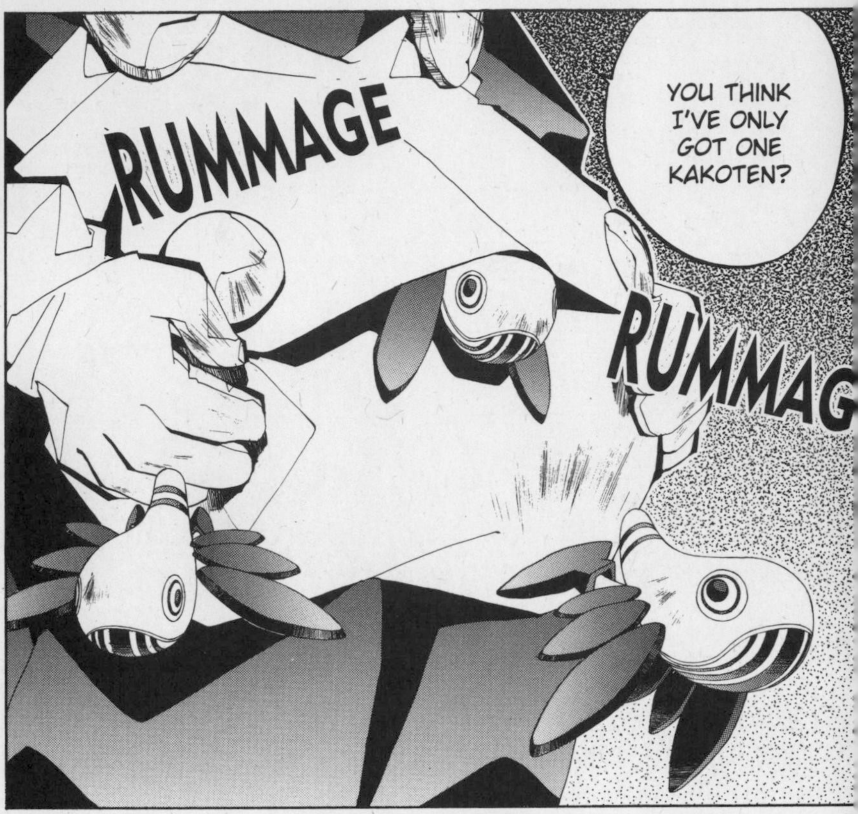
YOU THINK I'VE ONLY GOT ONE KAKOTEN?
RUMMAG
RUMMAGE

Chapter 59

THE MAKA YONSHO, PART 5
A HERD OF KAKOTEN!

READ THIS WAY

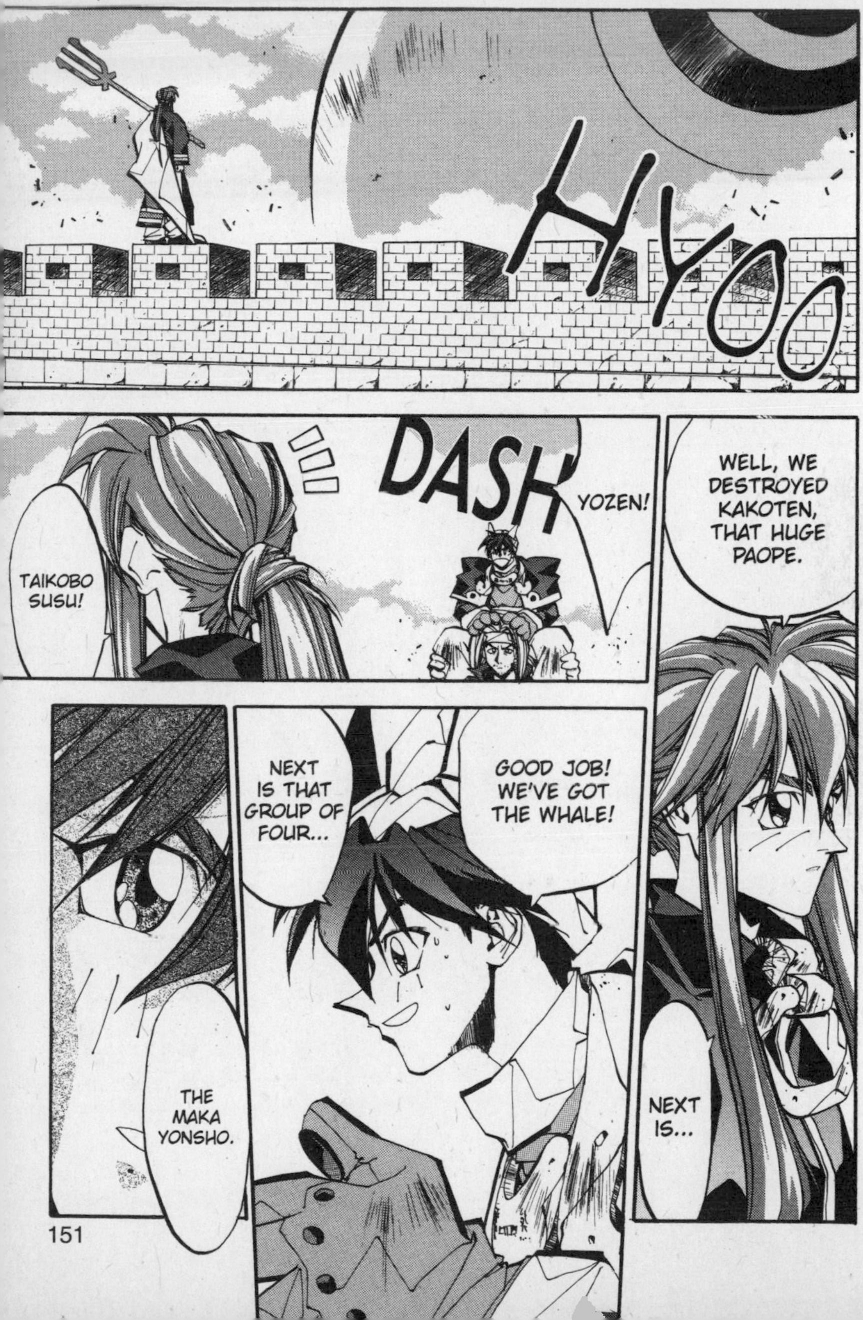

HYOO
WELL, WE DESTROYED KAKOTEN, THAT HUGE PAOPE.
DASH
YOZEN!
TAIKOBO SUSU!
NEXT IS...
GOOD JOB! WE'VE GOT THE WHALE!
NEXT IS THAT GROUP OF FOUR...
THE MAKA YONSHO.

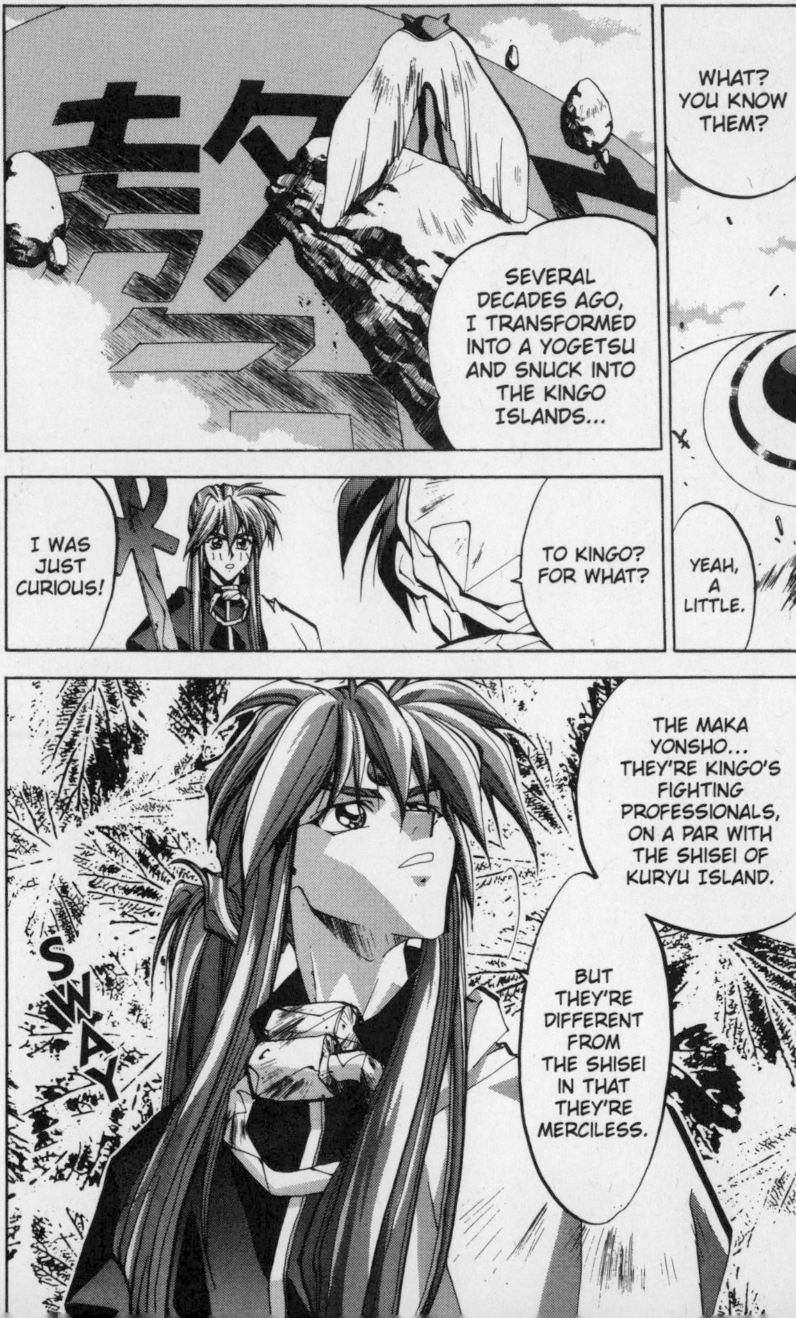

WHAT? YOU KNOW THEM?
YEAH, A LITTLE.
SEVERAL DECADES AGO, I TRANSFORMED INTO A YOGETSU AND SNUCK INTO THE KINGO ISLANDS...
TO KINGO? FOR WHAT?
I WAS JUST CURIOUS!
THE MAKA YONSHO... THEY'RE KINGO'S FIGHTING PROFESSIONALS, ON A PAR WITH THE SHISEI OF KURYU ISLAND.
BUT THEY'RE DIFFERENT FROM THE SHISEI IN THAT THEY'RE MERCILESS.
SWAY

READ THIS WAY

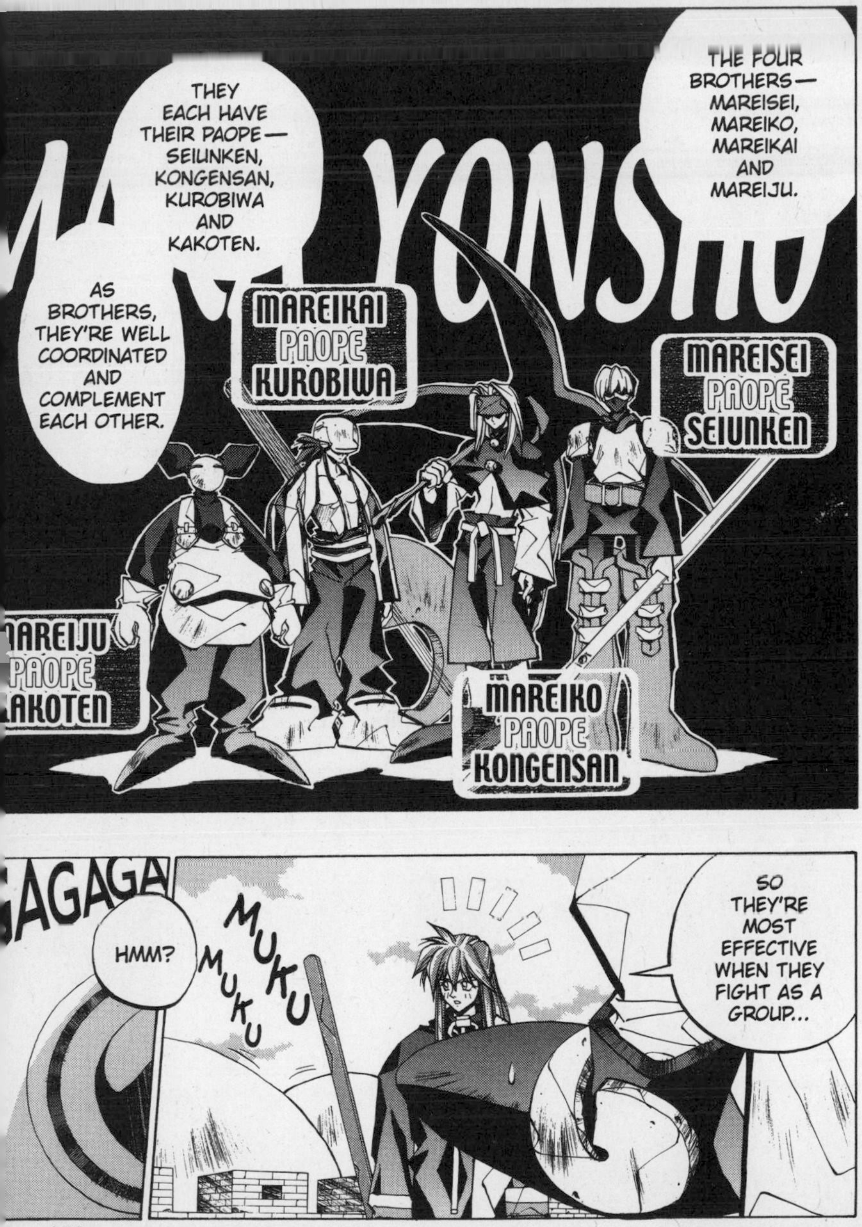
THE FOUR BROTHERS—MAREISEI, MAREIKO, MAREIKAI AND MAREIJU.
YONSHO
THEY EACH HAVE THEIR PAOPE—SEIUNKEN, KONGENSAN, KUROBIWA AND KAKOTEN.
MAREISEI PAOPE SEIUNKEN
MAREIKO PAOPE KONGENSAN
MAREIKAI PAOPE KUROBIWA
AS BROTHERS, THEY'RE WELL COORDINATED AND COMPLEMENT EACH OTHER.
MAREIJU PAOPE KAKOTEN
SO THEY'RE MOST EFFECTIVE WHEN THEY FIGHT AS A GROUP...
MUKU MUKU
HMM?
GAGAGA

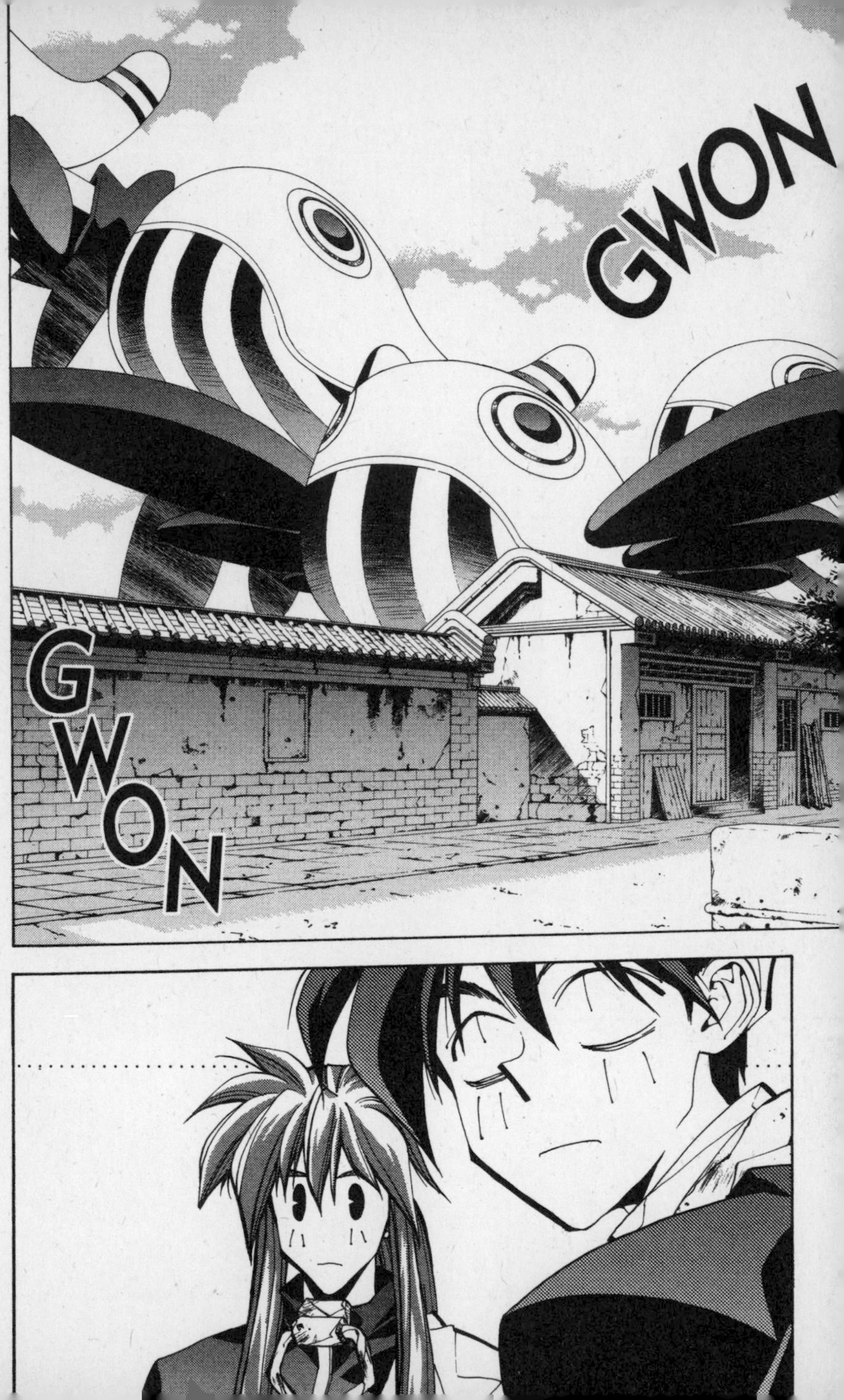
GWON
GWON

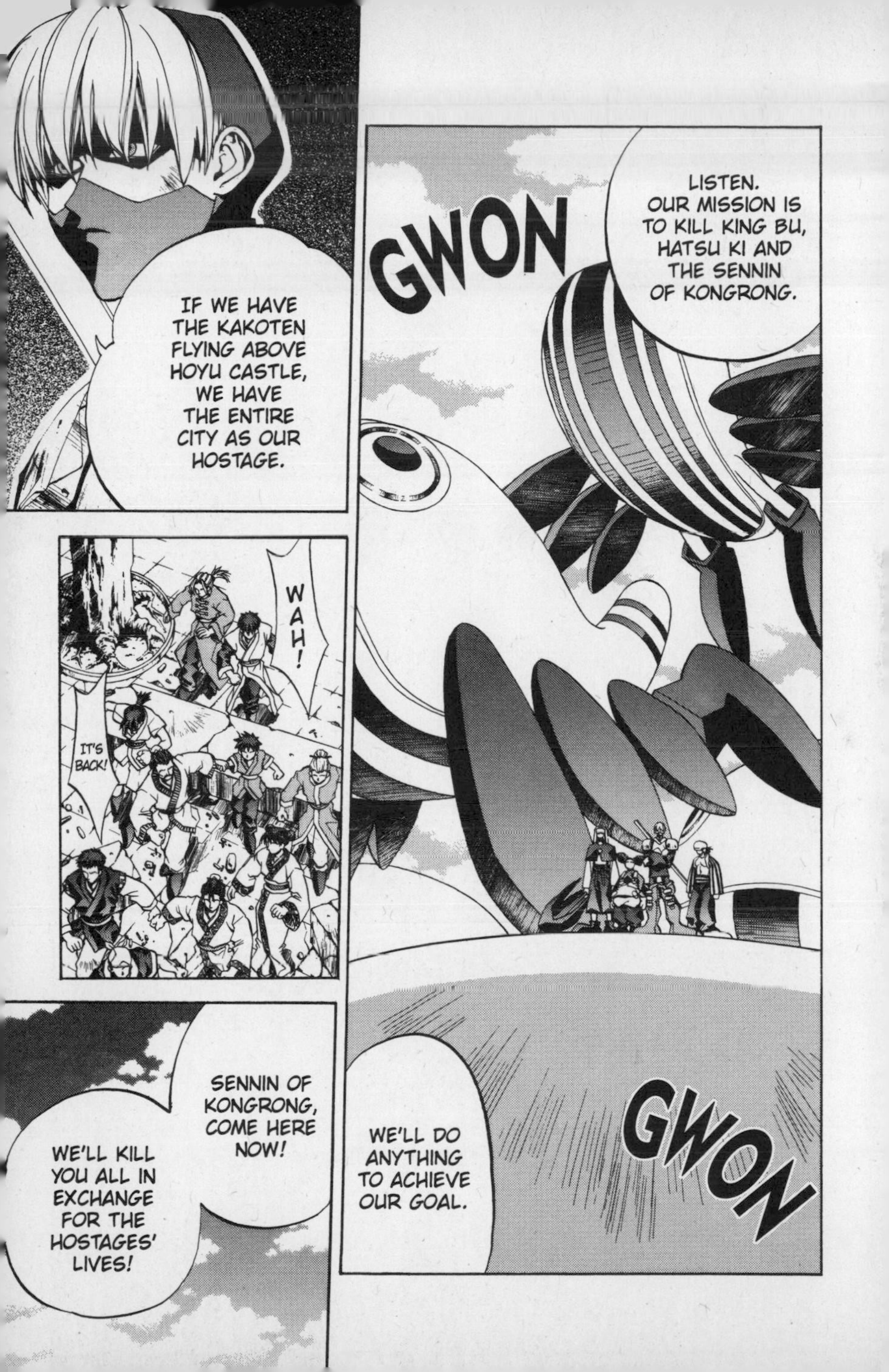
GWON
LISTEN. OUR MISSION IS TO KILL KING BU, HATSU KI AND THE SENNIN OF KONGRONG.
IF WE HAVE THE KAKOTEN FLYING ABOVE HOYU CASTLE, WE HAVE THE ENTIRE CITY AS OUR HOSTAGE.
WAH!
IT'S BACK!
WE'LL DO ANYTHING TO ACHIEVE OUR GOAL.
GWON
SENNIN OF KONGRONG, COME HERE NOW!
WE'LL KILL YOU ALL IN EXCHANGE FOR THE HOSTAGES' LIVES!

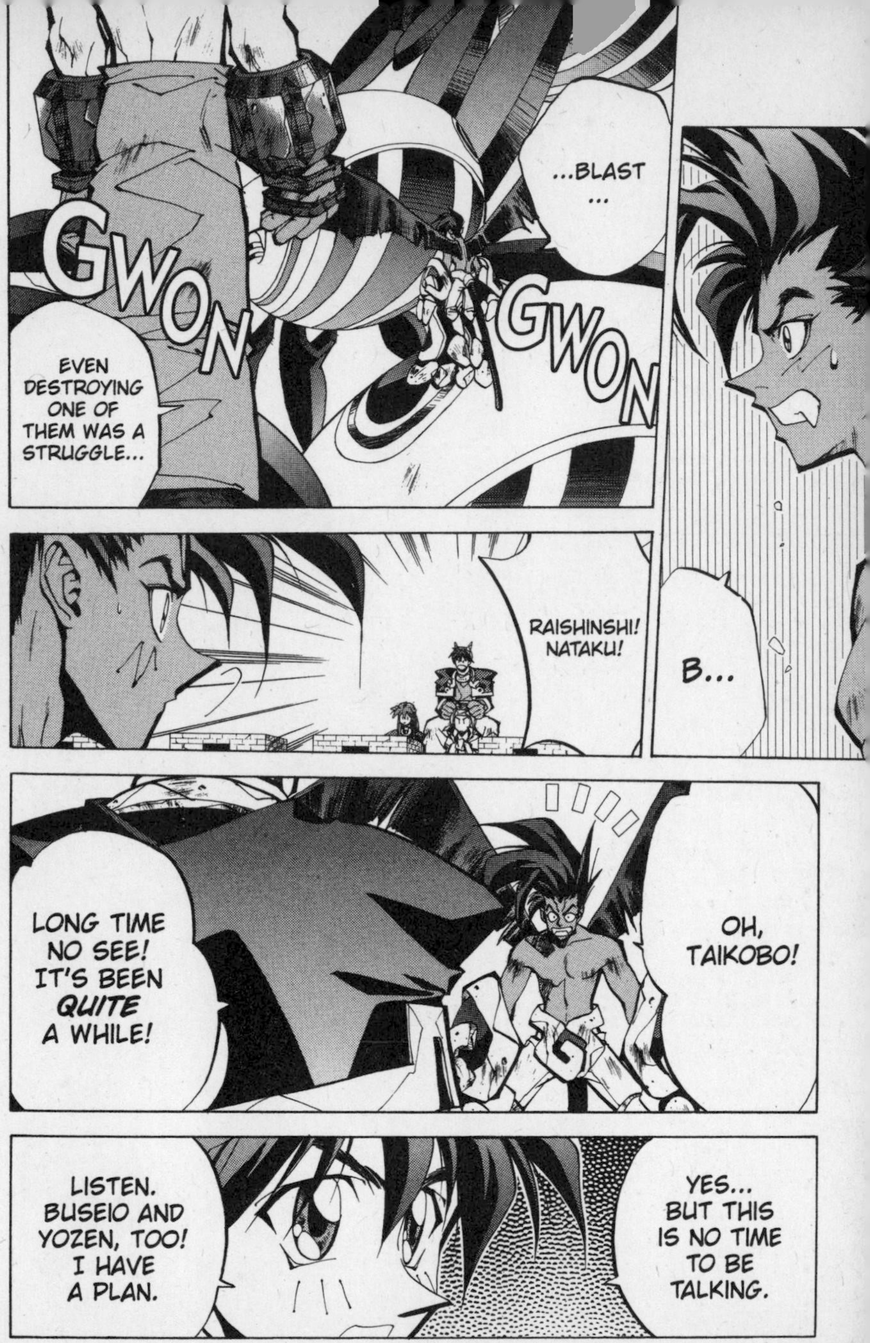
...BLAST ...
GWON
GWON
EVEN DESTROYING ONE OF THEM WAS A STRUGGLE...
B...
RAISHINSHI! NATAKU!
OH, TAIKOBO!
LONG TIME NO SEE! IT'S BEEN *QUITE* A WHILE!
YES... BUT THIS IS NO TIME TO BE TALKING.
LISTEN. BUSEIO AND YOZEN, TOO! I HAVE A PLAN.

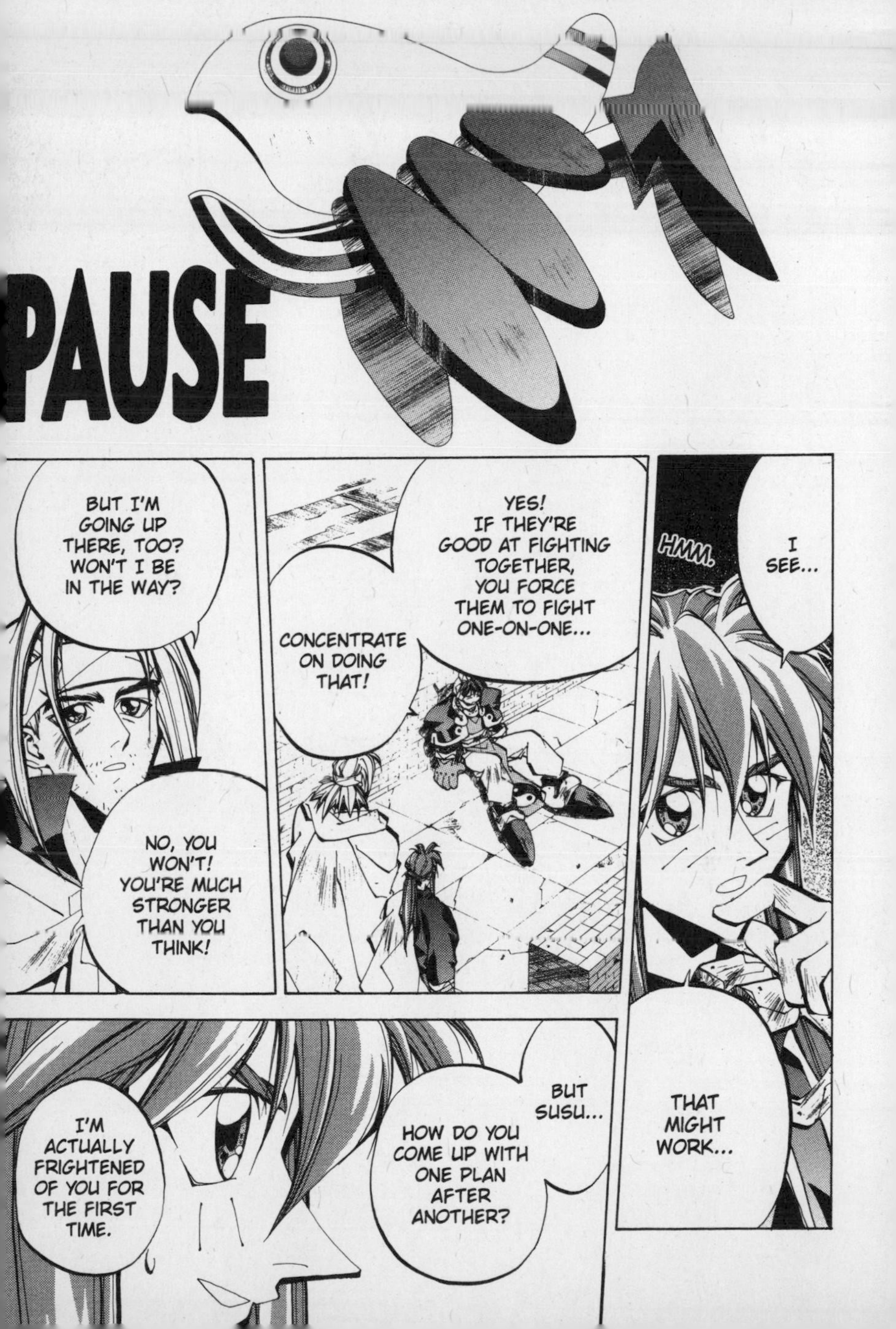
PAUSE
HMM.
I SEE...
YES! IF THEY'RE GOOD AT FIGHTING TOGETHER, YOU FORCE THEM TO FIGHT ONE-ON-ONE...
CONCENTRATE ON DOING THAT!
BUT I'M GOING UP THERE, TOO? WON'T I BE IN THE WAY?
NO, YOU WON'T! YOU'RE MUCH STRONGER THAN YOU THINK!
THAT MIGHT WORK...
BUT SUSU...
HOW DO YOU COME UP WITH ONE PLAN AFTER ANOTHER?
I'M ACTUALLY FRIGHTENED OF YOU FOR THE FIRST TIME.

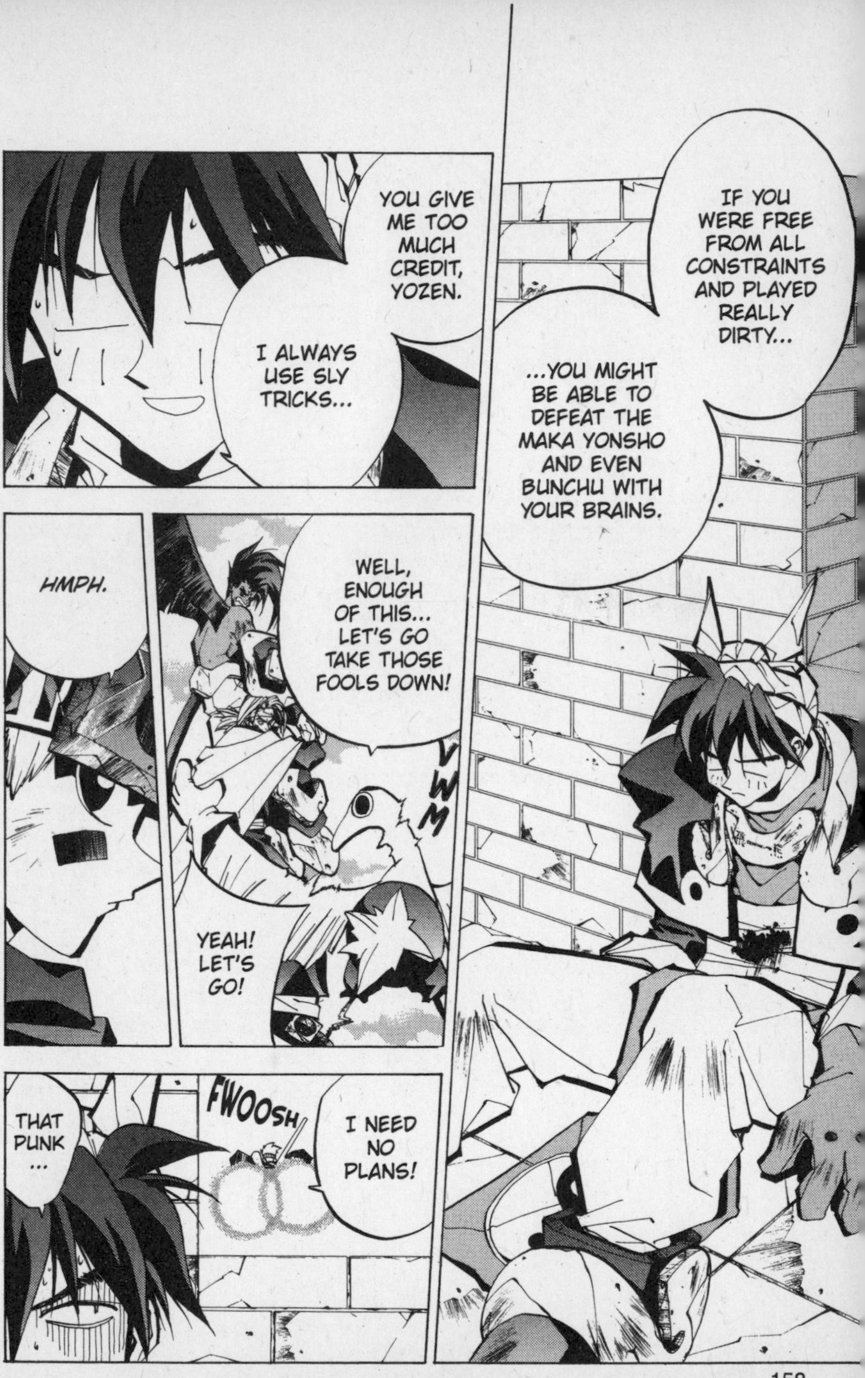
IF YOU WERE FREE FROM ALL CONSTRAINTS AND PLAYED REALLY DIRTY...
...YOU MIGHT BE ABLE TO DEFEAT THE MAKA YONSHO AND EVEN BUNCHU WITH YOUR BRAINS.
YOU GIVE ME TOO MUCH CREDIT, YOZEN.
I ALWAYS USE SLY TRICKS...
WELL, ENOUGH OF THIS... LET'S GO TAKE THOSE FOOLS DOWN!
VWM
YEAH! LET'S GO!
HMPH.
FWOOSH
I NEED NO PLANS!
THAT PUNK ...

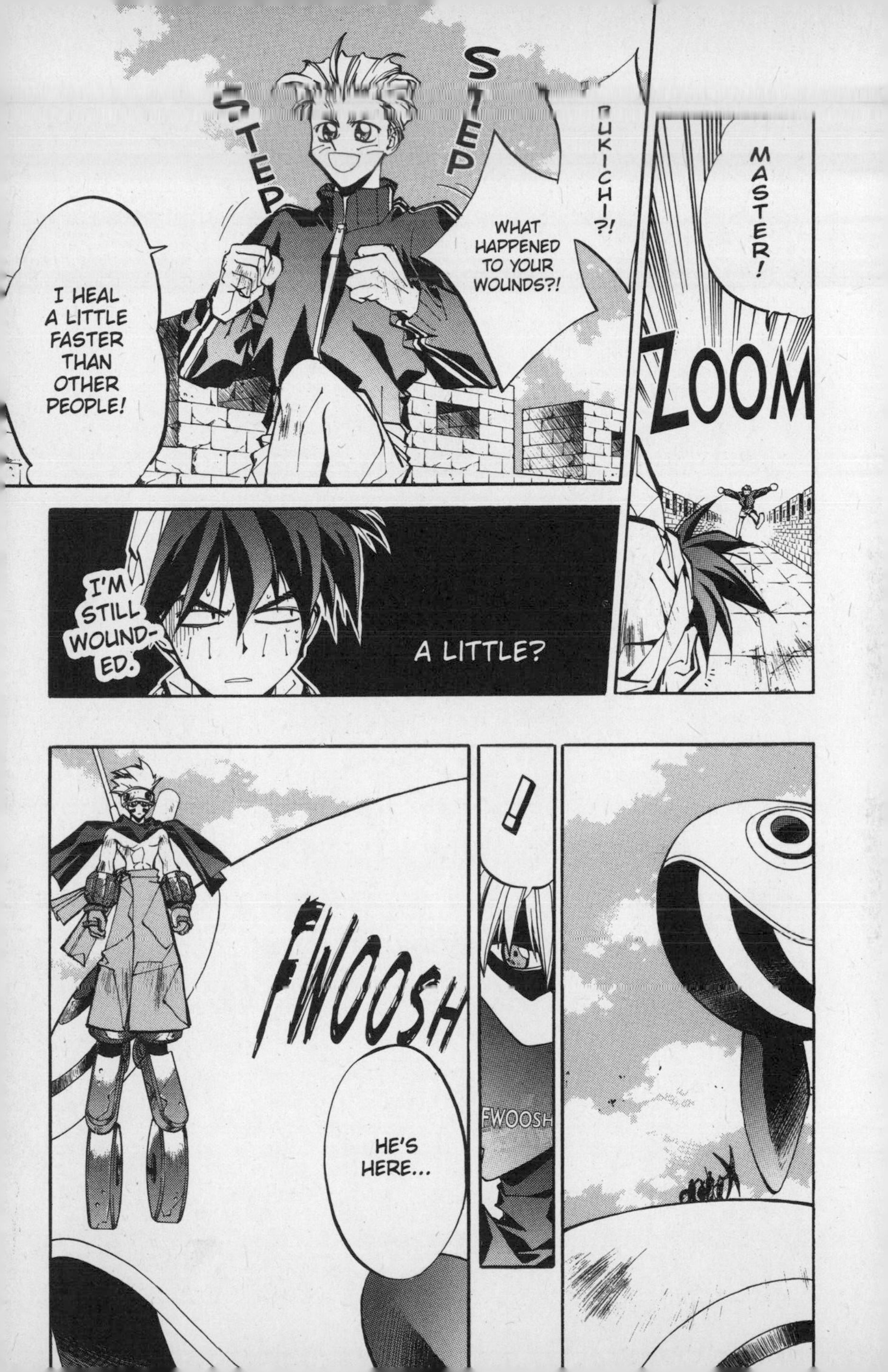
MASTER!
ZOOM
STEP STEP
FUKICHI?!
WHAT HAPPENED TO YOUR WOUNDS?!
I HEAL A LITTLE FASTER THAN OTHER PEOPLE!
A LITTLE?
I'M STILL WOUND-ED.
!
FWOOSH
FWOOSH
HE'S HERE...

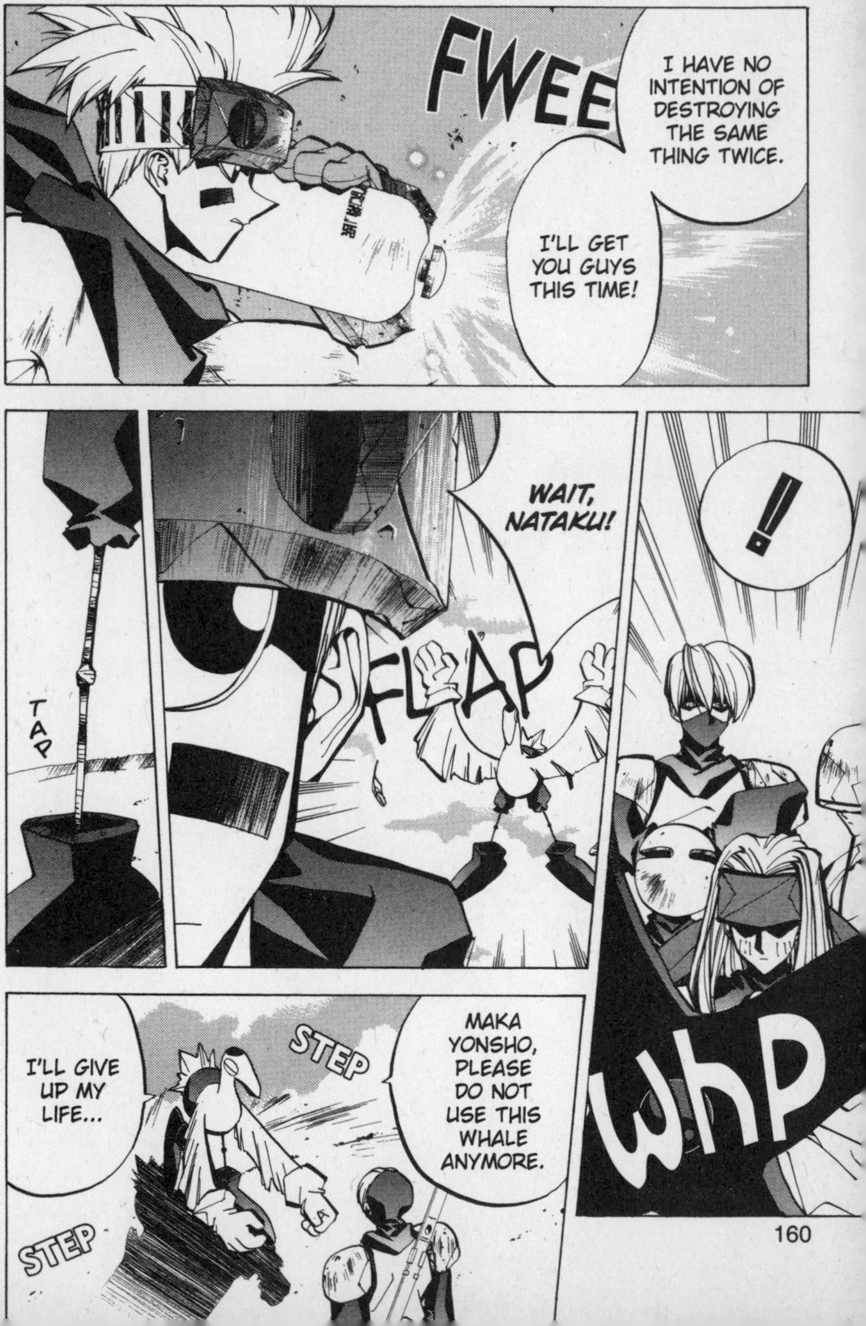
FWEE
I HAVE NO INTENTION OF DESTROYING THE SAME THING TWICE.
I'LL GET YOU GUYS THIS TIME!
!
WhP
WAIT, NATAKU!
FLAP
TAP
STEP
MAKA YONSHO, PLEASE DO NOT USE THIS WHALE ANYMORE.
I'LL GIVE UP MY LIFE...
STEP

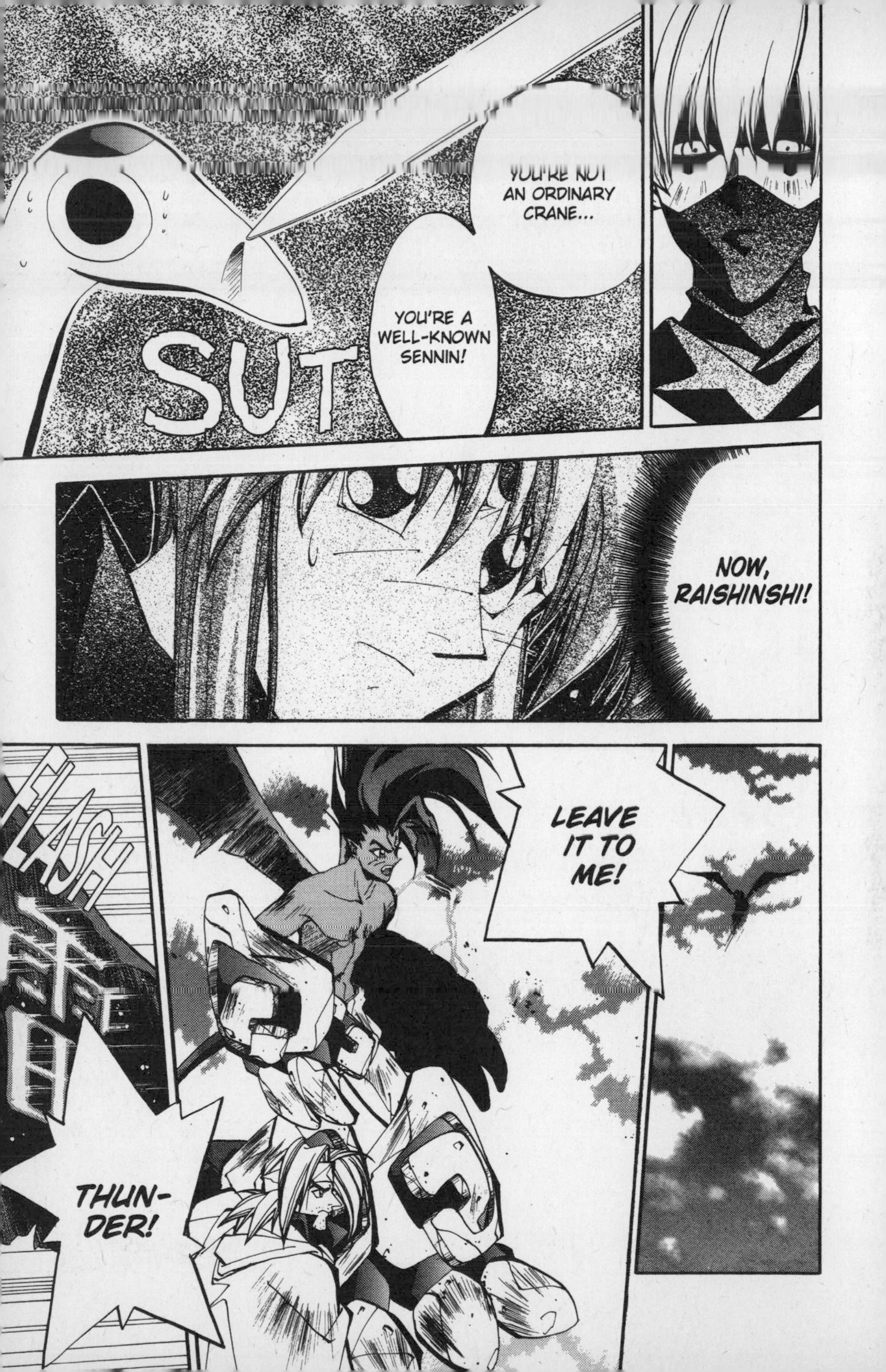
YOU'RE NOT AN ORDINARY CRANE...
YOU'RE A WELL-KNOWN SENNIN!
SUT
NOW, RAISHINSHI!
LEAVE IT TO ME!
FLASH
THUN-DER!

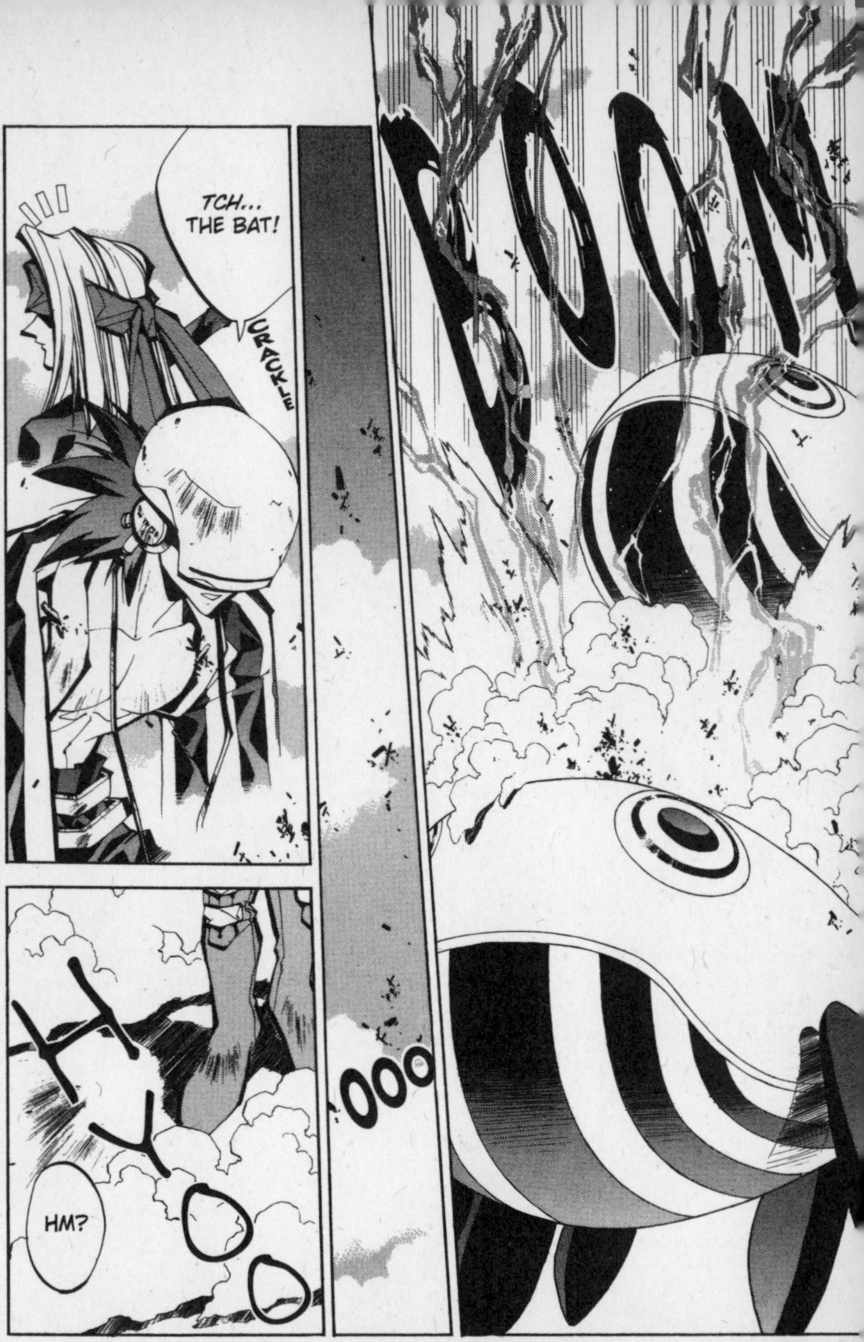

BOOM
OOO
TCH... THE BAT!
CRACKLE
HYOO
HM?

READ THIS WAY

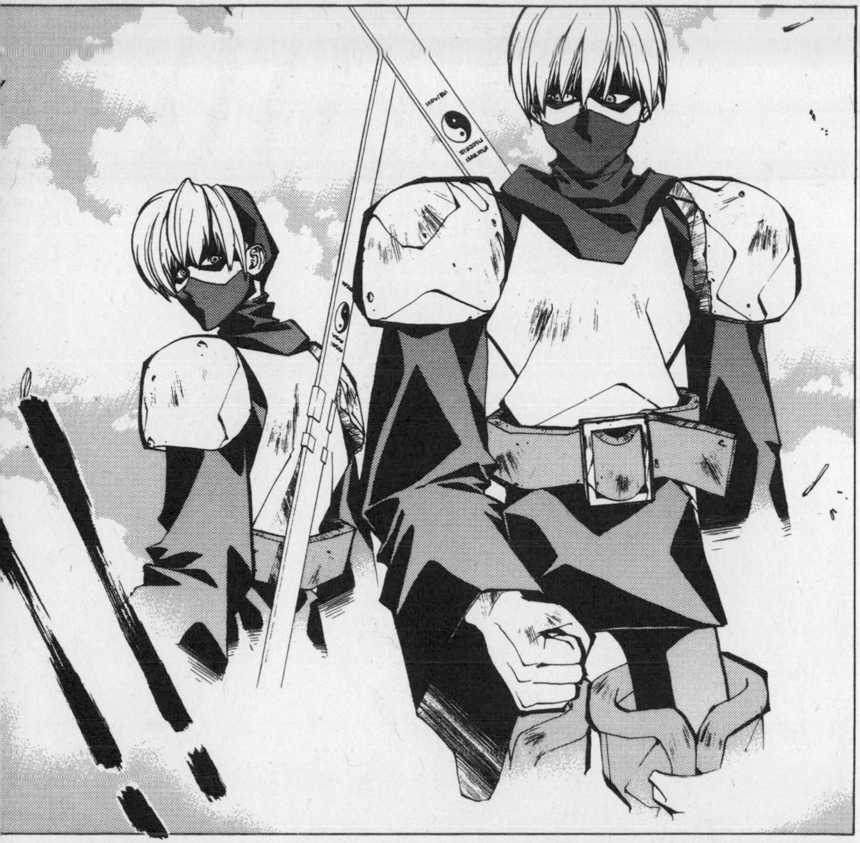

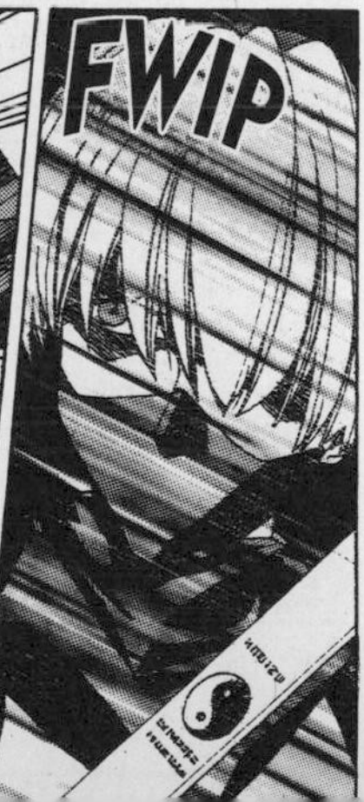
FWIP

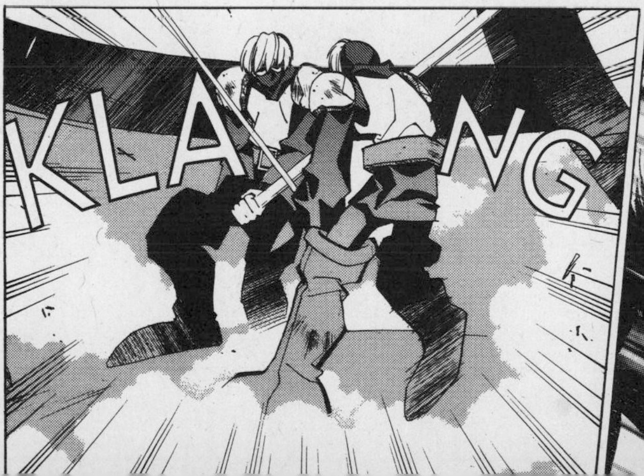
KLANG

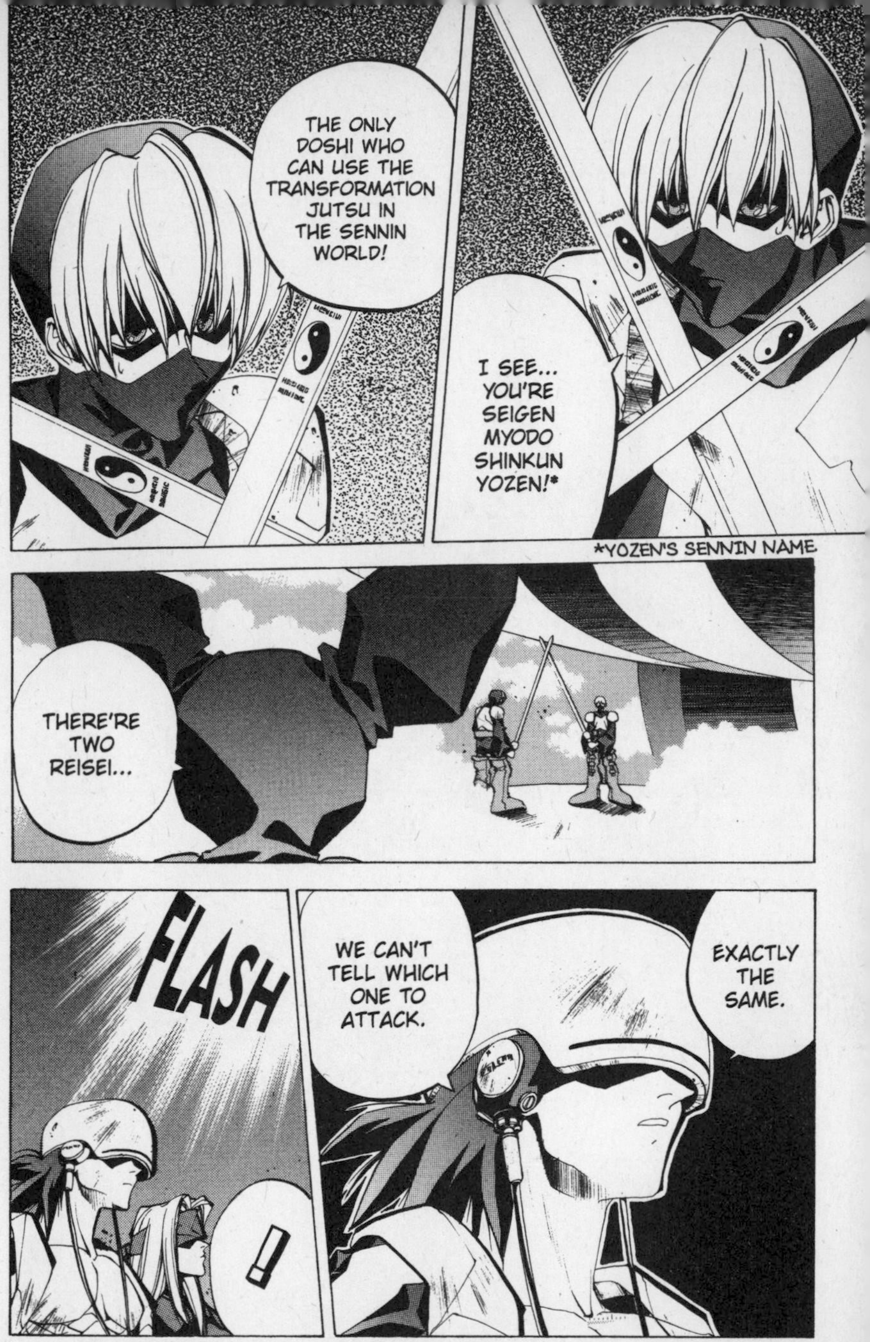
I SEE... YOU'RE SEIGEN MYODO SHINKUN YOZEN!*
THE ONLY DOSHI WHO CAN USE THE TRANSFORMATION JUTSU IN THE SENNIN WORLD!
*YOZEN'S SENNIN NAME
THERE'RE TWO REISEI...
EXACTLY THE SAME.
WE CAN'T TELL WHICH ONE TO ATTACK.
FLASH
!

READ THIS WAY

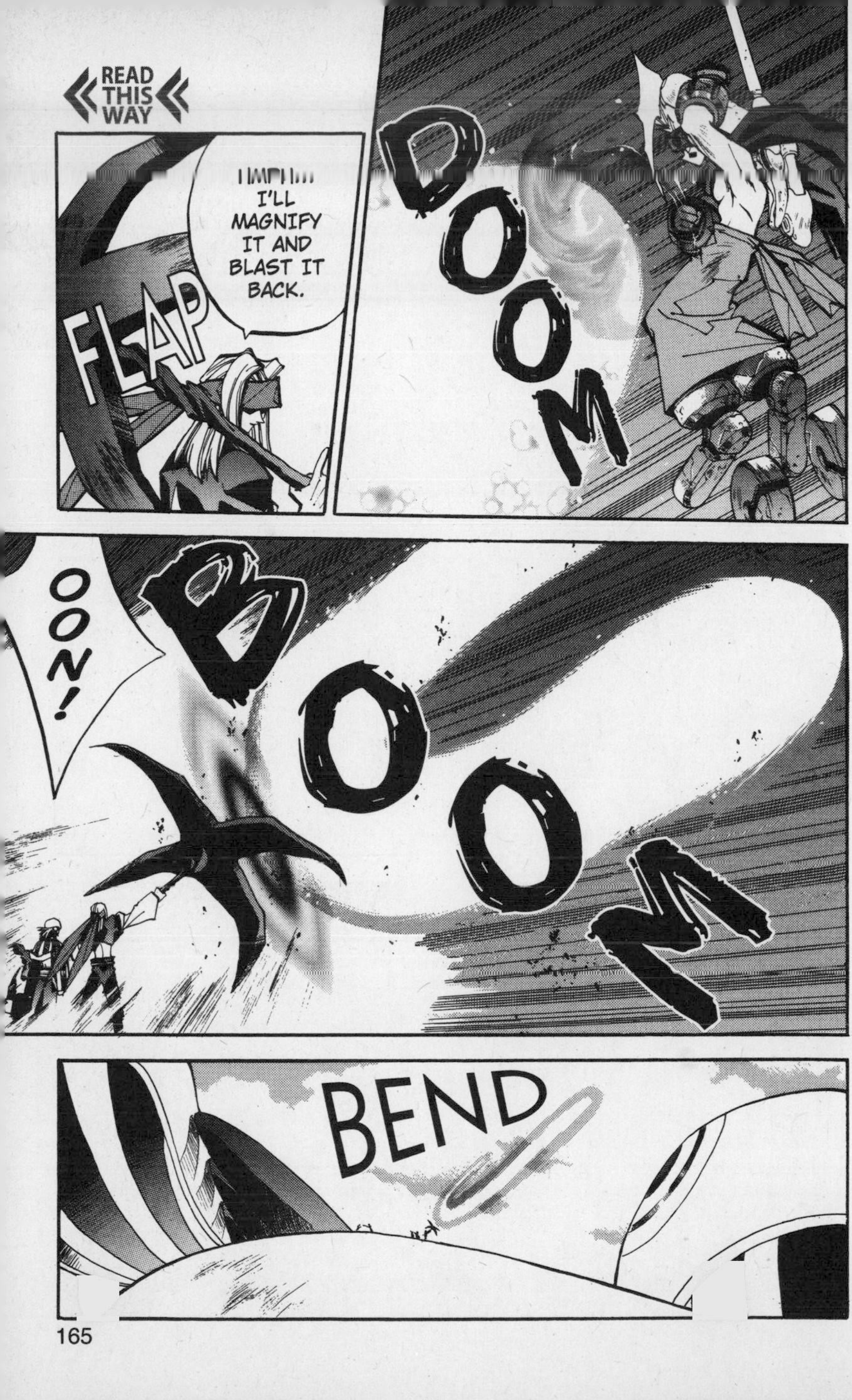
DOOOM
I'LL MAGNIFY IT AND BLAST IT BACK.
FLAP
BOOOM
OON!
BEND

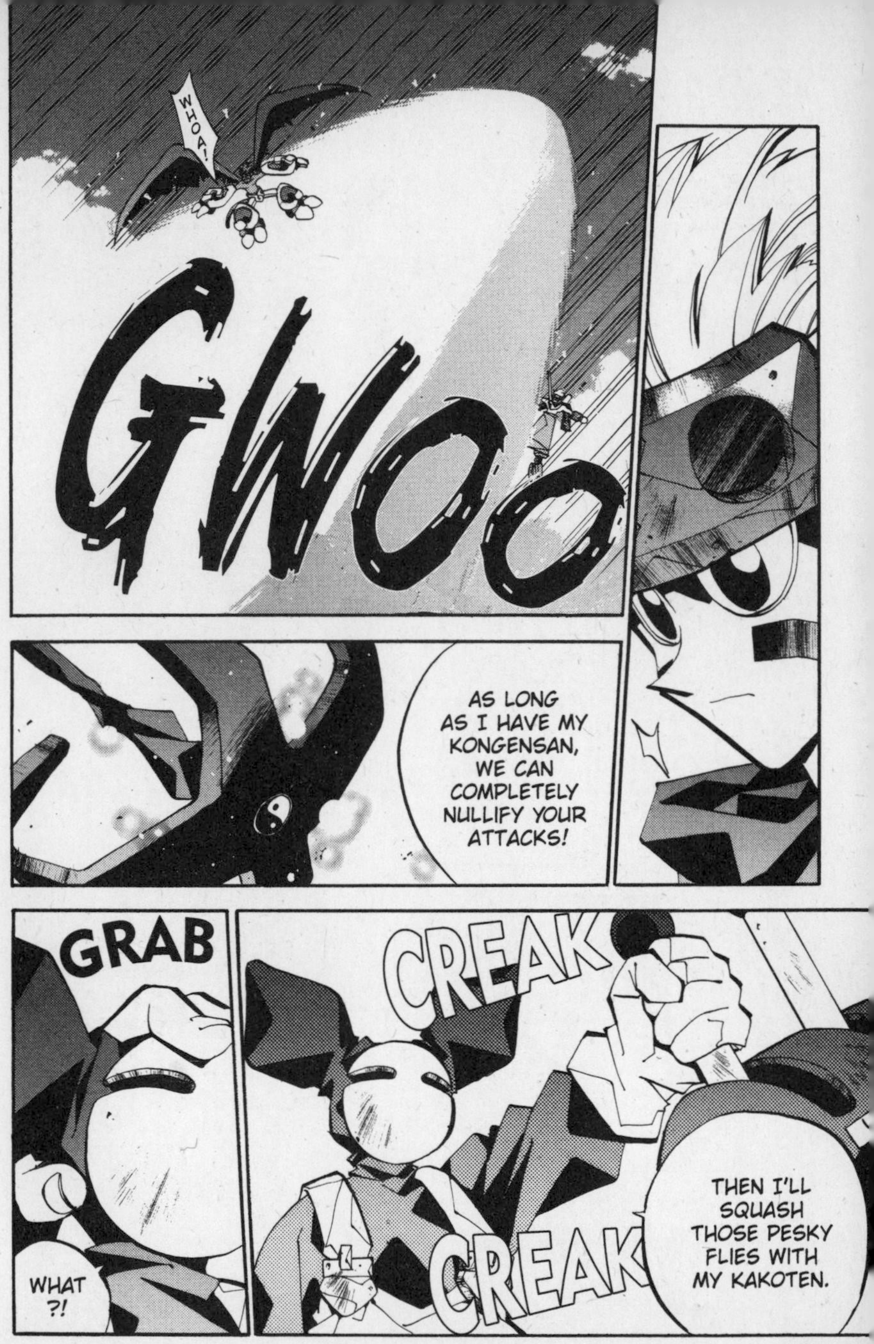
WHOA!
GWOO
AS LONG AS I HAVE MY KONGENSAN, WE CAN COMPLETELY NULLIFY YOUR ATTACKS!
CREAK
THEN I'LL SQUASH THOSE PESKY FLIES WITH MY KAKOTEN.
CREAK
GRAB
WHAT ?!

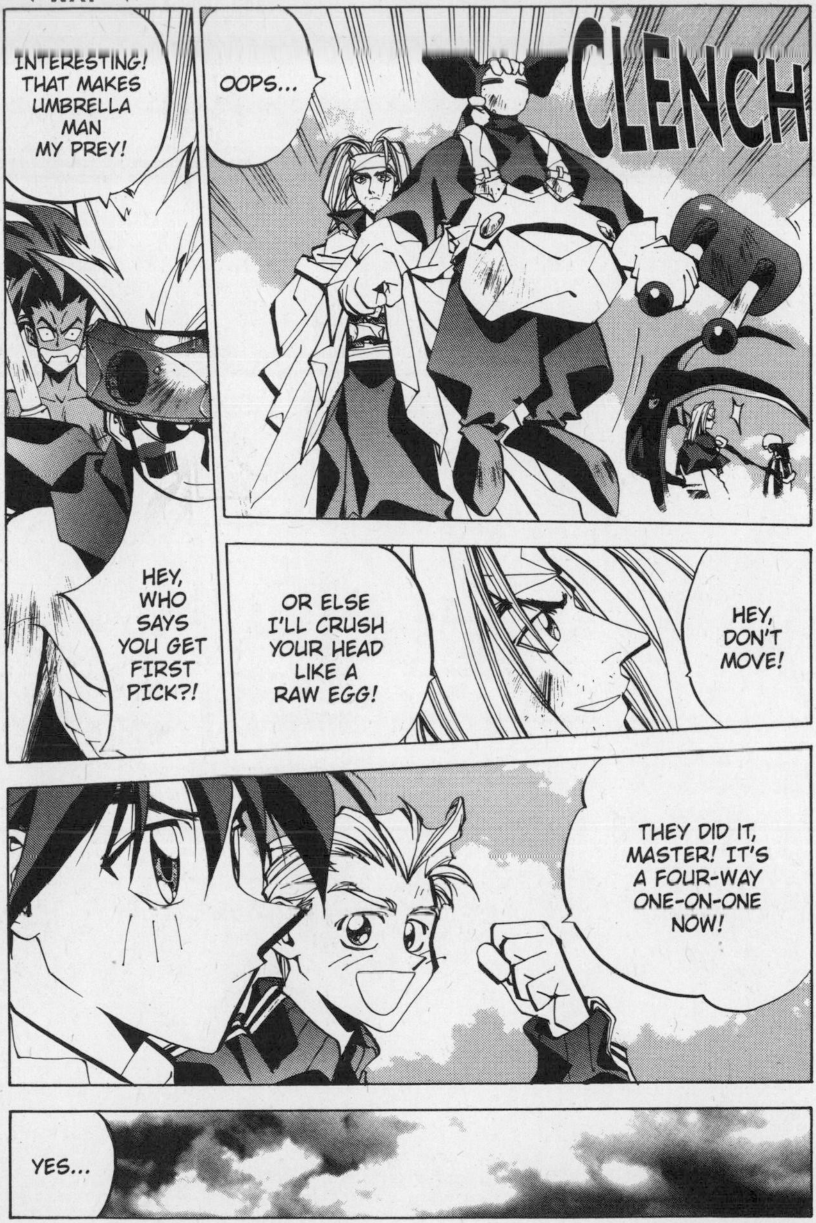
CLENCH
OOPS...
HEY, DON'T MOVE!
OR ELSE I'LL CRUSH YOUR HEAD LIKE A RAW EGG!
INTERESTING! THAT MAKES UMBRELLA MAN MY PREY!
HEY, WHO SAYS YOU GET FIRST PICK?!
THEY DID IT, MASTER! IT'S A FOUR-WAY ONE-ON-ONE NOW!
YES...

封神演義

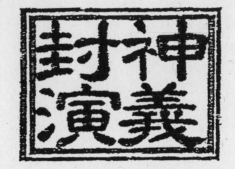

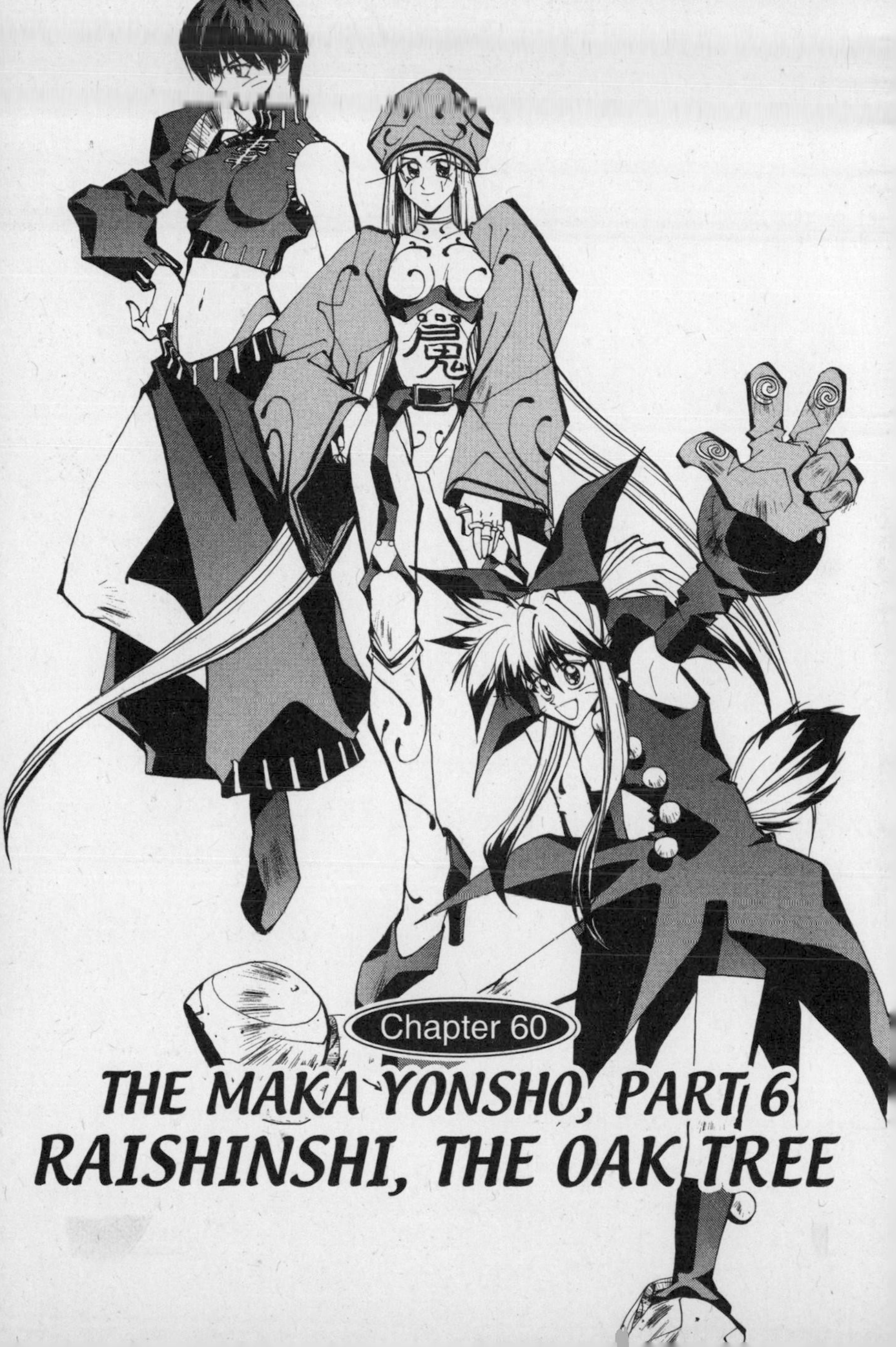

Chapter 60

THE MAKA YONSHO, PART 6
RAISHINSHI, THE OAK TREE

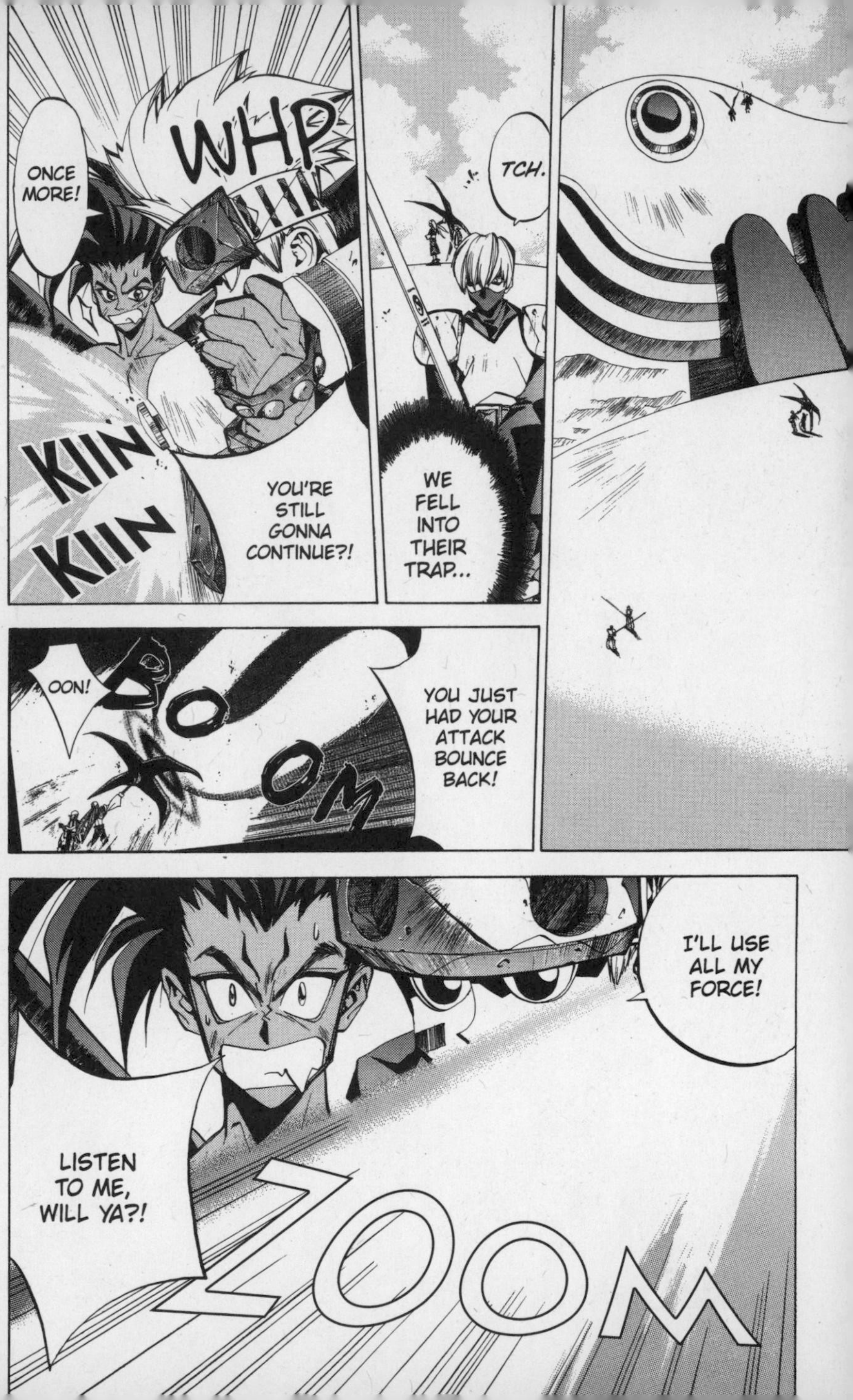
TCH.
WE FELL INTO THEIR TRAP...
WHP
ONCE MORE!
YOU'RE STILL GONNA CONTINUE?!
KIIN
KIIN
YOU JUST HAD YOUR ATTACK BOUNCE BACK!
OON!
I'LL USE ALL MY FORCE!
LISTEN TO ME, WILL YA?!
ZOOM

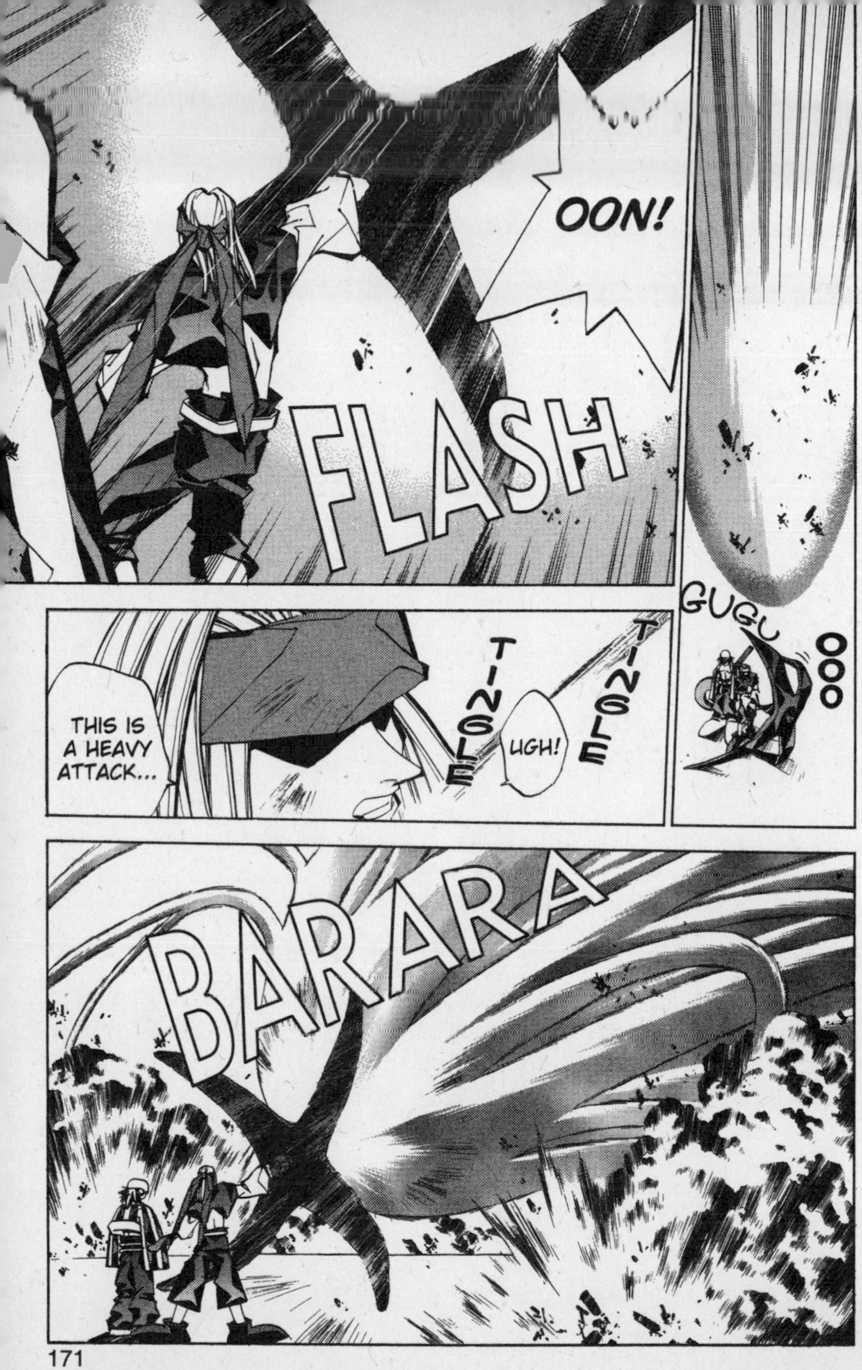
GUGU
OOO
OON!
FLASH
TINGLE
UGH!
TINGLE
THIS IS A HEAVY ATTACK...
BARARA

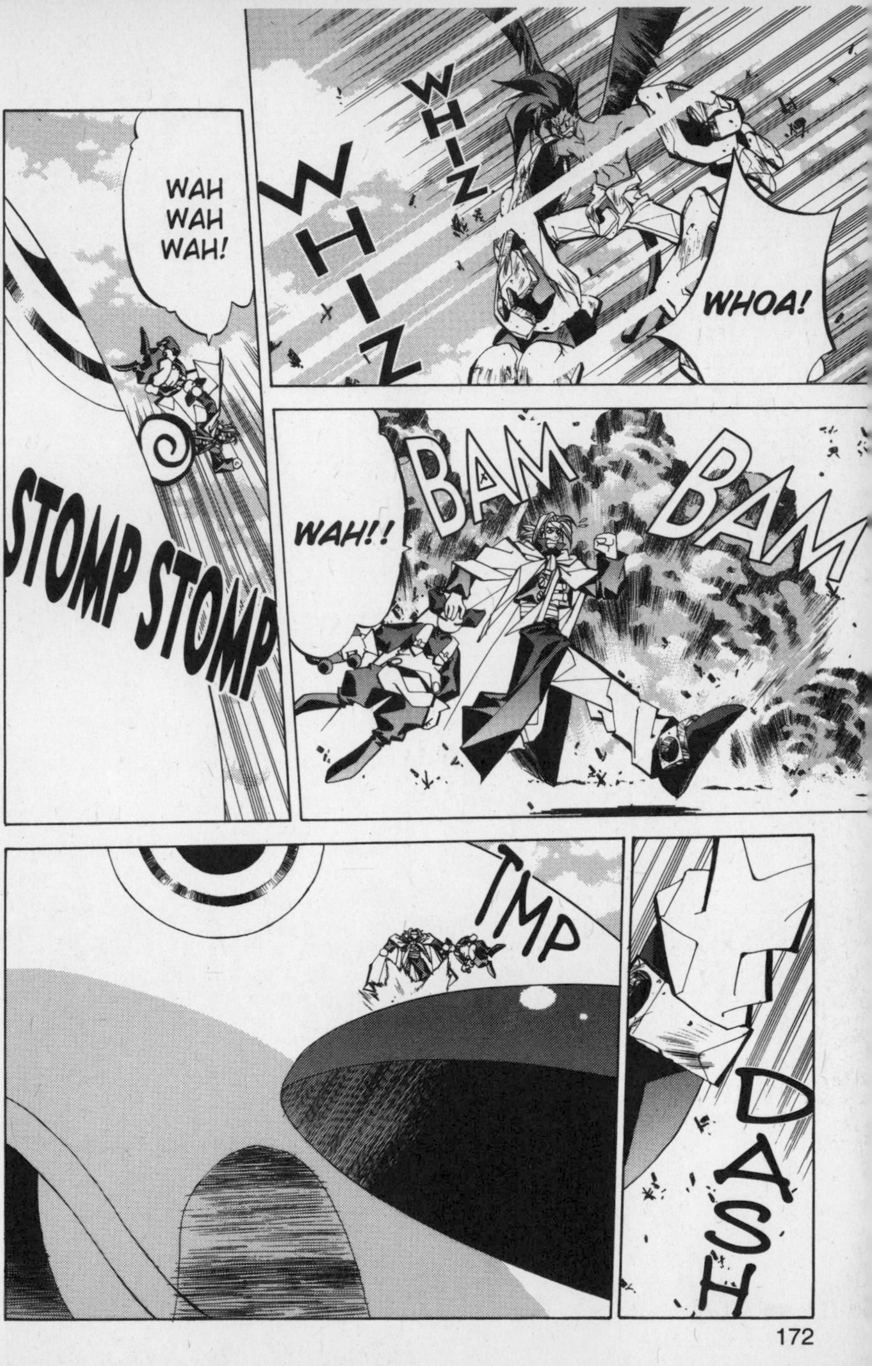
WHIZ WHIZ
WHOA!
BAM BAM
WAH!!
WAH WAH WAH!
STOMP STOMP
DASH
TMP

READ THIS WAY

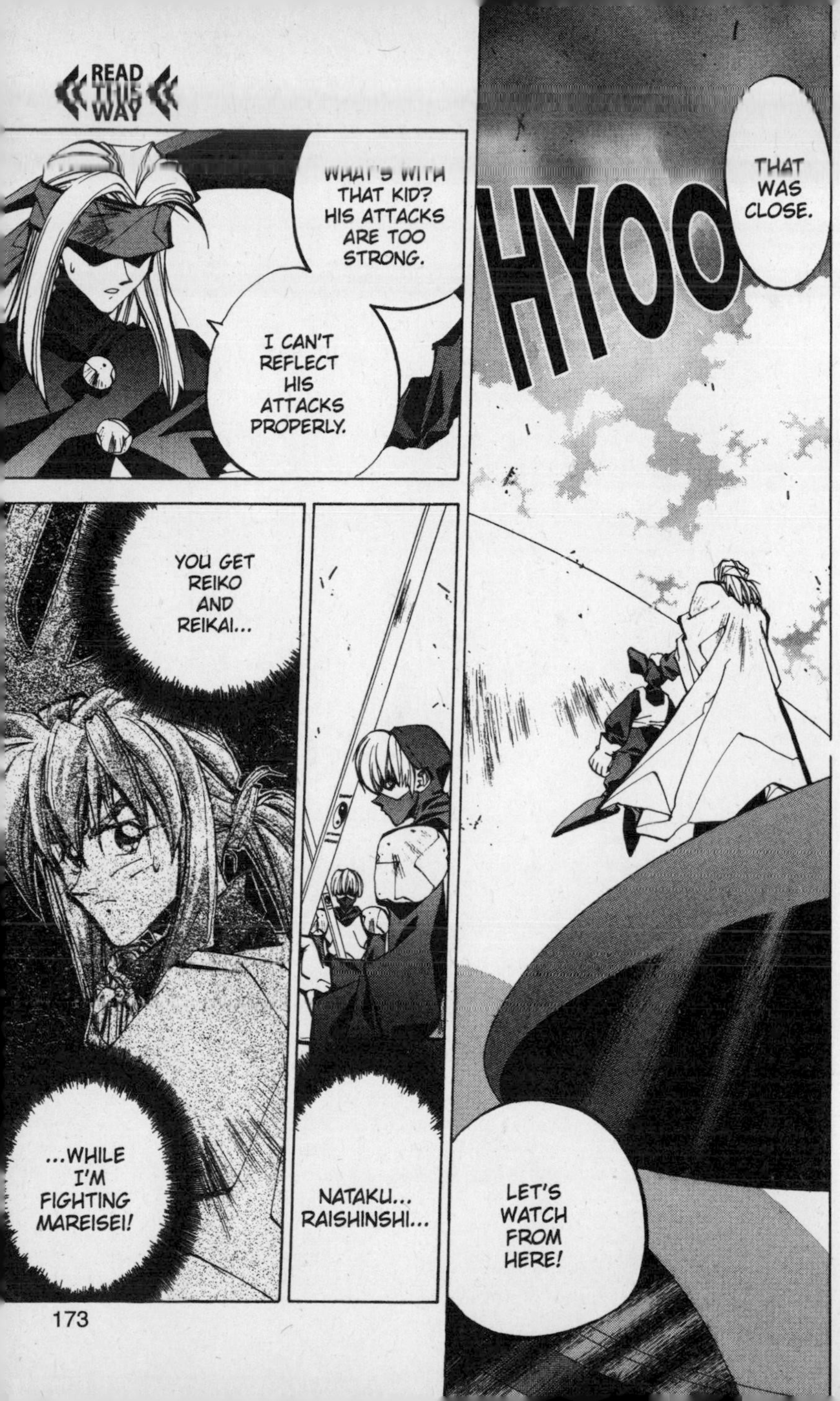
THAT WAS CLOSE.
HYOO
LET'S WATCH FROM HERE!
WHAT'S WITH THAT KID? HIS ATTACKS ARE TOO STRONG.
I CAN'T REFLECT HIS ATTACKS PROPERLY.
NATAKU... RAISHINSHI...
YOU GET REIKO AND REIKAI...
...WHILE I'M FIGHTING MAREISEI!

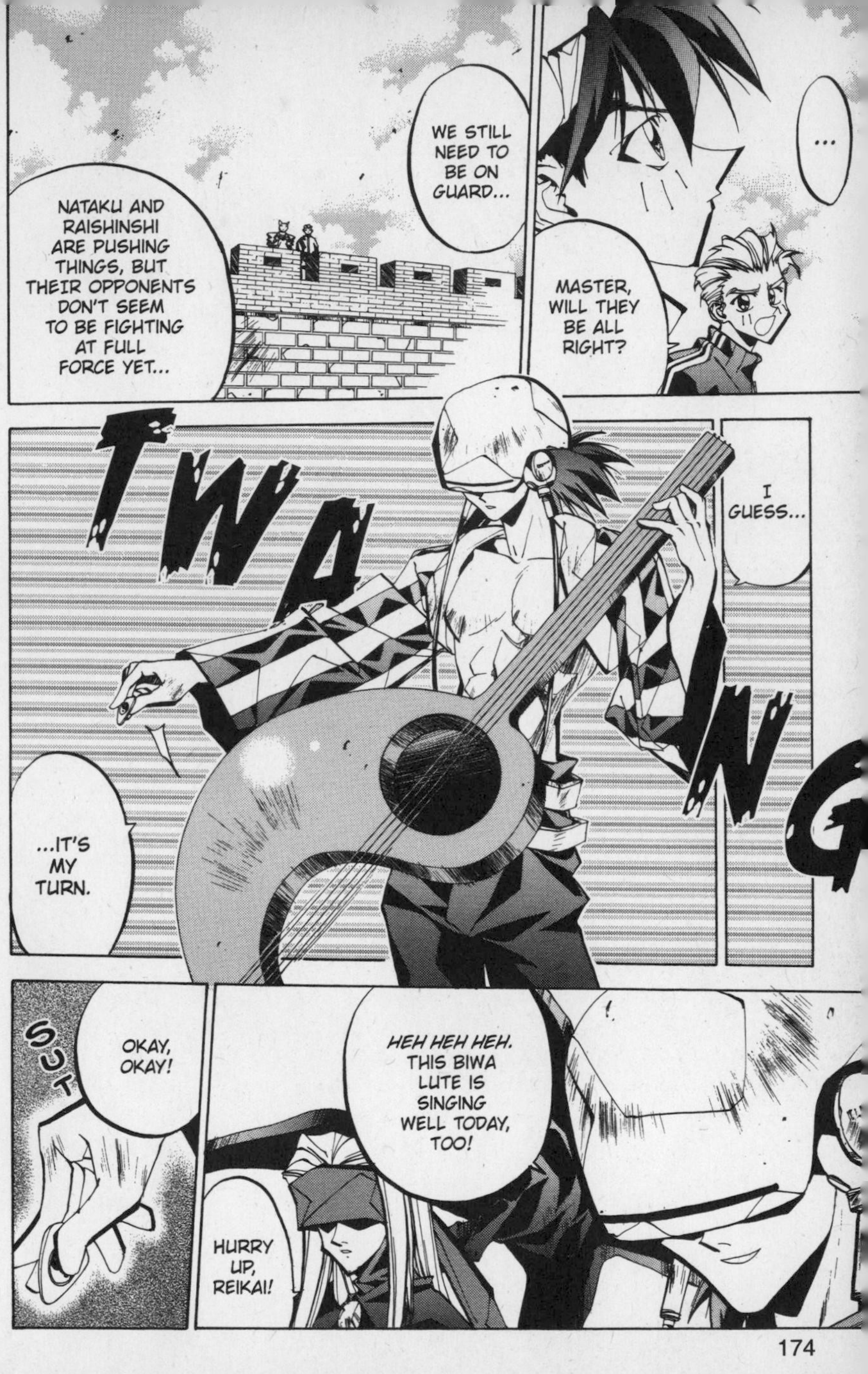
...
WE STILL NEED TO BE ON GUARD...
MASTER, WILL THEY BE ALL RIGHT?
NATAKU AND RAISHINSHI ARE PUSHING THINGS, BUT THEIR OPPONENTS DON'T SEEM TO BE FIGHTING AT FULL FORCE YET...
I GUESS...
TWANG
...IT'S MY TURN.
HEH HEH HEH. THIS BIWA LUTE IS SINGING WELL TODAY, TOO!
HURRY UP, REIKAI!
SUT
OKAY, OKAY!

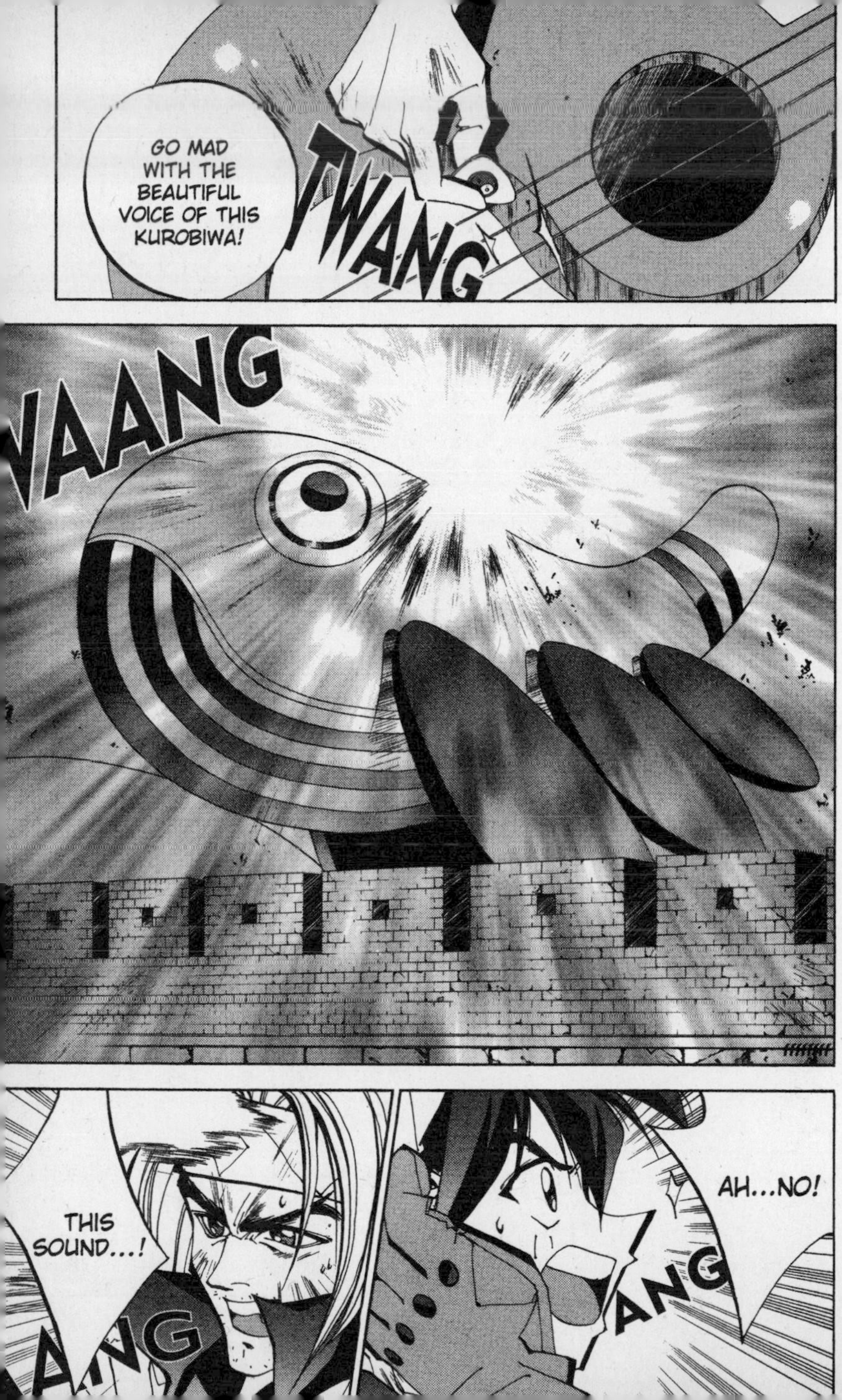
GO MAD WITH THE BEAUTIFUL VOICE OF THIS KUROBIWA!
TWANG
WAANG
AH...NO!
ANG
THIS SOUND...!
ANG

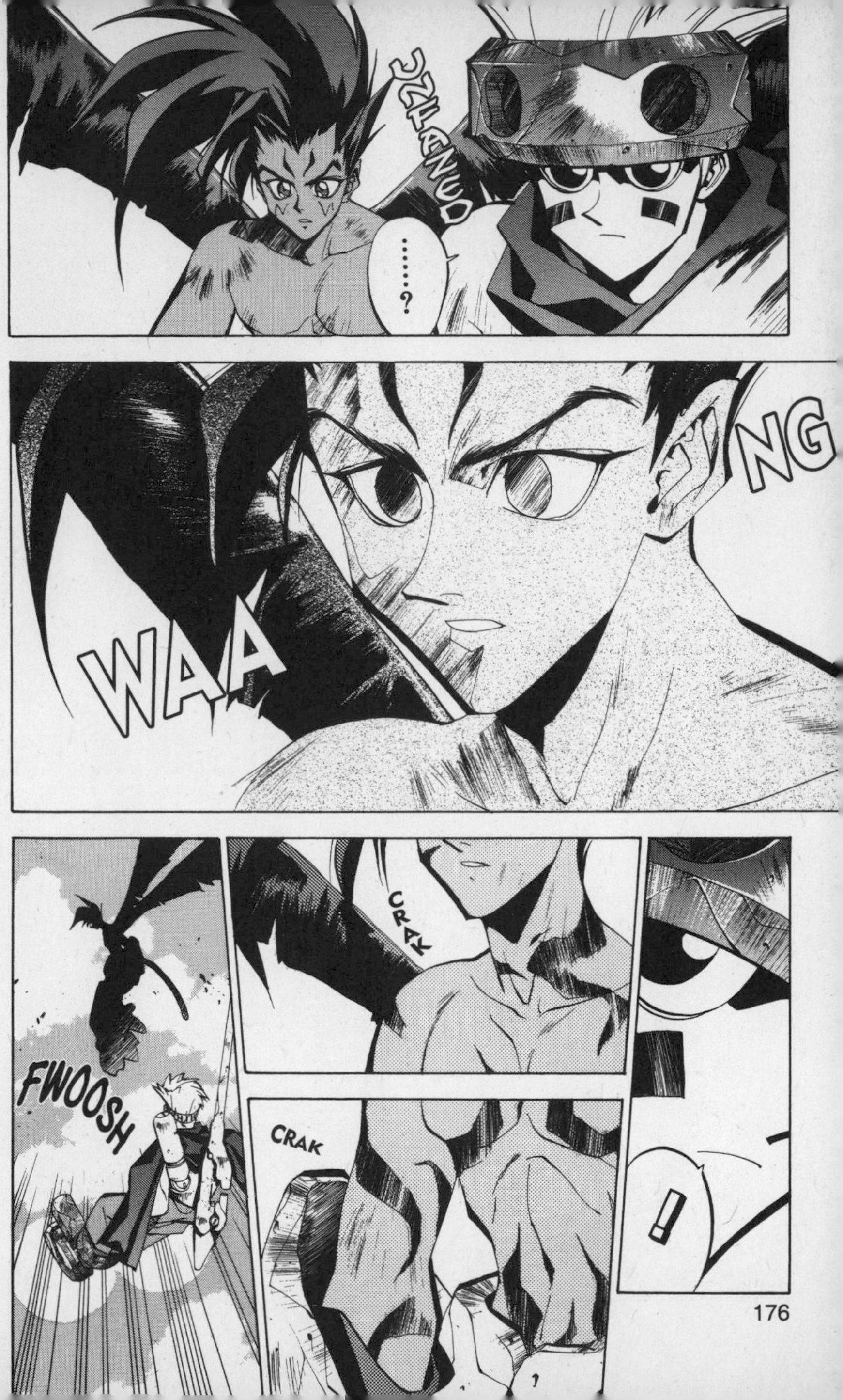
......?
WAA
NG
!
CRAK
CRAK
FWOOSH

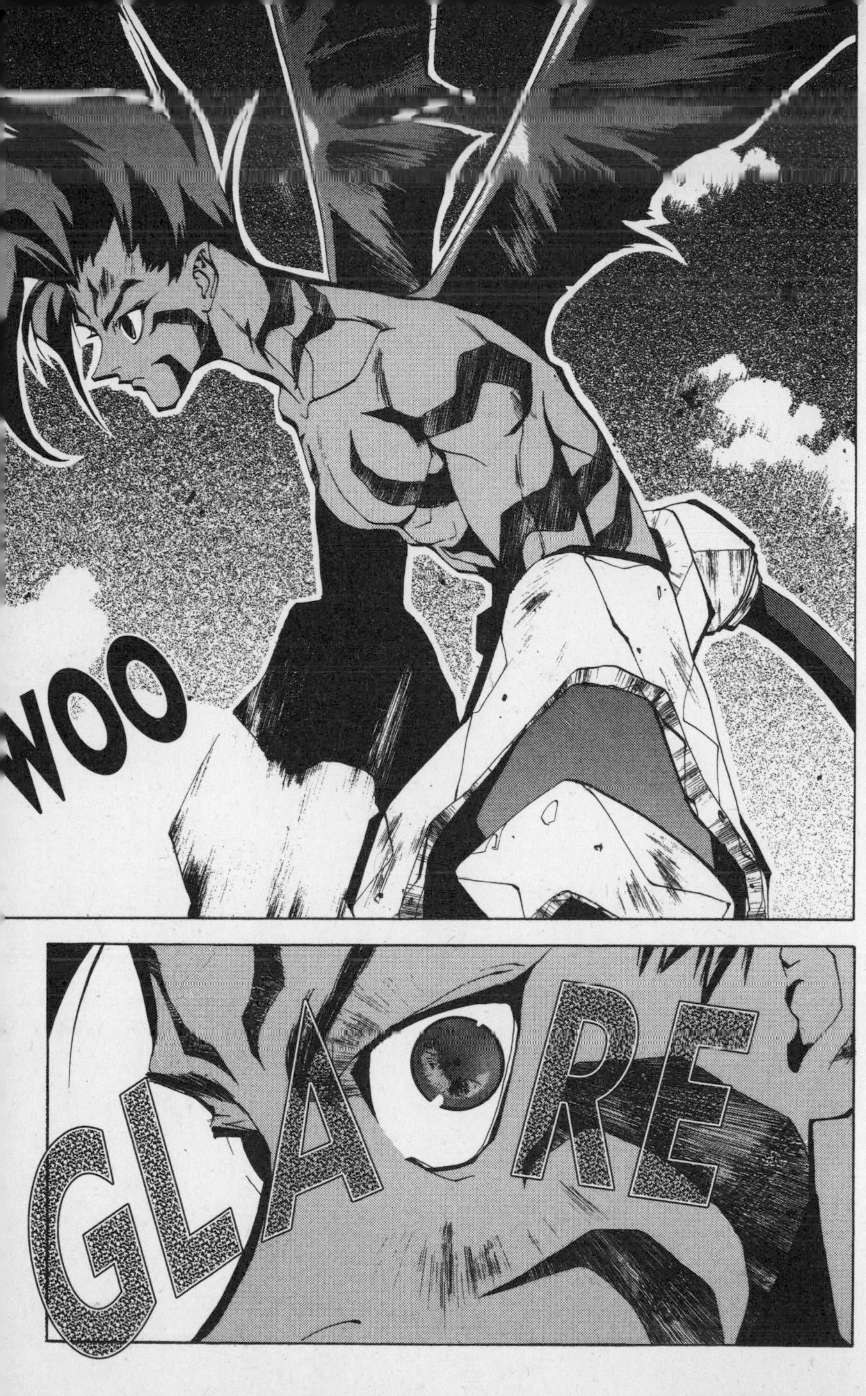
WOO
GLARE

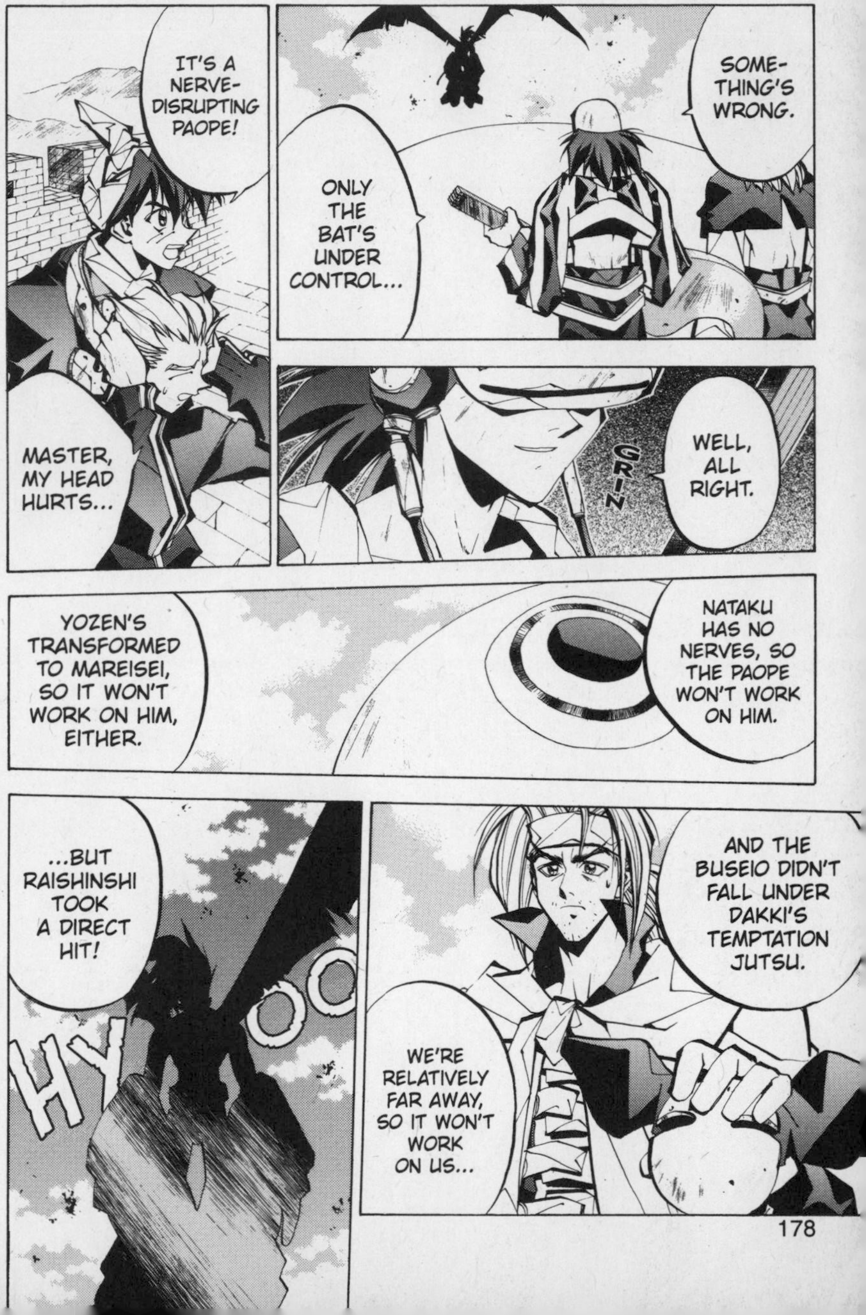
SOME-THING'S WRONG.
ONLY THE BAT'S UNDER CONTROL...
GRIN
WELL, ALL RIGHT.
IT'S A NERVE-DISRUPTING PAOPE!
MASTER, MY HEAD HURTS...
NATAKU HAS NO NERVES, SO THE PAOPE WON'T WORK ON HIM.
YOZEN'S TRANSFORMED TO MAREISEI, SO IT WON'T WORK ON HIM, EITHER.
AND THE BUSEIO DIDN'T FALL UNDER DAKKI'S TEMPTATION JUTSU.
WE'RE RELATIVELY FAR AWAY, SO IT WON'T WORK ON US...
...BUT RAISHINSHI TOOK A DIRECT HIT!
HYOO

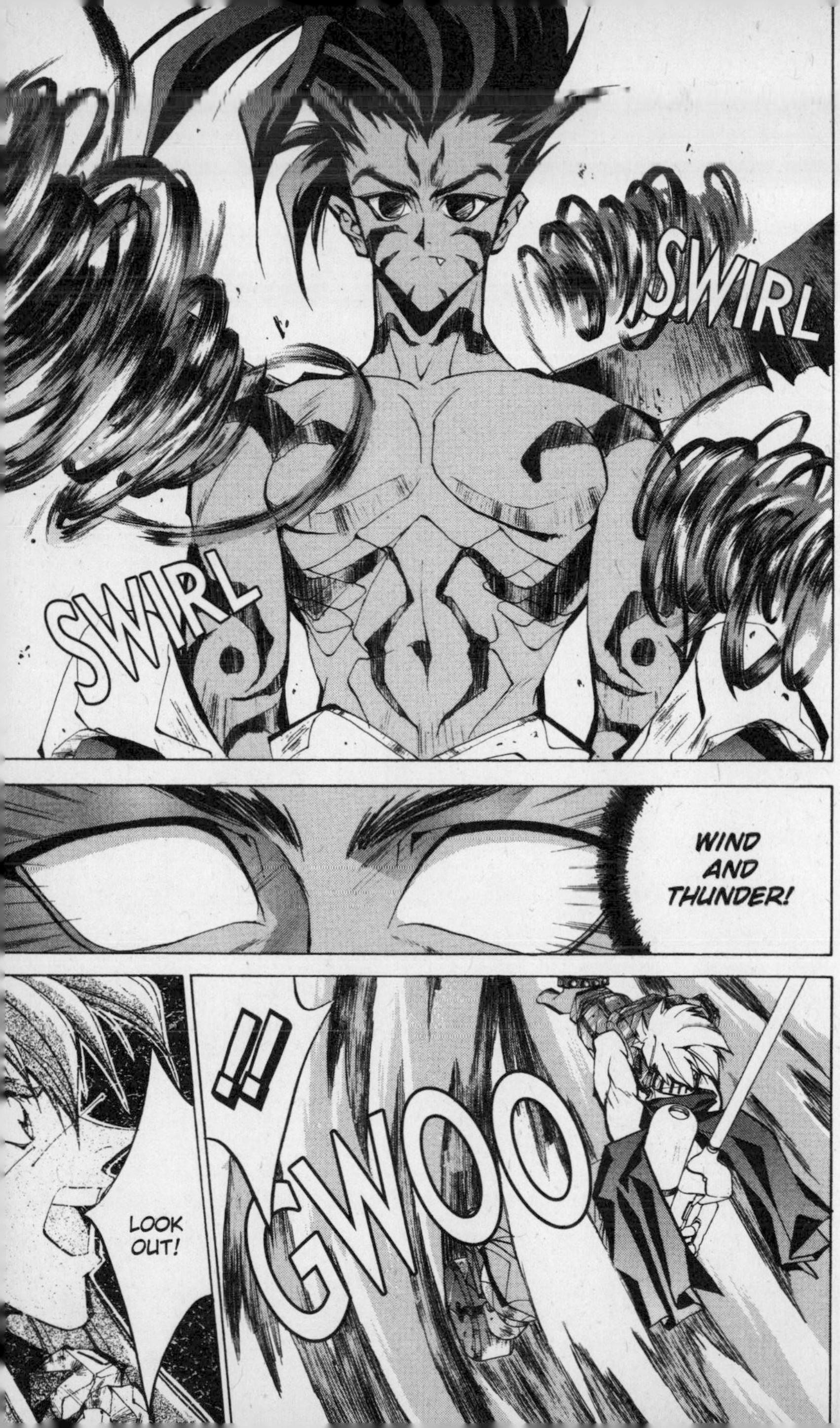
SWIRL
SWIRL
WIND AND THUNDER!
!!
GWOO
LOOK OUT!

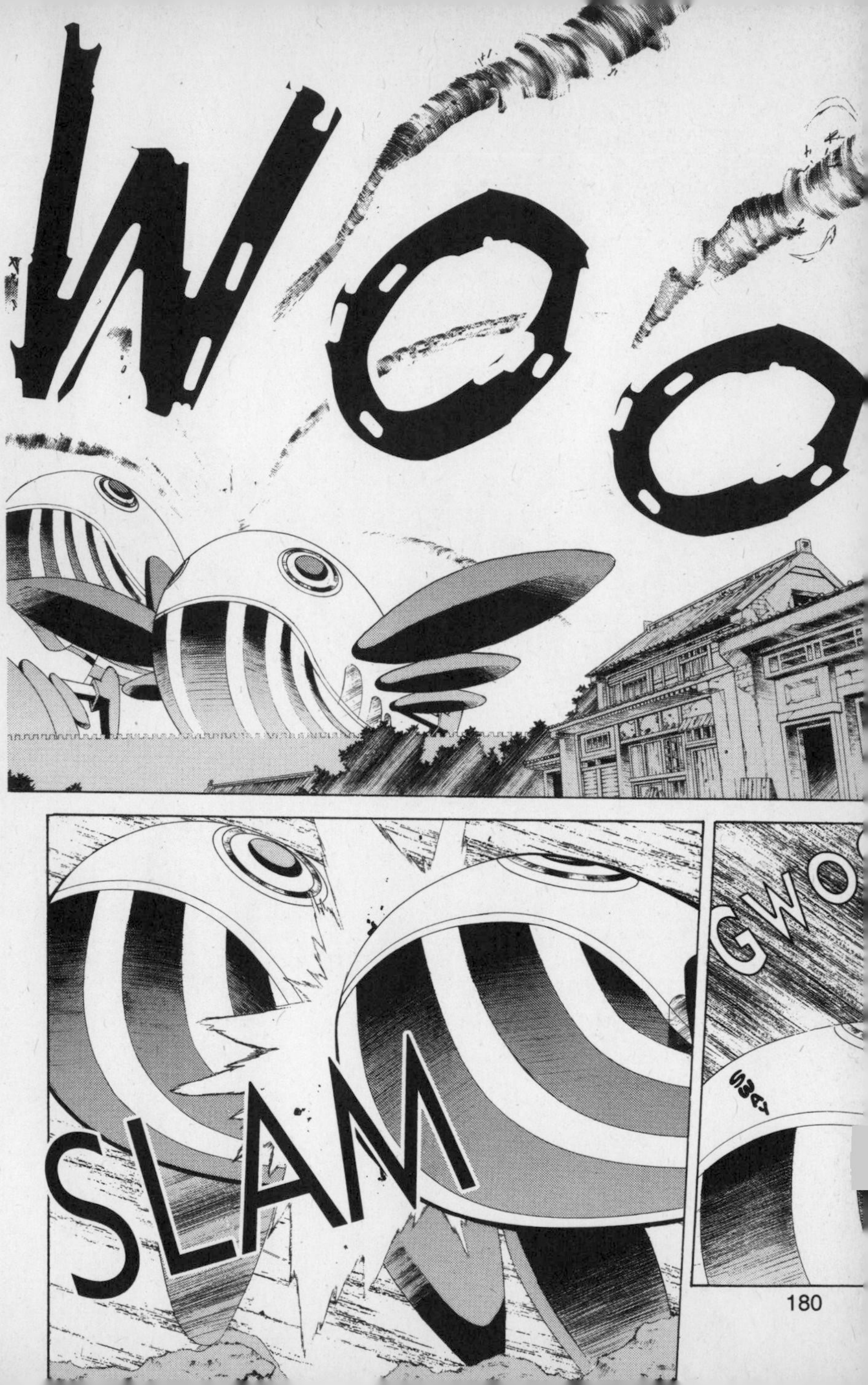
WOOO
GWO
SLAM

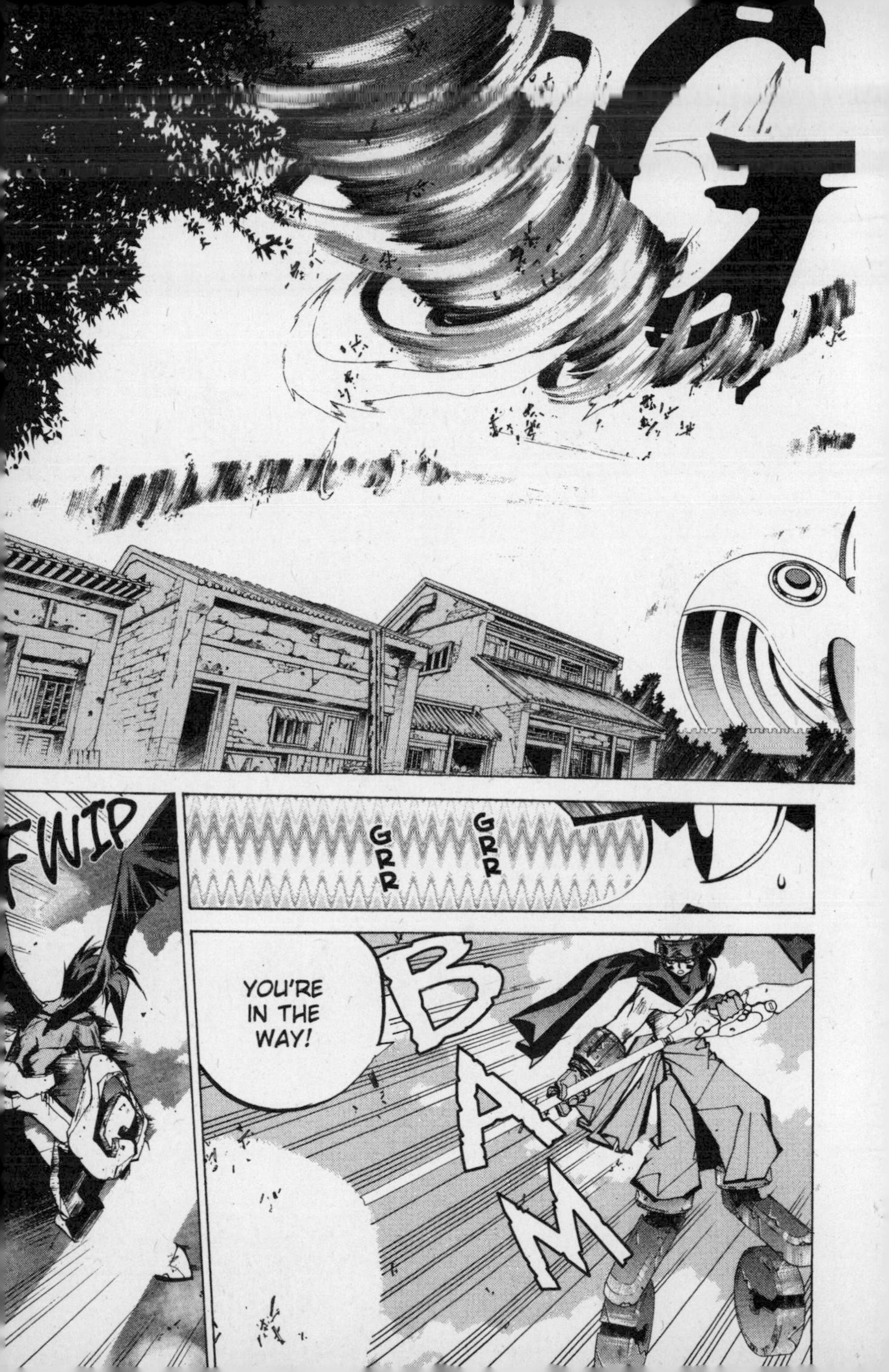
GRR GRR
YOU'RE IN THE WAY!
BAM
FWIP

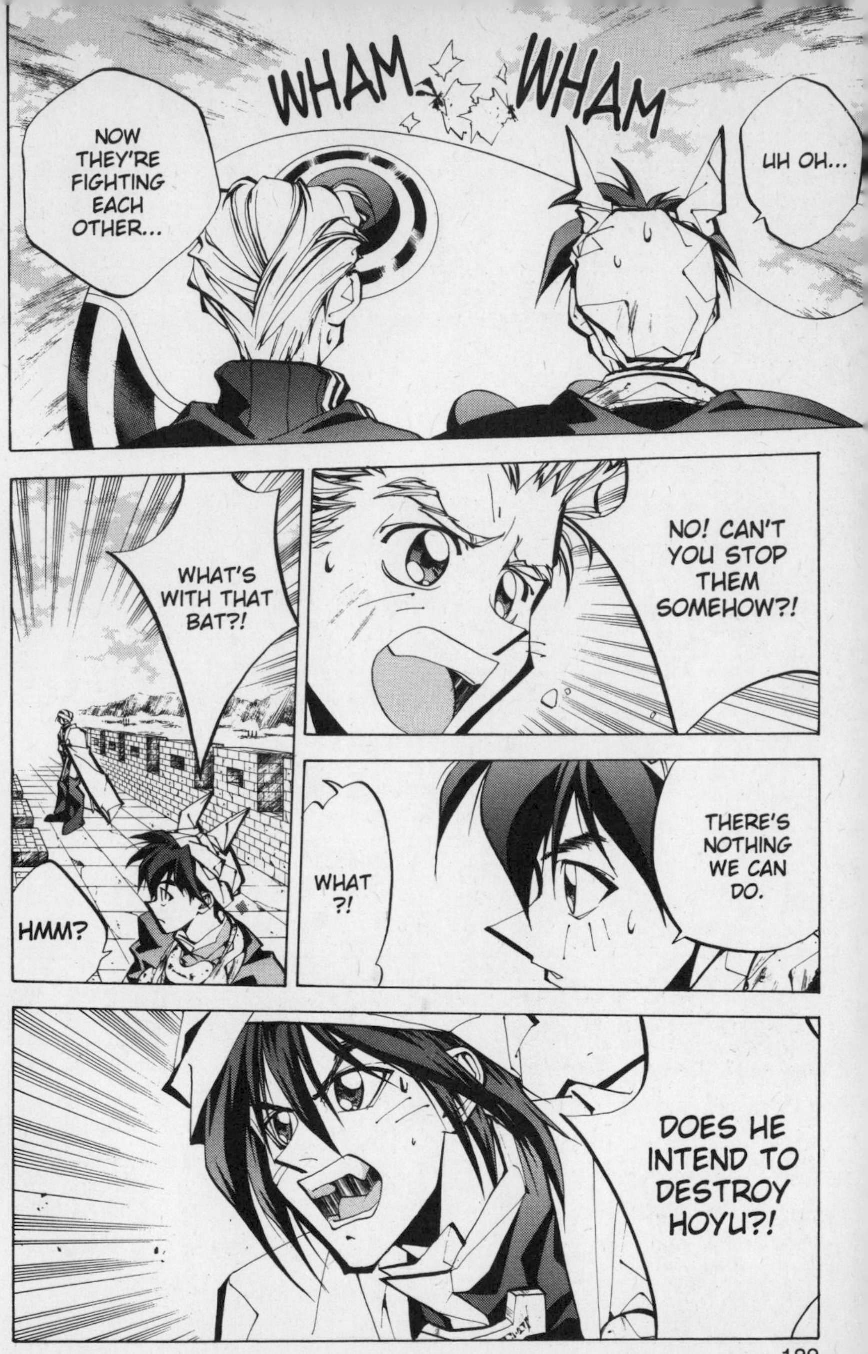
WHAM WHAM
UH OH...
NOW THEY'RE FIGHTING EACH OTHER...
NO! CAN'T YOU STOP THEM SOMEHOW?!
THERE'S NOTHING WE CAN DO.
WHAT?!
WHAT'S WITH THAT BAT?!
HMM?
DOES HE INTEND TO DESTROY HOYU?!

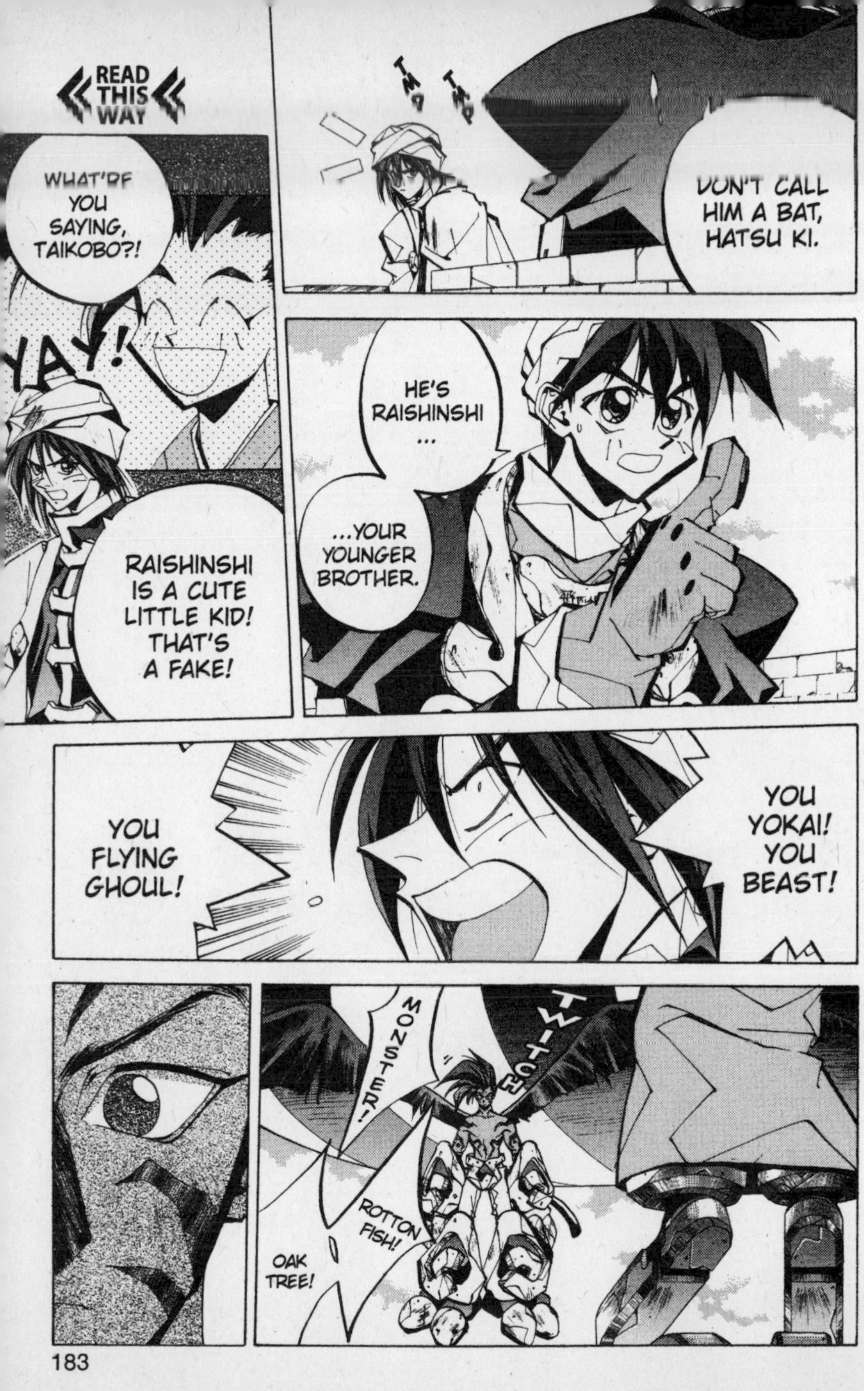
READ THIS WAY
TMP
TMP
DON'T CALL HIM A BAT, HATSU KI.
HE'S RAISHINSHI ...
...YOUR YOUNGER BROTHER.
WHAT'RE YOU SAYING, TAIKOBO?!
AY!
RAISHINSHI IS A CUTE LITTLE KID! THAT'S A FAKE!
YOU YOKAI! YOU BEAST!
YOU FLYING GHOUL!
TWITCH
MONSTER!
ROTTON FISH!
OAK TREE!

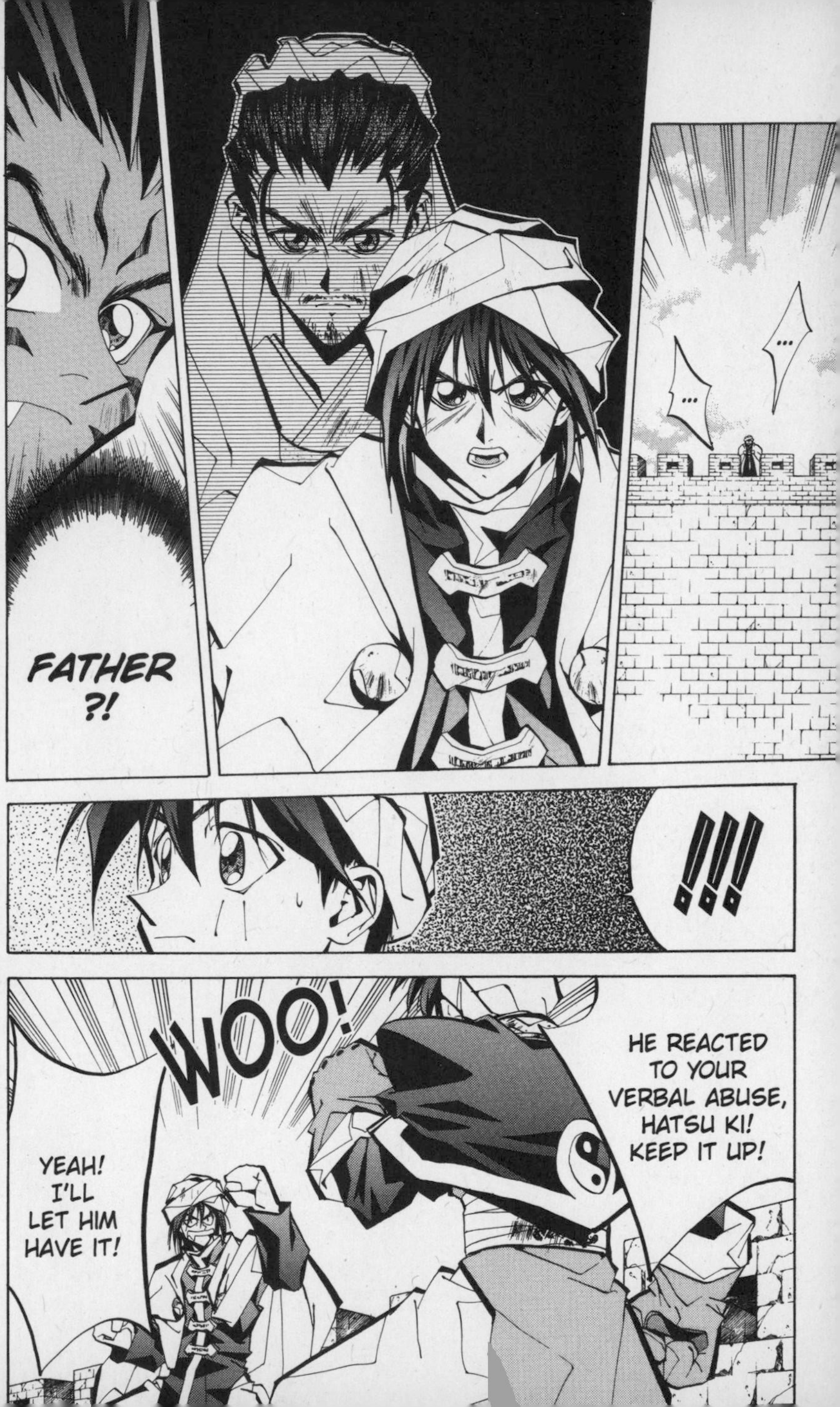
...
...
FATHER ?!
!!!
HE REACTED TO YOUR VERBAL ABUSE, HATSU KI! KEEP IT UP!
WOO!
YEAH! I'LL LET HIM HAVE IT!

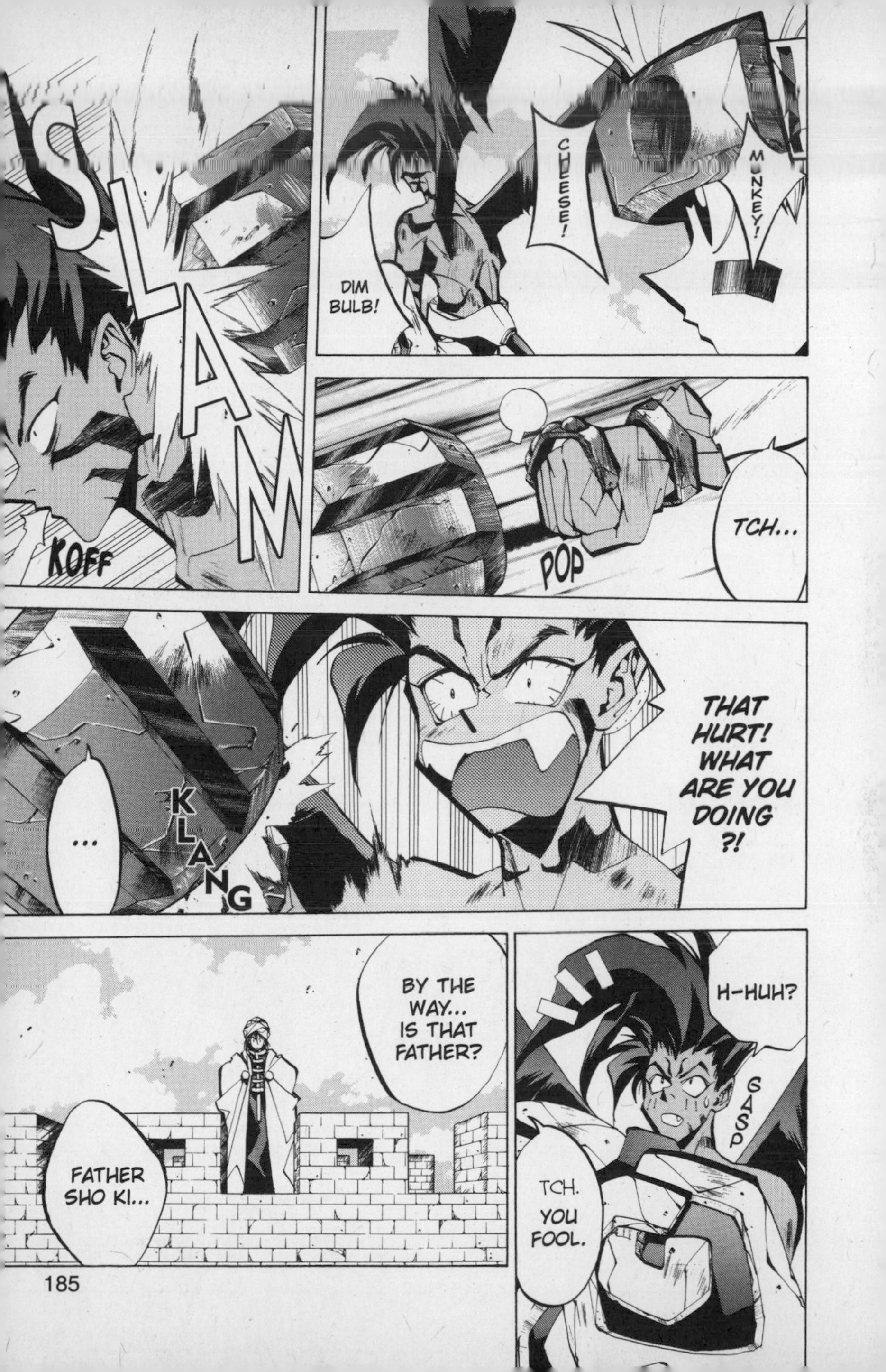
MONKEY!
CHEESE!
DIM BULB!
TCH...
POP
SLAM
KOFF
THAT HURT! WHAT ARE YOU DOING ?!
KLANG
...
H-HUH?
GASP
TCH. YOU FOOL.
BY THE WAY... IS THAT FATHER?
FATHER SHO KI...

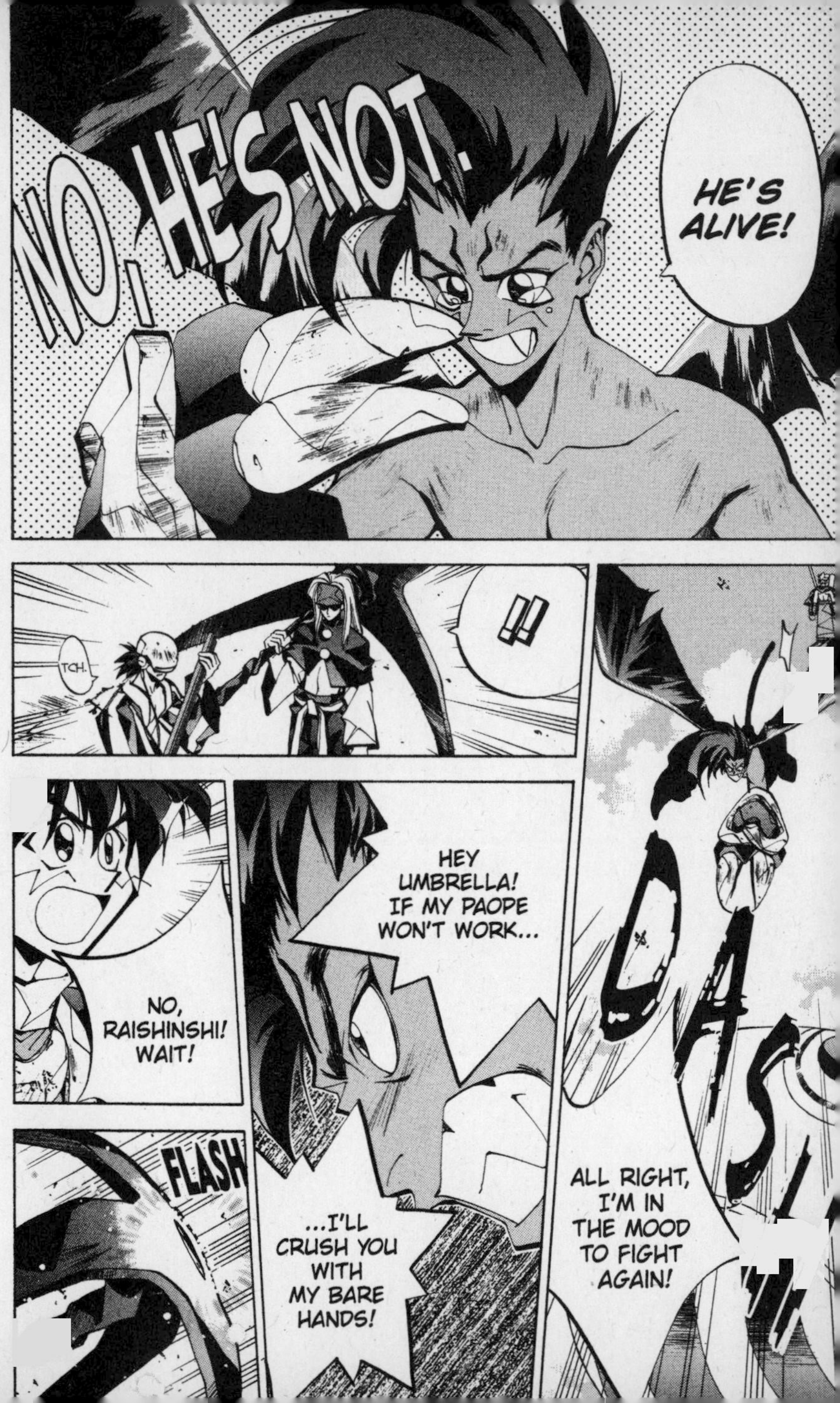
HE'S ALIVE!
NO, HE'S NOT.
DASH
ALL RIGHT, I'M IN THE MOOD TO FIGHT AGAIN!
!!
TCH.
HEY UMBRELLA! IF MY PAOPE WON'T WORK...
...I'LL CRUSH YOU WITH MY BARE HANDS!
NO, RAISHINSHI! WAIT!
FLASH

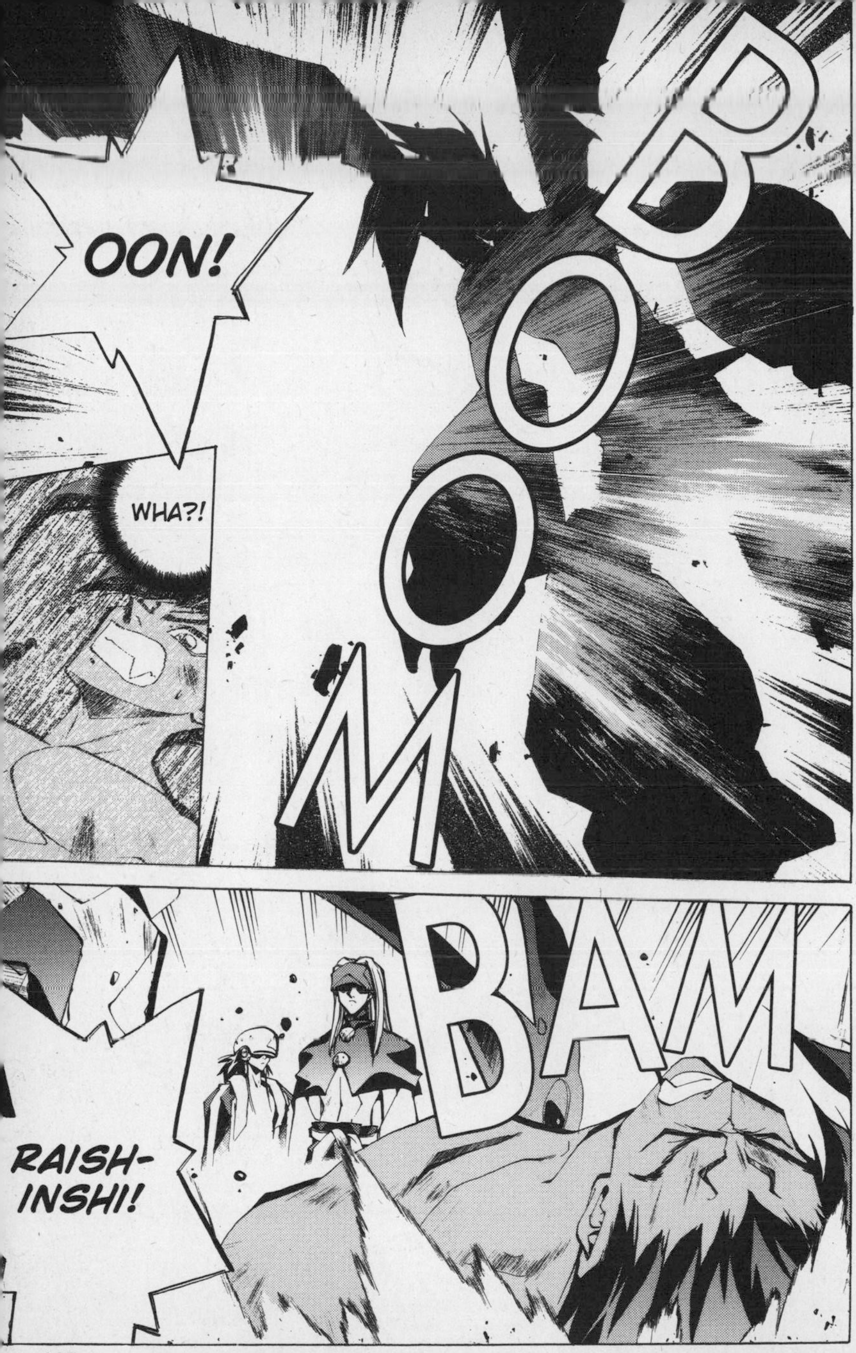
BOOM
OON!
WHA?!
BAM
RAISH-
INSHI!

HOSHIN ENGI, VOL. 7 - THE END

封神演義

Hoshin Engi Grand Travelogue!!!

Weekly Jump **Version**

Confidential Materials! The origin of *Hoshin* is in China!!

This past July, Fujisaki-sensei traveled to China for research! We covered his trip in detail in *Akamaru Jump, Weekly Jump's* supplementary issue. In *Weekly Jump,* we cover additional information that is being published for the first time!!

File 1 Taikobo Was Sealed!

Locally, he is considered a Taoist Deity.

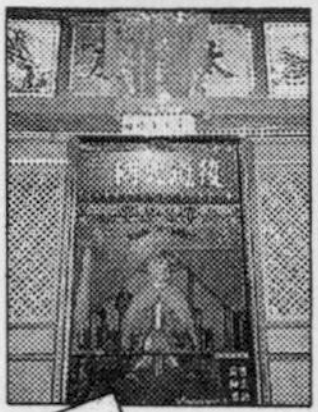

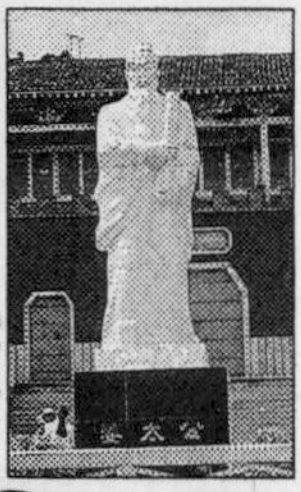

▼ At the entrance of Diaoyutai is a statue of Taikobo about five meters tall. The place is famous as a tourist attraction.

▲ Taikobo is enshrined in the sacred temple. He looks like a genial old man.

Diaoyutai is located in Baoji, near the ancient capital of Xian. Surprisingly, Taikobo is enshrined as the local god. What we found *there* was...

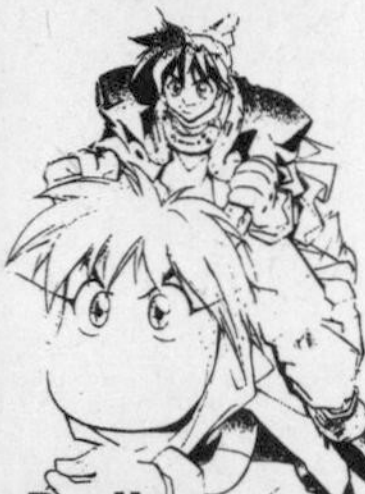

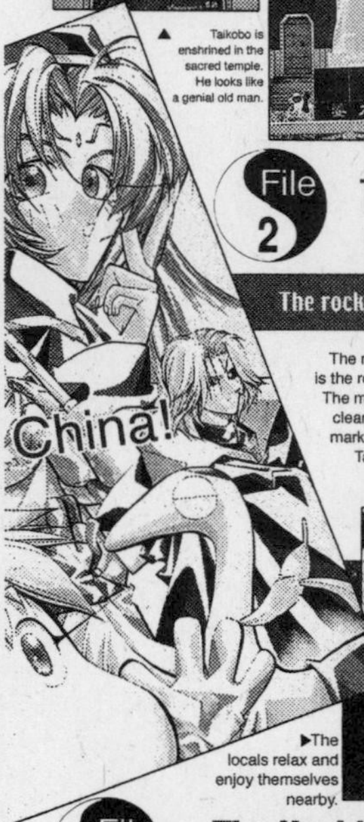
China!

File 2 Taikobo Really Loved Fishing!

The rock Taikobo sat on exists in China!!

The must-see at Diaoyutai is the rock that Taikobo sat on. The marks his thighs left are clearly visible.From those marks,we can imagine that Taikobo was a very well-built man.

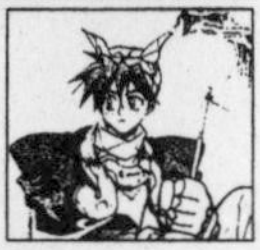

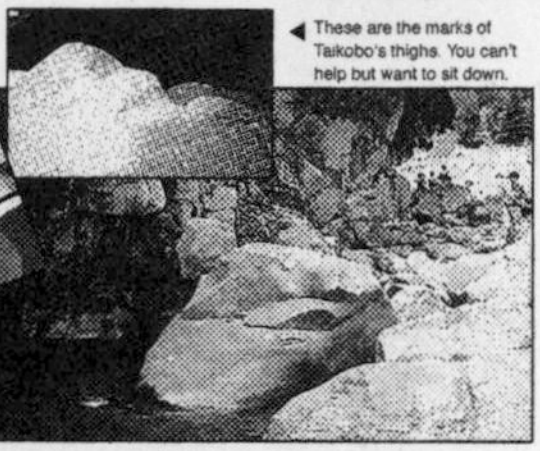

◀ These are the marks of Taikobo's thighs. You can't help but want to sit down.

▶The locals relax and enjoy themselves nearby.

File 3 The Hoshindai Exists, Too!

It's so new, you wouldn't think it has existed for 3000 years!!

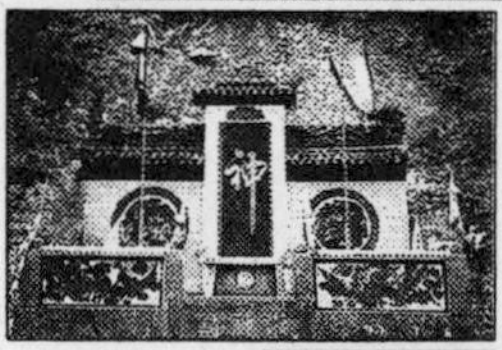

The Hoshindai, where Sendo were sealed by gods during the war between Yin and Zhou, exists at the Diaoyutai. It is new, and doesn't look as if it's existed for 3000 years, but it's one of the main tourist attractions. There are carvings of animals of the Chinese zodiac around the Hoshindai, and the atmosphere is sacred.

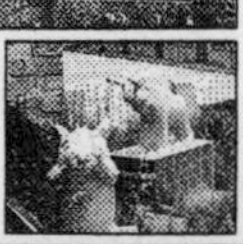

▲▶ It is more like a monument related to *Hoshin Engi* rather than a historic structure. You need to pay an entrance fee.

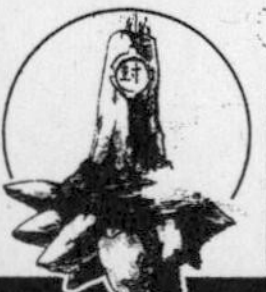

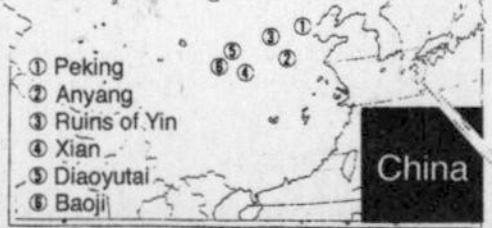
① Peking
② Anyang
③ Ruins of Yin
④ Xian
⑤ Diaoyutai
⑥ Baoji
China

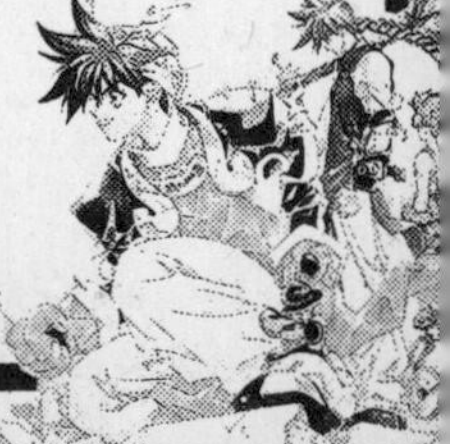

This article was originally published in Weekly Shonen Jump, No. 44, 1997.

Chinese Manga versus Japanese Manga!!
Which do you prefer?!
A comparison of *Hoshin* characters!!

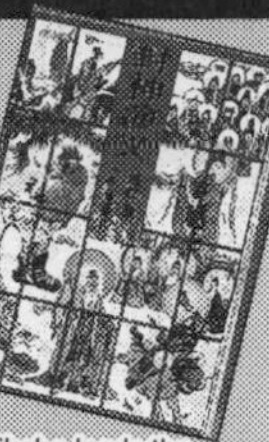

Several translations of *Hoshin Engi* are available in Japan. In China, the story is adapted for young people as well as for children. In Peking, we bought the version published by Shonen Jido Shuppansha.

1. Taikobo: Taikobo leads the Seiki army to subjugate Choka. (In the original, Taikobo is Shiga Kyo.) He looks like an old man. Does he look depressed because he's afraid of the Choka army?

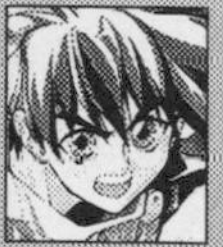

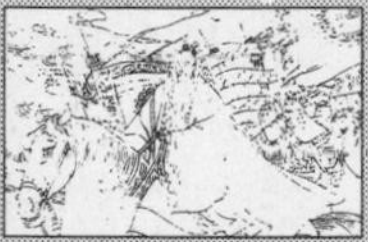

2. Dakki: The Chinese version of Dakki is surprisingly a simple-looking beauty. The Fujisaki version of Dakki is sexier, but when you consider that her original form is a fox, the Chinese version looks more like it...

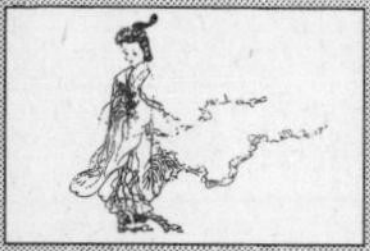

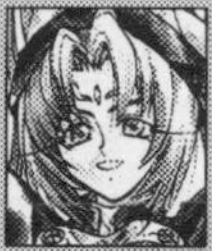

3. Nataku: The battle between Nataku and Chokeiho. The Fujisaki version portrays it in Chapter 35 (Volume 5). Pay attention to the difference in paope such as the Kenkonken, Fukarin, and Kasenso rather than the difference in their looks.

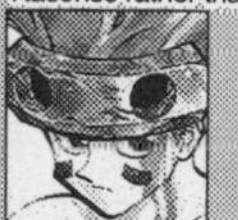

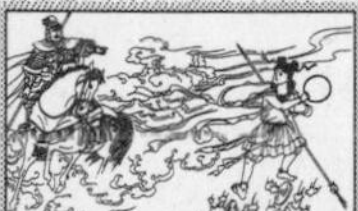

4. Yozen: The battle between Yozen and Kakoten. Kakoten is of course the paope of Mareiju, one of the Maka Yonsho. The Chinese version of Yozen is manly and dignified. He is different from the Fujisaki version, but it makes sense that he is so popular...

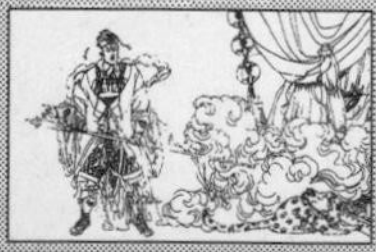

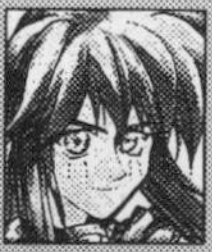

File 4 Seiki's Cuisine Depends on "Paste!"

Seiki's cuisine is hotter than Choka's? This is an episode from Chapter 48 (Volume 6). With Xian cuisine, paste is placed at the side as seasoning...as you can tell from the photo, the food all looks really hot.

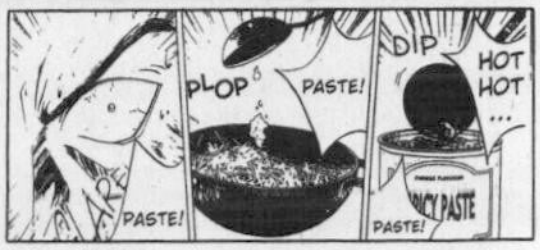

PLOP
PASTE!
DIP
HOT HOT ...
PASTE!
PASTE!

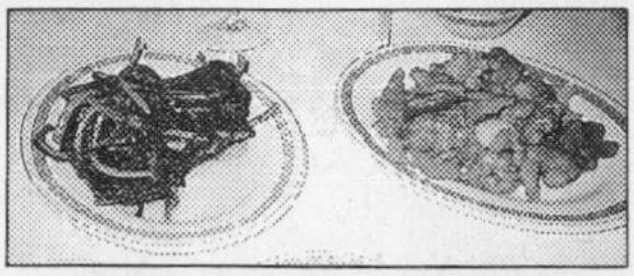

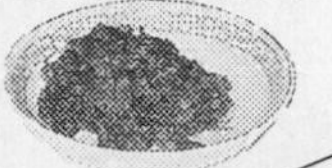

◀▼ When we ate the foods, they weren't as hot as they looked. The paste itself was pretty hot, though.

File 5 Was There a Model for Young Bunchu's Comrade, Shushi?

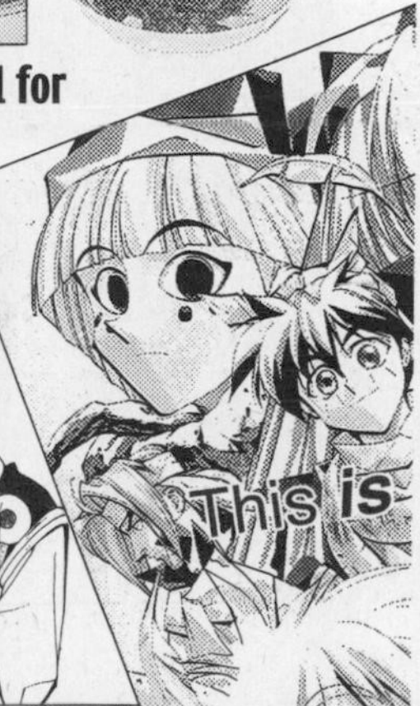

This is

The fighting queen! The grave of Yin's queen, Fuko was in the Ruins of Yin!!

Shushi, was the queen who appeared as Bunchu's comrade in Chapter 51 (Volume 6) and fought beside the king on the battlefield. She is modeled after Fuko, who is enshrined in the Ruins of Yin in Anyang.

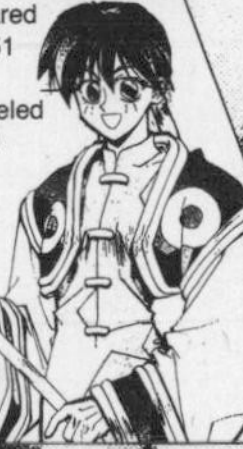

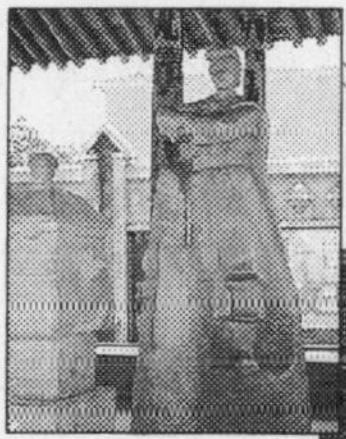

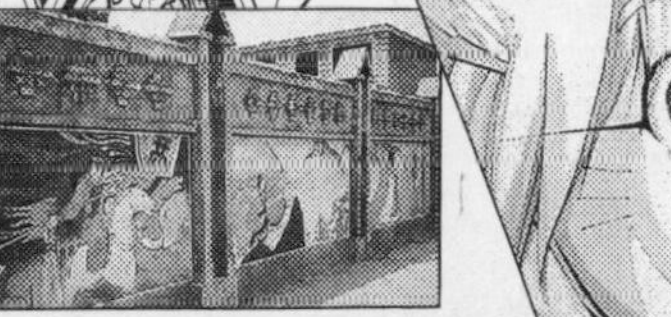

▲▶ Fuko was a queen as well as a warrior. Her accomplishments are recorded on statues and murals.

File 6 A Coincidence?! The Designs of Reiju!

Shin'yo and Kokutenko lived in the Yin era?!

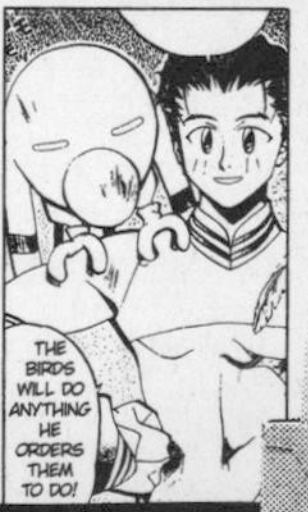

THE BIRDS WILL DO ANYTHING HE ORDERS THEM TO DO!

Shin'yo is the Reiju that Su Kokuko, the acting Hokuhakuko, uses in Chapter 52. There are common features with the statues in the Ruins of Yin in the original roundness of the design.

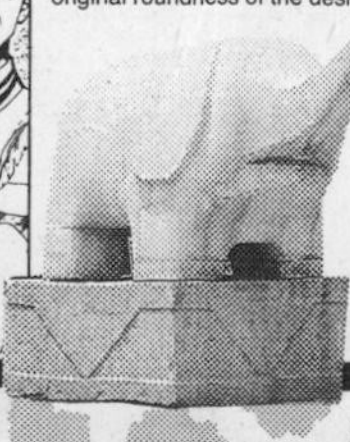

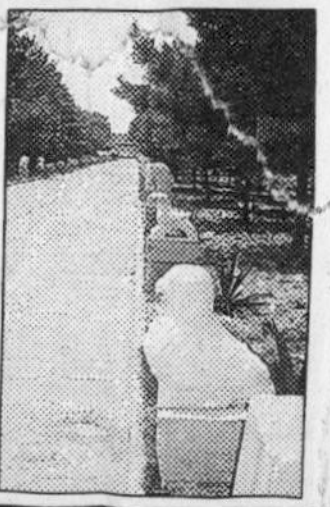

◀▶ There are lots of statues that look like Supushan and Kokutenko.

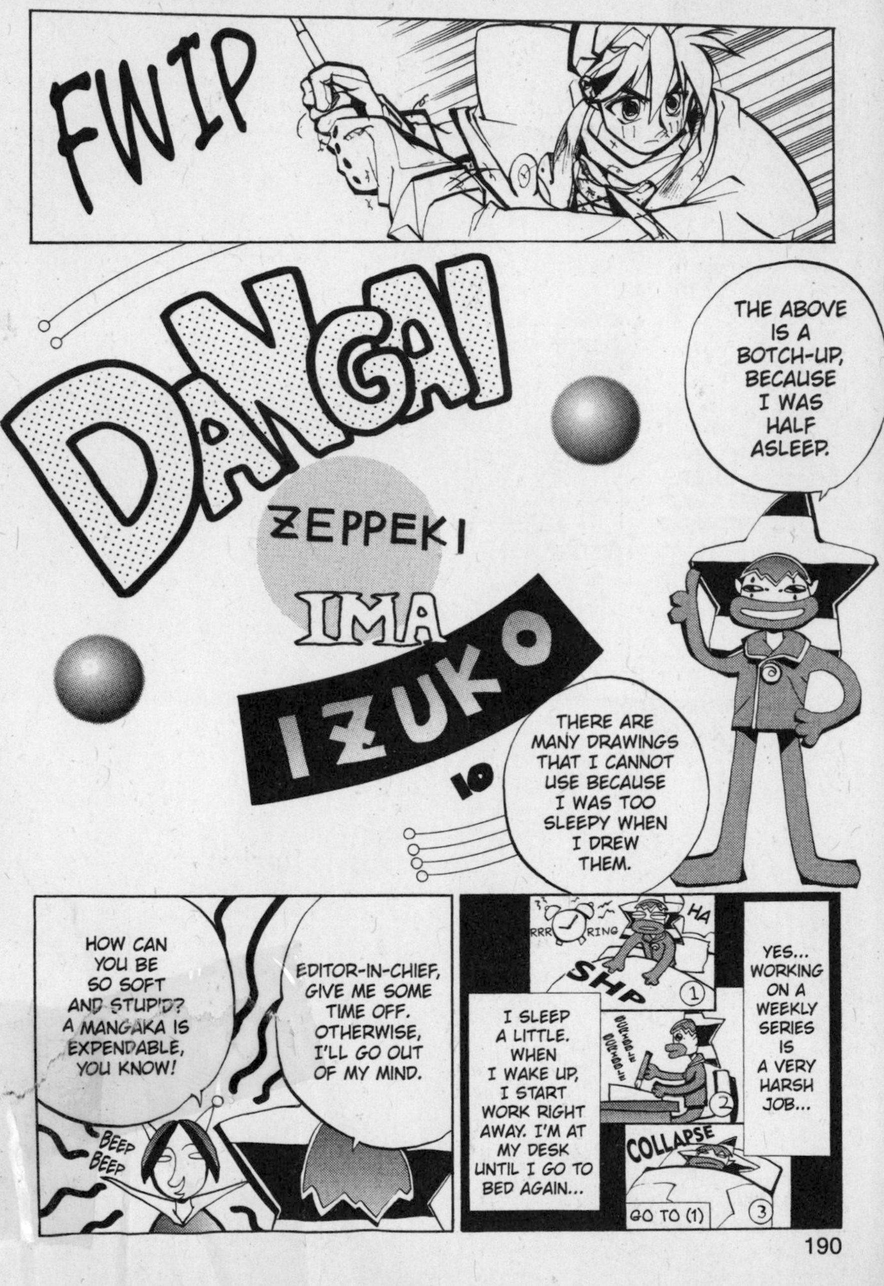
FWIP
THE ABOVE IS A BOTCH-UP, BECAUSE I WAS HALF ASLEEP.
DANGAI ZEPPEKI IMA IZUKO 10
THERE ARE MANY DRAWINGS THAT I CANNOT USE BECAUSE I WAS TOO SLEEPY WHEN I DREW THEM.
YES... WORKING ON A WEEKLY SERIES IS A VERY HARSH JOB...
HA
RRR
RING
SHP
1
I SLEEP A LITTLE. WHEN I WAKE UP, I START WORK RIGHT AWAY. I'M AT MY DESK UNTIL I GO TO BED AGAIN...
2
COLLAPSE
GO TO (1)
3
EDITOR-IN-CHIEF, GIVE ME SOME TIME OFF. OTHERWISE, I'LL GO OUT OF MY MIND.
HOW CAN YOU BE SO SOFT AND STUPID? A MANGAKA IS EXPENDABLE, YOU KNOW!
BEEP BEEP

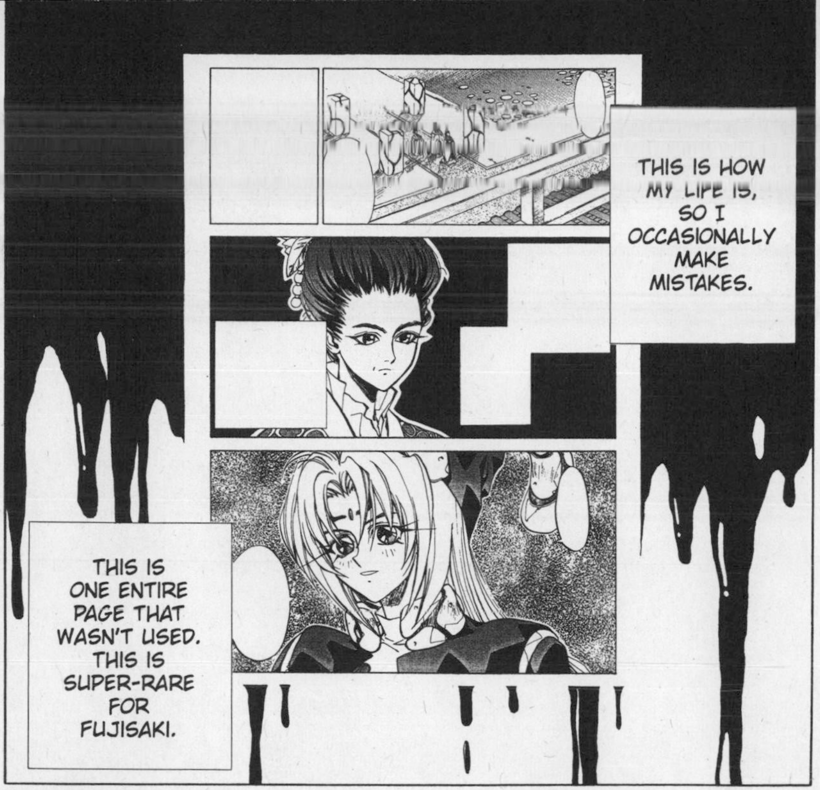
THIS IS HOW MY LIFE IS, SO I OCCASIONALLY MAKE MISTAKES.
THIS IS ONE ENTIRE PAGE THAT WASN'T USED. THIS IS SUPER-RARE FOR FUJISAKI.

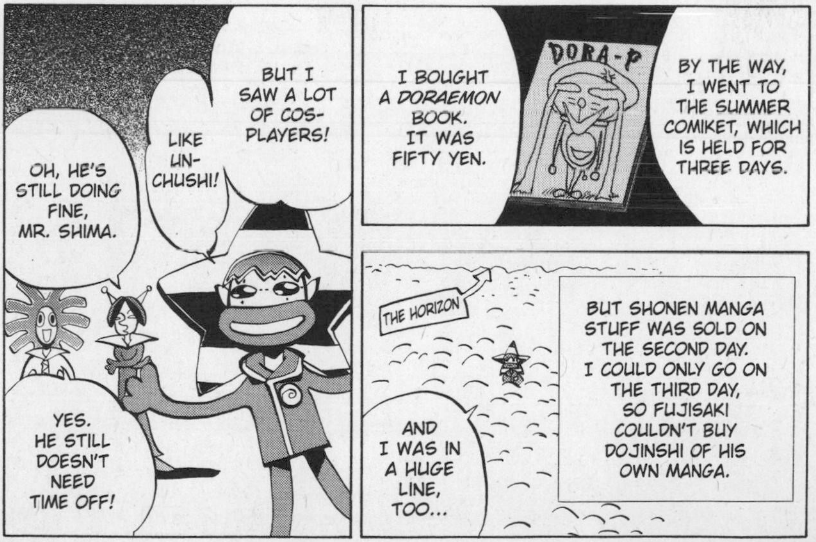
BY THE WAY, I WENT TO THE SUMMER COMIKET, WHICH IS HELD FOR THREE DAYS.
DORA-P
I BOUGHT A *DORAEMON* BOOK. IT WAS FIFTY YEN.
BUT SHONEN MANGA STUFF WAS SOLD ON THE SECOND DAY. I COULD ONLY GO ON THE THIRD DAY, SO FUJISAKI COULDN'T BUY DOJINSHI OF HIS OWN MANGA.
THE HORIZON
AND I WAS IN A HUGE LINE, TOO...
BUT I SAW A LOT OF COS-PLAYERS!
LIKE UN-CHUSHI!
OH, HE'S STILL DOING FINE, MR. SHIMA.
YES. HE STILL DOESN'T NEED TIME OFF!

Hoshin Engi: The Rank File!

You'll find as you read *Hoshin Engi* that there are titles and ranks that you are probably unfamiliar with. While it may seem confusing, there is an order to the madness that is pulled from ancient Chinese mythology, Japanese culture, other manga, and, of course, the incredible mind of *Hoshin Engi* creator Ryu Fujisaki.

Where we think it will help, we give you a hint in the margin on the page the name appears. But in addition, here's a quick primer on the titles you'll find in *Hoshin Engi* and what they mean:

Japanese	Title	Job Description
武成王	Buseio	Chief commanding officer
宰相	Saisho	Premier
太師	Taishi	The king's advisor/tutor
大金剛	Dai Kongo	Great Vassals
軍師	Gunshi	Military tactician
大諸侯	Daishoko	Great feudal lord
東伯侯	Tohakuko	Lord of the east region
西伯侯	Seihakuko	Lord of the west region
北伯侯	Hokuhakuko	Lord of the north region
南伯侯	Nanhakuko	Lord of the south region

Hoshin Engi: The Immortal File

Also, you'll probably find the hierarchy of the Sennin, Sendo and Doshi somewhat complicated. Here, we spell it out the easiest way possible!

Japanese	Title	Description
道士	Doshi	Someone training to become Sennin
仙道	Sendo	Used to describe both Sennin and Doshi
仙人	Sennin	Those who have mastered the way. Once you "go Sennin" you are forever changed.
妖孽	Yogetsu	A Yosei who can transform into a human
妖怪仙人	Yokai Sennin	A Sennin whose original form is not human
妖精	Yosei	An animal or object exposed to moonlight and sunlight for more than 1000 years

Hoshin Engi: The Magical File

Paope (宝貝) are powerful magical items used by Sennin and Doshi. Sometimes they look like regular objects, like a veil or hat. These are just a few of the magical items, both paope and otherwise, that you'll encounter in *Hoshin Engi!*

Japanese	Magic	Description
打神鞭	Dashinben	Known as the God-Striking Whip, Taikobo's paope manipulates the air and wind.
霊獣	Reiju	A magical flying beast that Sennin and Doshi use for transportation and support. Taikobo's reiju is his pal Supu.
雷公鞭	Raikoben	Reduces an opponent to ashes with a huge clap of thunder.
哮天犬	Kotenken	The Howling Dog can fly and be used as an attack paope.
莫邪の宝剣	Bakuya no Hoken	Tenka's weapon, a light saber.
禁鞭	Kinben	A powerful whip that can attack anything in a diameter of several kilometers.
花狐貂	Kakoten	An object that consumes people and cities for its energy source.
青雲剣	Seiunken	A sword with a blade that splits into many blades when swung.
混元傘	Kongensan	Absorbs the enemy attacks and uses them against the attackers.

Coming Next Volume:
The Revolution

A new character appears in Seiki—Sengyoku, a beautiful Sennin more powerful even than Taikobo. But is she there as an ally, or as an enemy agent? Taikobo must use all his cunning to find out.

AVAILABLE AUGUST 2008!

Read Any Good Books Lately?

Hoshin Engi is based on *Fengshen Yanji* (*The Creation of the Gods,* written in the 1500s by Xu Zhonglin) one of China's four classic fantastical novels of adventure, magic and mystery. The other three are *Saiyuki* (*Journey to the West* by Cheng'en Wu, late 1500s), *Sangokushi Engi* (*Romance of the Three Kingdoms* by Guanzhong Luo), and *Shui Hu Zhuan* (*Outlaws of the Marsh,* by Shi Nai'an, mid-1500s).

Want to read these books? You can! They're all still in print, more than 500 years later!

These books are North American in-print editions only.

NARUTO 1

SHONEN JUMP GRAPHIC NOVEL

Story & Art by **Masashi Kishimoto** volume

Read where the ninja action began in the manga

NARUTO

INNOCENT HEART, DEMONIC BLOOD

SHONEN JUMP FICTION

Fiction based on your favorite characters' adventures

JOURNEY INTO THE WORLD OF NARUTO BOOKS!

UZUMAKI
The Art of **NARUTO**

ART OF SHONEN JUMP

Hardcover art book with full-color images, a Masashi Kishimoto interview and a double-sided poster

Tell us what you think about SHONEN JUMP manga!

Our survey is now available online.
Go to: www.SHONENJUMP.com/mangasurvey

Help us make our product offering better!

THE REAL ACTION
STARTS IN...

SHONEN JUMP
THE WORLD'S MOST POPULAR MANGA

www.shonenjump.com